CW00521776

KOHL

Genius of the Present

KOHL

Genius of the Present

A Biography of Helmut Kohl

Edited by
Karl Hugo Pruys

Translated by Kathleen Bunten

edition q, inc.
Chicago, Berlin, Tokyo, and Moscow

Photo Credits
dpa Bildarchiv, Frankfurt/Main (81)
Ullstein Bilderdienst, Berlin (12)
Archiv des Autors (10)
Laurence Chaperon, LASA, Bonn (1)

Author's Note
During the completion of this book, friends stood by my side unselfishly. They supported me unasked, helping when they saw the need. Special thanks are due to Dr. Jürgen Schebera of edition q, and to my colleagues Carolin Dietrich and Christine Schatzmann, without whose efforts the work could not have been completed.

Library of Congress Cataloging-in-Publication Data

Pruys, Karl Hugo, 1938–
[Helmut Kohl. English]
Kohl, genius of the present: a biography of Helmut Kohl / by Karl Hugo Pruys.
p. cm.
Includes bibliographical references and index.
ISBN 1-883695-10-4
1. Kohl, Helmut, 1930– . 2. Heads of state—Germany—Biography. 3. Germany—Politics and government—1982–1990. 4. Germany—History—Unification, 1990. I. Title.
DD262.P78 1996
943—dc20 96-23379
CIP

© 1996 by edition q, inc.

edition q, inc
551 North Kimberly Drive
Carol Stream, Illinois 60188

All rights reserved. This book or any part thereof may not be reproduced, stored in a retrieval system, or transmitted, in any form or by any means, electronic, mechanical, photocopying, recording, or otherwise, without prior written permission of the publisher.

Printed in the United States of America

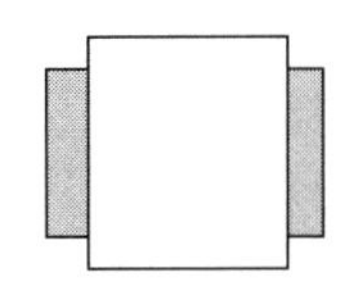

Contents

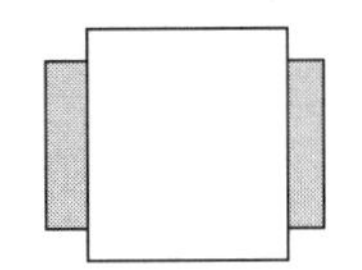

Introduction

On Being the Genius of the Present

Helmut Kohl, the first chancellor of a united Germany, is one of the world's most respected personalities of the late twentieth century and is perhaps the most influential politician of all. U.S. President Bill Clinton, who is of the younger generation and is not necessarily along Kohl's lines politically, has called Kohl "one of the greatest statesmen of our time." Not only have Israeli universities awarded the German leader honorary doctorates, but a Helmut Kohl Institute for European Studies was founded in Jerusalem in the spring of 1995. Neither his media advisers nor Kohl himself are surprised anymore when opinion polls clearly show him to be "the most important German." He probably considers this epithet "completely self-evident" by now.

The French rate Helmut Kohl and Nelson Mandela well to the fore of present-day statesmen, and eighty-five percent of Spanish voters favored him as president of a united Europe. Indeed, Kohl's enthusiasm for Europe, which is probably far too great for the right-wing nationalists of his own Union party, remains unabated. Cees Nooteboom, the internationally respected writer from the Netherlands, praised Kohl's "very well formulated speech" during the latter's sensitive visit to the war memorial in Rotterdam. Looking to his powerful neighbor, Nooteboom said that one must be "grateful that someone like him is able to influence things in such a large country."

Though scarcely anyone would have believed it for a long time, Kohl is able to touch the spirit of people, especially very unsophisticated ones. Russian women who walked with him through a military cemetery in Moscow on May 9, 1995, had tears in their eyes when they met the great German; others honored their guest from Western Europe, crying "Helmut, Helmut!" The usually unsentimental German leader did not disguise the fact that he was moved when he embraced his friend François Mitterand—possibly for the last time—after Mitterand had described the role of the

Germans after the Second World War in a sympathetic way in the remembrance service at the Berlin Schauspielhaus on May 8.

The positive image of the Germans, as well as the unexpressed fear of a resurgence of Prussian hegemonic aspirations, had grown strongly after German reunification. The tall man at the head of this country's government has come to symbolize such growing interest, and has increasingly become the focus of the rest of the world's attempt to heap more responsibility onto Germany than may be good for it.

Helmut Kohl, an icon? The stuff of legends surrounding him seems to be on the upsurge since he was re-elected chancellor for the fourth time in 1994. Those scoffers who once called him "the man without qualities," "not authentic," and "a man without a secret," have been silenced. The news magazine *Der Spiegel* titled a hurtful story about him "*Die Machtmaschine*" (The Power Machine). At the same time, however, the magazine and the collective left wing of Germany were forced to admit that they had greatly misjudged the man from the Palatinate and his ability to endure. Once dismissed as provincial, the man who has been at the top of the German government for more than three legislative periods—longer than his "ancestor" Konrad Adenauer—could be trusted to be able to do just about anything.

"Whoever really loves power does not speak cynically about it," said Johannes Gross, who might have been even—or especially—thinking about Helmut Kohl when he said it. Friedrich Schorlemmer wrote aptly about the supposedly power-hungry chancellor that when it came to power, an opera singer could certainly not be faulted for actually singing in an opera. Kohl's critics frequently attack him for his national preponderance, though it is secretly admired by the majority of Germans. The "Kohl system" has penetrated the subconscious of a generation. The solitariness and almost loneliness of the role Kohl plays lends the man from the Palatinate an authenticity which up until now only his staunchest admirers would have ascribed to him.

It is still true that Kohl does not stand for a particular policy, nor for a concept, a specific program, a *Weltanschauung* or philosophical credo, a vision—call it what you will. He is a pragmatist *comme il faut*, the "genius of the present," as Lothar Gall described it. Kohl has never expressed an idea which was worth pondering for more than two minutes. He has not written any programmatic books, which, above and beyond memoirs, almost all his predecessors have done, with the exception of Adenauer, who was a welcome role model for his "grandson." Therefore it is quite fitting to say that Kohl does not write books, but history.

Kohl's progression has suffered interruptions, and still does. When his course is examined more closely, a five-year cycle emerges, with ups and downs—or more aptly—temporary setbacks or steps backward, situations in which the hero always rises like a phoenix from the ashes, only to stumble a half decade later.

Start with 1961. Two years had passed since he had entered the CDU *Land* parliamentary party (*Fraktion*) in Mainz; Kohl's political career had clearly begun. But he then had his first setback, which even he acknowledged, hardly storming the heights of the chairmanship, but being elected to the board with a slim majority. Five years later he failed to get a seat in the CDU presidium at the government level, which was a blow to his already well-developed ego. Again, five years after that in 1971 he made a singularly silly mistake during the debate on co-determination at the party conference in Düsseldorf, where he proved unequivocally to his internal party rivals that he did not yet have the makings to reach the top. But he had a real stroke of luck two years later: Rainer Barzel, leader of the party and the *Fraktion*, lost his nerve and resigned from both positions, leaving the field open for Helmut Kohl to campaign for the chairmanship of the party at the government level. In retrospect, all the indications show that the CDU party conference elected him chairperson because there was no chance of an imminent change in government in Bonn and no one had to worry about the possibility of Kohl becoming chancellor.

Five years after the Düsseldorf disaster, the greatly underestimated man from the Palatinate achieved brilliant results in the *Bundestag* elections in 1976. Nevertheless the election did not give him the desired chancellorship because of the strong Social Democratic–Liberal majority. This blow was all the more bitter in light of the 48.6 percent vote. In 1981, one year after Franz Josef Strauss had become a candidate for chancellor and Kohl had gone through what he called "the valley of humiliation," the CDU leader was on the way up the ladder again. The party conference in Mannheim confirmed him as chairperson for the fourth time with an overwhelming majority.

Still in keeping with the five-year theory, in 1986, Kohl's fifth year in office, there were openly expressed doubts that Kohl would again lead the Union to victory in the 1987 *Bundestag* elections. Despite many humiliations, Kohl the pragmatist heeded the signs of the times and went ahead with the reunification of Germany. After that—and exactly five years passed since then—the party, supported by influential voices in the media, was considering an early replacement for him. People talked about the "autumn of the dinosaur"; Kohl himself spoke resignedly and pondered his succession, but without any result. The "giant," as he is often referred to, is "large, strong, and powerful." Nevertheless, as Johannes Gross correctly points out, he is "not always the victor in the battle." Though no one needed to express this openly, in late 1994 and early 1995, the chancellor of the Federal Republic of Germany appeared to be a larger-than-life Napoleonic "consul for life."

Kohl has no true friends. His personality is such that he always needs to be at the center of things no matter where he is. For this reason he never likes to confide in anyone, which further strengthens his political position. Kohl's press officer from his Mainz days, Hanns Schreiner, is probably correct that "from time to time he was so direct it was almost fatal. I was frequently uncomfortable about his self-presentation at the expense of others, and in the typically brash Palatinate manner. . . . This swaggering at others' expense—he did that to a lot of people, including friends. He didn't mean anything wrong by it. I fear that he didn't have any feelings about it."

Anyone in politics has rivals, and in the CDU, as in other parties, the cynical saying still holds true that there are "enemies, deadly enemies, and party friends." Nevertheless, there have been and still are some friends to whom he is close, but mentioning them would always result in an incorrect sequence. Perhaps Kohl's real friends are not in politics at all, so that he does not have to fear that they could do him out of his living. The president of the German Employers' Organization, Hanns Martin Schleyer, and Alfred Herrhausen are among these, as are the media mogul Leo Kirch and the actor Günther Strack. A friend from his youth, Heinz Schwarz, who also came from Rhineland-Palatinate, is said to have "understood" that a chancellor must do without the usual friendships. But Schwarz and others who have dealings with Kohl all agree that he is incapable of being open and completely honest in times of crisis, for example in parting, which is unavoidable sometimes in politics. At such times, even when he thinks they have come, Kohl is remarkably shy, even weak, and indecisive about saying what needs to be said. He seems to panic about having to be the bearer of bad tidings. On the other hand, praise for him can never be obvious enough, or bald enough, to give him the greatest pleasure.

Hence Kohl's perception of reality remains selective, depending on whether he is being flattered or reviled. He needs applause without having to be loved. When Werner Mauser pondered whether a biography could be written about someone who is living, he asked himself rhetorically, "What does Kohl want? Does he want to be praised?" What a question: naturally he does! In his book *Der Deutsche Kanzler* (The German Chancellor) Maser does Kohl this dubious favor well above the required measure.

The most firmly entrenched stereotypes about the man and the politician are that he is larger than life, indestructible and at the same time completely normal. It may be true that his contemporaries at first did not see anything unusual in him, but Helmut Kohl today is one of the most unmistakable figures on the world stage. Over the years the large man has gained pound after pound, almost as if he were developing impenetrable armor to protect himself symbolically against all kinds of attacks. There is a reliable witness to the fact that he needs this. Wolfgang Schäuble, a close associate who has studied him carefully, says that "He can never hide anything. . . . If you know him, you can read everything in his face." The Social Democrat Wilfried Penner, a man who observes closely with a quiet sense of humor, says much the same: "Even today, Kohl is still different from others who have formed a *cordon sanitaire*, a no-touch zone, when they are in parliament. He still takes part in debates, nodding in agreement when his adherents fiercely defend him. Even today he still reacts when he has been hit: his ears go red as if he has been caught at something." He appears to be vulnerable and of course irritable, as his many outbursts behind closed office doors show; in public or semipublic circles he stifles obvious reactions. He seldom appears exhausted, but often has a look that could be described as "not on form." He yawns openly when he feels like it, and when his stomach still permitted it, he would put his feet up on the table in front of his colleagues.

The number of illnesses experienced by Kohl in his sixty-five years—just a few minor operations, most recently on his knee—can be counted on the fingers of one hand. Kohl appears to be indestructible. He can be extremely sensitive, like most people who overestimate themselves and make it seem like humor when they laugh about others. Kohl also has handy physiological characteristics such as being able to sleep "sitting up as if he were in bed" on the many long flights that a chancellor has to make, according to Peter Boenisch. "But when he needs to be, every gram of his easily hundred kilograms is wide awake." The caricature of him as a "pear," which came from sketches of the French Citizen King, Louis Philippe, in nineteenth-century French newspapers, is inaccurate, because Kohl's head is not pear-shaped. According to the Chinese practice of determining a person's character from the shape of his head and face, Kohl has a so-called earth face: a broad, chiseled chin with a slightly smaller forehead. The Chinese consider the earth person to crave knowledge and be energetic, clever in tactics, and programmed for success. If he gets a chance, he shows what he can do. The negative sides are that he is quickly insulted, has only a few friends, and tends to dominate.

There are politicians who have based their careers on their rhetoric and others who have to do without this talent. Helmut Kohl belongs to the latter group, and Nina Grunenberg, a journalist with *Die Zeit*, understated it when she said that aesthetics get no satisfaction from him. One looks in vain for original phrases from him, with the exception of inapt metaphors, which—looked at in gentle irony—provide amusement. One of the best ones was "the warm sofa of freedom," on which the citizens of the German Democratic Republic were able to sit after 1990. One of the most frequently quoted phrases, "the grace of a late birth," is still regarded by many people as a Kohl original, but it actually came from Günter Gaus, the *Südwestfunk* moderator who later became the permanent representative of the Federal Republic in East Berlin. Kohl adopted the phrase without quoting its source and made it known, first in Israel and then at home.

Der Spiegel wrote in June of 1995 that "Kohl's effect is not based on what he says, but how he says it, namely, with the absolute certainty of citing the final and generally valid truth," which is a view that has become prevalent. Kohl is at his most authentic when he is complaining publicly about the lachrymose character of the all-too-sated and comfortable Germans. Since his youth, self-pity and a woebegone attitude have been an anathema to him, a characteristic he shares with very few people. One of his indisputable virtues is that he is completely uncorruptible when it comes to material goods. Ever since the beginning of his political career he has given a wide berth to anything that smacks of corruption or attempts to influence with money or goods. On the other hand, he can be enticed with loyalty, flattery, and repeated praise, which gains his gratitude and dispels his intrinsic and deep mistrust.

It would take a trained psychologist rather than a biographer to describe Kohl's relationships with friends and colleagues, women and family, the old and the young. Kohl's wife Hannelore says of him, "Whoever has him, has him for a long time," which can also apply to his political persistence. "The women elected him," Peter Altmeier, the "father of the *Land*" said indignantly in 1961, when he recognized that the talent of the younger generation, Helmut Kohl, elected to the board of the parliamentary party in the Mainz *Landtag*, would be his future challenger.

Kohl and women? The general opinion is that with the opposite sex the man from the Palatinate is either reserved or jovially condescending, with a somewhat altar-boyish reticence. Others think that they see something in the older man that makes him susceptible to full-bosomed women: perhaps it is a motherly ideal. The obligatory indecent remarks about women and sex are never heard from Helmut Kohl even in a social context.

Politics is an existential question for Helmut Kohl, quite literally. Although it is difficult to describe in detail, he is sort of like a monster who feeds spiritually in an ominous way on the substance of politics and the people who are part of it. This may have caused some of his colleagues who left him or who were "cast off" by him to reach the damning conclusion that he is a cynic without parallel. Such feelings are likely to have stemmed from deep hurt, which can turn into just the opposite as soon as the person returns to the patronizing love. Kohl has used many companions and friends, colleagues and helpers on his way to the top. While this fate inevitably was shared by his political companions, Kohl is, in the twilight of his political career as chancellor of the Federal Republic of Germany, without serious heirs and successors in his own ranks.

In the fall of 1994 there was a spirited discussion about Kohl's possible successor, especially in leftist intellectual circles. The chancellor and CDU chairperson received a sidelong defense from the writer Gabriele Wohmann, of all people, who could not necessarily be counted among his admirers, in a jab that made his sniping rivals look silly: "One effect of succession I could live with: the pundits (if one of *them* became head of state, I'd emigrate) lose what currently passes for a joke—the one about the amazing leader who eats more than his fellow citizens but carries no more weight."

Helmut Kohl: The Biography does not purport to be a global analysis of the political achievements and failures of the first chancellor of a united Germany, nor is it intended to be a comprehensive appreciation of his historical significance. Both of these must be left to future generations. The necessary distance from his personality and actions in the present can only come with time. Johannes Gross, the insightful and always critical observer of Kohl, wrote in 1976 that "if Adenauer was the father of the republic, Erhard its fosterer, Brandt its saviour, and Schmidt its preserver, then Kohl is a new type who does not define himself, but points to the future in returning to the beginning of the circle. He regards himself as the heir, son or grandson, or at least the executor of Adenauer." Is there any more to be said?

The book is rounded off with an essay by the German correspondent of the French daily newspaper *Le Figaro*, my friend Jean-Paul Picaper, who knows Kohl well. He writes about the Franco-German relations during the Kohl administration, which up until 1995 paralleled that of François Mitterrand, who retired from politics several months before his death in early 1996. The relationship between Germany and France is at the heart of the European policies of the federal chancellor and chairperson of the CDU, the undeniably great European, Helmut Kohl. If the biographical part of this book does not look in detail at the European question, it is to allow Jean-Paul Picaper to present this succinctly in his essay.

Karl Hugo Pruys
Bonn, August 1995

1

Childhood and Youth

1930–1950

In Praise of Ancestry

Helmut Kohl's father and maternal grandfather were middle-ranking civil servants whose profession brought them into direct contact with the people. All his life, Kohl's sense of family has made him extremely proud of and grateful to both. His frequent references to his ancestors, particularly to these two, casts a favorable light on this patriotically inclined man who history books will one day record as the longest-serving German chancellor.

Grandfather Kohl, on the other hand, was strangely shrouded in obscurity. The politician Helmut Kohl, writing many years later in a collected biography about the parents and childhoods of prominent contemporaries,[1] said that his father came from a "farming family of thirteen in Lower Franconia," but nothing else. His father, who he called Hans, probably his nickname, was baptized Johann Kaspar and left home at fourteen to live with a master miller and his wife, who treated him like a son. His paternal grandparents' farm had burned down, and the suddenly impoverished family was undoubtedly relieved to have one of its many children placed safely elsewhere. The "blessing of children" spoken of by pious families in those days had thrust a farmer without a home or a farm into an untenable position. Five children did not reach their tenth birthdays and two died just before their second year.

Hans Kohl went to the same school in Greussenheim, near Würzburg, that was attended several years later by Adam Stegerwald, the famous social politician of the Weimar Republic and later leader of the Christian Democratic Employees' Organization. After leaving school Hans served in a Bavarian regiment and at the end of the war found a secure job in government. By 1921, after a few years as finance secretary, Hans Kohl's career was well enough established to allow him to marry the second daughter of Peter Josef Schnur, a teacher who came from the Hunsrück area.

Helmut Joseph Michael, the third and last child of Cäcilie Elisabeth and

Hans Kohl, was born on April 3rd, in the unsettled year of 1930, in Ludwigshafen, a city dominated by the chemical industry. The family's circumstances, though by no means luxurious, were not uncomfortable. The Kohls had a house of their own in Friesenheim, a suburb of Ludwigshafen, with seven main rooms, a kitchen, a cellar, and several other rooms, including a large storeroom. The garden provided everything a housewife needed in the way of potatoes, vegetables, and herbs. Kohl's grandfather Schur, from whom his parents had inherited the house, had left forty fruit trees, most of which he had grafted himself. Helmut never knew his grandfather because he had died shortly before the future chancellor was born.[2]

The memory of this teacher with his love of the arts was kept alive by Kohl's parents. Peter Josef Schur, who came from a long line of teachers, loved to play the organ and had been the church choir director. Even many years after his death people spoke of him as being well respected and even loved. He may or may not have been a "gifted" teacher—a number of well-meaning Ludwigshafen citizens at least said he was when they talked about their favorite son, Helmut Kohl. Such statements often come from a rosy view of the past. Be that as it may, Helmut considered his grandfather to be "the epitome of a teacher" once he began thinking about his family history. Helmut was spiritually drawn to this man, with his artistic inclinations, but seemed to forget his paternal grandfather, perhaps because he himself is not artistic, though he appreciates talent all the more for this reason.

Peter Josef Schnur attended the teacher-training school in Speyer. He first taught in Trier and then moved to Ludwigshafen, where he married and became head of a middle-class Catholic family which was free of religious intolerance. The family discussed the Bible but also studied literature, played music, and sang the praises of God—all at the appointed time. The daughter Cäcilie, Helmut Kohl's mother, grew up in this benevolent climate to be a well-behaved child without the need for parental strictness and attended a girls' boarding school for a few years.

Cäcilie Kohl communicated her love for her home in the Palatinate to her husband Hans and they moved permanently into the spacious house built by her grandfather. Nine years passed after their marriage. The economic and political situation in the republic forced even those people who would otherwise not be inclined to live closely together to live in a tightly knit circle. Even in those days, long before family planning, the Kohls decided that three children were enough. Helmut was the youngest. The oldest was his sister Hildegard, followed by his brother Walter, who was four years older and was killed at the age of eighteen, only a few months before the end of the war, in Westphalia. Christmas of 1944 was overshadowed by the news of Walter's death, which profoundly affected the fourteen-year-old Helmut. It traumatized him and possibly even destroyed his idyllic youth. Even as an adult Kohl will not speak about his brother.

Kohl becomes almost melancholy when he thinks about the war, which "abruptly and mercilessly ended an almost ideal childhood. . . . Daily life became different; it was darker, more painful, more constricting."

These experiences should be seen against the background of a fairly sheltered childhood in the well-run family of a civil servant. Kohl's father was an upright, hard-working, thrifty, and modest financial secretary who would only buy a streetcar ticket in bad weather—otherwise he rode to the office on his bicycle. He bought beer from a local public house, as was the custom in those days. However, he did so only on Saturday evening, "in order to celebrate the coming day off," as the son remembers fondly.[3] On the other days of the week the rule was moderation, circumspection, and doing without, just as Helmut Kohl urges in government statements on budget cuts. Nobody in the family got more than anyone else, except Helmut when he was small and turned his nose up at a Christmas goose because he did not like poultry. His mother made him a beef roulade, after which the young boy, who looked to his parents for harmony, was happy with them and his world, despite the war shortages. The good life meant tasty food for the child and later for the man as well: a plentiful source of food, comfort, and warmth from people he is close to or who are loyal to him. Comfortable surroundings took on overriding importance for the boy. In summer, when the garden supplied fresh vegetables, salads, herbs, and fruit—in short, everything for the German table—the growing boy found his life to be Lucullan.

His main job was looking after the chickens and turkeys, but his real love was raising rabbits. He rode his bicycle as far as thirty kilometers to take a doe to a premier buck rabbit in order to obtain good breeding stock. On a trip to the Far East almost half a century later, Kohl told the buck story to Kai Diekmann, a journalist for *Bild*, who enriched *Max* and other illustrated magazines with the tale. It became a real source of amusement because it showed an unexpected side of Helmut Kohl, although the incident had been briefly touched on in his article on the childhoods of prominent contemporaries.

Oddly enough, Kohl was the smallest boy in his class until he was fourteen. He shot up after that and was nicknamed "*der Lange*" (the tall one). However, in his school picture in 1937 Helmut looked almost like a dwarf, with extremely dark eyes in a slender face. At eighteen he was a good-looking young man who could attract the girls.

When Helmut was nine, his father, an experienced officer who had

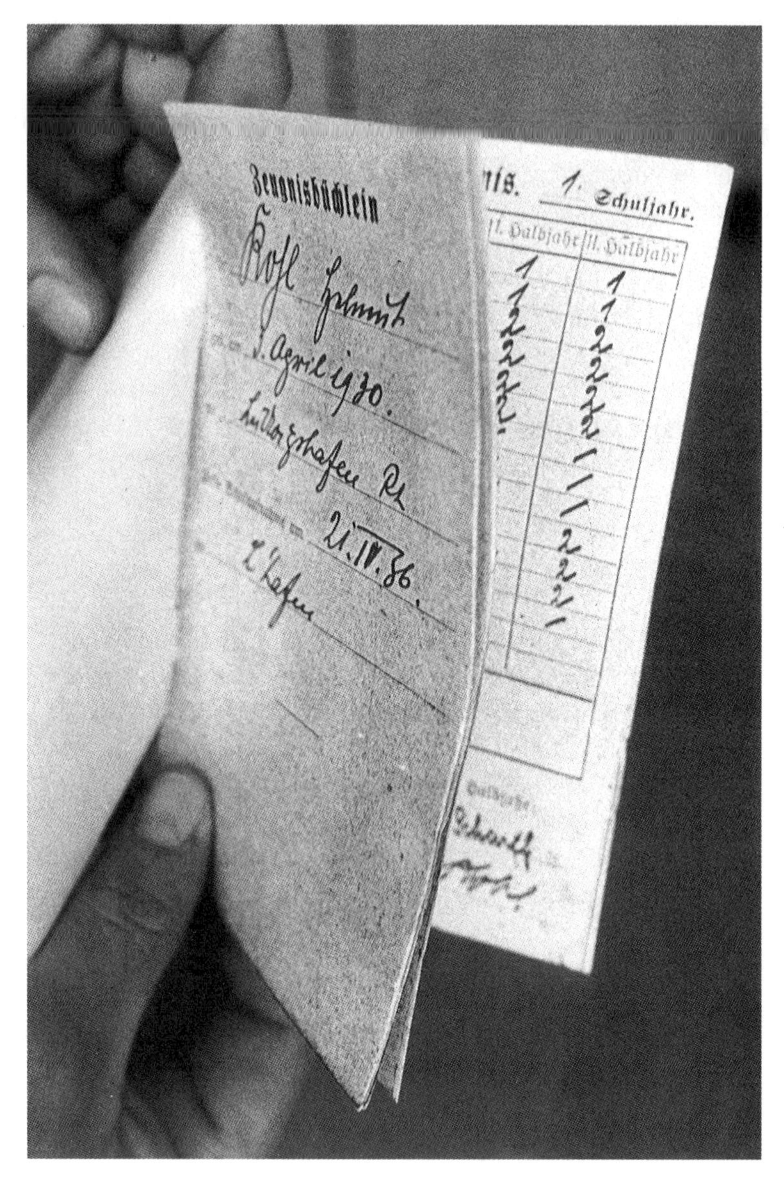

Kohl's first-grade report card. Helmut was still a model student here, in contrast to later years.

served on the front in the First World War, was called up again to fight a war that was not his, because he hated the National Socialists. Hans Kohl was already over fifty, but his country called. He did not return home until almost the end of the war. In the meantime his wife ran the large household alone.

Twelve-year-old Helmut joined a school fire brigade, "inexperienced, but ready to take a risk, even foolhardy," the other participants recalled as adults. The boys not only helped put out the many fires started by incendiary bombs but also helped recover the dead and injured. These experiences would continue to affect them as grown men, especially Kohl the politician. And whenever the industrial city was not being bombed, the barely fourteen-year-old boy found a niche with the *Deutsches Jungvolk* of the Hitler Youth. Helmut, the son of a Catholic civil servant, obviously took part only in a half-hearted way, because he never made it to the rank of *Fähnleinführer,* according to Willy Zirngibl, a journalist the same age as Kohl and the Bonn correspondent for *Westdeutsche Allgemeine Zeitung* (WAZ).

Helmut enjoyed the many school hikes which have now gone almost out of fashion. He frequently roughhoused with the other boys in the class and played a lot of tricks, since he liked making fun of other people's surprise.

Birthdays were always celebrated in style. The Kohls had a full house then, with plenty of homemade cakes and gallons of hot chocolate, despite shortages. Even years afterward Kohl could recall exactly the cookies his mother baked for Christmas: spicy speculatius, butter cookies, and cinnamon waffles: "The whole house smelled of almonds, vanilla, candied peel, and melted butter, and even the unbaked cookie dough tasted wonderful."

This was the beginning of Kohl's lifelong love of good food and drink. When he was opposition leader in the *Bundestag* (federal assembly, or parliament) he constantly asked Juliane Weber, his executive secretary, whether there was something to eat in the refrigerator. Even as chancellor he hired the chef for the chancellor's office himself. Kohl's memories are most vivid when it comes to food. At the age of sixty he said he could still taste his mother's lemon and caramel puddings.

The Good Life

Despite material shortages, day-to-day life in Germany during the 1930s and the war years was comparatively comfortable. Nevertheless, those with a strong thirst for freedom and self-determination felt constricted by the rules and regulations of National Socialist ideology or merely those of the times. These included the famous, or infamous, requirement that every German family eat stew on Saturdays without fail whether they liked it or not. Members of the Hitler Youth were known to go from house to house to check up on whether this socially imposed rule was being adhered to. Otherwise, the Kohls, at Hohenzollernstrasse 89, had meat twice a week, but egg and flour dishes on "normal" workdays, and on Fridays the obligatory fish, since Catholics were not allowed to eat meat on that day. Shellfish was served often and it became one of Helmut Kohl's favorite foods. In a small civil-service family, his mother had to watch every penny to keep within the budget. Her son recollects that she went to market only when traders were beginning to take down their stalls and were knocking down the prices.

Nevertheless, those years were good for the schoolboy and growing teenager. As a grown man, Kohl is always quick to point out that his was a completely normal family, a typical small family of a civil servant just like millions of others. That is most certainly the case, since he seems to exude normality, which can be read in every gesture. Unlike parents of eight or ten children, his parents never had to worry about having enough for their children. The Kohls were able to give their children presents from time to time; Helmut got a secondhand but still very good bicycle for his fifth birthday. Gifts for first Communion, including a wristwatch, were not to be worn and thrown away; they were put away for safekeeping and for wearing later on. As in millions of other families, the children got practical gifts for Christmas: pullovers, coats, and socks. However, Helmut's parents once surprised the young boy with a medieval castle, to which were added year after year the usual small figures and wagons.

The schoolboy loved to play and eat, especially in those lean years, and he loved to snack. Kohl has had a lifelong weakness for sweet things; comfort and security came from a constant supply of good food. It is inconceivable what sort of malnutrition phobia the war and shortages may have caused in him.

Helmut's childhood was thus, with very few exceptions, almost out of a picture book, giving the man great self-confidence but also a strong desire for harmony. His mother also fit this pattern. Kohl described her as "optimistic, courageous, and extraordinarily lively,"[4] and she had a great influence on her youngest child. She did not show her feelings, but was considered reliable and inspired confidence in others, a woman from whom other people sought advice and help. She did not parade her Catholic faith, but lived it in the liberal way typical of the tolerant Rhineland. She often went to Mass in "her" church, but preferred to listen to a Protestant church service on the radio; Cäcilie thought the Protestant sermons were more profound, serious, and more deeply rooted in faith. Kohl's parents thus did not have any difficulty later on in accepting the Protestant Hannelore Renner as a daughter-in-law.

The good life continued in elementary school and secondary school. Helmut's grades were average and in primary school he was still the smallest in the class, despite all the good food. Nevertheless, he was mischievous and encouraged the other boys in practical jokes. He was often beaten in school, which was a customary punishment, especially when the principal caught him smoking.

At ten Kohl entered the secondary school on Leuschnerstrasse, very near his home. Of his school days, Kohl had "friendly-reserved" memories, as he told journalist Willy Zirngibl. "I wasn't an outstanding student . . . because school didn't really interest and challenge me."[5] Speaking candidly, he said, "I didn't really like going to school and fear that I didn't bring much joy there either." Nevertheless, after much internal debate, Kohl became the class spokesperson. He was not afraid of speaking out frequently against tough teachers, an approach to those in high position which stood him in good stead during his later political battles.

Despite the many meetings and exercises required by the *Deutsches Jungvolk* of the Hitler Youth—he achieved only the lowest rank, *Jungenschaftsführer*—Kohl had a lot of free time. Like millions of other boys during the Third Reich, he read books by Karl May, from the three Winnetou stories to *Durch die Wüste* (Through the Desert). He took care of his small collection of animals, especially his twenty blue-and-white Viennese rabbits. He built their hutches himself and had to find food for them every day. He also had a peacock and a tame fox, which had to be given up because of its strong smell. A raven with a broken wing was also cared for by the animal-loving boy.

Just before the end of the war, when the Third Reich lay in ruins, Kohl and his friends from Ludwigshafen were sent to a camp in Berchtesgaden to be trained as anti-aircraft *Flakhelfer*, all part of the "total war," which didn't even spare children. On his fifteenth birthday, Kohl and his friends of the same age were sworn in by *Reichsjugendführer* Arthur Axmann in the stadium at Berchtesgaden. Kohl never forgot the Nazi leader's loud screaming during the ceremony. Many of his comrades fainted from lack of food in the final weeks of the war.

Germany surrendered just five weeks later. The murderous specter was laid to rest, leaving in its wake bewildered people living in ruins of apocalyptic proportions and a young generation which faced a disorienting future. Ludwigshafen was two-thirds destroyed. Kohl's brother was killed in the war, and his father had a bad heart from his service on the front. In the final, confusing days of the war, Helmut and his friends had fled Berchtesgaden in the face of the approaching American troops. The fifteen year old boys spent the last few days of the war near a matte field near Augsburg. They were quickly surrounded and beaten up by Polish forced laborers. Still wearing the Hitler Youth winter uniforms, they, like many thousands of young people, felt the wrath of victims of the Nazi terror. They were turned over to the local American command and ordered to work on a farm, but were released to make their way home after three weeks.

Since the boys did not have identification papers they ran into trouble with the American military police. After walking for many weeks they gazed across the Rhine at their destroyed city. The military authorities had blocked the river crossing, so the boys holed up for a while in the old Mannheim castle bunker until the small, hungry band managed to make its way to Ludwigshafen. After a big hug from his mother, the boy asked her for some peach preserves, which he devoured greedily.

History in His Head

Kohl's parents were not explicitly his role models, but he learned a great deal from them. His father's temperament, albeit constrained by easygoing bureaucracy, was inherited by the son. The family was Catholic, but more in a secular sort of way, open to other ideas or philosophies, tolerant in the manner of the Rhineland—in short, satisfied with itself and the world.

"The fact that you thought in national terms also went without saying," Kohl recalls in his retrospective about his parents' politics. "The feeling of nationalism at home was without any missionary zeal or even sectarianism. My parents felt a bond with the country they were born in; they identified themselves with its interests without denying 'the others.' They had historical dates in their head, were proud of Germany's cultural achievements; they loved their homeland, its customs and traditions, its language."[6] In language he himself has remained firmly rooted in his homeland, the Palatinate. To use Kohl's expression, one had "history in one's head"—but perhaps less so in one's heart? No, he could not have meant that, since whenever this man speaks of history he unwittingly becomes enthusiastic. He speaks almost in romantic terms about history as "exquisite," an expression which, like so much else in his life, has associations with food and drink.

Tradition does not make you blind, Kohl's father told him. Once, on leave from the front during the war, he wanted to listen to the "enemy radio broadcasts" on *Radio Beromünster* or Radio London—at that time strictly forbidden—and he sent the children out of the room. It was an extremely unusual event, which is why the son still clearly remembers the strange occurrence decades later. "As we were leaving the room we heard something about Jews." Another time, in describing his experiences "outside on the front," his father ended with a sentence which the son never forgot: "God have mercy on us, if we ever have to pay for this." This is a good Catholic thought, and has nothing in it of Rhineland liberalism. Kohl's father had his principles and he stuck to them. His son inherited his sometimes serious, sometimes mocking skepticism, all his life making fun of those who brag about their country, although "fatherland" still remains one of Kohl's favorite words, and in his opinion one which cannot be replaced by any other. Even as a child he was impressed by the fact that his father was prepared to do his duty "without any great speeches." That may sound heroic in retrospective hero worship and glorification of the self-evident, but it is not: he also speaks of his "grace of late birth." This rather strange statement by the Christian Democrat could be taken as a hidden incrimination should he be found guilty by virtue of having been born earlier. Is it perhaps even an attempt at a general absolution for all those of other generations who became fellow travelers or even activists, and who nevertheless played a role in postwar Germany? However, one looks in vain for qualification or differentiation in regard to Nazi crimes in Kohl's words in a historic speech made on January 25, 1984, before the *Knesset* in Jerusalem.

"I would like to make the point clearly at the very beginning, especially since I am the first German chancellor of the generation after Hitler—I lived through the war as a child; I experienced the Nazi period quite consciously in the home of my parents, who were against the Nazis." In presenting a painting by Reuchlin to the Israeli president, Helmut Kohl remarked, in trying to describe his stance toward the present and the past in regard to the woeful Nazi past, "He [Reuchlin] embodies part of the great humanistic tradition of our people and of our republic, which exists in this spirit. That is true for all, especially for the younger generation. . . . I say this as someone who could not have incurred any guilt during the Nazi era because of the grace of late birth and the good fortune of a remarkable home."

Kohl had spoken about the "grace of late birth" as early as the 1970s, as quoted by the *Frankfurter Allgemeine Zeitung* on June 17, 1978. But it was his spectacular appearance before the Israeli parliament that made this political-historical metaphor a media splash. Months later, Werner Nachmann, chairperson of the Central Council of Jews in Germany, expressed astonishment at the chancellor's repeated use of the phrase.[7] Historian Werner Maser's attempt to ascribe meaning to this awkward matter is unsatisfactory, since it stops short of delving into the possibly deep psychological aspects of this self-interpretation. "Helmut Kohl, with his knowledge of history and awareness of how easily young people can be led astray, openly admits that he escaped such dangers by grace of his 'late birth' and was lucky in this instance."[8] Only lucky? Clearly Kohl means that his childhood, rooted firmly in religious principles and politically close to the center, would "not have provided the basis for totalitarian ideologies." In 1933, and disregarding the consequences for his career, Kohl's father had left the

Stahlhelm (steel helmet), the German nationalist organization of soldiers who had served on the front, to which he had belonged for many years.

The confused economic situation in the industrial city of Ludwigshafen was favorable to the growing National Socialist movement. Unemployment at twelve thousand out of a total of thirty-five thousand workers at the beginning of the 1930s was way above average. After the First World War the dissatisfied populace hated the French occupation troops which had been stationed there since the end of the 1930s. Maser says that the people's reaction to this unsatisfactory situation since 1918 was "often neurotic." The "damaged continuity of history," Maser writes, led in Ludwigshafen to a specific feeling of nationalism. In other words, the people of this region at that time were more rebellious, restless, and recalcitrant about attempts to dominate them than elsewhere in the republic. They were open to political insinuations and watchwords which would promise them a radical departure from the prevailing circumstances and a return to the lost feeling of national identity. The National Socialists must have realized this early on, since they founded the first group outside of Bavaria—where the movement started—in Mannheim, near Ludwigshafen, as early as 1922. The NSDAP had been active in this heavily populated area long before Hitler came to power, and long before anyone could say what the role of the NSDAP would be in German politics. Nazism attracted not only workers, but even in the very beginning academics, civil servants, and the middle class. Religion alone allowed many people to resist the temptations of a totalitarian ideology promising solutions to all material and national problems. This was true of the Kohl family and many hundreds of thousands of other families in Germany at that time. This was the reason that the politician Helmut Kohl could say later that his parents "took their religion seriously."

A Horrible Job

At age fifteen, Kohl had experienced everything that anyone could or should have at his age and at that time, growing up in an ordered home in a large city in a provincial homeland with an industrial background. He was an average student, rabbit breeder, altar boy, reader of Karl May, and member of the Hitler Youth. Now he was to experience farming, since war had destroyed the cities and displaced their populations.

It was uncertain when his school would reopen. Food was extremely scarce in Ludwigshafen, two-thirds of which was destroyed in the bombing, and thousands of people turned to the land. At least on the Düllstadt farm belonging to the company Süddeutscher Zucker AG the hungry boy had regular meals and learned how to work harder than he ever had before. His job was to look after the cows, and he learned how to plow with a team of oxen, a difficult job involving control of the six animals needed for a full day's plowing. "A horrible job," Kohl recalled. However, he did it with a certain amount of dogged pleasure since he secretly enjoyed farm life and even considered becoming a farmer someday. However, he probably did not mean this too seriously, since his schoolboy enthusiasm had gotten ahead of his hands, which were unused to the heavy work.

The farm was only one memory from his youth, though one of the most important ones. At least temporarily, the first carefree days of his childhood seemed to be gone forever. The fight for existence, begun very early, took on serious proportions. It reached existential proportions once growing numbers of farmers and farm laborers from the eastern and central part of Germany streamed into the West. They came from the land and wanted to return to it. Not only that, but they knew their job, and a fifteen-year-old could hardly compete.

Thus Kohl returned home just before onset of the winter of 1945–46. His old school received the subdued boy after his half-voluntary, half-enforced interlude in the countryside. The former secondary school on Leuschnerstrasse had become a scientific secondary school; it was later renamed Max-Planck-Gymnasium. The briefly considered apprenticeship in farming was shelved because it did not offer much of a career for the fifteen-year-old. In the months on the farm Kohl had shot up, presaging the epithet "giant," to which was later added the party-political adjective "black."

A local newspaper wrote in the late 1930s, "Ludwigshafen, as it is today, is a rather bleak monument in stone to its city fathers' lack of foresight."[9] After the war, in this city of workers, there was not one stone on top of another. The school too had not been spared by the bombing, and had to be rebuilt. As a reward for successfully repairing their classrooms, the students were told by the teachers that they would be able to use the rooms until the end of their time at school. Helmut, now nicknamed "*der Lange*," was said to have been good in organizing things, a talent he began to demonstrate and develop more and more.

However, he did not like the scientific bias the school had adopted. Math, physics, and chemistry were almost as important as German, French, and English. He was fortunate in having an understanding math teacher in Otto Stamfort. A Jew, Stamfort had joined the French resistance during the Nazi era. He was captured by the gestapo and thrown into a concentration camp. After his release and employment at the secondary school in Ludwigshafen, this man of many interests soon became one of the leading communists in the French Occupation Zone.

The Great Organizer

The boy found math boring, without any substance, and a real torture. His teacher was patient; himself only in his mid-thirties, he had a lot of understanding for his students' disinterest in the dry subject. Aside from that, his own real interest was politics and philosophizing about life and contemporary history.

Stamfort took an unusual approach, one which was already common in some schools and unknown in others: he started a two-hour discussion group on philosophy which met every Wednesday afternoon after school. Naturally Kohl was enthusiastic and he and a dozen others took part. Within a few weeks the relationship changed from a student-teacher one, since Stamfort's family lived in a house whose backyard bounded that of Kohl's parents. His teacher's revolutionary thinking did not bother the seventeen-year-old in the least, although he had absolutely no use for communism. He liked Stamfort, a good man who looked at matters of state with naive idealism. Fruit and vegetables were exchanged for books and good advice over the garden fence. If there was enough tea, coffee, and baked goods in the CARE package, Stamfort invited his student over to his house. The young man did not find him doctrinaire, but deeply convinced that communism would bring about earthly salvation. Stamfort gave the seventeen-year-old Kohl the works of Karl Marx.

The communist Stamfort was probably the first person Kohl had met who awakened in him the pressing need for political clarification and participation. Kohl was deeply distressed when his math teacher moved to Thuringia in 1948, where he worked for the local government on school reform along communist lines. The politically involved teacher embarked on a successful career, soon becoming a respected professor at the Friedrich Schiller University in Jena. Later he was chairperson of the Organization for German-Soviet Friendship.

After Stamfort left, the boy had to put his nose to the grindstone. The new math teacher was also the school director, and was a strict man who did not like fun, did not want to know about philosophy, but rather wished to concentrate on his own subject. Kohl received a grade of six in math in his *Abitur* (roughly equivalent to an American junior-college diploma), which was the worst grade in the *Abitur* in math in Rhineland-Palatinate in 1950. This was offset by a grade of very good in German. (By then a co-founder of the *Junge Union* [Young Union] in Ludwigshafen, he was able to inject many of his own thoughts into his essay on the highly controversial topic, "Is the social question a market question?")

The standard of the centrally administered *Abitur* in French was much higher than it is today, which is why one of Kohl's oldest friends, Heinz Schwarz, from Koblenz, later interior minister of the *Landeskabinett* (cabinet of the *Land*, or state) under Minister-president Kohl, thought the insinuation was "idiotic" that Kohl does not speak French and for years had to have an interpreter for his conversations with François Mitterrand. Kohl only felt that if people he was meeting with simply assumed their language should always be spoken, then German should also be used from time to time. At any rate, he would stick to his German.

Kohl was the first student in his class to become involved in party politics. Influenced by the father of a school friend, he joined the fledgling Christian Democratic Union (CDU) in 1946, at the age of sixteen. He was practically a founding member, with number 00246.

A number of Kohl's former schoolmates respected his spirit vis-à-vis his teachers, especially those in high position. As class spokesperson he was considered "insubordinate in principle" and sometimes even provocative; his friend Heinz Schwarz from the *Junge Union* says Kohl's behavior was simply "fresh." But this freshness impressed most people, because it showed that the young man actually tried on a day-to-day basis not to let inculcated respect for authority—after all, his father and grandfather were civil servants—devolve into subservience.

One of his fellow students, Karl-Otto Freisberg, recollected that "*der Lange*"—he was also called "Helle," a shortened form of his first name—once took on the new geography teacher. This teacher had adopted a harsh tone that was very unpopular with young people after the Second World War. Following procedures, the class spokesperson took the teacher to task: what did he mean by using such a tone from the barracks; those times were gone forever. That made an impression! Abashed, the teacher excused himself by referring to his long time as a prisoner; also, he said, he had no intention of giving credence to false authority.

Another fellow student, Karl Cunz, said that Kohl was generally respected in the class not because he was spokesperson, but because he took care of other students who could not count on regular meals. He ensured that Cunz, an orphan, was given "Hoover meals," the school food that came from U.S. army supplies.

Religion teacher Günther Schmich remembers "Helle" Kohl as a pugnacious and fearless debater. He turned the classroom forum into a local party meeting. The class would hear, "I would like to address the chair," whereupon a tall boy stood up, according to Schmich. "We have two questions to pose. . . ." After the end of the religion lesson the boy stopped Schmich at the door and asked him, among other things, "Is our currency hard?" Another anecdote relates that Kohl asked his religion teacher how the Catholic church regarded "sexuality among secondary-school and university students" and what the teacher himself thought.

Without going into detail about the particular question, the historian Maser relates in his biography of Kohl the following anecdote, which was characteristic of the secondary-school student with political aspirations. "Once, when Schmich and Kohl disagreed because the latter would not accept a number of the teacher's interpretations, Schmich demanded that Kohl go with him to the bishop's office in Speyer and debate the problem at a higher level. Even with the church leader Kohl did not mince words. He argued just as before—and literally drank his debating partner under the table. Kohl, Schmich recalled in 1990, remained the winner."[10]

"Helle" kept a watchful eye on his fellow students' behavior. Whoever tried to get out of work, cut classes, or otherwise behave improperly, had to pay for it, after consultation, of course. Not letting your neighbor copy your work was considered against the code of comradeship. "*Der Lange*" opted for the practical solution in this case as in many others: get school over with to finally have a free life and to test one's talents. Each one had to get through as best he could, even with a neighbor's help.

It was probably then that the cornerstone of Kohl's practical philosophy was laid. It could be summed up as "Everything can be organized, especially that which is reasonable," meaning that which is the most efficacious in each instance. "Reasonable" sounds more pretentious, and it thus became one of Kohl's favorite expressions, which he later repeated frequently.

The "great organizer," as he was called in the senior classes, was able to pull off a lot of things others had not dared to do, for example, going to a special performance of *Götz von Berlichingen* with about fifteen hundred other students at the Mannheim State Theater. The young man, well versed in the party political apparatus of the city, knew better than his fellow students and sometimes his teachers where the appropriate offices were, where a small subsidy or a stamp for an official permit could be gotten.

At that age, culture was not the only order of the day. At age eighteen one also organizes tea dances with the girls of the neighboring high school. It was at one of these events that Helmut Kohl met the blonde fifteen-year-old Hannelore Renner at the Weinberg guest house in Friesenheim, and he fell in love with her at first sight. She became his wife only a few years later.

A Circle of Cake around the Main Question

In 1972, three years after being elected national deputy secretary of the CDU at a party conference, Kohl remarked that Dean Johannes Finck, the first chairman and actual founder of the CDU in Rhineland-Palatinate, "was certainly a great influence on me. I would almost call him a foster father." However, he admits that many people influenced him, "so that I couldn't say that one person or the other had the greatest influence."[11]

Others who influenced the seventeen-year-old student, already politically active, were Prelate Martin Walser, journalist and culture minister; Albert Finck, the brother of his "foster father"; and Josef Schaub, the newspaper publisher. The churchmen were all liberally ecumenical in a way which came to the forefront in the Catholic church only in the 1960s, but which already had some staunch supporters. At that time, when there was never enough to eat and day-to-day life was plagued by acute hunger, the student Kohl was grateful for the occasional meal he was treated to in the restaurant of the Hubertus Hotel by Walser, Finck, or Schaub. Material and spiritual things, body and soul—how closely they are linked.

The mayor of Ludwigshafen, Ludwig Reichert, and his CDU parliamentary party leader, Ludwig Reichling, were role models and furthered Kohl's career as well. The venerable city councillor and archdemocrat of the chemical-industrial city, Betty Impertro, says that "There were a lot of people I had to stomp on, but I only had to stroke Helmut." Kohl's parents did not stroke him when he confessed that he had joined the newly formed CDU. Though they were not exactly faint-hearted people, they had their doubts about party politics, whatever the motives. The Third Reich and its totalitarian society, with its all-embracing, propagandist single party, probably frightened the former centrist man and his wife, and certainly disillusioned them. Perhaps they only thought that at his age, Helmut should concentrate on his schoolwork and not run around so much. Their son proved again that one can despise or ignore unwarranted demands of authority, but at the same time orient oneself on true authority. "Helle" did exactly that in sticking to his role model, the much older and more experienced Johannes Finck. Finck had run the Catholic parish in Limburgerhof, on the edge of Ludwigshafen, since the 1930s. In the 1920s he had gained a reputation as a centrist representative in the Bavarian *Landtag* and was a vocal spokesperson for the Catholic parliamentarianism of the Weimar Republic. The division of the conservative Christian party into the center and the Bavarian *Volkspartei* (People's Party)—which had a parallel in the late 1970s Union parties—became the fiasco of the principled Finck's life. One of the many unpleasant consequences of this party strife was that it also made the founding of a Christian *Volkspartei* after the war all the more difficult. Finck gained kudos as one of the founding fathers of the CDU in the Rhineland-Palatinate. Already in the final autumn of the war, in 1944, he had started planning how to unite the Christian conservatives, generously leaving out the revival of the center, in order to open the door and give Protestants a party along their own lines. Finck himself gave up his political functions in 1946, as priests were not supposed to be involved, and devoted himself to his pastoral duties and his writing.

Kohl had had a good instinct that in this man's nonmaterial roots was something the Christian Democrats could always call upon: conservatism with a Christian outlook and the precept of tolerance toward others with different religious beliefs and views. Later he would say staunchly that the Union had "conservative, Christian, and liberal roots" and that these three roots could not be denied. It fit in with the young Kohl's view and his sometimes boisterous temperament that his role model, Johannes Finck, had bravely tackled the French occupation forces. "Helle" liked that and tried to follow suit. During the Nazi period Finck had made his rectory a meeting place for resistors. He himself remained in the background until his death in 1953, a priest with a door always open to the workers of his industrial city.

Johannes Finck is the person most frequently mentioned when Kohl talks about the past, often with barely suppressed emotion. Finck did not leave party politics voluntarily in 1946. At any rate, from his rectory he continued to be a great influence on the people and programs of the young CDU, though the people themselves were not so young and the driving force was older men and women. This was a contentious issue and the reason why "Helle" devoted so much time outside school to politics and the CDU.

What happens when someone retires from public office? He or she founds a circle of like-minded people. Finck asked his fellow priests in the region whether they knew any suitable candidates for the political circle. The name Helmut Kohl was mentioned in the parish of St. Joseph in Friesenheim. Kohl joined Finck's small circle in 1947; undoubtedly he was attracted to the meetings at the Limburgerhof rectory partly by the cakes. He also showed up on time for meat and sausages from black-market home butchering.

There was no greater influence on Helmut Kohl, who headed the *Land* government twenty years later, than Johannes Finck. The meetings were run like seminars with the dean, and each participant had to give a paper.

Since there was no other materials available they used booklets published by the People's Organization for a Catholic Germany. In this atmosphere, outside the narrow confines of school, the young man was almost an adult in a group of adults, as his political arguments were soon to prove so annoyingly to the older members.

For hours the group discussed major issues—Catholicism, socialism, liberalism, conservative and revolutionary thought, government authority, and the sovereignty of the people. Though Helmut Kohl's natural pragmatism made him love to attack ivory-tower thinking, he enjoyed the sessions at Johannes Finck's more than anything he had known before. He became his master's favorite pupil and remained loyal to him until his death. "A fatherly friend," the up-and-coming CDU man called Finck in his retrospective. Finck was even more than that and was certainly one of the few men who gave direction to Kohl's life.

Dawn over the Truly Hollow Place

Even as a young man Helmut Kohl's thoughts and feelings echoed those of Johannes Finck, with deep discontent about the difficulties in day-to-day life brought about by the French occupation. Forty years later in a televised ceremony marking the anniversary of the capitulation of the Third Reich, he said, "It was a bad time in Ludwigshafen. There was hardly anything to eat. The French occupation was like nothing anyone could imagine today. It was the time when Charles de Gaulle still dreamed of occupying the left bank of the Rhine for France and I started to become active politically."

This conclusion, viewed with historical introspection and laced with some ridicule, sounds like an unintentional parallel to the inauspicious statement by the *Führer* in *Mein Kampf*, "And then I decided to become a politician." Kohl could not have intended the parallel. There is no such thing as an hour of awakening; this view stems from the rosy retrospective of those people who win in the end, having sought clarity and signposts to avoid becoming bogged down in the mire of life. Kohl sought political life for a number of reasons and found it with resounding success.

The French, to nationally minded Germans, especially those on the border, were a great annoyance. Kohl endeavored more than any other German chancellor since Konrad Adenauer to reconcile the two countries. Recent history has erased the division. The anger and humiliation that many people must have felt did not last. Germany not only recovered, but soon was a well-respected nation in the heart of Europe, largely erasing the memory of everything that once separated it.

However much the patriotic Kohl would like to have humiliated the French occupiers, he was also proud of a passionate Social Democrat such as Kurt Schumacher. Using a false passport, Kohl left Ludwigshafen, in the French Occupation Zone, and went to Mannheim, which was already under U.S. administration, to hear Schumacher, who was then chairperson of the Social Democrats. "It was an incredible experience hearing this man with all his passionate beliefs in a painstakingly repaired hall," he told the historian Maser. "At that time I was a young man but was already a member of the Christian Democratic Union, but this man made an overwhelming impression. . . . Despite his broken body, he was full of vitality. He gave us renewed hope. I became a fan of Schumacher then and actually still am, naturally with greatly differing ideas about political detail, but his personality fascinated me."

Naturally Kohl exaggerated, since as an already adept CDU member it was only Schumacher's showmanship that fascinated him. Schumacher was at that time the most eloquent Social Democratic leader, at least in presence and personality, and knew how to hold his audience in the Rosengarten in Mannheim. Kohl's obvious respect was for a nationally minded Social Democrat, just as he had a high regard for Georg Leber.

The evening in Mannheim listening to Schmacher was not the sort of experience that caused him to enter politics. Kohl probably wished he possessed the almost demonic eloquence of a Savonarola found in this man, who still bore the traces of his years in a concentration camp. There was another reason why Schumacher did not influence Kohl's political future. Kohl is a German, but not as nationalistically minded as this passionate Social Democrat, who later made the terrible accusation against Adenauer in the Bonn parliament, "You are the chancellor of the Allies." That was phrased aptly, almost nastily, but it was not the truth. And of course "Helle" thought so too. As a schoolboy his political credo had been "freedom" and "Europe." In order to make this part of public life, he joined the newly founded *Europa-Union*, which was quickly dissolved by the French occupation forces, putting a rapid end to his career as deputy chairperson.

Kurt Schumacher would not have regarded such a European debating club as a good venue in postwar Germany. But there was something moving about the founding of a group of young Europeans at this historic time. The Ludwigshafen high-school students who met in the *Brücke* (bridge) for the founding of the European Union were keen and excited. Kohl's name was soon mentioned when it came to voting for chairperson. Not wanting to leave things to chance, "Helle" had brought his friends with him and as a matter of honor, the Friesenheimer students voted for him unanimously.

"He not only wanted our votes, he wanted to be loved," recalls one of the friends from his youth.

The group, very quickly forbidden by the occupiers—the French greatly opposed the concept of a united Europe at the time—had an effect well beyond Ludwigshafen. It could be termed a kind of dawn. Ernst Bloch, another of the city's famous sons, called the city "a truly hollow place" which must first be filled before it could assume form. This city, with which the Marxist philosopher had a love/hate relationship, leaned toward the elegant residence of Mannheim on the other side of the Rhine, which is "happy and friendly just as in the time of Hermann and Dorothea" (a reference to a play by Goethe). This was Bloch with his sense of loathing, which perhaps explains why he became a philosopher and not a politician, who at his or her best works for change and the achievement of the possible, and who is not mired down in introspective analysis. "In the end, Ludwigshafen remained the factory ruins forced into becoming a city: a helpless victim of circumstance, cut in half by the railroad, a Zwickau without inhibitions, in a false day à la Biedermeier in its inception, a heavy, rainy day." The apparent hopelessness prompted a philosopher to reflect about the world and provided a politician with a challenge to make the future better. It is not surprising that Helmut Kohl remained true not only to himself but to his city, in keeping with his enduring desire for security, conditioned by factors that reveal something of his personality.

In 1928, Bloch wrote about his native city, "Places like Ludwigshafen are like the first cities founded on land: fluctuating, easygoing, on the shores of an unsteady future."[12] Plundering the old to rebuild the new, Bloch says, "is best done in such a place. A crossroads of worker and entrepreneur, clearly and factually between them and the future." And thus we see, despite the suppression of a wonderful initiative for which the time had not yet come, a "dawn over the truly hollow place." "Don't despair," was the almost heroic motto of the citizens, who did not want to stand still with the Marxist precepts.

2

Political Steps

1950–1960

The Higher School of Wasting Time

From the very beginning, Helmut Kohl had only one idea: go into politics and make a name for himself, no matter what the cost. No other thought obsessed him quite as much in his younger or later years. He began studying law at the Johann-Wolfgang-Goethe University in Frankfurt without much enthusiasm, and also studied psychology, which was fashionable at the time and would gain increasing importance. Economics was added to create a mixture that was not entirely satisfactory in the long run. Kohl was happier when he transferred to the university at Heidelberg, because the faculty included such famous professors as philosopher Karl Jaspers, sociologist Alfred Weber, cultural sociologist Alexander Rüstow, and political scientist Dolf Sternberger. Moreover, it was only one hour on the Lambretta to home in Ludwigshafen, where the party politics which was to become the cornerstone of his career awaited. Even then Kohl was convinced that his career would take him to Mainz, and then to who knew where. The tall young man on the small motor scooter caused a lot of amusement, but at least the young university student from Ludwigshafen had transport, an unusual thing in those days.

Hence Kohl was able to keep up with his friends, who, though they may not have regarded him as a role model, at least looked to him for inspiration. "*Der Lange*" was out to make a name for himself and attracted a number of followers. Heinz Schwarz, a young bank employee from Koblenz, knew his friend Helmut would not say no if it meant gaining political power. Kohl was one of the few who admitted that he found power attractive and that he was after it, not mincing his words.

Schwarz, later Kohl's interior minister in the *Landeskabinett*, met the seventeen-year-old at the CDU *Land* party conference in Kaiserslautern and again at the first seminar of the *Junge Union* in Bendorf, before the currency reform. They soon became friends, joined by Heinrich Holkenbrink, a

The 23-year-old Kohl with Margret and Heinz Schwartz in Ludwigshafen, 1952.

teacher-in-training from Neuenahr, in Westphalia, to form a triumvirate, a force to be reckoned with in *Land* politics. A fourth was Heinz Korbach, later *Regierungspräsident* of Koblenz. Kohl was the youngest of the small group but still the most hardworking of all. At that time, since he was attending university, he was thought to be the secret number one. Heinz Schwarz, of short stature and quick temper, almost exclusively looked after the younger, up-and-coming members of the CDU and became the secretary of the *Land* CDU. Kohl was trying to make a name for himself in the main party. Younger people joined the CDU in order to topple the older members as soon as this was realistically possible. At the party conference in Kaiserslautern a *Junge Union* member termed the party leaders "collec-

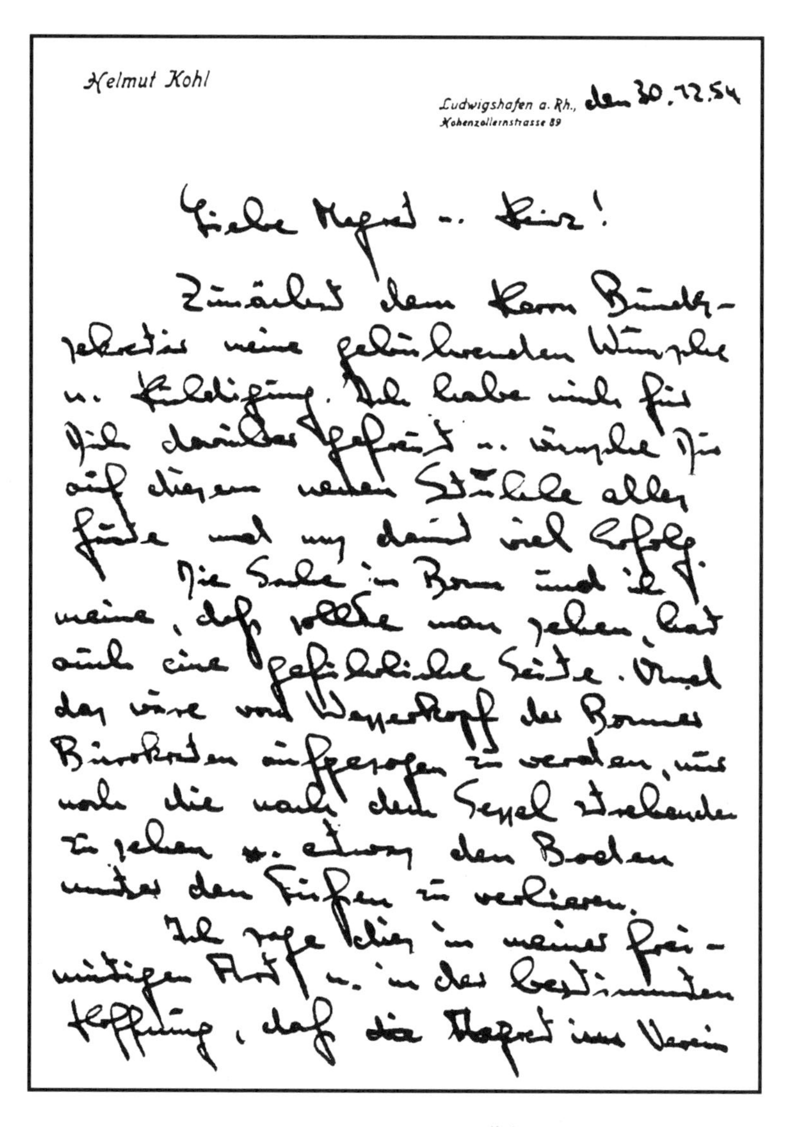

Helmut Kohl

Ludwigshafen a. Rh., den 30.12.54
Hohenzollernstrasse 89

Liebe Margret u. Heinz!

The first page of a letter to Margret and Heinz Schwartz written on December 30, 1954. Kohl congratulates his friend on his appointment to secretary of the Junge Union, *but also warns, "The matter in Bonn . . . has a dangerous side as well, which would be to get caught up in the top-heavy Bonn bureaucracy, to pay attention only to those seeking the position, and to lose touch with the ground beneath your feet."*

tive geriatrics." The main target of this vituperation was Peter Altmeier, the "father" of the *Land* party, who the younger generation planned to oust from power. The merchant Altmeier, who had not forgotten how to count, soon had to admit that the younger generation knew "at least as much about power" as he did.

In these first years after the end of the war and the collapse of the Third Reich, politics was as much about learning democracy as anything else. Social democracy, with its long-standing traditions, began to reassert itself. In the Soviet-occupied zone it was put to flight and finally swallowed by the communists; those who resisted lost their freedom or even their lives. The Christian Democratic Union, the response of Christian-minded people—a fusion of Catholics and Protestants—was formed in Bad Godesberg, at that time a separate spa town south of Bonn. Local branches were formed all over in a Germany destroyed by the Reich. The Union provided an impetus to the Parliamentary Council that was forming the constitution, as did SPD men such as Carlo Schmid and Kurt Schumacher.

Young people again began to read newspapers, which were produced only in limited numbers because of paper shortages. Politics gripped the imagination most of all. Everything was rationed during the time of the black market, especially food. Heinz Schwarz had to ensure that there was enough food for Bendorf to be able to continue the seminars. Strictly rationed meat, skimmed milk, and spinach were the only things he could get. "You could always get potatoes," Schwarz recalled half a lifetime later, "but organizing the rest was a real problem for me."

The constitution of the *Land* of Rhineland-Palatinate was accepted on May 18, 1947, though the differences between people from the Rhineland and the Palatinate, such as the *Rheinprovinzler*, were by no means smoothed over. A day before that, Heinz Schwarz and some of his friends from Leubsdorf joined the CDU "so that no one could say afterward that we joined because the Union won."

Kohl was not interested in pursuing a career in the junior branch; he was content simply to be a part of it. He could easily have become chairperson of the *Land* organization, but remained deputy. Schwarz, the main organizer, became the secretary of the national *Junge Union* and as such was able to impress "*der Lange*" with his Mercedes 170.

The Higher School of Letting Oneself Go

"He had a way with words and would tell people in authority just exactly what he thought." Heinz Schwarz was quite firm in his opinion of student and fellow party member Helmut Kohl. That way with words soon dispelled any inferiority complex Schwarz may have had because he was not a student: "Don't let it bother you, you're an intellectual too, just without a degree." This was the end of the matter for both. Kohl soon came to believe that the mixed background of the small CDU group was good for its image.

Heinz Korbach, a colleague at that time, said, "Even as a seventeen-year-old he had an astonishing thirst for political power." At another time he said, "He spent many hours defending his political views, staunchly and with fervor, backing them up with new reasons all the time. He regarded the Catholic church as a religious power with some distance, though with favor; he by no means condoned unquestioning adherence to this authority."

As Korbach says, "It is difficult to believe that Kohl as an eighteen- or nineteen-year-old made any substantial contribution to the fundaments of the German constitution. However, his belief in the social market economy and in the first German chancellor, Konrad Adenauer, was unquestionable." On the other hand, Korbach stated euphemistically, at that time Kohl "did not stand unreservedly behind the minister-president of Rhineland-Palatinate, Peter Altmeier." It was Schwarz who attested that he, Kohl, and many others of the younger generation "came on the scene in order to topple Altmeier and his cabinet, even if this would take many years."

First Kohl had to finish his degree. Since he had not done the *Grosses Latinum*, he had to cram vocabulary before his history professors would even accept his seminar papers. At Heidelberg he majored in history and minored in public law, government law, and political science. He was in good standing with the prominent historian, Fritz Ernst; his other professors were Conze, Gollwizer, and a former professor from Leipzig, Maschke. Kohl wrote a seminar paper entitled "The Popular Front in France" for Professor von Albertini. He also attended lectures by the well-known cultural sociologist Alexander Rüstow and seminars by Waldemar Burian on Soviet politics. Kohl was successful in getting into Sternberg's seminar and, recommended by this well-known political scientist and publicist, he was appointed an assistant at the Alfred-Weber-Institute at a salary of 150 marks, a boost to his income.

Walter Peter Fuchs, the renowned expert on Ranke, became Kohl's dissertation advisor. His thesis dealt with recent history: "Political Development in Rhineland-Palatinate and the Resurgence of Political Parties after 1945." This basically descriptive work that examined recent events and political movements was not groundbreaking in nature, but the doctoral candidate nevertheless achieved the distinction *cum laude*. This was quite an achievement for someone like Kohl, who already at that time was the leader of the Ludwigshafen CDU and one of the most active Union politicians in

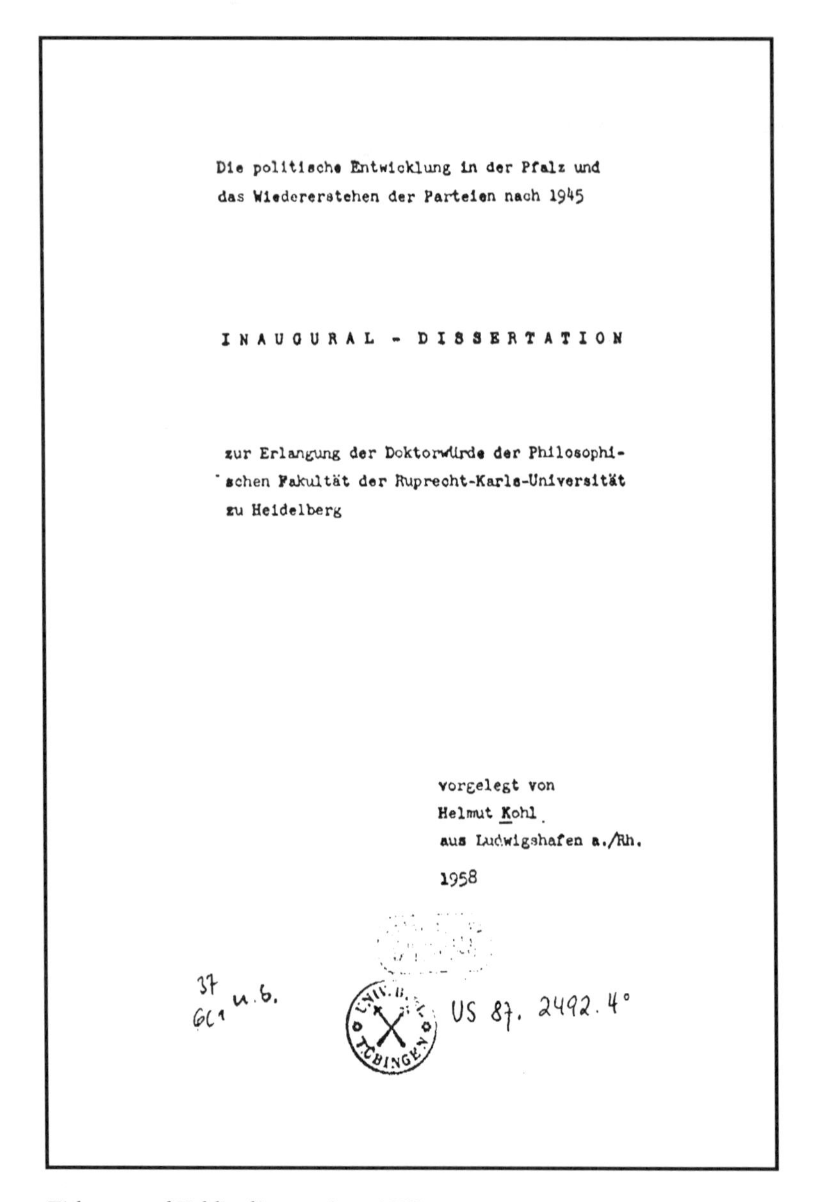

Die politische Entwicklung in der Pfalz und
das Wiedererstehen der Parteien nach 1945

INAUGURAL - DISSERTATION

zur Erlangung der Doktorwürde der Philosophischen Fakultät der Ruprecht-Karls-Universität
zu Heidelberg

vorgelegt von
Helmut Kohl
aus Ludwigshafen a./Rh.

1958

37
6C1 u.6.
US 87. 2492.4°

Title page of Kohl's dissertation, 1958.

Rhineland-Palatinate. His dissertation was backed up with many private and official documents from well-known politicians of the *Land*. Many of the documents were from the estate of his great mentor, Johannes Finck, thus maintaining the teacher-student link long after Finck's death. Kohl, though quick enough to grasp concepts, was not prone to linger over a task longer than necessary and finished his studies part time. His fellow student

Erwin Faul, professor of political science at the University of Trier, described Kohl at the time: "The doctoral candidate reacted with impatience to the ins and outs in the process of obtaining a doctorate, and to the criticisms of his dissertation readers about the way he formulated things."[13] The already experienced local politician was able to get his material "from his immediate experience." Kohl believed that the doctorate might give him greater standing in politics, his only real aspiration.

Looking back at his university years after becoming adviser to the

Lebenslauf

Am 3. April 1930 wurde ich in Ludwigshafen am Rhein als drittes Kind des Finanzbeamten Hans Kohl und seiner Ehefrau Cäcilie geborene Schnur geboren.

Nach dem Abschluss der vierten Volksschulklasse besuchte ich vom 28.3.1940 bis zum 8.7.1950 die Oberrealschule an der Leuschnerstrasse in Ludwigshafen am Rhein, an der ich am 8.6.1950 die Reifeprüfung ablegte.

Im Wintersemester 1950/51 begann ich an der Johann Wolfgang Goethe Universität in Frankfurt am Main mein Studium. Im Wintersemester 1951/52 bezog ich die Ruprecht Karls Universität Heidelberg, an der ich meine weitere Studienzeit verbrachte. Zunächst beabsichtigte ich eine Juristische Laufbahn einzuschlagen, im Verlauf meines Studiums folgte ich jedoch meinen historischen Interessen und wählte Geschichte als Hauptfach; in diesem Sachgebiet fand ich auch das Thema meiner Dissertation.

Seit Herbst 1956 arbeitete ich in der Forschungsgruppe des Politischen Seminars der Universität Heidelberg unter der Leitung von Professor Dr. Dolf Sternberger. Als Stipendiat der Deutschen Forschungsgemeinschaft verfasste ich eine Studie über die Bundestagswahlen 1957 unter besonderer Berücksichtigung des Landes Rheinland-Pfalz.

Meine Lehrer an der Universität Heidelberg waren vor allem die Professoren Walter Peter Fuchs, Fritz Ernst, Johannes Kühn, Werner Conze, Dolf Sternberger und Walter Jellinek

The curriculum vitae that accompanied Kohl's dissertation.

Organization of the Chemical Industry, he spoke almost disparagingly about the "higher school of wasting time."[14] By this the graduate, now looking for a job to earn money and start a family, meant that although his alma mater gave him a lot of time and intellectual relaxation, it did not provide the impetus for his role in the world. Kohl regarded his time studying as a kind of self-imposed, semicloistered existence, and the long nights with fellow students discussing seminar papers and planning their lives as pretty much a waste of time. He chafed at the bit, which is why his pocket diary became his constant companion, adviser, and tempter. Before Kohl starts a session or a fairly formal discussion, he still gets out his pocket diary and examines it. Kohl's behavior in his professional and private life became almost identical, following the same pattern of meetings, travels, and consultations in small groups. Otherwise he had not learned anything and continued more or less in the same vein, even though his improvised studies left some traces, particularly in a historical-critical regard. The almost thirty-year-old politician trying to get a seat in the Mainz *Landtag* shared the fate typical of the political class as a whole. He began to admire Adenauer, now in his third term and beginning to show some signs of weakness; Kohl admired him at least for his stamina in holding onto office in Bonn.

However, he also attempted to topple, little by little, the other older office holder, the minister-president Peter Altmeier. Sometimes he enlisted others to undermine Altmeier, who he believed would soon lose office, and sometimes he did the work himself. More than once Kohl was accused of arrogance. He answered this charge almost with amusement, such as in an interview with the *Mannheimer Morgen* published in the August 28–29, 1966 issue: "I've heard this accusation. I'm not, however. But my height of 1.93 meters doesn't do anything optically to dispel this notion." Konrad Adenauer once chided him, "Watch out that you don't become a cynic." Kohl reacted with characteristic alacrity and lack of respect for the older man: "The fact that it is you that says that really surprises me. But I don't have any talent for cynicism."[15] But not all of his contemporaries were convinced of that.

Those in politics also have to earn money on the side. The financial compensation of the time was extremely low; a councilor in the Ludwigshafen city council was paid only fifty marks and a member of parliament of the *Land* only five hundred marks. Thus Helmut Kohl had to look for a steady job, having worked previously like hundreds of other students in the Badische Anilin-und-Soda-Fabrik (BASF) as a stone grinder in the workshop of the chemical company, and finally for contract salary in the woodwork shop. With his newly awarded doctorate and no experience in commerce, Kohl was able to get a job as assistant to the management at the Willi Mock iron foundry, a medium-sized company. He was paid eight hundred marks a month; the position was obviously created for Kohl, the rising star among the new generation of *Land* politicians, "since he had to be helped," the wife of the company's director recalled thirty years later. The assistant to the management was responsible for bookkeeping for the firm's 250 employees, as well as negotiating deals on property with the company's neighbors—the director said he even had some success there.

Sorry, I Don't Have Time

Kohl's job as adviser on economics and tax policies with the Organization of the Chemical Industry in Rhineland-Palatinate became a long-term one, with a salary of one thousand marks per month, rising to three thousand in just ten years. He knew by then that he was born and bred to be a politician. After entering the CDU *Landtag* parliamentary party (*Fraktion*) in 1959 he looked to the future with confidence. A journalist once asked him what his dream career would be. "Mine of course!" was the answer.

He was the youngest person in the *Land* CDU but became one of its leaders within two years. Party work for the twenty-nine-year-old was his first real challenge outside of his home city. Right from the start he had his eye on the head of local government, Peter Altmeier, a real challenge for the pugnacious Kohl. He probably needed that in order to feel the pinpricks that proved he was making progress, in order to show himself and the world what he could do.

No inferiority complex ever caused this man to have doubts; he was the way he was and that was all. Others had to take him as he was, though often enough they tried to get around "*der Lange*" with a smile. Altmeier as a person and a symbol was just the right type for a parliamentary neophyte to try to topple from the saddle: not only was he the oldest, he was also the longest-serving German minister-president. At first this attempt seemed laughable. Altmeier, a businessman born in the nineteenth century, was an unparalleled example of a successful politician in postwar Germany. He always dressed formally, wearing silver-gray ties even when it was not necessary, and vests which were long out of fashion, and he had the slightly disapproving look of a strict Catholic priest regarding a poor but repentant sinner. Altmeier was also the only survivor in office from the first conference of minister-presidents in 1947 at the Rittersturz, near Koblenz, to which he was invited and which he led. Thus there were reasons enough for Kohl to believe that Altmeier, though worthy of respect, had outlived his time. Heinz Schwarz, who became a member of the *Landtag* at the same time, called him "a representative of a bygone age."

Kohl moved into an office of the chemical organization in his home city of Ludwigshafen. He drove to his political appointments in the capital of the *Land* in a French-built car which he had bought at a good price with help from relatives in the Saarland. Naturally Kohl envied his friend Schwarz, who had a plush Mercedes by virtue of his position with the national *Junge Union*, and he never missed an opportunity to tease his friend about it.

They "worked like animals" according to Schwarz, never missed an appointment, and chided their political opponent almost to the point of freshness or even chutzpah. The reactions to this were mostly gratifying. A leading article in the Mainz SPD publication *Die Freiheit* threw light on the political scene in the *Landtagsparliament* in a tone that seemed almost grandfatherly and finger-shaking. The article was entitled "Bad Style" and was written by "*Pfiffikus*" (artful dodger), a pseudonym which must have greatly amused Kohl.

> Our publication's discovery that the clocks of the Mainz government are slow or standing still has greatly enlivened discussions about the budget in the *Landtag* to date. They moved the government bench and the speaker of the CDU party. However, instead of actually doing something about this, it was polemically defused by this group. It was in particular Drs. Kohl and Schwarz from the Christian Democratic nursery for up-and-coming politicians, the *Junge Union*, who went about things in the wrong way in their tone and arguments. . . . A democratic parliament is no place for statements such as "Your grinning doesn't change anything" to a political opponent, or the fanatically blinding assertion that the Social Democrats are agitating and speculating with German unity, as stated by that zealous CDU foal, Schwarz. Or is this a response to Social Democratic concerns about the cultural and education policies in Rhineland-Palatinate, when the CDU know-it-all, Dr. Kohl, said to the SPD speaker, "You just want the minister's chair yourself!" Now, Dr. Kohl, permit a question to be directed at you: What position in government are you aiming for? The meteoric rise to speaker of the CDU for the minister-president's budget and that for culture seems to leave two possibilities open. It almost appears that the previous [sic] minister-president, Altmeier, despite his successful appearances on television, will not have to worry so much about the SPD winning his beloved position as elder statesman in the next *Landtag* election campaign will about the "Dr. Kohl shock troop."[16]

The Social Democrats had the upper hand and the Altmeier regime had passed its prime. The opposition in the *Landtag* ate into the CDU with the exception of only three seats, and the bastion of Peter Altmeier, in place for almost a generation, began to crumble. These were ideal conditions for a newcomer with excellent prospects to turn later campaigns to his advantage. Klaus Dreher wrote about Kohl's challenge to Altmeier: "He was almost an unknown outside of Rhineland-Palatinate. In the *Land* he is referred to with a slight shudder, but also with admiration. Some people think he will be the one to lead the CDU to new heights, others are afraid of his rough approach. The younger generation likes to identify itself with him and regard him as a youthful hero on the political stage, which has been dominated almost exclusively by the older generation for one and a half decades."

When the young Kohl strode through the assembly of the *Landtag* and someone wanted a word with him, he said more and more frequently as the weeks went by, "I'm sorry, I don't have any time." A proper parliamentarian plans for himself if others have not already done so for him. But he had not reached that stage in the early 1960s. The three men from the *Junge Union*, Kohl, Holkenbrink, and Schwarz, still formed a small group within the overwhelmingly more settled CDU *Land* party. They stuck together as well in the evenings, when they met for a glass of wine on the Neubrunnen square in Mainz, where they could speak their minds openly and sometimes really slander some people. "*Der Lange*" relaxed only with those of like mind, young men in politics, lobbying organizations, and parliament. One evening Heinz Schwarz and Heinrich Holkenbrink dragged him into a bar; Heinz, always ready for anything, eyed the striptease dancer with interest, but Kohl and Holkenbrink were completely immersed "in their philosophical discussions," according to Schwarz. All his efforts to draw attention to the movements of the naked dancer had no effect on Kohl: "He was enough to make me despair!" The same drama was played out with different actors during a trip with the *Junge Union*, when a beautiful blonde tried persistently to gain the attention of "*der Lange.*" Kohl ignored her. Schwarz could not understand his friend's obstinate behavior until afterward. "He already was going out with Hannelore, which Helmut found reason enough." He was probably also fairly reserved, although he appeared otherwise.

By the early 1960s Germany's tough times were over. The "eating binge" was followed by the desire for luxury goods, which for Germans meant having a good radio or record player. Some people even had televisions but Kohl still did not have a working refrigerator. This was to change. His engagement to Hannelore had lasted thirteen years and was to lead to marriage with a roof over his head. For Kohl, this naturally meant one's own roof. It was important to have connections, and anyone working for an influential organization who was also a parliamentarian in the *Landtag* could get credit without security based on recommendations. Kohl's philosophy of life is founded on security and there he did not have any problems. Hannelore Renner and Helmut Kohl married at a time when the politician of the younger generation stood a good chance of getting ahead in his party and in parliament, in this regard too Kohl was a steady pragmatist who left nothing to chance.

Hannelore, three years younger, came from Leipzig. It is possible that they might never have met except for the war and the fact that the Renner family fled from the East to the West in May 1945. Hannelore's father, a talented engineer, had developed the Panzerfaust portable antitank weapon, capable of penetrating tank armor, in his munitions factory in the final year of the war. The Renners had to abandon everything in the face of the advancing Soviet Red Army. When Helmut and Hannelore first met at a tea dance organized by the high-school senior in the Weinberg guest house, Hannelore was wearing a dress made out of three flags. Hannelore's mother had cut out the swastika from two of the flags and the third had come from a church. Both young people admitted they were terrible dancers with two left feet. Hannelore Kohl said, "We were a pretty sad pair."

She later reckoned that they had lived in different places for eleven years, but each had inwardly made a commitment to the other. As a schoolboy and university student, Helmut had written her as many as three letters a week, almost two thousand letters over the years. The marriage was a happy one, and for Kohl, by nature monogamous, a source of self-confidence and security.

In public life Kohl also sought loyalty and commitment, reported Jockel Fuchs, one of his most prominent rivals at that time in internal politics and the subsequent long-serving lord mayor of Mainz. Fuchs used the meticulous, patronizing tone that politicians from opposite camps adopt.

> Kohl made contacts, not only within his own party, but also with members of the opposition in parliament, from the SPD. You could discuss things with him coolly and in confidence, often over a glass of wine in the restaurant of the *Landtag*, even after the most heated debates in the assembly. Sometimes he gave the impression of wanting "the warmth of the nest" in day-to-day politics. Thus it became a regular thing that the so-called "pipe-smoking colleagues" met after work in the restaurant of the *Landtag*. Prominent among them was Helmut Kohl; his parliamentary manager, Willibald Hilf, who later became director of the *Südwestfunk* radio and television network; the manager of the *Land* SPD parliamentary party, Karl Thorwirth; and myself. At that time we all smoked pipes. We discussed an awful lot of decisions ahead of time there, and whatever was

agreed was mutually adhered to. You could always reach an agreement with Helmut Kohl, and he stuck to it. These conversations over a glass of wine shouldn't make anyone think that there weren't also some heated political debates if necessary. If Helmut Kohl was speaking he could really let loose, though it all remained within the rules of democracy. We younger politicians of the time looked at the world a lot differently from our older colleagues, who were still under the influence of the Weimar Republic, their years as emigrants, or persecution by the Nazis.[17]

3

Climbing the Ladder

1960–1966

A Palatinate Temperament with a Pipe

It was 1961, and Helmut Kohl was elected deputy chairperson of the forty-one members of the *Landtag* parliamentary party by an extremely narrow majority. Altmeier had favored his supporter from Koblenz, Heinz Korbach, and, feeling certain that he would have a majority in the party, Altmeier vehemently opposed the expansion of the leadership to two deputies. That suggestion had been made to avoid having to make a decision between the two friends. It was Altmeier's bad luck and Kohl's advantage; he and not Korbach took the lead.

Kohl's way up the ladder was determined from that moment. However, the gaps between the individual steps in his career differed greatly: it took him only two years to become chairperson of the party, but then six years until he became minister-president. The next stage, chairmanship of the national party, took four years; after that he had to wait nine years until he became chancellor. It cannot be said that his rise was rapid. Everything took time, and the man from Rhineland-Palatinate did not have it any easier than anyone else. Often the opposite was the case, since he always had more potential opponents than admirers and supporters. Nevertheless, Kohl made the history books by becoming the youngest chancellor. But none of his predecessors had entered politics at such an early age. Kohl began his career at sixteen and by twenty-two he was actively engaged in politics. Now, at thirty-one, he was established, and from then on none of his political colleagues, and almost none of his opponents, ever seriously doubted he would unseat Altmeier within the foreseeable future.

From then on "*der Lange*" had his eye firmly fixed on the Zeughaus in Mainz, where the minister-president had been rooted to the chair for the last fifteen years. Two years later, Kohl was able to score his first real triumph: in the elections as leader of the parliamentary party in the Mainz

Landtag he came just short of one hundred percent, with two abstentions and one vote against. Kohl interpreted this victory as a signal to mobilize all his friends and forces and start the fight for the top. His friends often play a role in his methods as is usual in politics—which allows the instigator to remain under cover. At the same time he attacked the ministers of culture, as Heinz Schwarz likes to recall, since "*der Lange*" felt that he had been cheated in his *Abitur* and wanted to even the score.

When Kohl's friends in publishing call him a "thoroughbred politician," which he was already at the time, the outbreaks of temper by the young giant were probably only the release of pent-up aggression from his years as a student, when he was not as active in politics as he wanted to be. That is the reason he spoke almost angrily about "the higher school of wasting time" when he could not make an impact on the politics of the day. Klaus Dreher, a journalist who followed Kohl's rise to power over two decades, adopted a tone in 1965 suitable for a mild description of a genre, which later devolved into sharp analysis and criticism. "He has the bubbly personality and active imagination of the Palatinate temperament. In his first political moves he lashed out against some politicians who were his friends, and also against Altmeier, which he regrets today."[18]

Nothing made Kohl sorry—otherwise he would not have become the man he was made by history and the political situation in Germany. The cliché of "the angry young man" also did not fit the facts: he was not that angry. At thirty-three, Kohl did not love life any less than he did at sixty-five. He played the role of an angry young man because he enjoyed frightening others, particularly his older party friends. Kohl consciously allowed the press to say that the parliamentary party was the "second center of power" after Altmeier's state chancery. For Altmeier, from a middle-class background, the Rhenish *Windthorstbund* and in later years the (Catholic) Center party had become his spiritual and political home. His lack of contacts was legendary; his lifestyle—in contrast with that of Kohl, who was half his age—almost spartan; and his tone dry, sober, and distant.

Altmeier's isolation increased as the younger man's challenge seemed to become more and more open, although perhaps the greatest achievement of this man was his undoubted ability to integrate things. Persistently and patiently, using his knowledge of the region, the party cornerstone united the *Land*, with its regional differences and economic orientations, without merging or erasing its beloved peculiarities. By moving from Koblenz to Mainz, Altmeier proved that the Rhineland-Palatinate belonged together and that old dreams should not have too great a sway. "Of course always with the belief that the people of Koblenz were better," Heinz Schwarz said about Altmeier's stance.

There could hardly have been two more different men than Altmeier and Kohl. This was not due just to the age difference, but to their characters. The younger man had the same degree of ambition which the former was able to satisfy. Kohl said then, as today, that "A politician has to be ambitious. However, the ambition has to be kept in check, but it must be there, just as you would expect from a hunting dog. You shouldn't have to carry him to the hunting field."

While Altmeier's style was conventional and even reserved, "*der Lange*" acted with the unconcern of the youthful hero in a bungled attempt at banter in Schiller's play *Don Carlos*. There is, however, no evidence that the young man was thinking at that time about the Marquis de Posa, who, despairing about the rigidity of his emperor, cries with pathos, "Grant freedom of thought, sire!" But pathos is not a characteristic of this man, even in his youth, though a friend from his days in Mainz recollected, "When a large man with a pipe showed up at a boring meeting of the *Junge Union*, it guaranteed an argument."

Unlike the head of government whom people wanted to remove, Kohl had a number of good friends, not as head of the CDU, but as a person. For over ten years in the *Landtag* these were Heinz Schwarz, Heinrich Holkenbrink, Heinz Korbach, and Otto Theisen; Heiner Geissler and Bernard Vogel came later. They formed a clearly honorable but sometimes noisy group in the CDU, attracting some but sometimes repelling others.

Kohl started to learn how to think tactically and proved this during discussion of a reform, which was ahead of its time. The SPD in the *Landtag* had proposed that school fees be abolished. Parliamentary member Hülser (a friend of Kohl's father) and Heinz Schwarz said they would support the proposal. Holkenbrink and Kohl, as well as Altmeier, were against it. The CDU establishment thought a split had developed in the "Kohl group." Not in the least! They continued to eat lunch together in the canteen and drank a glass of wine in their favorite pubs, where they had the opportunity to come up with new plans and work on new proposals. The move by the opposition fell apart as expected and school fees were not abolished until the mid-1960s.

The CDU majority in the *Landtag* became less and less secure with every election. Nationally, the CDU/CSU lost its absolute majority in the election of 1961, and a dark shadow was cast over Konrad Adenauer's last year in power by the painful "*Spiegel* affair." On October 26, 1962, police occupied and searched the offices of *Der Spiegel* (West Germany's largest and most influential news magazine) in Munich and Hamburg, remaining in occupation for over a month. *Spiegel* publisher Rudolf Augstein was arrested, along with Conrad Ahlers and several other editors, and charged with "suspicion of high treason" because of an article on the inadequacy of the national defenses.

The Federal High Court eventually dismissed all charges owing to insufficient evidence, and Defense Minister Franz Josef Strauss was compelled to admit before the *Bundestag* that he had played a vital part in the arrests. Adenauer's favorite, Strauss, was forced to resign. At that time, Friedrich Sieburg, the co-publisher of the *Frankfurt Allgemeine Zeitung*, wrote cuttingly in an editorial, "Yesterday Adenauer was said to be standing *behind* Strauss. Today he is said to be standing *in front of* him. Some clarification is needed here." There are no comments by Kohl to parliament or the public about the shattering admissions by the highest-ranking members of his party in this scandal. However, the man from the Palatinate had a lifelong aversion to the Hamburg-based news magazine.

Reforms, Reforms

> By *reforms* we mean continuity and progress. We interpret the word to mean that the house built over two decades, the Federal Republic of Germany, will continue to meet our needs in the coming decades. In so doing we must also understand each new generation which seeks to move into its "parents' home." I must warn against those who believe that politics is a drawing board. Politics has to do with people, and thank God, people do not let themselves be designed on a drawing board."[19]

Kohl's analogy to a "parents' house" into which the younger generation moves reflects his own experience. Everything is concrete, and can be felt and sensed. There has rarely been a politician who thinks less in abstract terms than Helmut Kohl. "Politics has to do with people. . ." That is of course only a mild version of the claim ascribed to the restless, active, ambitious politician that "politics has to do with human flesh." Politics creates possibilities and paths for men and women in society, but it also opens the door to the all too well-known ravages of power, or at least influence, mild blackmail, coercion, and betrayal. But that is as inconceivable without publicly documented strife, political self-presentation, even sometimes the sacrifice of personal interests and doing without the pleasant aspects of life, as is the church of salvation without the Inquisition and the spiritual and physical torture.

Helmut Kohl, the force and initiator behind the small power base in the *Landtag*, was a far cry from the experienced politician of the 1970s and 1980s. But he learned quickly. Beginning in 1966, Kohl headed the *Land* CDU as its *Landesfürst* (regional prince), and the CDU gained 2.3 percent in the *Landtag* elections of 1967. It thus narrowly missed achieving an absolute majority. In Mainz at that time it was an unwritten rule that no government coalition was to be attempted against the strongest party in parliament. This continued to be the case, since already on election night Jockel Fuchs, the top SPD candidate and later lord mayor of Mainz, declared categorically, "It goes without saying that it is up to the strongest party to lead negotiations on forming a coalition!" Thus the CDU had free rein to resurrect the old coalition with the Free Democrats. Kohl nodded and grumbled a barely binding assent to continuation of the Altmeier regime. The man from the Palatinate placed some of his trusted fellows in the cabinet without too much difficulty—Bernhard Vogel as culture minister and Heinrich ("Heiner") Geissler as minister for social affairs. Both were with him for many years on his way to the top.

The thirty-seven-year-old extracted a promise from Altmeier, "*der Alte*," as Kohl called him with some irony, that he would make way for him in the middle of the legislative period, precisely on Constitution Day, May 1969. Altmeier agreed reluctantly, but had he not kept his promise, anything could have happened, including a public confrontation and a fall from power.

The CDU often cleverly left it to the opposition SPD to denigrate Altmeier on the ruling bench, Jockel Fuchs recalls clearly. "Peter Altmeier was in the habit of always having the last word after debates in the *Landtag*. We younger members didn't like that, so we got together and agreed that he wouldn't have the final say. Thus we younger SPD members spoke up again and again after Altmeier, who finally gave it up after several weeks. The front bench of the CDU grinned about it—no one jumped into the breach."[20]

The aspiring minister-president soon proved his political talents. Those who do not know his personality say that in public life he is anything but considerate, even sentimental. The land reform was carried out with an iron will, despite opposition. The idea of a larger population concentration, which was uncautiously announced during the fervor of a general reform, remained only on paper. "Wherever wood is planed, there are woodshavings," Kohl was wont to reply to political opponents who remind him about political promises.

Kohl brought party pressure to bear when he discovered that the "*Altvater*" (old father) was not ready to leave his office at the agreed time and was visibly hesitating. Altmeier had probably grossly underestimated the solidarity of the *Land* CDU, which was no longer "his" party. While the minister-president carried out his final tasks of office, the state chancery cellar was being rebuilt under Kohl's orders.

The farewell ceremony which the patriarch planned for himself on May 16, 1969, in the ceremonial hall of the chancery gives an idea of the spirit of the times. Altmeier's former agriculture minister, Oskar Stübinger, praised the celebrant, calling him "a man of the people." Altmeier had just spent hours, clearly moved, shaking hands with several hundred people. His designated successor stood unmoved the whole time with an inscrutable expression, as observers reported, in front of the windows in the hall, letting events take their course. Kohl listened to Altmeier reminding his audience about his twenty-two years in office and the hungry population of the early years after the war. He emphasized as his greatest accomplishments the Rittersturz conference, reintegration of the Saarland, and the founding of German Television Channel Two in Mainz, actually a great accomplishment of the *Länder* against Adenauer's claim to the media. The departing minister-president listed all his colleagues and political friends by name, including his trusted chauffeur Paul Geisel, who "once helped do a somersault," an allusion to a minor car accident. The only one not mentioned was Helmut Kohl. "Obviously neither of them had anything more to say to each other," Jockel Fuchs said. Kohl was noticeably the first to leave the hall, without shaking hands with Altmeier.

Change in government in Rhineland-Palatinate, May 1969. The departing minister-president, Peter Altmeier, and his successor, Helmut Kohl, regard one of the going-away presents.

The first Kohl Cabinet in Mainz poses for photographers. From left: Bernhard Vogel (culture), August Wolters (interior), Fritz Schneider (justice), Otto Mayer (agriculture), Heinrich Geissler (social), Minister-president Kohl, Herman Eicher (finance) and Hans Neubauer (economics and transportation). May 19, 1969.

"Woe unto anyone who didn't show up for a cabinet meeting," said Heinz Schwarz, interior minister in Kohl's second *Land* government. Unlike the legend, Kohl's style of government was not "predominantly friendly and jovial," but strict, aimed at efficiency and brevity. "Kohl wanted to avoid any sort of heated debate in cabinet meetings. He hated it when an argument seemed to be brewing and he deflected it immediately. You had to be informed about individual questions ahead of time and these had to have been agreed ahead of time with other departments," said Schwarz. Under Kohl there was little discussion in the classical sense; decisions were made between alternatives, which were presented succinctly. On the other hand, general issues, even philosophical ones—basic issues, that is—were discussed at even greater length. Kohl bothered with day-to-day matters only reluctantly. He would fly at a minister who brought along documents from his department to discuss. "Why are you bringing along that nonsense from your department? Is that your opinion or your people's? We're not into administration here, we're governing. That's the difference."

The cabinet took its time with important issues, the ministers discussing details. One example was the decision on the nuclear power station at Mühlheim-Kehrlich, for which Kohl called a two-day closed session. The largely uninformed heads of departments were then able to question experts from all over the country before making a government ruling on this extremely important issue. The actual cabinet meeting took place at the round table in the chancery's wine cellar; tongues were loosened, ideas could take flight, one could speak openly among others from the *Land*; department heads felt they were among compatriots and called each other *du*—most knew each other from the *Junge Union*, and, with some differen-

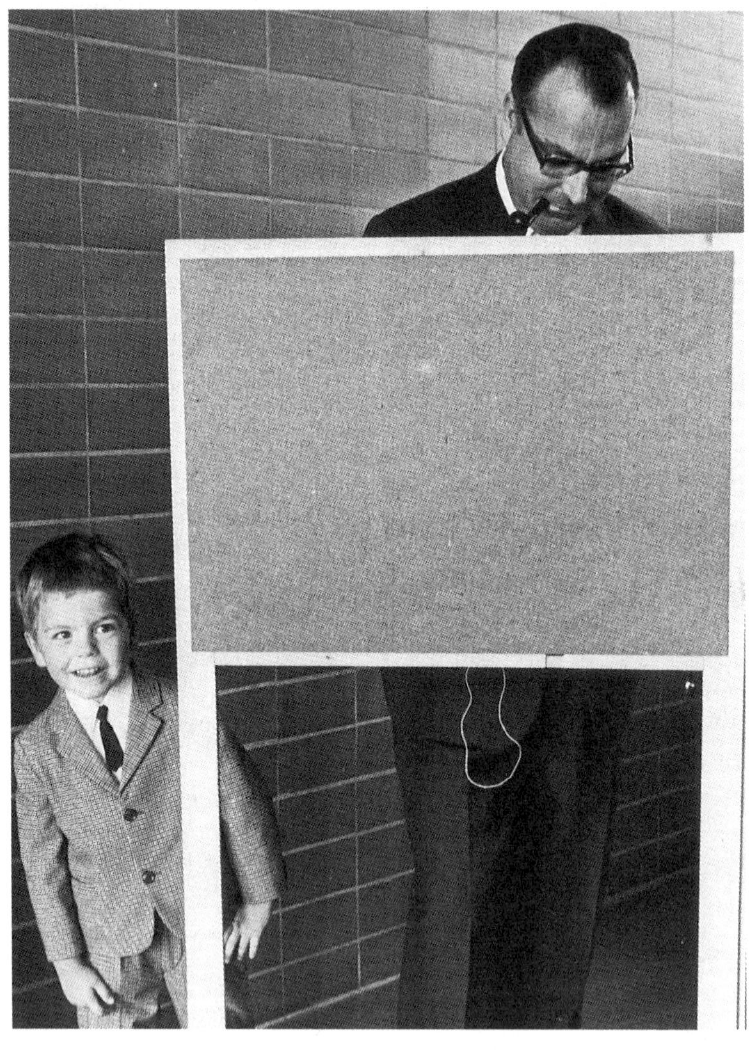

Local elections were held in Rhineland-Palatinate just four weeks after the change in government. Minister-president Kohl votes at the Ernst Reuter School in Ludwigshafen with his three-and-a-half-year-old son Peter. June 8, 1969.

tiation, acted like comrades. This personal atmosphere overwhelmingly characterized the *Land* governments of Helmut Kohl. The "black giant" gained the reputation for having a good instinct for people.

Not Born to Be an Ascetic

Did the up-and-coming Kohl also have a good position in the party? Not always an advantageous one, but one that was always in motion. His career in the CDU cannot be described as a steep line or curve, but more like an ascending flight of stairs with occasional landings. It was possible for him to rest for a moment and reflect, or look upwards as soon as he caught his breath enough to continue climbing.

Kohl frequently misjudged this progress, feeling that his early successes were carrying him upward instead of recognizing that everything has a price. A saying by the well-respected Social Democrat and academic Carlo Schmid was noted by Kohl early in his political career, but he did not allow himself to be slowed: "One must bend over far in order to achieve effects, just as far as the ground is under the forehead of the thinking person—that's where the stones and the undergrowth are which have to be cleared away before one can change the world."[21]

Naturally Kohl wanted to change the world, otherwise he would not have joined the CDU when he was just seventeen. The CDU was a party whose foundation "was in the air" according to some people, but whose way in German history was still not clear. "I do not believe it is possible to exist in the long run without recognition, unless one is born to be an ascetic. I'm not one of them," was Kohl's apt assessment of himself many years later.

His career, which satisfied him on individual points, but also sometimes made him feel that he had failed, continued apace. He was elected to the managing body of the CDU in the Palatinate at twenty-three, a remarkable achievement. In 1954 he successfully campaigned for deputy chairperson of the *Junge Union,* which he did not use as a springboard to further his career as he did the main party. Other milestones were his election to the executive committee of the *Land* in 1955, confirmation as chairperson of the county organization in 1959, and finally his election as chairperson of the district organization of the Palatinate in 1964. As such he entered the national executive committee the same year. In 1966 Kohl took over as chairperson of the *Land* CDU, and thus sweeping his great rival, Peter Altmeier, from the field, finally succeeding him as minister-president in 1969.

The rest of his road to the top of the party was not paved with success alone. Just as Carlo Schmid described, he had to clear away much of the stones and underbrush before he could proceed unhindered. It is practically forgotten that Kohl, in an early and insufficiently planned attempt, met complete defeat in the 1966 Bonn party conference as candidate for the CDU presidium. Delegates at this historic party conference chose Ludwig Erhard as the new chairperson to succeed Konrad Adenauer in March, primarily because he was chancellor and thus formally was the most powerful man in the CDU, although his colleagues did not hesitate to send him into the proverbial desert eight months later. It was certainly a crisis year for the CDU, but Kohl remembers well a date that he would like to have erased from his pocket diary. Erhard's first deputy was Rainer Barzel, leader of the parliamentary party in the *Bundestag* and secret conspirator among those members of parliament who wished to topple the one-time embodiment of the economic miracle. It was a Götterdämmerung in Bonn, a shake-up in Adenauer's party, which had escaped such things up to then. Assertions by the stymied regicide Barzel ("Erhard is the chancellor and will remain so") were shown to be hollow phrases, or were not taken seriously by anybody, including their authors, wrote Fred Luchsinger, the Bonn correspondent and later editor-in-chief of the *Neue Züricher Zeitung*. Erhard's popularity nosedived, and there were signs of decay within the bourgeois-liberal cabinet which virtually incited battles for succession in the center of power as well as on the party fringes. There were any number of aspirants to succeed Erhard. They styled themselves as such or were called so by "well-meaning" journalists. Gerhard Schröder, Paul Lücke, Eugen Gerstenmaier, and even Franz Josef Strauss were mentioned and dismissed time and again. A secret conference met at Gerstenmaier's hunting lodge in the Hunsrück, attended by the *Bundestag* president at the time, executive presidium member Bruno Heck, and the CDU *Land* chairpersons from Westfalen-Lippe and Rhineland-Palatinate, Josef-Hermann Dufhues and Helmut Kohl. Their presence at the conference was interpreted by at least some of the press as an indication of unanimity on the imminent fall of Ludwig Erhard, who was increasingly isolated at the top. Kohl was such an unknown figure to the media at that time that many newspapers called him "Hermann." Adenauer, who was vacationing in Cadenabbia, recommended Gerstenmaier to succeed Erhard in Bonn. During visits with the media, such as that initiated by Reinhard Appel at the *Stuttgarter Zeitung*, and in interviews with the press, the ambitious Swabian praised himself lavishly, though these statements were, strangely enough, mostly ignored.

For Kohl, the events of 1966 showed that the time had not yet come for a thirty-six-year-old in the CDU. Nonetheless, he did not always think so. He had hardly any connections with Bonn and only attended party committee meetings in "the small town in Germany." The man from the Palatinate began slowly but steadily to build up contacts with journalists who knew the Bonn scene. Klaus Dreher, then at the *Frankfurter Allgemeine Zeitung*, and later at the *Süddeutsche Zeitung*, and Peter Hopen, at the time important for Kohl as commentator and Bonn reporter for his house publication, *Die Rheinpfalz*, became positive and fair interpreters of the ambitious politician from the *Land* with thinly disguised government aspirations. Hopen, later the Bonn studio director of German Television Channel Two, recalled an evening barely two years after that, in the spring of 1968, when the drink flowed freely in the wine cellar of the Mainz state chancery at which Kohl, his press secretary Hans (Hännes) Schreiner, and Hopen himself held out the longest. Hopen recollected that heavy wines from the Palatinate were served. As they were leaving, Kohl, hanging on to the doorway, turned to his visitor again, and although his speech was slurred, he said carefully and clearly, "I tell you, I'll become the chancellor of the Federal Republic of Germany."[22]

4

From State to National

1966–1973

The Icy Coldness of Distance

Though Kohl's statement in the wine cellar of the state chancery was made after an evening of heavy drinking, there was a strong desire behind it. Nevertheless, the political circumstances were such that it remained absurd, even considering that it was made after several bottles of the noble grape.

Even though at thirty-eight he was already a member of the board of the national organization, but not yet in a deputy position, Kohl listened to the pressing recommendation of his political and personal friends to concentrate on short-term goals such as election as minister-president of the Rhineland-Palatinate. Kohl was realistic enough to know that someone other than the ambitious man from the provinces would be selected if there was a change in power in Bonn, where the former minister-president of Baden-Württemberg, Kurt Georg Kiesinger, cleverly moderated rather than ruled the Grand Coalition of CDU/CSU and SPD. Perhaps the person to be tapped would be Gerhard Schröder, who was the longest-serving minister in the Federal Republic of Germany. Or perhaps it would be Eugen Gerstenmaier, the eloquent Protestant churchman and parliamentarian who was sometimes involved in intrigue and was suspiciously vocal about his connections with the Nazi resistance. And there was Franz Josef Strauss, the powerful boss of the CSU, who always thought the Bavarians "should finally get their chance." Above all, there was the equally ambitious and vain head of the CDU/CSU in the *Bundestag*, Rainer Candidus Barzel, who was rarely passed over in any party decision.

Compared with these men, the man from the Palatinate seemed to be someone to be ignored. No one ever seriously considered that Helmut Kohl would soon play a role at the federal level, although some of the leaders of the national party undoubtedly must have noticed him. Kohl was taken with the Grand Coalition; or perhaps he was not. Two years before, as a thirty-six-year-old, during the decisive meeting of the board of the CDU in the autumn of 1966, Kohl had called the coalition with the Social Democrats, up till then in opposition, an "elephants' wedding." Oddly enough, the only board member who shared Kohl's view was the transport minister, Hans-Christoph Seebohm, who came from the extreme right wing of the party and who certainly did not fit in with the reformer Kohl. Kohl argued, prophetically, that allowing the SPD into the government was not only against democratic principles, but that there was also the grave danger that after a few years the Social Democrats could take over complete power in Germany, even if the coalition were agreed on a limited duration. This line of argumentation, behind which was a very pragmatic suspicion and a realistic assessment of the desire for power, seemed to stem from Adenuaer, Kohl's great role model.

The situation was very different when Kohl took office at thirty-nine as the youngest minister-president of a *Land* and also took a place in the presidium of his national party. Thus it was no wonder in the spring of 1970, a few months after he entered the armory of the prince-electors in Mainz, that the pipe-smoking party member began to express his ideas about party questions and the problems of the Bonn socialist-liberal government which had formed in the meantime. An interview in the *Süddeutsche Zeitung* in early February gave him ample opportunity to air his views.[23] The liberal newspaper was impressed by the candidness and self-criticism of the CDU presidium member, and by his forthright opinions on the difficulties an opposition party would have in the government. "A party like the CDU, which has held power for twenty years and which became far too dependent on the officials of the ministerial bureaucracy, naturally has an even more difficult time . . . ." The public understood even better Kohl's complaint about his party's lack of contact with intellectuals, "and with the mind per se," as Kiesinger would have said. "We have a lot to catch up on in the media and in the intellectual sphere." Since the CDU had continued to govern, but was now relegated to the opposition benches, the public paid little attention to it. Kohl had put his finger on a sore spot here, which was noted by only a very few in the union. All too many hoped for a quick return to power. For example, Rainer Barzel saw a chance for himself to replace Kiesinger as party leader and become a candidate for chancellor at the same time.

Kohl struck his interviewers as a "hopeful CDU candidate for chancellor." Though this description of the deputy chairperson of the CDU was perhaps a bit ahead of its time, it was not so wrong. Asked his opinion of the head of the CSU, Franz Josef Strauss, Kohl hit the nail on the head by saying he had "just as many opponents as supporters." This was a reason for Kohl to assume that Strauss was less dangerous than other rivals in the party. He was correct in this, as he was so often in regard to the temperamental and often incalculable Strauss.

He had his own views about the "human" climate in the party which he found dissatisfactory. "I have a number of friends in the party whom I would, ironically speaking, much rather have among the Social Democrats, and vice versa. But I consider that normal. You can't choose your relatives," he said on another occasion.

Then Kohl made a telling statement: "I'm not a preparer." What did he mean by that? In the view of the media, Kohl brought fresh air into day-to-day politics. The media regarded him positively and with a certain amount of respect, and considered him—compared to the many stale oldsters in the CDU family—dynamic and comparatively youthful and carefree. They began to invent alternative positions for the man who was not yet mature enough to reach the very top. These included the position of general secretary of the party, which the *Junge Union* wanted to make him. Kohl turned this down firmly, which was noted by many people. Others suggested him as a future minister under a government led by Barzel or someone else. Kohl discounted that idea as well, reacting sometimes with annoyance. When asked by Günther Gaus on his program *Fernsehgespräch* (Television Dialog) in Baden-Baden whether he liked the idea of being a minister in the chancellor's office, Kohl became annoyed and then, feigning nonchalance, said very seriously and with finality, "I am not a preparer."

No, that he was not. He came to an arrangement with the trappings of power politics, but did not hang back from his own political goal. He believed he was capable of being chancellor, that seemed to be clear, though he also regarded it as an office to which one should not aspire, because it is full of the "icy coldness of distance." He then played down his whimsical anxieties about the monstrous cold by saying that the chance to chart a course of action in this position was extremely attractive. Kohl knew that, at forty, he still had "an awful lot of time." He was also aware that government in Bonn was not up for grabs, and unlike his greatest rival, Barzel, he built that into all his considerations. In the autumn of 1970, a year after the SPD/FDP coalition was forged, Kohl praised the "team spirit of the Brandt government," though in the spring he had complained vociferously that the media were treating the new government with exceedingly great respect, even in a "euphorically positive" way.

Things had changed in the CDU, perhaps not profoundly, but in small ways. Discussions had been much more open since the Berlin party conference than they had been in Adenauer's time. "*Der Alte*" is dead, long live freedom of thought! The legendary campaign slogan "No experiments,"

With his wife, Hannelore, on vacation at the Wolfgangsee in summer, 1970. The dpa (Deutsch Presseagentur, *or German Press Agency) caption for this photo read as follows: "Against the backdrop of the renowned 'Weissen Rössl,' Kohl for once shows himself not as the government leader, but as a dinghy captain."*

which had found so much support in the past years, and which even years later sent old and gray party managers into raptures, had done its duty. Experiments were now wanted. Helmut Kohl, who scented the progression of time like a good hunting dog on the trail of a wild animal, took every opportunity to have a hand in the program.

"*Der Lange*," with his pipe and relaxed but cocky appearance, had undermined many an illustrious discussion group and started to break almost every taboo in the CDU. He called the "C" in the party name an impossible demand and said that reform of abortion laws was "well overdue" since, as he said openly, "we have to get out of a situation in which the legal demands of a state do not correspond fully to real life."[24] But he categorically denied the accusation that the CDU was charting a dangerous course to the left in social policies. In one CDU publication he committed himself to "a changed concept of women," to the principles of Catholic social teachings, and to the sacred principles of the Christian Democratic policies on pensions and education. At the same time, he spoke appreciatively and even respectfully of Bismarck, who once made the country great and strong, securing it from within and without. The publication praised Kohl, not least for his sense of history: "It appears that this thoughtful man, who tests the progress of our times without prejudice, will acknowledge even more strongly the traditional values of Adenauer's party—when he is more strongly compelled" (*Rheinischer Merkur*). The author did not say who was to "compel" this aspirant to higher party and government positions, but he did describe the circle which appreciated Kohl's statements about history and day-to-day politics: "Helmut Kohl is among the few 'reformers' in the CDU who do not react nervously and with annoyance when the word 'conservative' is mentioned." The *Frankfurter Rundschau*, critical of Kohl and his friends in the party, joined the strangely mixed chorus carrying his banner in the media, albeit with a different intention: "He is a pupil of Adenauer in style and content." In a question central to German politics as a whole, the paper played off the minister-president of Rhineland-Palatinate against one of his own ministers, the supposedly "more progressive" Gaddum. Kohl was not prepared to recognize the German Democratic Republic (GDR) even if its leaders in East Berlin made humanitarian concessions. Gaddum, the same age as Kohl, considered "narrow-minded thinking about territory and nationality" to be wrong and supported ratification of the treaty with Poland in spite of the reprimand by the head of his government.

In the committee he chaired, Kohl had to state the conditions under which recognition of the GDR was even possible. This question could only arise if "the citizen can decide freely and with self-determination whether or not he wants to live in the GDR." This insinuated achievement of a so-called "concrete utopia" to avoid giving a binding answer to the question of that time. To be sure, recognition of the state of the Socialist Unity Party was not an issue for someone anchored in CDU principles; it was merely a modus vivendi, a way of achieving better conditions for the people on the other side of the Wall and the barbed wire. For this reason it was logical that Kohl and others in the CDU answered in the negative the almost daily demands to increase the status of the GDR.

The Troubadour of Progress

The mood of the top leaders of the CDU in the winter of 1970–71 was more sad than lamenting, and could be described as "deeply depressed." Power on the Rhine had gone to the socialist-liberals and was thereby lost for the unhappy members of Adenauer's party. The situation was never more serious. Living in a villa on Rolandstrasse that was built after the Franco-German War and rented by the party for four thousand marks a month, former chancellor Kiesinger lived more against his will than in tune with the times, receiving guests in the manner of a private tutor dressed in a comfortable cardigan. The elder statesman involved himself in day-to-day politics only rarely when he was asked to do so by his political friends. When not working on one of his well-phrased *Bundestag* speeches he read his beloved Alexis de Tocqueville.

"A visit to the 'Winepfalz' minister-president," read the German Press Agency's caption from September 1971, showing Kohl in his Ludwigshafen apartment "in front of a cast-iron oven panel, of which he owns several."

Helmut Kohl respected his older party friend and chairperson from a distance and repeatedly insisted that he would become a candidate for leadership only if the great Swabian were to relinquish his birthright as firstborn. A skeptic might find this statement overly formal, but it was directed at those in the party who Kohl permanently suspected of wanting to revolutionize German politics. In the autumn of 1970 it became clear to the German public that for the first time there was a candidate for the leadership of the CDU who was not after the post of chancellor. Reinhard Appel, Bonn correspondent for the respected *Stuttgarter Zeitung*, asked the forty-year-old Kohl about this salient connection:[25] "Can you imagine that the future leader of the CDU would also be its candidate for chancellor?" Kohl, knowing the party would take a dim view if he went after everything at once, avoided a direct answer in a way that would become characteristic of his interview style: "I believe it is not a question of a principle for us or something which happens automatically. The decision must be made on a case-by-case basis. It has to be based on things as they are at the time."

But in this instance Kohl was pointedly suggesting a separation between the offices to his internal rival Barzel, who also wanted party leadership and who would definitely not accept the idea. Only the person holding all the threads in his hand and all the key posts of the party and *Bundestag* parliamentary party stood any hope of winning the battle for himself in the end. Well aware of his rival's lead, Kohl felt that his only hope was to lower his sights. When chided that a *Land* politician who had to stand for spring elections could not possibly go after the chairmanship in the government, he cited examples from the opposition: Willy Brandt had led the SPD for years from Berlin and Reinhold Maier had led the Liberals from Stuttgart, in Baden-Württemberg.

Kohl was celebrated as the "troubadour of progress" when he took over as minister-president in Mainz.[26] He now had to revise his Sturm und Drang image to appear to be a viable candidate for the party leadership in the *Bundestag*, not to speak of chancellor. No one seriously considered that the more conservative Christian Socialist Union of Bavaria would want a large say in the major decision for a joint candidate.

The selection of the CDU's chancellor candidate was a major issue at the party conference in late January 1971 in Düsseldorf. This conference resumed the Berlin program of three years earlier to shake the dust of decades off the comfortable, settled party that was used to having power. The party chairperson was to be elected the following autumn and the candidate for chancellor was thus by no means automatically determined. Most newspapers in Germany debated whether it would be Barzel or

Schröder: "There is no CDU politician who would be able to pull all the strands together for himself."[27] It was a piece of luck for Kohl. He is a master at disguising his true intentions, which is evident from his ingeniously spongy language. At that time he was for all directions, but especially the middle. Many joked about it, freely paraphrasing the saying "Wherever I sit, lie, stand, or decide: that's the middle!"

Kohl's answer to a pointed question by the *Süddeutsche Zeitung*, for example, could be interpreted any number of ways. "In the CDU/CSU and now in the SPD, the party leader and chancellor are always combined. Should the Union continue this practice in the next *Bundestag* elections, or do you believe that there are reasons for separating the two?" Kohl answered, "There is a lot to be said for the principle you mentioned. Basically both are possibilities. That is in part a question of personalities or one relating to the situation. I'm against making this question dogmatic. Furthermore, I don't believe that in the current situation it is possible to have a definitive opinion about the matter—at least I don't."

Naturally Kohl had an opinion, otherwise he could not have talked around the question. It was just that he did not want to be asked about it at that particular time. He knew that the way to become a candidate for chancellor was via party chairmanship. For tactical purposes he had Kurt Hans Biedenkopf, a lawyer and professor from Bochum, draw up a list of arguments slanted toward a separation of the two offices. At any rate, there was only one possible option in view of the internal party situation in which Kohl found himself in the spring of 1971. Kohl separated the fact that in Bonn Barzel led an extremely active party which was a powerful, if not unified, counterbalance to the shaky socialist-liberal coalition from the possibility of becoming a chairperson who hoped to integrate all the wings of the party. The illustrated magazine *Stern*, traditionally anti-Union, asked Kohl point-blank what qualifications he thought he had to become party chairperson. The man from the Palatinate did not hesitate and spoke candidly, soon becoming known as a clear challenger for the chairmanship of the CDU/CSU: "We will be electing the party chairperson at a time when we will still probably be in opposition. This seems to me to be an important starting point. The chairperson must be able to strengthen the party's ability to integrate. He must—and I think I am capable of doing this—further develop the CDU's concept for the 1970s. If I may use the old picture of party wings, he must be a man who stands in the middle, who is not tied to one side or the other." Kohl and his friends in the party proved this at the Düsseldorf conference, which was dominated by the socio-political controversy about the right of employees to have full co-determination.

Düsseldorf was a fiasco for Helmut Kohl, the up-and-coming party hopeful, and above all for the younger generation. The aspiring candidate for chairperson was increasingly suspected of being a political chameleon. The *Junge Union*, the more and more confident young generation of the CDU, accused the national party leadership, which included Kohl, of watering down the commission's documents for a program. Kohl's silence said much, and he retreated to his ambiguous statements about his position in the middle, which he strongly urged the party to follow. At the same time, the commission was working hard on continuing the Berlin program. In only a few months, they processed over seven thousand letters from all sectors of the CDU with suggestions for change or sometimes substantive deletions. Capital and work, however they fit together in the future social-political scene, became the overriding subjects of the Düsseldorf conference. Kurt Hans Biedenkopf, a lawyer and economic theoretician from the university of Bochum, and a recognized expert in co-determination, defined the controversial issue somewhat convolutedly, but in clearly thought-out words: "The unity of regulation in questions of co-determination means that the law and the political will it is based upon must take into consideration the direct correlation between reform of the Works Organization Act [which expanded the rights of workers] in the narrower sense, the revision of co-determination of the employee in the company, and the autonomy of tariffs."[28] Thus it was clear that the debates within the Union, which tended to support the employers, would continue for a long time, or at least not be ended by the conference in Düsseldorf.

Kohl, chairperson of the important commission with its task of showing the way into the future—"*Komm mit ins Jahr 2000*" (Come along to the year 2000)—took up his middle-of-the-road stance in the hotly debated co-determination discussion, but voted in the end for their concept as soon as it became apparent that the conservative line of some of the *Land* organizations would prevail. This was a tactical subterfuge which completely undermined his feigned sincerity. Kohl ran around the party conference like a wet poodle once tongues began wagging about his political somersault. He drank too much and thought about resigning from the presidium. Ernst Benda, a former minister of the interior who had a typical Berlin way of not mincing words, told host Heinrich Köppler, chairperson of the *Land* CDU in North Rhine–Westphalia, "Kohl is an idiot, and it's about time the public knew this."[29] The chastised one concurred, but did not wish to have his mistake continually discussed. However, he noted cold-bloodedly that political defeats are telling when they are due to one's own mistakes. The vote with such serious consequences was preceded by a debate in which the delegates proved that a people's party that is so used to being in power can still disagree and discuss things fairly.

Three proposals were to be voted on. One of these, from the left wing, was championed primarily by Hans Katzer, the leader of the Christian Employees' Organization and previous minister for labor and social affairs in the Grand Coalition. A second proposal, more in favor of the employer, was set forth by Schleswig-Holstein and the chairperson of its *Land* party, Gerhard Stoltenberg; it was also supported by other *Land* organizations such as the one from Hesse. The leadership's draft was initially supported by Kohl, who then switched sides. Once again it was proven that well-prepared speeches can make a politician. Alfred Dregger, leader of the CDU in Hesse, a proven conservative with a considerable gift for rhetoric, got a large round of applause for his theses. Dregger put the question of co-determination in the context of general social and economic development. Thus he maintained that the question of co-determination was "of fundamental importance for the self-image and future of the Union." Kohl's ears went red as he continued to listen to "Don Alfredo" say the left and right cupboard drawers should be kept closed, since "We all . . . reject socialism."

Dregger and his friends considered the equal or almost equal right of co-determination to be a threat to the right of ownership and the employer's freedom of disposition. Most people were not interested in the issue, since economic growth and continually rising incomes were of paramount importance. Dregger gained approval with his sharply formulated thesis "that our common political opponent, the socialists, want, with the aid of equality, to change co-determination from being an opposing position into an intermediate stage toward socialism—there is no doubt about that."[30] The extreme right wing assaulted its listeners without mercy with simplifications about the "dimension of equal co-determination which would change the system." They also applauded when Dregger dismissed his internal party opponents for looking like progressives.

Kohl's party conference speech made very little impact. It ended by stating meekly that there could be no continuing discussion about co-determination. It was very little from someone who set out to give his party a concept for the future, or at least the next few years, with the aid of a program of modernization. If Kohl had ever really spoiled his chances of successfully taking on his rival Barzel in the autumn party conference in Saarbrücken, it was at the Düsseldorf party conference. However, the optimistic career man, realistic and pragmatic, was already saying the next day in his local Mainz paper that for the most part he was satisfied with the program party conference. The question of co-determination had been debated "at a high level, even if the voting mechanism had broken down before the end," an attempt *par excellence* to deflate the Düsseldorf disaster.

Victor on the Field of Emptiness

In the months after the Düsseldorf party conference, a Helmut Kohl was to be seen in Bonn, Mainz, and elsewhere who obviously did not believe in himself much anymore. At least this was the fatal impression he gave friends and colleagues in government and party offices. However, appearances were deceptive; one tactical mistake and a low period afterward are not enough to make someone give up completely, and the man from the Palatinate was not known for being chronically depressed.

Journalists who regarded him favorably tactfully avoided mentioning more often than necessary the candidate for party chairperson who had been recently announced. But other papers recalled that Kohl had two years earlier hinted at his interest in becoming a candidate for the highest party office, and that he would write the date down in his beloved pocket diary when the time came.

The CDU, traditionally divided on the question of personalities, did not give a particularly favorable impression in the spring of 1971, even though there were friendly voices in the media which heaped praise on the "effective" opposition in the *Bundestag*. Among these was the publicist Johannes Gross, who considered Barzel the best party leader the CDU/CSU ever had and "the most efficient party leader ever in the history of the *Bundestag*." The malleable and busily calculating Barzel attracted a half-dozen members from the Social Democrats and Liberals over to the Union side, all economic realists with nationalist convictions. The opposition leader intended to use them to topple the shaky coalition majority by a constructive no-confidence vote, which was permissible under the constitution but had never before been attempted.

Kohl could not stand the stilted Barzel, whose oratory was routine. Herbert Wehner, taskmaster of the unruly SPD party in the *Bundestag* and an "old master of political defamation" according to Kohl, had the habit of interrupting the *Bundestag* debates of his counterpart with remarks such as "Oil change!" Kohl avoided frequent meetings with the party leader in the *Bundestag* and limited discussions in party committees to those that were absolutely necessary. Basically these two politicians had nothing to say to each other; they were completely different in origins and career, philosophy of life, and innate political abilities. While Kohl was unable to make up any ground against his hated internal party rival, the mood on the home front was good. Voting in the *Landtag* election in late March gained the CDU from six to eight percent in the heavily populated cities. Kohl cleverly decided not to press home this advantage. He was happy about his results but rather pensive about the bad showing by the Liberals. The minister-president's retention of the Liberal Hans Friderichs as state secretary in the *Land* government, possibly intended as a way to get the Liberals on the side of the CDU again, proved a bad move. Friderichs soon moved over to the Social Democrats in Bonn, where he did well as economics minister, later getting a well-paid position with the Deutsche Bank.

Kohl, the boisterous campaigner with lots of ideas, achieved an absolute majority using an American method. CDU election campaigners canvassed men and women on the street and in their homes. The top candidate himself put flyers on car windshields. This greatly boosted Kohl's image on the national political level; he was taken seriously and he was soon was on the government political agenda again.

Heinz Schwarz, Kohl's interior minister, was pleased that "the CDU was now together again." The average age of cabinet ministers in Mainz was under forty, a unique situation. Kohl continued to focus on the October election party conference in Saarbrücken. Since in early summer he reckoned that his chances of successfully defeating the powerful Barzel to be very slim, he said in an interview with the German Press Agency (*Deutsche Presseagentur*, or dpa) that he would consider the position of executive chairperson, which had once existed under Konrad Adenauer. If necessary, Kohl probably thought, he could work himself into the real title given time. Sooner or later, he would have to be reckoned with. He regarded rising within the political system as the work of Sisyphus, which did him good, since it dampened his *Sturm und Drang* approach and forced him to go step by step with a measured pace.

The concept of the executive chairperson was basically nothing but a diversion to avoid always publicly competing with the same zeal as his rival Barzel, who was completely different and already held an important national government role. In a television interview with the *Deutsches Fernsehen* Kohl said that if the CDU/CSU won, he would "naturally work together loyally with whomever the joint CDU/CSU committee selected as chancellor candidate." When Barzel was mentioned, Kohl said evasively, "naturally for every candidate."

Kohl had fewer problems with Kurt Georg Kiesinger. He knew that the eloquent Swabian with his great love of history and literature would sooner or later withdraw. For that reason, the man from the Palatinate could say openly that only if his respected friend Kiesinger became a candidate again would he refrain from going after the chairmanship himself. However, no serious party friend reckoned that Kiesinger would run again, most especially Kohl. Kiesinger had become leader of the CDU because that was what CDU chancellors did.

Losing office was a hard blow to Kiesinger and for months he gave the impression of being very irritated. Being in the opposition was not his forte. He remained a "victor on a field of emptiness," as the papers wrote. Kiesinger, a learned man, had already produced scientific papers in Ribbentrop's foreign ministry, as Kiesinger related in his biography for the *Bundestag* handbook. In fact for a time he had been a liaison adviser of the foreign ministry to Goebbels' Ministry of Propaganda, which caused him some difficulty in the beginning after his move from Stuttgart to Bonn, until Conrad Ahlers, the editor of *Der Spiegel,* found a *Persilschein* [proof of a clean bill of health; a reference to a brand of soap powder] for Kiesinger in the Hamburg-based magazine's vast biographical archives. One of Kiesinger's bosses in the old days had made a note that the young legal adviser was "slightly unreliable in National Socialist terms," which was turned to his advantage twenty years later. The retirement of Kiesinger, made fun of as "King Silver Tongue" because of his meticulous speech, deprived the *Bundestag* of a great orator.

The Race Is On Again

Kohl realistically assessed his chances of beating Barzel in the early summer of 1971 and only went after the party leadership. His still weak or even nonexistent image at the national political level did not allow him to take any bigger steps.

Barzel, on the other hand, had made it very clear that he was going for broke. He wanted to retain the parliamentary party leadership in the *Bundestag,* take over party chairmanship, and go after or wait for candidacy for chancellor. Gerhard Schröder, a long-serving government minister with a good reputation to defend and considerable influence in the Protestant working group of the CDU/CSU, had made his candidacy for party chairperson dependent on the combination of the two positions—chancellor candidate and chairperson—whether the CDU liked it or not. For that reason, Hans-Otto Kleinmann's comment in his *Geschichte der CDU* (History of the CDU) is apt: "Paradoxically it was exactly this issue which subsequently alleviated the problem of deciding on a person, and, due not in the least to strong pressure by the CSU and its chairperson, Franz Josef Strauss, who had great influence on the nomination of the joint top candidate for the CDU/CSU, the trend toward the separation of party chairmanship and chancellor candidate began to gain a hold. Schröder took this as a signal to drop out of the race. Thus the dice had to be thrown at the Saarbücken party conference: Barzel or Kohl. It was also a decision for or against combining the Union's two highest offices."

This ended the open feud in the CDU; both rivals for party leadership were set and the battle could begin. Kohl said at a press conference in Mainz that he was optimistic about his candidacy for the highest party office at the Saarbrücken conference. Whether he was actually as optimistic as he said in the capital of "his" *Land* is difficult to say. All his life, Kohl has acted with great confidence, conviction, and optimism, making an exact interpretation of his words impossible. At such times he always has a serious expression, as if he wants to give the impression that he is very confident about a matter. At this press conference Kohl spoke in general but not very well thought-out terms about foreign policy. Though he emphasized that priority for the immediate future "should be given to foreign matters," he actually meant that Europe and the Third World would be absolutely in the forefront. He told journalists that he supported reconciliation with Eastern countries, but that this should not be top priority in foreign-policy issues—a serious miscalculation.

The media had just started to assess Kohl's chances more positively after virtually dismissing him as a serious candidate for months after the Düsseldorf disaster. Barzel seemed at first to have succeeded in pushing through his concept of "all the offices in one hand," but by mid-summer, Kohl was able to tell Rolf Zundel, Bonn correspondent for *Die Zeit*, that he

In conversation with Chairman Kurt Georg Kiesinger during the CDU party conference in Düsseldorf, January 25, 1971.

believed "he would become a good party chairperson." Lounging in an enormous leather armchair in his office in the Mainz state chancery, Kohl gave an impression of self-confidence: "If I'm right, I think there is a growing trend toward separation of the offices."

Speaking to the conservative *Rheinische Post* in Düsseldorf, Kohl said that the first test for the new CDU national party chairperson would be the next *Bundestag* elections. And, hypocritically, he added that it would be "unthinkable" for him, in view of this difficult task, to "waste time and energy on petty jealousies." Kohl is exceedingly ambitious but only a tiny bit vain—but he never acts selflessly.

In the meantime, Kohl had secured Gerhard Schröder's support after the latter dropped out of the running. The race between him and Barzel seemed to again be a completely open one. Bruno Heck, the CDU general secretary, now said that he did not agree with the CDU chairperson in the *Bundestag*. Kohl's formulation was that he would be "against the obsolete chancellor-electing body of the CDU," pointing out that even as early as 1973, the majority of voters were people who had not consciously experienced the time before the founding of the Federal Republic. The Union parties, he said, could also no longer count on the traditional surplus of women. The head of the planning commission was annoyed that the CDU had the reputation—wrongly, he thought—of favoring the employer and not the employee. At any rate, it irked him that the media presented it that way, and thus distorted the image of a party which was committed to Christian socialist precepts. Correctly assessing the situation of Konrad Adenauer's party in the early 1970s, Kohl demanded a better and more effective organization of the CDU, in keeping with the wishes expressed by many party members. The CDU was a body with many self-willed and some brilliant thinkers, but was also a people's party without a real head. That had to change, and he—who believed he knew the party sufficiently well—was the one to do it.

The Union, still much too comfortable and often self-righteous, with its established membership predominantly of older people, badly needed to be reformed. Kohl had been thinking about a reform concept for a long time, even if the result tended to be more commonplace, or at least not that exciting. The practical Mainz "regional prince" decided the first step was to manage the party budget. To win votes you have to make investments. It is like a business; enterprises without funding cannot hope to succeed. The CDU's debts had to be paid off as quickly as possible and spending brought under control. The highest priority was certainly good campaign funding. This would be the key, since the great rival, the SPD, held the purse strings in Bonn to which the CDU, as opposition, had no access.

That was a bitter but undeniable fact, even if daydreamers would have it otherwise, such as many in the party's left wing in the Christian Democratic Employees' Committees. As soon as he took over party leadership Kohl also wanted greater understanding from the members. The time of almost patriarchal ruling of political groups and their associated organizations was probably past, and it made good sense to keep in mind that by the next *Bundestag* elections more than half of the electorate would be of the younger generation. This had consequences for politics. Moreover, social-psychology research and opinion polls showed that an increasing number of people did not necessarily want to remain with one party. Politicians would have to heed this in public debates and in the fight for political issues and messages. Kohl was ready to do this, while his internal party rival concentrated almost exclusively on his day-to-day work in the traditionally difficult *Bundestag Fraktion*.

Kohl already had a detailed plan: he did not want to present the party with a wholesale package. He suspected the SPD would use the next employee-council votes in the spring of 1972 to prepare for the next *Bundestag* elections. Kohl believed that the CDU should not "just sit back and watch" this development; he told journalists the CDU should itself "further the expansion of groups in companies." The man from the Palatinate liked to mix practicalities with moral issues, a tack which is always well received in Germany.

Germany in the early 1970s was a highly industrialized, prosperous country with good economic growth and a more and more sophisticated social-political "self-service" system. At that time, the relationship between the citizen and the state had broken down to quite an extent. For Kohl, this meant that things were no longer as they should be. People who were well established often proved bad examples for the younger generation: "Whoever thinks tax evasion is a cavalier crime should not be surprised when others think that trying to get out of serving in the armed forces is also a cavalier crime," Kohl said.

Kohl considered the 'C' for "Christian" in his party's name to be very modern, although the number of people who were leaving the churches was rising. A little bit of persuasion is always good for a party politician, who sometimes interprets the signs of the times differently from what the dates and facts show. "The CDU has always understood the 'C' in its name as a self-imposed obligation, as a measure for its own actions, and has never claimed to be exclusively the party of Christians. The obligation entails not accepting the world as it is, but changing it, that is, improving it."

The minister-president in Mainz became more optimistic as the party conference in Saarbrücken approached. He said openly that his work often gave him a great deal of pleasure, even though he still had to admit that he had made a colossal blunder at the Düsseldorf party conference. He had to make amends for that, if not this time, then definitely the next. Despite this starting point, in late summer he still correctly and calmly assessed the competition with his rival, who still had the lead in some respects: "A defeat wouldn't mean tragedy for me. I have time." The CDU regarded the competition between its chairperson of the program commission and *Bundestag* parliamentary party leader to represent a genuine alternative.

Kohl became increasingly immune to enmity and vicious gossip; the only thing that really appeared to bother him was being considered provincial. Even though Germany has always been composed of provinces, which give the nation its strength and cultural richness, to be thought provincial pained Kohl, especially since he had been after a national reputation for some time. With self-satisfaction he launched a barb at Barzel by saying that involvement with foreign policy did not necessarily prove that a person was cosmopolitan.

On the other hand, Barzel, the extremely well-controlled *Fraktion* leader in the *Bundestag* who was versed in foreign policy, "had an extremely complicated relationship with himself and his environment," with completely different advantages and disadvantages than Kohl. Ten days before negotiations began and before the elections for the board in Saarbrücken, Rainer Barzel once more cited in newspaper and television interviews the advantages that would make it almost impossible not to elect him for the top CDU position: Adenauer had already given him the task of producing a study about the missions of the Union! Even as party chairperson, he said, he was involved in party work. The combination of CDU/CSU was "the spearhead of the Union acting on a governmental political level."[31]

Kohl argued that the Union was in a new situation, that of opposition in the *Bundestag*, and therefore needed a new concept. The party, as the future embodiment of the political will of millions of voters, needed to be vigorously mobilized, which could not be done by the parliamentary party in Bonn. He told *Der Spiegel*, "I consider the party to be an open political community which is prepared to discuss issues, and whose ability to act is very much dependent upon the willingness to cooperate."

Barzel adopted a style more typical of the CDU's past, preferring a more vertical line; that is, he advocated clear-cut leadership and a structure organized from the top down. The reformer Kohl sought a horizontal line of intraparty democracy, which allowed opinions to develop from the bottom up. This sounded risky, because such theses leave more questions open than they answer.

At the party conference itself on October 4–5, as with the issue of co-determination at Düsseldorf, a well-formulated, defiant speech decided the race for the party leadership, up until then regarded as being between two very different candidates. Rainer Barzel convinced the party conference plenary session with the statement "The pre-eminence and contribution of the party are guaranteed if we all think of ourselves as a party, and have not only fundamentally decided, but have also decided fundamentals."

Barzel was elected party chairperson over Kohl with a resounding vote of 344 to 174. Fritz Ulrich Fack, co-publisher of the *Frankfurter Allgemeiner Zeitung*, called the selection "a logical way out of a leadership dilemma" which the Union had been caught up in since Adenauer left. He also considered Barzel's election a further step toward emancipation from the overshadowing figure of its founding chairperson. "Now the fourteen-hour day instead of charisma" was called for.

Kohl was disappointed and humiliated. After all, he had shown the flag, as is customary in politics when there is an opportunity to show that one is still there. Perhaps, as many in the party said, he had started too early, even though no one could tell him which other day and year he should have aimed at.

Barzel's two-thirds majority also decided the question of the chancellor candidacy. Kohl recognized that immediately and thus he could answer journalists' questions without hesitation: "The candidate for chancellor has also been decided: it will be Rainer Barzel."

The Prince-Elector of Mainz

The forty-one-year-old Helmut Kohl—many thought he looked fifty when he was thirty-five—was again able to lean back in the massive armchair in his office in the former residence of the prince-electors in Mainz. He even had time if there was no pressing state business to listen to a little music on his stereo. Kohl loved baroque music, especially Vivaldi and especially that played by the master of the Bach trumpet, Maurice Andre. He actually put Bonn am Rhein aside and felt comfortable in his Mainz domain. The "Black Watch on the Rhine," as Peter Brügge titled his fulsome article on Kohl's style of government in the Rhineland-Palatinate,[32] was doing well; at least he did not need any help or support from outside.

Kohl made such a good impression at the party conference at Deidesheim that reports even reached the Bavarian affiliate, where some CSU people even suggested that he had the right stuff to become chancellor. Naturally this view was not shared by Franz Josef Strauss, who in the

Wirtschaftswoche denigrated him as "a carpet-slipper politician," Barzel's deputy party leader Richard von Weizsäcker as an "ecumenical worldly bishop," and the party leader's advisers as "Mickey Mice." Nonetheless, Kohl regarded the candidacy for chancellorship as being Barzel's by virtue of his sweeping victory in Saarbrücken.

Mainz remained Mainz, and every day Kohl saw in this a confirmation that he and his staff had accomplished a great deal at a fairly young age. In the *Land* between vines and turnips Kohl did not simply govern, he ruled more like "the prince-elector in the state chancery at Mainz." Kohl's governing style must have been due to the baroque appearance of the "black giant," his love of life, and his epicureanism ("*Einer druff mache,*" in his Palatinate dialect), so that all over the *Land* his "regency" was described in feudal terms. In reports and commentaries about citizen Helmut Kohl there are references to "Prince-Elector," his "baroque residence," and the "courtly state." In the usual elections for the board, the head of government is not chosen by a vote (*gewählt*), or given the task of carrying out the duties of his office, but is rather elected (*gekürt*—a reference to the system of prince-electors), as if he still wore the long wig of the Sun King, Louis XIV. Before Kohl took over as minister-president of the Rhineland-Palatinate, at the time of Peter Altmeier, his colleagues in the province considered him Altmeier's crown prince. Kohl's rise to power seemed like a fairy tale, so that he naturally was called "the black giant." And he did not just govern the *Land* in a backwater, but "ruled over Kurmainz, Kurpfalz, and Kurtrier," and to the north over parts of "Kurköln" (Cologne). In so doing, some people think he was looking down the Rhine toward Bonn, his ultimate political aim. The endless hours in the office were lightened by a couple of glasses of wine at lunch, evenings were sometimes given over to revels in cheerful company.

The high-spirited Kohl took a fiendish pleasure in leaving the state chancery later than anyone else and driving home via the Deutschhaus square, looking over toward the opposition's parliamentary office. "It's already dark again over at the Sozis. They always go home by five o'clock." The younger-generation CDU man and successful *Land* leader's reputation for being hard working and being everywhere at once preceded him. Working during the day and enjoying the evenings became Kohl's way of life. Right from the beginning in Kohl's "power chancery" the pleasure principle held sway, although this also included an appropriate measure of disorganization. Juliane Weber, Kohl's efficient executive secretary, who has worked with him in this capacity his entire career, learned everything she needed to know in the state chancery in order to further in her own way with a sure hand the sheer unstoppable rise of her impetuous boss.

This government dignitary often tended to make fun of others just like a badly behaved boy. His mostly younger advisers probably shook their heads when they heard that their political idol stripped off his shirt in front of a display window when shopping for shirts in downtown Mainz, much to the amusement of the passersby. Mrs. Kohl knew that her husband was relatively well behaved during large state receptions in Mainz. The rest of the time she hoped for the best, with the understanding that she was allowed to take him home when he "started to break the china."[33] On warm summer days Kohl came to work in light sandals and, if he felt like it, took his secretaries to the closest ice cream store. In short, he turned on its head just about everything in the residence which had been done by the generation of the reserved Altmeier, who carried out his governmental duties with painful exactness.

In order to assure the "children" of his *Land* that he was firmly ensconced in the Rhineland-Palatinate, he told every other interviewer he would not be taking on any additional duties (in the party at national level), which could "adversely affect in any way my duties as minister-president of this *Land*." This was a typical statement for local newspapers, but outside the Rhineland-Palatinate he often spoke differently, since he had no doubt that he would make a second try, or as many as would be needed, to become chairperson of the national party. In the *Deutsches Monatsblatt*, a publication for CDU members, he let it be known in an article entitled "Dr. Kohl Elected Again" that Dr. Helmut Kohl had been elected for the fourth time "with an overwhelming majority" as chairperson of the *Land* CDU at the seventeenth *Land* party conference of Rhineland-Palatinate. Two days before the eagerly awaited vote of constructive no-confidence initiated by the CDU/CSU in the *Bundestag*, which was to become a Waterloo for Rainer Barzel, the CDU's own *Deutschland-Union-Dienst* reported: "Minister-President Kohl: Outstanding Results for the CDU" in the local elections in Rhineland-Palatinate. Reality is more curious and sometimes insidious than any whimsical fantasy or dramatic intrigue. The day before the controversial vote of no-confidence, Kohl's office in Mainz issued a short statement to the CDU's press office in support of the position of the opposition in the *Bundestag*. The seminal statement: "The coalition in Bonn no longer has a majority among the people as a basis of trust for its policies." The CDU/CSU was capable of governing and better able to work with a small majority than the federal government of SPD and FDP, said the deputy chairperson of the national party coolly. At the same time, the man from Rhineland-Palatinate did not underestimate the great risk involved in toppling the incumbent chancellor.

This attitude was extremely aloof and it was meant that way, since Kohl would undoubtedly not have been happy if Barzel had become chancellor by such a risky parliamentary method—the vote was also controversial within the party.

The Teacher of Political Platitudes

Decision making about the constructive vote of no-confidence ended in a fiasco: the CDU/CSU members under Barzel's leadership thought they knew how the voting would go and that they would achieve the so-called "chancellor's majority," but they failed by two votes. One of these was from Julius Steiner, a corrupt CDU member of parliament from Swabia, who a few months later revealed his vote to Paul W. Limbach, the Bonn correspondent of *Quick*. This sensational statement to the press caused a parliamentary investigation. The matter could not be explained, however closely looked at and whoever was blamed for buying the vote. It was only in 1989–90, after the fall of the Berlin Wall, that it was revealed that the Ministry for State Security had played a dirty role here.

Barzel, at first depressed, soon regained his old composure. Kohl, who is uncomfortable coming into close contact with people he does not like, turned a cold shoulder to his number-one internal party rival during his first visit to Mainz, the *Land* capital, in the summer of the unhappy year of 1972. Furthermore, he let his guest from Bonn, the party chairperson and *Bundestag* opposition leader, know almost physically that he was unwelcome. The almost five hundred guests in the residence of the prince-electors also felt the frosty atmosphere at the reception, at which meager refreshments (pretzels and fairly sour wine) were served. The host pointedly avoided a speech of greeting or a toast to the leader of the CDU in the *Bundestag*. After only a brief handshake during the necessary pleasantries required by protocol, which Kohl found onerous, he kept his distance from Barzel.

While Barzel's public speeches had a sharp edge, the head of government in Mainz played the role of the reconciler who sought compromise and wanted to avoid confrontation in any form. He spoke about the "broad spectrum of the people's party, the CDU/CSU," and warned expressly against a "friend-foe relationship in these confused and agitated times." Ostensibly he did not like at all the irreconcilable rift with the socialist-liberal coalition in the *Bundestag* which was perpetrated by his friends in the party. He disapproved of the all-pervading self-righteousness of his party friends, who from time to time expressed doubts about his political competence, suspecting that Kohl's preferred liberal-progressive stance on many controversial issues relating to domestic politics merely hid a modernist attitude. It fit into the picture when Wilhelm Dröscher, who was leader of the SPD opposition and the CDU counterpart to an extent, stated regretfully that "Kohl has had it too easy in Mainz for many years, because he is a tree on the political level." However, he never listened, the "good man from Kirn" sighed, but only "presented himself."[34] This indeed reflected Kohl's attitude toward life: he wants to have, show, and build on that which he wants. His critics in the auditoriums and parliament called him the "teacher of political platitudes,"[35] which he trots out as if he were speaking to a forum at a congress of political scientists about epoch-making results of sociological field research.

On the other hand, Kohl's answers to questions about the state, state authority, or such a serious issue as the right of pardon are more convincing. He also criticized those who do not trust themselves to be an example of authority to their contemporaries: "I believe that we have a crisis of self-image of those who want to have authority. Our democratic form of government presupposes the functioning of political parties. But only four percent of the voters in the Federal Republic of Germany belong to a party. And of these four percent, only one tenth is involved in the political work and elects the leadership potential for our country."[36] He answered honestly that the right of pardon, granted to the minister-presidents of the *Länd*, weighs heavily: "Of all rights conveyed by this office, that of pardon most certainly carries the greatest burden. Weighing up guilt and expiation, the right of the individual to have a chance to learn from his experience and the right of the general public to be protected against repeated crime, must be assessed against one another. However, despite the burden on me, I am against changing this procedure. The right of pardon must continue to rest with one person. The person who has the right of letting mercy come before right must also bear the full weight of this right." This sounds almost philosophical, based on authentic experience of life; it showed the forty-two-year-old to be a responsible politician with no inclination to make unpleasant issues more palatable, to diminish exalted or serious issues only because the times saw fit to denigrate them.

However much Kohl as minister-president could be scrupulously honest and even unreservedly open—for example, as the one to exercise the complicated right of pardon—he could also be ruthless as a party politician. He did a complete about-face on whether it would make more sense and promise greater success to hold the new elections for the *Bundestag* in November or wait until the following spring. These elections had appeared necessary to the opposition and the shaky parliamentary majority as a result of the failed vote of no-confidence. Surprisingly, in July Kohl championed the idea of November elections, having earlier clearly supported elections for the following year. It appeared, however, that he must have favored the idea of November elections all along, assessing the mood in the *Land* objectively and figuring that his despised rival Barzel could end up looking like a guilty, premature entry only a few months after the no-confidence vote.

Thus he quickly made all the necessary arrangements in his *Land* party organization so that he could throw himself into an election campaign right after the summer recess. This campaign was not exactly furious. The CDU motto alone, "We're building progress on stability," had fatal associations with a well-known German editorial writer, whose journalistic works read like they have first been written in Latin and have lost something in the translation. Kohl campaigned harder and with a stronger public image than his role demanded. He was panicked about not giving the impression of a lack of solidarity with the national party led by Rainer Barzel. Thus the people from Rhineland-Palatinate were the first to put up their candidates and prepare for the big battle, for party reasons. The "black giant" campaigned long and hard, not sparing himself or his health. When he became short of breath, he had himself "squirted up," as he termed it, in the Mainz university clinic. No one could chide him for lack of solidarity in difficult times. In this point he is unrelenting even with his friends: "The CDU is not the party of Rainer Barzel or Helmut Kohl, but is the party which I joined as a schoolboy and which is my political home."[37] That also sounded good to those who wanted to provoke him against his rivals. So that his major rival to the south would not think that Kohl was ignoring him (since he knew anyway that no one achieves high office without the CSU), the "Sozis" were also assailed in the November elections, which ended disastrously for the Christian Democrats: "You've put Brandt on a pedestal of general reverence . . . and now you need a devil, so you make one of Franz Josef Strauss out of cardboard. That's simply stupid."[38]

Since the *Bundestag* elections gave the ruling coalition of Social Democrats and Liberals a clear majority, it was able to continue to govern with greater peace of mind, but was still hard pressed by the opposition. Despite disagreement in the CDU/CSU, Barzel still looked to the *Bundestag* and the media to be an effective challenger. But gradually and unmistakably, his pugnacity, physical strength, and nerve gave out. At the same time, the chances of the opposition before the election were not bad: inflation, rising building costs and cost of living, recession, and a completely miserable budget situation—which ended up driving a Social Democratic finance minister and an economics minister out of office—seemed to promise success. After the vote—which seemed to promise Brandt and Scheel so much—nothing changed at all.

Barzel's more astute colleagues recognized that renewing the somewhat old-fashioned Union would not happen overnight. No one seriously believed that it would happen "like early spring." It was more likely to be a long and drawn-out process, and the party slogans were correspondingly somber. "Politics means service and duty" was somewhat dry and dusty, but was in keeping with the seriousness of the time. "An opposition without animosity" was difficult for most CDU parliamentarians, but they had to go through this "hard school"; the way through this troubled period would last longer than most had feared. The unsuccessful Barzel did not spare self-criticism in speeches before his party. However, his listeners had the feeling that he wanted to unmask not himself, but someone else, "the great unknown one." "Did we counter the others' idealistic and emotional elements—reconciliation, peace, and reforms—and their pathos with too little theory, principles and emotional fundamentals? Have we been incapable of this for a long time?" When Barzel spoke like that, he appeared to say to his followers, "What we need is radicalism in principle from our substance." However, there was deep division about just what this substance was in the Union in the early 1970s.

Perhaps it is an exaggeration to say that Helmut Kohl did not have too many problems with reversal in the November elections. On the other hand, neither his philosophy of a new, younger, and more up-to-date CDU, nor especially his personality, had been at issue. Not yet for disposition were all those things that a man like him, who many in Bonn still thought of as provincial, was ready to fight. He had demonstrated solidarity with his despised rival at the head of the party in his stout-hearted campaign. What more could one want? Kohl magnanimously told journalists in Mainz—since there was no date set and none anticipated for the next party conference—that the preconditions for a debate about personalities did not yet exist. Nonetheless, Kohl saw his rival's failure as clearing the way for his own rise to the top, and so he could afford a little generosity. The others would see to it that he was on his way.

Heat Lightning in the *Bundestag* Party Sky

There were signs of anger in the CDU/CSU parliamentary party in the *Bundestag* even before the newly elected house sat for the first time. This union of the two parties must be formally confirmed by contract after every *Bundestag* election. This agreement covers among other things the division of the funds allocated in the federal budget to the parliamentary parties.

Once again the vociferous Bavarian section had harsh words to say about what it considered weaklings in the north, meaning the CDU with its "carpet-slipper heroes." Hans-Erich Bilges, one of the sharp correspondents on German politics from the Bonn daily newspaper *Die Welt*, got Richard Stücklen, incumbent head of the CSU *Land* group, to half admit, though he would not confirm or deny this, that the CSU intended to end the Union with the CDU in the *Bundestag* effective immediately. This caused a sensation for a few days, but reliable Bonn analysts and well-placed observers of the internal processes of the Union parties were skeptical about a rift between the CDU and the CSU. Helmut Kohl too was skeptical. Speaking to the *Südwestfunk* (Southwest Radio and Television), obviously unaffected by the excitement, he announced a closed conference of the CDU in late January 1973. The CSU was also planning such a meeting. Kohl said that he was "absolutely optimistic" about the near future and the coherence of the two parties. Kohl was accused by people in the party of having a desire for harmony and a bad habit of trying to cover up all obvious problems. But his words reflected more than just these traits. Kohl played for time in order not to give the CSU any opportunity to get out of the alliance without a plausible reason, because if the parties did split up, they would lose their almost uninterrupted parliamentary dominance. They went separate ways in day-to-day politics and banded together to prevail in the *Bundestag*. This strategy had worked for a long time, and a little bit of heat lightning in the *Bundestag* sky would hardly change this. Stücklen, with his volatile Franconian temperament, had only been toying with the idea of splitting the alliance, probably with the intention of getting a few pennies more for his *Land* party, and two or three speaker positions.

From then on time worked in Kohl's favor. He had begun to put on weight, later giving him the undeserved and contemptuous reputation of "sitting," despite the fact that in riding terms the rider sits firmly in the saddle at the gallop. Around the turn of the year "young, interested members of the CDU" said that the party needed a chairperson "who looked after the party work and did not just nominally carry out the duties of his office." Making this demand was a five-person team of authors writing in the quarterly *Sonde—Neue christlich-demokratische Politik*. These included the political scientists Helmut Pütz, Wulf Schönbohm, and Peter Radunski. Only a few months later all three had key positions in the CDU at the national level.

Kohl broke cover as he had two years before and again spoke up as a candidate. If Barzel wanted to become a candidate again for party chairperson, he, Kohl, was ready to put himself up as a rival. This pleased the press, since personal debates make good headlines. Kohl no longer beat around the bush, but said clearly what he thought was important for the party and himself. The candidacy for chancellor, he said, could be forgotten for a few years because the SPD/FDP coalition was more firmly entrenched than ever. "We have entirely different problems at the moment." Kohl recognized correctly that it would be a long time before the Union returned to power.

Unlike Christian Schwarz-Schilling, the CDU general secretary from Hesse, Kohl did not believe that the Union parties had lost the intellectual leadership of the Federal Republic. As he often did to hide his innermost thoughts and feelings, Kohl retreated into a complaisant, but typically German and rather pessimistic view: even though politics without vision was not realistic politics, he wanted to expressly warn the Union not to seek the blue flower of romanticism. When he referred to his own career, which would soon make him party chairperson, the forty-three-year-old talked big about democracy, which could not exist without authority: "Whoever has political office has to have the authority of office and especially personal authority."[39]

Rainer Barzel did not seem unduly impressed with the recent challenge by his rival in Mainz, since he continued to be "available to become party chairperson."[40] At the end of March Barzel and Kohl met privately in Bonn to discuss the candidacy for chairperson in detail. Kohl had asked for this meeting in a letter in order to again give his reasons for the separation of the two offices. They knew each other well from numerous CDU executive committee meetings, but Kohl especially was eager to have this discussion, which was meant to show fairness and openness, although the public was not informed about the meeting.

The candidacy for chancellor was touched on only indirectly, since both Kohl and Barzel were aware that the elections in October for the new chairperson would also be a preliminary decision on the next candidate for chancellor. The concept of separating the offices did not seem completely convincing anyway, since Kohl's argument would be trouble if his position as minister-president were brought up. At any rate, up until March 1973, he had not agreed to give up this position if elected chairperson of the national CDU.

On exactly the same day Kohl had chosen for his meeting with Barzel, a remarkably laudative article was published in the European edition of *Time* magazine about the politician from Rhineland-Palatinate who represented the younger generation. It was entitled "Leaders Who Can Turn the Century." The article was a seventy-line-long piece, suitable for saving to show the grandchildren. The American magazine said that Kohl was a man who "looked more like a jovial university professor than one of the most ambitious politicians of the younger generation in West Germany." He was said to be "popular with the youth of West Germany" and have been "successful as an energetic reformer" who, though Catholic, had abolished the church school in his *Land*. The key sentence was, "If he gets the opportunity in October to lead the Christian Democrats, Kohl will almost certainly put more emphasis on the very necessary willingness for cooperation and initiative in relations with the U.S." The analysis was correct, since the Brandt-Scheel administration was regarded with some suspicion in the United States. Washington hoped that the return to power of a conservative party in the not too distant future would revitalize the friendly atmosphere that had once characterized U.S.-German relations.

The Business of Criticism

It would be wrong to say that Kohl had attempted to chase after the spirit of the times. However, in that spring it looked like the spirit of the times had caught up with him.

In the first issue in May, the respected Hamburg-based weekly newspaper *Die Zeit* devoted a whole page to the deputy chairperson of the CDU in an article on "The Intellectuals and the CDU."[41] For Germany's left it was slightly embarrassing that the publisher of their favorite newspaper was a former CDU member of parliament, though he did leave the party under protest to be an independent thinker.

Kohl's article was well-written; cool, and distanced, his spiritual dispassion lurking behind every line. The draft of this rather remarkable confession of a leading Christian Democrat's "productive conflict" with the intellectuals, as the headline said, was forged in the rhetorical-political scientific workshop of Kohl's talented press secretary, Wolfgang Bergsdorf. Concisely and accurately, the author said after seventy lines, "The behavior and thinking of politicians and intellectuals, their ways of arguing and acting, are fundamentally different. Both fulfill different functions and play different roles in society. " The *Zeit* article made a few polemical sideswipes at intellectuals' admiration for a chancellor such as Willy Brandt as a "symbol of this new reconciliation of spirit and power." "This renewed synthesis which the SPD believes itself to have achieved frees the politician from the odium of power, and it absolves the intellectual from the contradictions in politics." The price of this apparent harmony in the relationship between politicians and intellectuals was "dangerously high." In the end, intellectuals might criticize, but decision making was well vested in the politicians.

Having fully tackled the opalescent facets of social democratic spiritual relations, the CDU deputy chairperson—somewhat surprisingly—came to a brief and fairly lame conclusion. It consisted in the main of the depressing guess that the relationship between the CDU and intellectuals "will not be without problems in future." In this tone he continued by saying that there was a vague chance of improvement if the CDU in future could justify its political aims "theoretically and convincingly." And the intellectuals for their part should "not make the business of criticism dependent on the current political trend." Here Kohl made reference to the Social Democrats, clearly favored by the (leftist) intellectuals. It was an unstated admission that there was still no clear explanation why the CDU had so deeply alienated the intellectuals.

The month of May saw the resolution in quick succession of the fates of Kohl and his bitterest rival. Rainer Candidus Barzel threw in the towel just before the final debate in the *Bundestag* on May 9 on the basic agreement between the Federal Republic and the German Democratic Republic and on the law on United Nations membership. Discouraged by the endless, and what he considered pointless, debates in the parliamentary and national parties about a resolution to this extremely controversial issue, Barzel resigned as head of the parliamentary and national parties, a move which surprised his friends and opponents alike. However, on the previous day, Barzel had suffered a defeat in a vote which decided everything. Against his recommendation to reject the basic agreement but vote for U.N. membership, the majority of the party also rejected the latter in a trial vote. For Franz Josef Strauss's CSU, the scales were tipped by a part of the Hessian *Land* group led by Alfred Dregger and the politicians representing displaced Germans, Herbert Czaja and Johann Baptist Gradl. The way to the top was thus opened, and preparations were made quickly for an extraordinary party conference in Bonn on June 12.

Barzel retained the right of final decision as party chairperson only until the election of his successor as speaker in the *Bundestag*. Kurt Georg Kiesinger, one of the Union's leading figures, took over leadership of the *Bundestag* party, which elected Karl Carstens as Barzel's successor by a clear majority.

Carstens, a fifty-eight-year-old professor of international law, was a former state secretary in the chancellery. His rival, Gerhard Schröder, had made the mistake of writing a personal letter to all Union members of parliament in which he outlined his unparalleled qualifications for the top post. Carstens did nothing of the sort, and Kiesinger considered him to have won the day.

After the dramatic events in the party and *Fraktion* at the meeting of the CDU social committees in Bochum, in the Ruhr region, Kohl learned that it is possible to be nominated for top posts in the Union but still have to fight for support. Barzel got a long ovation from the delegates, but Kohl received only weak applause. Again it was made clear to him that he had only just started. Because he had long ago focused on the time beyond his party chairmanship, he was suspected by the Christian Democratic employees' wing of being a secret "disciple" of the conservatives Strauss and Dregger, without whose support he would never reach the top.

At this party congress Kohl cleverly played on the party as a binding and overriding institution against his party rivals Barzel and Hans Katzer, who was confirmed as head of the social committees. "In the present situation, which threatens to tear the party apart, I do not want to open up new breaches, but must try to get agreement from the other groups as well to achieve a model of co-determination."

The same thing had occurred a few days before at a CDU community-organization conference in Mainz. Barzel was greeted with applause, Kohl with silence. However, the day was saved by a speech; Kohl ensured that he spoke much longer than his former rival, the retiring party chairperson. Furthermore, in a flash of genius, he called the CDU the "classical people's party, which was, is, and remains the reform party." Up to that point there was nothing incorrect about that, but Kohl's repertoire in the meantime had been expanded to include rhapsodies of similar statements, recitations of pat phrases in measured tones. Later he would add, "That's our politics," which he would emphasize with an almost angry gesture, meaning "There's no use contradicting."

He soon got used to the grumbling from various groups in the party. Indeed, it became almost indispensable, because criticism from the left and reservations from the right within the Union provided slogans for his speeches. Hence his party-political profile remained unclear for the most part, for which he was criticized, but this did not anger or faze him.

Only when he speculated did the CDU chairperson sparkle with originality. For example, Kohl spoke of the idea of European citizenship, which he "wanted to see tested" seriously in the European Community. He was thinking of the foreign guest workers in Germany; the problem of the guest workers, Kohl said a few days before his initial visit to Brussels, "has taken on a European dimension." The fundamental thinker, with aspirations of inspiring the party to new heights, was obviously philosophizing about "a new phase of integration policies," though he added, almost as an excuse, that "the fundamental issue is again being debated."

Kohl's political statements became more unclear, general, and nonbinding as the extraordinary party conference approached. He knew he had to convince many of the delegates of his qualifications. A bad election result would greatly hamper someone who wanted to use the party chairmanship as a stepping stone to the chancellery.

By the beginning of June the "black giant" was hoarse from speaking. At a press conference in Rhineland-Palatinate, he tried to extract a promise from the journalists present that they would follow his actions to see that he was not neglecting his duties as minister-president after he became party chairperson. This confidence begs the question of how he came to have such a high opinion of his ability to do the two jobs. The saying "good performance is doing work over a long time" also held true for him, and time is always limited.

Kohl made a long appearance on television on the eve of the elections. He was puzzled to still be asked if he had his own opinion. The public had the impression that he was between two fires and would not consider having his own view. Astutely, Kohl said it was certainly not the time to go chasing after a laurel wreath. But he also said with feigned sincerity that it went without saying that it was exactly at this time that he had to make a bid.

Looking to a future political career, Kohl responded, though not in great detail, to questions about the lack of control over the CSU, which along with the CDU had an acceptable opposition leader in the *Bundestag*. Kohl said that the CSU and CDU did not stand a chance in the country unless they always worked together, and that neither he nor Strauss would have the final say: "We want power again in this country, and to lead the country politically in this way."

5

The Party Chief

1973

A Question of Psychological Self-Advancement

The twelfth of June arrived, an extremely hot day in the Bonn "greenhouse," and the Beethovenhalle was filled to overflowing, as is usual at such times. Most of the CDU delegates recognized on this auspicious day that the strategic leadership of the opposition switched from the *Bundestag* CDU/CSU to the national party.

It was a brief and almost hectic party conference which took place under unusual circumstances and left a lot of disappointed or angry faces. Kohl garnered 520 votes, an impressive performance, although no one seemed very surprised about this. The CDU had no alternative at this point, and the Kohl/Biedenkopf team had some attractions for the younger party members, being a *tableau de raison* for those people disappointed with Barzel's decision to get out of party leadership (though not politics).

Ritual has it that at such times the maiden speech of the new party chairperson is praised as being "programmatic," although it was anything but. Kohl's general secretary, Kurt Hans Biedenkopf, a man of keen intelligence and absolute candidness in judgment and rhetoric, later admitted that he "would rather have not become a candidate if he could have read the speech sooner than just a half day before in the state chancellery wine cellar."[42] Kohl had called the professor from Bochum and asked him to come to Mainz so that he could read the draft of his speech for June 12. Biedenkopf, who clearly had other ideas about a new beginning, change, and party leadership, held his head in his hands after reading the first ten pages. Was there any chance of going back? No, the only thing to do was close one's eyes and go for it!

Biedenkopf ("Bieko") got nine more votes for general secretary than his "boss," who he later only nominally recognized as such, and who also soon regarded himself as "executive chairperson." He never did manage to get over the second part of his title as general "secretary."

The old and the new CDU chairmen at the twenty-first party conference in Bonn, July 12, 1973. Rainer Barzel on the way to the podium. In his farewell address, he called for the party to "get back into step through renewal and reform."

Biedenkopf, a university professor with great political aspirations, put behind the bourgeois life of six years at the University of Bochum, in the Ruhr region, where he had been founding dean, and his two years as a member of the central management of the Henkel concern. At first disappointed by Kohl, the forty-three-year-old Biedenkopf began to see his new role as the most challenging one of his life. His management experience, outstanding analytical abilities, and talents as a speaker allowed him to lead the bourgeois Christian Democrats as he would a large company hoping to capture the entire public market.

Kohl spoke for two hours, in keeping with the adage that "whoever gives a lot will give many people something."[43] The minutes note "heavy applause" only in three instances, although a lot of clapping is usually appreciated at CDU events. The first two instances were when he praised his "friends" Kiesinger and Barzel. Almost at the end, the audience applauded thunderously when the newly elected chairperson roared out with double meaning, "Understand that we will never again regain a majority capable of governing if we do not realize that the tone and ways of dealing with each other in this party must correspond to the principles of the Christian Democratic Party."

Had the party taken leave of Kiesinger and Barzel too soon? The question was not relevant to them, since on that Sunday in June they had no other choice. Kohl offered the delegates a standard menu, nothing special, with scarcely any ideas, or "visions," to use his words. Biedenkopf had read the speech ahead of time, but had not revised any of it, and had not expressed his opinion of it to Kohl himself or the Mainz clan.

In keeping with the adage that "the person is always at the center," Kohl showered his listeners with democratic platitudes for over thirty

The newly elected CDU chairman's first visit to Federal President Gustav Heinemann at Villa Hammerschmidt, June 19, 1973.

minutes: "The respect for the dignity of the person is the foundation of our politics." Nevertheless, a platitude from the broom closet of Christian social ethics garnered applause: "We dare to formulate our politics out of a sense of Christian responsibility."[44] Such statements then ended in stringent exhortations that sounded like they came from a secondary-school religious education class: "We know that people can err in their recognition and actions. Thus we do not believe in the total power to do everything in this world. In history whoever has attempted to create heaven on earth has made a hell out of it." Kohl did not suggest any reforms, but only a "compass" for possible change in social conditions. The main point was that the speaker himself was given the impetus which he tried to convey to the others. Kohl was fascinated by some of his own ideas: "My friends, we can see the dynamics of our principles; we must further develop these dynamics with greater courage and conviction. In our party program we ascribe to dynamic democracy; that is, to a further development of this democracy. It is exactly because of this understanding of democracy, and of the question of the democratic formulation and the creation of will in all areas of our nation and our society, that we must ensure this further development."

This thought came from the rather conservative political scientist Richard Löwenthal, who had understated social democratic leanings but was nevertheless the party's "crown lawyer" in questions of political science and theory. Löwenthal had been a professor of Horst Teltschik, Kohl's colleague in Mainz, who had come up with the concept of "dynamic democracy" in one of the brainstorming sessions in the state chancery wine cellar.

The domestic and foreign policies Kohl propounded at the extraordinary party meeting in Bonn, whose one and only purpose was to elect and hear a new party chairperson, did not differ significantly from those of his predecessor, keeping carefully to the precepts of the current socialist-liberal government coalition. "We must determine our own foreign policy on the basis of the present situation," Kohl said. "Whether we like it or not, 1973 is not 1969. When I say that we have to adjust to the new situation, this does not mean that we have to just accept it, because we cannot and will not accept the division of our country."

The man from Rhineland-Palatinate urged his listeners to consider the treaties on relations with the Eastern bloc with the same realism that could have come from his internal party rival Barzel: "Treaties which have been legally made are binding to us as well, since we are a constitutional party. The Basic Law and the joint decision by the *Bundestag* of May 17, 1972, give us the chance to apply the treaties in accordance with our foreign-policy goals."

The editor in chief of the self-appointed "court paper" of His Majesty's

Opposition, Herbert Kremp, moaned after the rhetorical tirade in the packed Beethovenhalle to the Bonn correspondent of the Springer paper that "The CDU is in awful straits." However, his restrained commentary published the next day was more friendly and encouraging, which Kremp of course thought the worst possible form of verbal onslaught.

The response to the party conference, and especially to Kohl's speech, ranged from diffuse to lukewarm. The new chairperson had not yet convinced the bulk of the party members and the journalists had already started to nitpick at Kohl's language. For a while, the exception to this was the Springer press, which was steering a Unionist course slightly to the right as long as the Christian Democrats continued to give so much as an impression of guaranteeing that the country would not be completely plunged into a socialist morass. However, these papers did not have full confidence in Kohl's ability to chart an entirely new course and stuck with such people as Franz Josef Strauss, Karl Carstens, and Alfred Dregger.

Oddly enough, stories about Kohl in those days still contained phrases such as "sincerity" or "a dose of humor." There was no denying that the "black giant" came from a bourgeois background, had had a fairly ordinary Catholic upbringing, and grew up in a reasonably restrained atmosphere, but "sincerity" and "humor" were not his salient characteristics. Kohl styled himself repeatedly as someone for whom power was "the chance to change and form things, and not a question of psychological self-enrichment." By this he meant the actual desire for prestige which is necessarily bound up with high-ranking office. It was better to appear modest to the world at large than to be caught beating your chest in front of the mirror.

The chance to change things: Kohl had learned a long time ago what was important. It was not clear whether he had picked this up from the Social Democrats and their chairperson, Willy Brandt, who was a moderate chancellor and was highly respected in other countries. The party leader had to take the undisputed top position in the Union hierarchy and put an end once and for all to the so-called *Fraktionspartei* (the party in the *Bundestag*). "The party creates the party in the *Bundestag*, and not vice versa. In all questions which are of long-term . . . significance, the party committees must speak out. But the party in the *Bundestag* is the important spearhead," he said on the radio station *Deutschlandfunk*.

There was at least one person in the country who did not know what to make of this: Karl Carstens, the parliamentary party chairperson. Only the party membership card bound the man from Bremen to the party. He had not made a career for himself in the party during his long service as state secretary in the chancery and the defense ministry. Perhaps he had never attended a party conference aside from when he was speaking.

After the "takeover of power" in the CDU, changes had to be made in the Konrad-Adenauer-Haus in Bonn, the nerve center of the party on the federal level. However, no one was able to say that there had been a "night of the long knives." Barzel's general secretary, Konrad Fraske, had to give way to Biedenkopf, and after a grace period Ottfried Henning, the government manager, also turned over his post to the quiet but effective leader of the political-policy department, Karl-Heinz Bilke, who admired Kohl and had wanted to work for him for a number of years. Kohl's adviser on the press and media in Mainz, Wolfgang Bergsdorf, moved to Bonn to run the chairperson's office and thus to act as Kohl's listening post in the Konrad-Adenauer-Haus. The organization department devolved onto Günter Meyer, a chain-smoker whose temper was of Old Testament proportions. Later, whenever Kohl approved the line-up of his party conference committee, he regularly lost his temper, leaving Meyer red-faced at the scene of his supposed mistake. Though Kohl considered himself a perfectionist and his chief organizer a genius in improvisation, the opposite was more likely the case. But it seemed to be fitting to start a party conference with an explosion.

The important position of heading the political department was at first given to Kohl's trusted associate Dorothee Wilms from Cologne. After two years, General Secretary Biedenkopf appointed her government manager "without a department" and replaced her with his highly gifted friend, Meinhard Miegel, who had up to that time headed a rather insignificant department within the main department for politics. Peter Radunski, from the CDU *Land* organization in Hesse, was appointed to handle public relations, being responsible for all campaign strategy of the party central organization. He was a young man of the progressive wing of the Walther Leisler-Kiep school, determined to successfully hone Kohl's unformed image.

The newly elected party leader reserved two days a week for appointments in Bonn, although it was often only Mondays, on which the party committees met in turn. He had promised the people of Rhineland-Palatinate that "no one would suffer the slightest loss of his work for the *Land*." Despite strong denials that there was any connection with Kohl's move to Bonn, there were negotiations as early as June between the head of the *Land* representation of Rhineland-Palatinate and its neighbor, the Chamber of Industry and Commerce. The Mainz resident Roman Herzog wanted to expand the offices of the representation to the *Bundesrat*, which had become too small, and make them more comfortable. This move was of course at the behest of his colleague from the *Land*, Helmut Kohl, who had gotten him involved in politics. "This has absolutely nothing to do with

Kohl's new role in the federal government," the man in charge of the building volunteered.

However, the pleasures of wine drinking were to be provided by the Mainz "embassy": the wine cellar became a meeting place for everyone who was anyone in politics and the media after the autumn of 1973. Even if Kohl had not brought along a prominent political image with him from Rhineland-Palatinate to Bonn, the residence of his *Land* always had good wine available for visitors and guests. Wine tasting at the representation of the Rhineland-Palatinate soon became an important social event on the Bonn political scene. Anyone invited by the Mainz economics minister could consider himself or herself to have been accepted. The bibulous hazes from the Gründerzeit villa in Schedestrasse were some of the best to be had in Bonn, and they were legion.

The newly elected party chairperson waited only forty-eight hours before he informed the press that he was not only the top man in the CDU, but also (practically) its candidate for chancellor. The next *Bundestag* elections would probably take place in the fall of 1976, with the next ones for the *Landtag* in Rhineland-Palatinate a year before that. Thus the party had to settle on a candidate, with whom to go forward into the great battle by mid-1975 at the latest. He was to be "the candidate who had the best chance of beating the SPD." In order to successfully deflect any criticisms that the offices had not been separated, Kohl suggested as early as June 1973 that he would "possibly" relinquish the post of minister-president to a successor before the election year 1976. As long as he still held the post, however, he wanted to make the most of the opportunity to speak in the *Bundestag*. He would have difficulty there maintaining his ground in rhetoric against the likes of federal chancellor Willy Brandt, and even more so against Helmut Schmidt a year after that.

Not Everything Is Possible

Kohl felt like he had never felt before. He wanted to express some thoughts emotionally, in keeping with the new situation which had so rightly made him the chairperson of the second largest people's party: "The first and most important thing seems to me to enable our many members, friends, and adherents in the country to again be liberated. That is, they should be informed about what the party wants, they should be able to participate in discussions about the party's political path, and they themselves should participate, so that they can thus show the CDU flag so to speak at work and in all areas, in families, associations, and organizations across the whole society."[45] The new chairperson, who indeed differed from his predecessors in many ways, allowed himself to recommend to the good old Christian Democratic Union that it should look over the shoulder of the socialists and take a leaf out of their book in regard to strategy and tactics. Indeed, the totality of Kohl's organizational aspirations appeared to be borrowed from the Social Democrats, though the new CDU head believed that their basic mistake was to think that almost everything was possible in politics and life.

Kohl hit the nail on the head when he drew a parallel between the "communal socialism" of the venerable SPD man August Bebel and the long-term theories of Helmut Schmidt.

Still not experienced and confident in foreign politics, Kohl did not like to get involved in the debates on the treaties with Moscow and the Warsaw Pact and the basic treaty with the GDR. However, the former "provincial prince" of Mainz with federal-level aspirations did not hesitate to demonstrate what the Union intended to do in the future—often to the annoyance of the Bavarian sister party. He repeated Rainer Barzel's words with only slight variations: the "new" *Ostpolitik* of Willy Brandt and Walter Scheel certainly had not sprung from the soil of the CDU/CSU, but it carried the stamp of a constitutionally elected federal government and was therefore "to be respected."

He who wants power in the republic has to adjust to situations as quickly as possible. Thus Kohl was as outspoken as he wished only among friends, where he would not provoke controversy. Briefed by experts, Kohl expressed deep concern to the in-house Konrad-Adenaur-Stiftung about the dramatic arms build-up in the Soviet Union and its client countries: "The air forces of the Warsaw Pact have changed from a defensive role to an offensive one . . . and the Red fleet has been built up to such an extent that it would have taken the breath away even from Grossadmiral Tirpitz."[46]

The climate in the party scene in the Federal Republic of Germany was not exactly favorable to Helmut Kohl in the early fall of 1973. It tolerated the somewhat old-fashioned looking man with glasses, though the average citizen thought him much too young to bear the dignity of a party chairperson. But they placed the "black giant" far behind Social Democratic leaders such as Brandt, Schmidt, or Wehner. To use the words of the man appointed to look after the image of the Mainz minister-president, Kohl as the "biggest" among the giants automatically caught the eye. However, with his glasses, conventional appearance, and conservative dress he did not make an outstanding impression. Even worse, caricatures published of Kohl did not have the stereotyped, characteristic exaggerated features.

The illustrated magazine *Stern*, which traditionally vilified the Christian Democrats, published the strictly confidential career tips, compiled under

Kohl's watch, from the Interscal agency in Bad Honnef. Whoever commissioned this advice should have known that such material could not be kept secret. The whole matter was embarrassing to the chairperson's advisors, although those charged with looking after the image of the new man in the Konrad-Adenauer-Haus had to say that the advice was realistic for the most part and would probably not cause too much damage. Naturally the magazine published by Henri Nannen—who had emphatically greeted the "social-liberal" coalition when it was installed in 1969—did not miss the opportunity to garnish the text with a number of unflattering photos. In addition to this somewhat immature text there were career tips such as, "Dr. Kohl must not ignore fashionable and youthful accents." The comment was directed at Kohl's sartorial style, which did not differ in the least from that of his conventional role models (his clothes should be "a little less unobtrusive"), and at his dark glasses frames "which in their present form leveled his physiognomy too much." The head of the Mainz cabinet and CDU chairperson was insulted; he lost his temper because someone in his immediate circle had commissioned the silly study. Above all the fairly transparent recommendation that he should show himself more clearly to be the "representative of the new generation in the CDU," culminating in the ridiculous suggestion that he should distance himself from "older politicians such as Kiesinger, Strauss, and Schröder" met with resistance from the person they were directed at.

Kohl immediately issued a strong statement about the article, even threatening *Stern* publisher Nannen with legal action and canceled on short notice a lunch appointment with the Hamburg magazine head. Kohl was easily able to do without the lunch. However, the chance to hold a private conversation with the *Stern* head, in view of the conceit rightly ascribed to Henri Nannen, could only have proven useful. Kohl made an irreparable mistake; the magazine not only continued its anti-CDU tack, it stepped it up.

Two years later the target of the "career tips" actually followed one of the suggestions, which he had forgotten in the meantime: the horn-rimmed glasses were replaced with rimless ones, giving him a completely different appearance. Those who mocked him referred to his "Peter Pasetti look" which was to be seen on the posters during his first election campaign as CDU chairperson.

Before Kohl sat down at his desk on the tenth floor of the CDU skyscraper in Friedrich-Ebert-Allee to familiarize himself with his work, he first considered his eating habits. There was a café near the party headquarters where the "black giant" could buy his strawberry cake and cream for seventeen marks (out of his own pocket). He would hand the cake out to the secretaries in the reception area, who were completely unused to such jovial treatment of personnel. The obligatory lentil soup and a large selection of cakes were always on hand for breaks from committee meetings. No nickname resulted from this, though "the sweet one" or similar might have been applied; "*der Dicke*" (the stout one) was not applied until later.

The beginning of the week belonged to the commuter from Mainz; otherwise the chairperson was scarcely to be seen in the building. Kohl proved to his colleagues that he meant it when he said he wanted teamwork. Indeed, he avoided completely the experts in the party apparatus. Even though his critics felt that he would take little advice, they soon got to know and appreciate his direct way of working, the same way he lived life.

Kohl appreciated right from the start that the ordinary party conference in Hamburg scheduled for the fall would be his first acid test, and started to work toward that with the help of his brilliant general secretary. The topics for Hamburg had been determined and set for decision by his predecessors: co-determination, land rights, long-term savings, and reform of education and vocational training. Burdened with these issues in advance, Kohl was most keenly interested in co-determination. Therefore the CDU chief, always somewhat chatty in interviews, began talking around this debate—expected, hoped for, or feared—as a "reasonable solution to a difficult problem." At the same time, Kohl rightly regarded co-determination as not being decisive for the party conference, since it was not possible to implement it in the immediate future, not even by the SPD-led coalition which represented the interests of the workers.

Kohl had not been a great theoretician in the past, nor would he be in future, even though he can tenaciously argue about programmatic issues in smaller groups. Thus, for example, he did not appear as an author in a respected publication of this time, *Die Union in der Opposition—Analyse, Strategie, Programm* (The Union in Opposition—Analysis, Strategy, and Program), though some of his closest associates did, including Richard von Weizsäcker, Elmar Pieroth, Rudolf Selters, and Philipp Jenninger. Weizsäcker, correctly assessing the situation, pointed out that the governing Social Democrats, while united by a "progressive rhetoric," had a "pragmatic leadership" and, moreover, an "ideological wing." The latter was far less of a threat to the Union parties than the coalition's pragmatism, which could attract middle-class voters. Thus Kohl's first public speeches as CDU leader directed only as much ideological criticism of the SPD as was necessary for semantic effect. Exaggerations would have cost him credibility. That was better left to the "Sozis" themselves, who had enough trouble with their "conservatives" and their "market economists," such as Karl Schiller ("Comrades, do you want another republic?") and Alex Möller ("Comrades, leave the cups in the cupboard!"). They alone had to unmask themselves.

The CDU gradually rediscovered its old problems, which gave it a lot of grief in the months leading up to the congress in Hamburg: insufficient solidarity in its ranks and the grudging creation of loyalty to its leadership. Weizsäcker, who had decided to hitch his inner political career to Kohl, began to have a gloomy vision—admittedly, a rhetorically exaggerated one. During the tense week before the nervously awaited first party conference under the new leadership it resulted in the assertion that the CDU had reached a dangerous point at which "history would ruin its own characters and consume them."

Kohl's only theoretical contribution was a book published three months before the party conference with the bland title *Between Ideology and Pragmatism*. It contained vague recommendations for the Federal Republic of Germany such as a "third way," in the form of "critical rationality" (possibly taken from the work of the philosopher Karl Popper). The small book was published by the radio journalist Alois Rummel, who was actually a supporter of Kiesinger, but who also wanted to be on the winning side of the internal party competition. Even Bernt Conrad, a Springer publishing group correspondent who was inclined toward the CDU, asked himself "why people had persuaded Kohl to publish such a superfluous book." The liberal-conservative journalist Hartmut Klatt dismissed the book as a "seminar paper which displays profound views" which his colleagues applauded only lightly because the tract was completely "removed from any political reality." Kohl did not repeat such an easily avoided mistake. It was not until many years later that his most bitter opponents and his very best friends were able to say with gratitude, "he does not write books, he writes history."

The Little Professor as Kohl's General

"The CDU's 'real' time in the opposition began with Kohl and Biedenkopf," said Wulf Schönbohm, one of the most competent and at the same time most critical chroniclers and analysts of CDU history. Before he left his position as adviser in the party's central organization, he wrote a caricature of the CDU family in a roman à clef which was eagerly received by the public. Schönbohm later wrote his dissertation in a dry, scientific tone, since *ira et studio*: "Not only because of the constellation of personnel, but also because of the fundamentally changed political conditions, there was a good basis for the first time for political and organizational regeneration of the CDU in the opposition after the Bonn party conference, in contrast to the time before."

Schönbohm then compared the situation in 1973 to that in 1969.

- The *Bundestag* election results in 1972 did not offer the opposition any other prospects for at least four years (Schönbohm was right; it was ten years). There was no possibility that the government would change before that. There was widespread recognition of the fact that the CDU would have to draw wide-ranging consequences from this new situation if it wanted to run the government again.
- The election of Karl Carstens as chairperson of the parliamentary party and Helmut Kohl as chairperson of the national party finally separated the holders of these two offices, and there was no smoldering leadership crisis. There was in reality no rivalry, as might be supposed, between the chairmen of the national party and the parliamentary one, because Kohl and Carstens worked well together and Carstens did not show any inclination toward greater political ambitions of becoming a chancellor candidate in 1976, chiefly because the candidacy also did not play a role in internal party discussions.
- The controversy between German domestic policy and *Ostpolitik* which had dominated the previous legislative period had for the most part been laid to rest through ratification of the most important treaties. Though opinions in the party still differed about these, German domestic issues increasingly dominated internal party debates. The sometimes stormy confrontational politics of the Union in regard to German politics and *Ostpolitik* had proven not to be sensible, and thus there was a shift to a more moderate form of argumentation and concentration on major issues of domestic policy.
- These changes also caused a shift in party leadership from the parliamentary party to the national party, and after 1973 the party organization was finally able to become emancipated from the parliamentary party. The national party made the political decisions on basic issues and questions of medium- and long-term implications, while the parliamentary party, as the party's "spearhead," translated these

into parliamentary practice. For the first time in the history of the CDU the successful functioning of the party as a whole was essentially dependent on the achievements of the party organization.
- The change in generations in the mid and late 1960s from the *Land* to the federal level enabled the new party leadership to implement political and organizational changes because the up-and-coming generation of functionaries and mandators had greater understanding of fundamental reforms.

The increase in membership had also helped break up the crusty structures of the party organization at the local and regional levels, an important prerequisite for the activation of the party organization. Kohl himself underestimated the CDU party membership in 1973, incorrectly assuming that the CDU would have about 500,000 members by 1976; at that time membership was already over 650,000.

The new party leadership chose four main goals which the party also regarded as urgent:

- Elucidation of the CDU's political profile by implementation of political programs and elaboration of concepts;
- Increasing membership;
- Integration of the party organizations, particularly at the community level; and
- Expansion of an effective party apparatus at all organizational levels.

These passages from Schönbohm's dissertation aptly describe the situation of the CDU when Kohl and Biedenkopf took over party leadership. The general secretary practically had to become the "managing" chairperson by virtue of his permanent presence at the party center. The telephone lines between Bonn and Mainz were glowing because of possible votes, but the "little professor," as Kohl liked to call his "general," had the advantages of geography. Having turned his back on the university, he did not have any other mandate or office and was thus free to do the job for which he had been chosen by his chairperson and the party conference. His function as general secretary became an important one in the party in those years, and also in the eyes of his rival. He had been in his position barely over a year when those in the SPD "barracks," the Social Democratic Party headquarters, started speaking enviously about a "streamlined leadership" in the CDU, even stating this in key party publications.

The relationship between Kohl and Biedenkopf was tense right from the beginning, the intensity of their direct cooperation relaxing after the two very different men came into closer geographic proximity, standing shoulder to shoulder as chairmen of the presidium and executive meetings, holding the necessary discussions, and appearing in public. The party conference in Hamburg was a key success; perhaps for the first time in the congress center of the Hanseatic city the CDU showed it could handle controversial discussions, some of which were extremely heated, but at the same time achieve impressive compromises. The congress ended—also for the first time—with the playing and singing of the national anthem.

Views of a Faun

With a successful party conference and the favorable reports in the press behind him, Kohl, the forty-three-year-old up-and-coming politician, was able to explore the political terrain and make himself known and popular, gain points, and be the hero of the day. The glitter had largely worn off the ruling SPD/FDP coalition, more and more ministers and state secretaries resigned, differences of opinion split the SPD parliamentary party, and a major crisis seemed almost inevitable.

It was time to look around the internal political scene, breathe a little foreign air, and poach in the gardens of political opponents. Temporarily, Kohl became vain and arrogant, which was not like him at all. He acted like an unbridled faun who was susceptible to everything he could get his hands on materially and symbolically. His first internally controversial move was to target the office of the federal president, for which there was to be a new appointment in the spring of 1974. Kohl declared abruptly that the head of the state was "not a post which was the private property of the party in the majority in the government." What does "private property" mean here? Naturally this does not exist per se in politics. However, a majority is a majority, and that belonged to the "social-liberal" coalition—as it called itself—in Bonn. Kohl was after something else: having a part in finding a candidate and gaining a bit of power, which his political opponent had to deny him if it was not to call itself into question. However, the Brandt-Scheel government was a long way away from doing such a thing, even though its susceptibility to crisis grew with every month. Kohl's advance in late 1973 and early 1974 was nothing other than an attempt to make the opposition reinforce its claim of being taken seriously by the public. Thus, in regard to a possible candidacy of Walter Scheel to succeed Gustav Heinemann as federal president, after the final meeting of the presidium in 1973, Kohl said only that the CDU had "not made a commitment one way or another at this time," although the party "had had its thoughts." All this meant was, "dear people, you must take us into consideration every day and every hour."

A few weeks later, in January 1974, Kohl was foolish enough to pose the question on television whether it would not be better "to return to direct election of the head of state." This was blatant populism, since Kohl knew just as well as anyone else who had read the German constitution even superficially that electing the president by popular vote would presuppose an entirely different government organization. A federal president without executive powers does not need a direct confirmation by the people; therefore, his advisers tried to make it very clear to him, it would be much better not to talk about a general election for the federal president if one did not want to turn the constitution on its head. Kohl later repeatedly said the "representative democracy had completely proved itself" even in this instance. This also entails that a representative organization such as the whole parliament should choose the federal president from among candidates proposed to it by the parties and their exponents in the parliaments. The states' rights proponent Theodor Eschenburg correctly spoke of the federal president as a "state notary." It should remain that way, thought Helmut Kohl only a few years after his unfortunate appearance on television.

The chairperson ran into some small semantic difficulties in regard to Germany and overall German politics, reunification, and relations with the Warsaw Pact. The national conservatives held against him his rather lukewarm conviction about national unity. Kohl made the fatal error of saying that the CDU wanted to "make itself the custodian of a future pan-German nation." That is naturally a lot less than, *expressis verbis*, a "united Germany," or, as was still said in 1973, a "reunited" Germany or "fatherland," later a favorite expression of the CDU chairperson in reference to everything having to do with the state, homeland, or history. At the Catholic Academy in Munich, he made people shake their heads when he shouted, "We're ready to accept the challenge of the GDR!" What challenge was that? That, wrote an enervated Wilhelm F. Mascher, was exactly why the academy's theme had been followed by a question mark: "CDU/CSU: Profile without a Program?"

During a visit to America, Kohl made another interesting suggestion which was on the periphery of the constitution and was a "personal view" of the CDU outside of official German diplomacy. It was aimed at boosting the status of the Konrad Adenauer Foundation in Washington, already a well-staffed institution which was used heavily by the conservative elements of the U.S. administration. President Richard Nixon did not receive the CDU leader, since reception in the Oval Office was obligatory only for chancellor candidates. Kohl was not yet in this position, so the German visitor had to be content with meeting Vice President Gerald Ford, Secretary of State Henry Kissinger, and former presidential advisers Arthur Schlesinger and Helmut Sonnenfeldt. Kohl also held conversations with an extremely long list of prominent people, including former secretary of state Dean Rusk,

Vacation in St. Gilgen, July 1974. German Press Agency caption: "Rubber galoshes are the only fitting footwear in wet weather at the Wolfgangsee. Son Peter stands at Dr. Kohl's side, ready to help him pull his boots on."

In 1974, Kohl was the first CDU chairman to receive an official invitation from the Chinese government. This photograph from September of that year shows Kohl in a pavilion of the industrial exhibition in Shanghai in front of a statue of the "Great Chairman" Mao Tse-Tung.

the top democratic leader Nelson Rockefeller, and Edward Kennedy. Kohl was especially pleased that he was able to round off his American trip by meeting U.N. general secretary Kurt Waldheim, since the Austrian reminded him somewhat of home: "When you enter the general secretary's office in the glass skyscraper on the East River, you think you're in Salzburg." Kohl also wanted to have "something along the lines of a party ambassador" in New York, just as he had for the American capital.

Kohl had barely returned from his trip to the United States when CSU boss Franz Josef Strauss started a "major dispute" (*Abendzeitung*, Munich) with the unpopular head of the larger sister party. In the Bundeshaus restaurant, a meeting place for parliamentarians, journalists, and lobbyists seeking drink and gossip, the Bavarian's well-known choleric temper exploded. After a discussion about tax and spending policies, a *tour d'horizon* through day-to-day issues of domestic and foreign policies as well as the associated differences in the views of the CDU and the CSU, Franz Josef, as his friends called him, shouted in front of a dozen witnesses that he "detested" Kohl.

This was a boon to the tabloids, which sought possible "reactions" by the leader of the parliamentary party, Karl Carstens, who everyone knew was not particularly fond of Kohl, but who would never say this in public except in very small circles and in veiled tones, with a characteristic clearing of the throat. "Did he have to say that so loudly?" the refined man from the Hanseatic city of Bremen had his colleagues comment on the incident. But Kohl's predecessor, Rainer Candidus Barzel, well used to such nastiness, did not wonder about it: "Strauss has always been that way. He beat Erhard to a pulp, left Kiesinger in the lurch, and the same sorts of things happened to me."[47] The CDU party chief who had been subjected to such vilification was not himself able to react since he was taking part in an event very important to someone from Rhineland-Palatinate: a carnival session with the motto "Mainz remains Mainz." The CSU *Land* press spokesman resorted to a culinary comparison that was "meant as a joke" (*kohl* is the German word for "cabbage)—there was nothing else he could do under the circumstances. "Strauss has always hated *Kohl* and it's his right. And on top of that, red cabbage. How can anyone serve red cabbage with roast veal?"[48]

Peter Boenisch, a friend of the Bavarian and likewise confidante of Helmut Kohl, wrote a decade and a half later, "There are confidantes of Strauss who say that he hated Kohl. It was worse than that. In the end, hatred implies too much honor. Therefore he acted like he despised the chancellor." Strauss's outburst in the *Bundestag* canteen was no accident: there was a method to it. The Bavarian had been angry for years about the fact that, in his estimation, the Union parties had not been able to cover the full conservative spectrum in the Federal Republic of Germany. The supposed leftist tendencies of influential circles in the CDU were held to be responsible for this, which is why Strauss and his friends put their minds to how this lack could be remedied in a campaign strategy for 1976 and beyond.

This was the inception of the concept of a "fourth party," which from then on dominated the intraparty "dialog" between the CDU and CSU, as well as interested circles on the right periphery of both groups. The concept was justified through the "national aspirations of the CSU," which no longer was content with having only "regional" significance. The party wished to expand in such a way that conservative voters "north of the Main River" who did not feel at home in the CDU or in a rightist FDP could turn to a CSU offshoot. Kohl did not wish to know about this; with good insight into the signs of a party break-up, he pointed out examples in the history of popular parties which had regretted such experiments. After the series of *Landtag* elections in the autumn of 1975, Kohl wanted to "finally determine" the personalities and programs within the CSU leadership for the decisive election.

At the same time, a fourth party was still discussed in the Union, seemingly never losing its attraction to the media, possibly because it could easily drive a wedge between the sisters who were supposedly enemies. Bad news is good news; there was no real animosity, even if some of their leaders could not stand each other. There were CSU party conferences which did not liven up until a speech by a CDU guest speaker. Karl Carstens had only to raise his beer glass during a social event on the periphery of a party conference in Munich or Nuremberg to be greeted with appreciative looks. Once when the otherwise reserved northern German allowed himself to get carried away and he put on a loden hat with chamois brush and directed a Bavarian band, the entire Bavarian-filled auditorium applauded thunderously.

The constant sniping between the CDU people in Bonn and the CSU people in Munich led, however, to some remarkably bad feelings which could not be explained by the facts or the atmosphere, or at all, for that matter. When General Secretary Biedenkopf had finally had enough, he got his press spokesman to tell the news agencies that "the CDU is prepared, having examined all the reasons for and against, to enter into diplomatic discussions with the CSU."

As assiduously as the Union parties looked inward, they neglected to react properly to internal political events. The opposition hardly commented at all about the spy scandal that caused the SPD/FDP coalition to change chancellors. The so-called "Guillaume affair," which caused a storm on the internal political horizon, flowed by like a brook, with the Christian Democrats staring helplessly into it. Only a few days after the relatively subdued changeover from Brandt to Helmut Schmidt, whose inaugural speech was presented under the rubric "Continuity and Concentration," Kohl admitted that "Schmidt took over quickly." However, the former middle-distance runner qualified this: "The question is whether his lungs will hold out."[49]

6

The Contender (I)

1973–1980

Drama in German Politics

Helmut Schmidt managed to hold his breath longer than his predecessor had, with his great but short-lived visions. The drama of German politics seems to dictate that the pragmatists survive longer. Thus Kohl predicted—either with inspiration or a good instinct—that Helmut Schmidt's term in office would be promising. "Helmut Schmidt is a man to whom it is very important to be seen as a quick decision-maker."[50] There was no doubt that the leader of the opposition considered him to be just that as well as someone who would do well in office. Even worse: only a few weeks after Schmidt took office, Kohl voluntarily referred to Schmidt as a "feared rival," something which would be confirmed in years to come. He denied vehemently having expressed this idea but the newspapers frequently repeated the statement.

While Kohl was adjusting to the new modus operandi of a chancellor very different from Brandt, things in his Rhineland-Palatinate home *Land* were going against him. The one thing he wanted to avoid happened: Culture Minister Bernard Vogel suddenly appeared as a candidate to succeed Kohl as head of the CDU party of the *Land*, challenging Kohl's own favorite, Heinrich (Heiner) Geissler. Kohl had supported Geissler, a good friend, in order to ensure having a more congenial party chairperson in his own *Land* in case he had to retreat from the federal government scene. Kohl wanted to do this without wanting to topple him as minister-president, which he could not be sure about with Vogel, who was intellectually brilliant and a skilled operator, but with a tactical low profile. The culture minister was already well known outside Rhineland-Palatinate and his attacks against political opponents were often rhetorically right to the point: "No one must attempt to collectivize the rights of the individual out of mistrust of him." Kohl's friend Heinz Schwarz recalled that the conflict about the candidates was "exceedingly bitter," making unanimity impossible before the party conference and a final battle over a choice inevitable. This was a bitter defeat for the "black giant" otherwise so used to success.

In the fall of 1974 Kohl and his family traveled to the GDR on a private visit. Hannelore Kohl, who had been born in Berlin and had gone to school in Leipzig, wanted to visit friends and relatives with her prominent husband. The Socialist Unity Party newspaper *Neues Deutschland* seized the opportunity to report this under the heading "Various." After he returned, Kohl summed up the visit by saying, "I can only recommend that everyone go there." He recalled that a student had told him that the people in the GDR considered themselves to be Germans just as much as those in the Federal Republic, regardless of whether it was in the GDR's constitution. The opposition leader had to recognize that the basic treaty had gone some way toward normalizing intra-German relations. The Bavarian sister party, the CSU, did not find this normal at all, most especially that someone like Helmut Kohl would lead the way in internal political issues. Ways of dealing with the controversy over proper strategy were published every Wednesday in the opening article in the *Bayern-Kurier*. The press spokesperson in the Konrad-Adenauer-Haus in Bonn bravely bit his tongue when he had to comment on the sometimes nasty, sometimes merely clumsy arguments of the Christian Socialist competition far to the south. The general formula for comments was to say that the CSU also knew that "only together can we defeat the internal political rival." The following Wednesday the report in the CSU paper completely ignored the statement replying to the latest accusations: "We will not present our better arguments like excuses." Kohl used a slightly mixed metaphor in a vain effort to counter the discussion about the fourth party which he hated so much: "The subject of the fourth party is now dead. It was always dead and now it is completely dead."[51] A day after the CDU head made this statement, the right-wing conservative party *Bund Freies Deutschland* declared it had been constituted as a regular party in Berlin.

As the end of 1974 approached, the personal fronts in the Union became more clearly defined. The decision would be between Kohl and Strauss; all other considerations just clouded the issue. People may not have believed in Strauss even in the south, because, although highly talented, his overwhelming personality polarized issues instead of creating the needed integration. Strauss worked to gain time. After the CSU's resounding victory in the Bavarian *Landtag* elections, he called Kohl to ask that he postpone his ambitions of gaining the official nomination as chancellor candidate until May 1975. Kohl understood that the veto against a quick decision on a chancellor candidate in the Union would have to be presented to the public as a unanimous one and that he was the one who had to do it. That was the way the game was played, and whoever reached the finish line first was the most important. The forty-four-year-old had a remarkable sense of security, and finesse was beginning to be shown by a man whose career had started more with the saber than the floret.

Kohl saw no serious competition in the CDU, not even from Gerhard Stoltenberg, who had sown dissension among the left, and most especially in Hans Katzer, the chairperson of the CSU social committees ("The mouth with a pacifier has to be avoided").[52] Nevertheless, the "tall blond from the cold north" appeared to be a real alternative to many people in the party. But Stoltenberg, the son of a pastor, was never a fighter; if someone kicked him in the shin he fell over and did not get up again. Helmut Kohl, with experience in the organization, a good memory for appointments, and a good dollop of chutzpah, defeated his potential rival by shortcutting his possible high-profile appearances in Bonn. If Stoltenberg planned a press conference in the government quarter, Kohl was guaranteed to schedule his media appearance after an executive board meeting at exactly the same time as his "friend." Only one of them could have a full house.

Kohl, who characterizes his temperament as a mix of the choleric and the sanguine, was able to live with the situation at the end of the year. It was true that Strauss caused trouble where he could, but the increasing laissez faire that Kohl's friends and colleagues noted proved an asset in dealing with someone of an entirely different disposition. He was not even bothered by the publication of a survey by the Infas Institute, with its ties to the SPD, which claimed that Strauss was the only Union politician who could give Kohl a run for his money. (Forty-one percent of those questioned favored Strauss, while only twenty-two percent favored Kohl.)

The pressure for demonstrated unity in the Union was such that even Franz Josef Strauss could not ignore it if he did not want to jeopardize the CSU's victory on the far horizon. Moreover, Strauss had said in a *Spiegel* interview that he "was not among the candidates." He did see three to five suitable candidates, he said, with the intention of showing clearly once again his dislike of the man from Rhineland-Palatinate.

A survey in the summer of 1975 showed that Kohl clearly lagged behind his rivals Strauss and Stoltenberg with regard to those qualities regarded as necessary for a statesman: knowledge, energy, strength, and decisiveness. However, a clear majority of Germans questioned regarded Kohl as being empathetic, reliable, and progressive. The survey concluded—perhaps not surprisingly, considering German attitudes in the 1970s—that Helmut Kohl was the ideal candidate for exactly these reasons.

Kohl avoided Strauss as much as possible, although he was normally inclined to slap political friends on the back and did not avoid close physical contact. Strauss's manner of talking with or about Kohl in top party leadership meetings frequently enraged Kohl. In this regard he had a much more sensitive and thoughtful nature, and any contradictions by Strauss tended to stun him for a few minutes.

There were, roughly speaking, two camps in the Union parties which were important for both of their futures, and especially for Kohl's political career. Kohl's supporters were liberal men such as Kurt Biedenkopf, Walther Leisler Kiep, Heiner Geissler, Richard von Weizsäcker, and the Bavarian culture minister Hans Maier, who could not be deterred, much to Strauss's annoyance. Strauss's adherents were the so-called hardliners, particularly in foreign-policy issues: Karl Carstens, Alfred Dregger, Gerhard Stoltenberg, and Werner Marx.

The Hamburg-based newspaper *Die Zeit* saw it the right way: "Kohl—that would be the way to solve the conflict. Strauss—that would mean political polarization." This view was largely shared by the Germans, as demonstrated by surveys and regional elections, and most especially the *Bundestag* elections in 1976 and 1980. As long as Franz Josef Strauss, the supposed power cynic, was a player in the political arena, his rival appeared to many people to be a more human and politically acceptable alternative to the Schmidt/Brandt government. Eduard Neumaier doubted the CDU's commitment to "follow Kohl's direction." This shows that its own principles had started to crack: "The spirit of Hamburg, in which the party had ostensibly said good-bye to a time without inspiration and of pure desire for power, is dissipating with every election."

Really? The rumor in the republic for a long time had been that Strauss would be content with the role of king maker. At the same time, for tactical and image reasons, Kohl said on television, "We have several candidates. I think that's good." The CDU had time on its side, and it also had a much more extensive public relations mechanism. It could thus automatically broaden consensus in public opinion. Small groups of CDU sympathizers also started to form which even in Bavaria were more drawn to a party led by Helmut Kohl than the CSU. Kohl considered these people foolish but was secretly glad about them. Every time there was an initiative in Franconia that favored the CDU it was threatened with being banned by the party central apparatus in Bonn. Groups sympathetic to the CSU to the north generally were limited to clubs which met regularly.

In spring there was a terrible incident which affected Kohl deeply and threw him off course emotionally for a time: his close friend Peter Lorenz, the head of the CDU and a candidate for mayor, was kidnapped in Berlin by terrorists. Kohl's official description of it was "a barbaric act of political vandalism." Helmut Schmidt spontaneously formed a crisis response team consisting of the justice ministers of the various *Länder* and the minister-president of Mainz. In his final two years in office (1981 and 1982) Schmidt was never able to completely get over Kohl's behavior during these dramatic meetings which were to determine life and death, depending on which decisions the officials made. At a "chancellor's tea" with the Bonn media, the quick-tempered Schmidt flew into a rage when the name of his challenger, Helmut Kohl, was mentioned: "The crisis meetings in the mid-1970s about the Lorenz case showed that *he'll* never be able to do it! He was really afraid for his friend and posed impossible conditions! This office is not for him!"

A Loser at the Top?

But the office was for him, as events showed just a few months after this outburst. Kohl had to prove himself against Strauss in the mid-1970s and the battle for the candidacy was crucial in Kohl's rise to power. He had to divorce himself from his predecessors and his rivals, trying not to be oversensitive. Since Kohl was generally not vain he was better able to shake off insults than others. It did not particularly bother him that Strauss was usually the first to attack. He was mainly concerned that things should work out all right and was ready to discuss any unpleasantness without being ruffled.

In March Kohl gained one of his most impressive victories in the election for the *Landtag* in Rhineland-Palatinate; even Strauss, the Bavarian lion, sent a telegram to "dear Helmut" congratulating him. Kohl was ready to share the point with anyone who would listen to his rather flippant comment: "One can only say that the man is right." Kohl made it clear to his friends on the eve of the election that only he was in a position to bind together the diverging strands of the Union and to integrate where there was blatant dissension. The only thing Kohl hated was the constant pre-election polls and the soothsaying of demographic monitoring, "this infantile game with tenths of percentages." Nevertheless, a year and a half later, on the eve of the *Bundestag* election of October 3, 1976, he "wanted to know exactly, right up to the last tenth of a percent" how things were going before he appeared on television.

Conceited or not, Kohl liked to read in the papers that he was "a tree among the bushes,"[53] even though his Social Democratic counterpart in Rhineland-Palatinate, Wilhelm Dröscher, only meant this relatively. The Mainz minister-president and most likely prospect to become the chancellor candidate felt himself vindicated when the co-publisher of the *Frankfurter*

Allgemeine Zeitung, Johann Georg Reissmüller, favored him before the final nomination: "Kohl's biggest trump is the fact that he comes closest to being the people's idea of the embodiment of middle-of-the-road politics without extremes." This was quite clearly directed against Franz Josef Strauss's tendency to use extreme political means, the Strauss who had been a former defense minister and later, in the Grand Coalition, an astonishingly middle-of-the-road finance minister. Strauss proved this tendency once again in a speech in Sonthofen, a small town in Bavaria, when he called up a vision during a closed session of the top CSU leaders, an apocalyptic one in internal party politics. Strauss said that "things would have to get much worse before the Germans finally realized that the Bonn SPD/FDP coalition would lead to ruin."

Strauss's speech could be interpreted in either of two ways. His words could be taken as a warning against a disaster of chasm and destruction. Alternatively—and his political rival wanted to interpret his words this way—Strauss could have *wanted* economic and social chaos *so that* Germans would look for a new leader, not just because he was warning against this. Holger Börner, the SPD party leader, viewed the Sonthofen speech as a heaven-sent opportunity for his party, whose public-relations work had suffered somewhat. "We'll engrave this speech in bronze and tout it round."[54] The metaphor was not exactly apt, but it was obvious that the man was happy. Chancellor Schmidt was also happy about it: "Surely the man could not have said such a thing." The Social Democratic economist Herbert Ehrenberg said, "I'll live with that until 1976."

Whatever the Sonthofen "strategy" or the Sonthofen "spirit," the damage that this unfortunate speech did to Strauss helped Helmut Kohl. The experienced CDU parliamentarian Georg Kliesing quickly concluded: "That solved the question of the candidate for chancellor pretty decisively."

Sonthofen also showed something else: the coalition took Strauss far more seriously than Kohl as a runner in the next *Bundestag* election. It wanted to see the probable loser at the helm, not a fighter who would ruin their fun. The vast majority of the public saw it this way, but the editors of the Hamburg-based news magazine were probably closer to the mark with their interpretation of the speech as having a double meaning: "The man who had been hesitating about becoming a candidate for chancellor up to now out of fear of possibly losing the election and thus ending his political career seemed visibly relaxed to his friends, since the decision was out of his hands."

A few weeks later the public also heard a different story from the Bavarian leader, who unexpectedly ascribed to his archrival "social-political competence and the ability to coordinate,"[55] qualities which Strauss himself was lacking despite his many talents.

Thus the matter was settled, even though a number of months passed with variations in the battle for the candidacy which provided more entertainment value than revelation of character. In late April Kohl allowed General Secretary Biedenkopf to go on the offensive by recommending his nomination before May 5 to the CDU. The top party manager believed that this would positively affect the final stages of the campaign in North Rhine–Westphalia and Saarland, where elections for new *Landtage* were being held on May 4. Originally the CDU and CSU had agreed that discussions about the chancellor candidate, his core team, and a party platform would not be held until after the *Landtag* elections, but this was scotched by the move. CDU circles believed that Biedenkopf's premature actions may have been due to a suspicion that he had encouraged Strauss to become a candidate, but that the latter had rejected this. The "general" had thus felt himself strongly compelled to save his good reputation by quickly furthering "his Helmut." Munich circles gossiped that Strauss had interpreted this as "extremely unusual flattery from Biedenkopf," who had, during a dramatic turning point in the internal party machinery of choosing a candidate, indirectly "encouraged" him to declare himself.

Events came to a head at the beginning of May. Those at the CDU party headquarters became impatient and wanted to sort out the facts. It was first rumored and then confirmed on May 9 by the press office at the Konrad-Adenauer-Haus that the top committees would discuss the nomination of the chancellor candidate at their next meeting, which would be devoted to preparation for the party conference in Mannheim, even though this would be trivial. As a party spokesman said, the CDU was already one hundred percent behind its chairperson. A spokesman told a correspondent for the *Frankfurter Rundschau*, probably in a moment of feigned desperation, that "with the help of God and the CDU Helmut Kohl will become the chancellor candidate."

The CSU executive-committee members were unimpressed with such zeal, since they still maintained that Strauss was the better candidate. It was not until a month later that the same spokesman, in his best "party-speak," said that the discussions by the CDU and CSU presidents on nominating a chancellor candidate would be held in a "spirit of comradeship and unity in the basic questions of German politics." This declaration had been preceded by a private meeting between Kohl and Strauss at which the latter promised his rival he would no longer stand in his way. The rest resembled a political drama with tragicomic overtones: while the

CDU nominated its chairperson unanimously as chancellor candidate as expected at a closed session at the Eichholz Academy, near Bonn, the battle of Kohl versus Strauss continued for another five weeks. Finally a meeting in the Bavarian *Land* representation in Bonn yielded a "joint" candidate just before the CDU party conference in Mannheim, which was to deal with "the new social question." The statement about a unified candidate was bitterly ironic, since it underscored not only that the battle for "the best" candidate was still bubbling under the surface, but that it would really break out in earnest.

Former chancellor Kurt Georg Kiesinger, who was respected by all sides, told the international press, "The CDU has proposed Helmut Kohl as a candidate for the office of chancellor. The CSU has acknowledged that the CDU, as the larger party, wishes to nominate the candidate. The CSU continues to believe that its chairperson is the suitable candidate. The CSU will support Helmut Kohl as the chancellor candidate, as does the CDU in the interest of common goals." These statements in a joint CDU/CSU communiqué were to "accompany the chosen candidate into a battle which the German opposition had long since declared to be a Herculean effort of secular significance to overturn the power structure in Bonn," as the sagacious Fred Luchsinger wrote with bitter irony. "A bad start for Kohl," wrote the Swiss journalist, who was highly regarded in the CDU. "Under the circumstances he [Kohl] will not be growing wings that quickly."

Party Conference in C Major

Kohl did not have to grow wings; he wanted to remain on the ground. At the same time a sigh of relief went through the entire CDU family. The government manager's office was extremely happy, posters with stickers (Chancellor Candidate of the Union) were already printed and on their way to Mannheim, where they would beam out at the delegates, guests, and journalists in the foyers entering the "Rosengarten." Head of press relations Peter Radunski had ensured that everything was up to snuff again. The party congress's message, "Alternative 1976," was also prominently displayed.

The party congress in Kohl's homeland was held in a beautifully decorated auditorium, having every sign of being led by a party chairperson who was determined to lead and confident of victory. Kohl carried through the conference on a theme that bore the marks of his general secretary, Kurt Biedenkopf. "Kohl could have read off the telephone book and still been applauded," Rolf Zundel wrote in *Die Zeit*. The self-assured chairper-

With CDU press secretary Karl Hugo Pruys at the Mannheim conference, 1975.

son confined himself, however, to speaking in generalities in the booming voice that he had begun to use more and more frequently. The forty-five-year-old paid numerous visits to a doctor who recommended that he take better care of his voice, but the "black giant" was unable to do this.

For the first time in his promising career as head of the party, Kohl received confirmation of his role as chairperson. His results were comparable to those of Adenauer: 696 out of 707 votes. *Die Zeit* summed up what other papers had also written: "The ovations seemed never-ending. He accepted the triumph with a hint of clumsiness which made the joy and the emotionalism believable. However, he was certainly not overcome with humble gratitude. Though he was pleased about the results, he also considered them to be right."

The undeniable primary theoretician of the CDU, Kurt Biedenkopf, had combined several theses under the heading "New Social Questions" and in the debate most of the congress speakers tried to elucidate their thoughts about possible answers to these questions in what was standard party procedure. The party conference theme was not exactly gripping but it certainly gave the media enough to comment on. Biedenkopf's thesis was that the rights of those people who did not have a lobby—primarily children, students, and older citizens—should be guaranteed. Such sentiments do not attract voters very easily; however, this topic harked back to the Union's "Christian" origins and commitments to which the other parties had not pledged themselves to date. That impressed a lot of people, since Biedenkopf proved himself to be a good analyst and orator, and the proponent of a good cause.

The "C major" played a larger role in many of the press reviews, more so than in previous party conferences. This pleased the fundamental thinkers in the party, including Richard von Weizsäcker, who was increasingly friendly to his "Helmutle." If Kohl asked his press secretary how a television interview had gone, and was reminded by him with great regularity that it was much more effective to look directly into the camera lens, "Richie," who also tended to avoid looking at the camera, told him "that everything had gone extremely well." In fact, nothing was "extremely well done," because Kohl's impact on the media was still not good, and he certainly did not have any illusions about this. Weizsäcker, the former president of the *Kirchentag*, however, always tried to have Kohl think well of him. Only at Kohl's side or with Weizsäcker's help would his political career succeed—that was the reason for the often exaggerated flattery of citizen Kohl by Freiherr von Weizsäcker.

Conservatives and progressives alike felt comfortable with Kohl's party conference speech. He conceded that everyone was right to an extent and avoided any prominent controversies. Those people in the *Bundestag* parliamentary party who were not completely against the treaties with Eastern Europe now believed that they could hope for a slow change toward more realism in the opposition's strategy. The conservative wing too got a nod with strong statements about freedom, work, and authority.

A confidential protocol that was an addendum to a parliamentary party agreement divided up responsibility for foreign policy between Karl Carstens, who represented the conservative wing, and Walther Leisler Kiep, the progressive. Carstens was responsible solely for Germany and Eastern Europe and Kiep for the other less risky areas. Despite this, the party leaders instructed the press department to announce the "appointment" of Kiep as the CDU's foreign-policy spokesperson. This led to some peculiar misunderstandings, because the press department in Konrad-Adenauer-Haus was not informed about the "secret note." For days the press spokesman defended an unusually mild statement by Kiep about the SED dictatorship in East Berlin "because Kiep had the official right to make such statements."

The CSU party leadership in Munich also was completely against it. The radio in particular pushed the issue to the limit by its frequent repetition of contradictory statements by both parties. Strauss called for a private meeting with parliamentary party leader Carstens to clarify the problem and Carstens's office head, Hans Neusel, was also invited. It was Neusel who

Kohl took part in "boisterous water games with the family"—according to the German Press Agency—during his summer vacation at the Wolfgangsee in 1975.

finally informed the CDU press spokesman about the cause of the unnecessary confusion. However, politics is not served by "secret notes."

Many people considered the new orientation of the CDU toward Christian values—presented in and commented on in many ways in party flyers and brochures—as a vain attempt to gain status. In reality, politics was put on an entirely different plane, for example in the *Bundesrat*, in which the CDU/CSU *Länder* had the majority. Helmut Schmidt himself, who Kohl did not particularly care for because of his baroque personality, "sought" a dialogue with the head man of the Union. Whether or not this was manipulated by the south, such a contact was reasonable in view of the political power balance. The chancellor wanted to find out what sort of resistance the Union parties were going to put up in the *Bundesrat*, and which legislative proposals they wanted to address. The proposed increase in value-added tax and unemployment-insurance contributions championed by the joint SPD/FDP coalition was turned down by the CDU/CSU. Had they remained adamant and instead demanded greater savings in the federal budget and not allowed a tax increase, the prospects for a lot of the coalition's projects would have been nil. On the other hand, with such strategies the CDU had very little leeway for new social utopias or for broad development programs, considering that the overall budget was already strained and the various factions were not yet collaborating,

The Bavarian delegates to the CSU party conference in September supported the CDU's chancellor candidate in good fashion, but Franz Josef Strauss again took the opportunity to give his rival a lesson. Strauss adopted

*In October 1975, the CDU chairman, accompanied by CDU-*Bundestag *representative Richard von Weizsäcker, and Werner Marx, traveled to Moscow for nine days, where he also met with Minister-president Kosygin. Here, with Hannelore and von Weizsäcker in a lecture hall at Lomonosov University.*

a direct tone in warning his "party friends" from the northern *Länder* that "promises and utopias could not be played off against one another." The interminable problems which the socialist-liberal coalition had created for itself through spending (especially under Willy Brandt) seemed to confirm Strauss's presentiments at Sonthofen.

Shortly after Kohl's brief visit to Munich there was a meeting between him and Schmidt which drew media attention. Kohl had prepared carefully for it and agreed beforehand on the topics to be discussed with opposition leader Karl Carstens. Since the CDU was then also preparing for a trip to Moscow, German-Soviet relations were on the table, along with other issues. Schmidt, however, was also keen to know the opinion of the CDU-dominated *Länder* in addition to the foreign-policy views of the minister-president of the Rhineland-Palatinate.

The SPD chancellor, who was much more popular with conservative voters, even in the CDU, than he was with elements of his own party, considered the CDU chairperson to be more important than the other Union leaders, even though he did not let Kohl know this at the time. Perhaps there would come a time when they needed one another, and tactical respect was a good thing.

Between All Chairs

Treading a careful line between real antitheses or only imagined conflicts between the CDU and CSU became a preoccupation for Helmut Kohl after that. From time to time, the Mainz minister-president's internal communications or public pronouncements appeared to have been made en passant. Kohl was said to be thinking of dismissing his "general," who often caused him difficulty, being a party chairperson who wanted more peace and quiet for his party on the front than Kohl, a power seeker, was furthering. The "little professor" understood this very well, and one of the consequences was that he soon had just as great a media presence as his boss. The professor's brilliant intellect often did not sit well with Kohl. By nature suspicious, the man from the Palatinate was inclined to see betrayal when another person would retreat into a momentary bad mood and then return to the business of the day.

"I have a strong relationship to the authority of this office," the chairperson told anyone who wanted or had to listen. Everyone who worked with or for him was made well aware of that point at party committee meetings. Mumbled snatches from those assembled could be heard before these meetings on the tenth floor of the Konrad-Adenauer-Haus: "He can't do this to us any longer," or "He really must say something concrete about

Frivolous joy, but only in front of the camera: The chancellor candidate, the CSU chairman Franz Josef Strauss, and the acting chairman of the CDU/CSU Fraktion, *Hans Katzer, at the strategy meeting for the 1976* Bundestag *elections, December 11, 1975.*

that." However, once Kohl entered the room and sat down in the chairperson's seat with its very high back, there was an almost worshipful silence, just as there would be in a high-school class when the principal entered. Once, after a trip to China, Kohl talked for two hours, more about his personal observations than about his political discussions with the Beijing leaders. "The women have such curious laced bodices to flatten their chests; these women wouldn't use anything like corsets, like our women." At a ceremonial dinner, "with a substantial and fatty Chinese meal" with the Chinese party leadership and government heads, each of the eighteen dignitaries toasted him individually with a highly alcoholic Gauliang and he had to keep up. How he got to bed he really didn't remember. He heard the next day that his Chinese interpreter had killed one of the many bicyclists on the drive home around midnight: "They don't have any lights on the bicycles." It was after this point that Kohl started to pay more attention to the Middle Kingdom.

Feelings of authority did not help, however, with the immense and constant stress caused by Strauss and his people. Kohl was able at least to quelch the Biedenkopf rumor believably, even though Heiner Geissler was already being mentioned. The social minister from Rhineland-Palatinate seemed to be exploring the Bonn terrain in the second half of 1975 in the form of a "social scientific" office in the federal capital, led by Ulf Fink, the former assistant head of section at the federal labor ministry under Hans

Katzer. Although the name "Fink" means "dove," this Fink certainly did not supplant a nightingale. Rather, to put it mildly, he lit a fire under the full-time staff of the political department of the CDU government office by publishing a gripping study on the future of the German social system. Geissler was (correctly) thought to be behind Fink's theories, which the press viewed as being completely unorthodox, judged against the rather slowly evolving ideas of the CDU. The CDU press department was faced with the almost impossible task of trying to explain over and over that Ulf Fink's theories "did not reflect the official party line."

Kohl read more frequently and with growing unease in the papers that he was no longer "master of the proceedings." Eduard Neumaier hit the proverbial nail on the head when he wrote that Kohl's weakness was his "political indifference, which made him hold back from making any pronouncements." Kohl was often heard mumbling to himself that he would love to see the day when he could "cut the legs off" anyone who crossed him.

But at the same time the party was doing splendidly. Membership had grown enormously, so that the figure had exceeded the 600,000 target months before the *Bundestag* elections. The increased respect of the CDU's rival political party was also noted with satisfaction. The Social Democrats had recognized that since Helmut Kohl had become chairperson, the Union was a political party organization to be taken seriously. The old "chancellor voting club" seemed to be a thing of the past. The CDU worked and showed a public image of being a propaganda apparatus which employed all the means of a modern service organization. "The secret of all success is the organization of the insignificant," Oswald Spengler said. Without knowing of Spengler's words, Kohl applied his principles and knew how to galvanize the right sort of people.

Politically, of course, Kohl had some stumbling blocks. He did not care, for example, that the media took him to task for his duplicity in the deliberations between Bonn and Moscow on the agreements on Poland, which were meant to draw a close to its painful history. In Machiavellian terms, he was more concerned that the Union parties should support him in his official rejection. At the same time, Kohl said "he respected the stance of its supporters." That is, he would have been happy if the package of treaties had been "blessed" by the *Bundesrat*, despite all the legitimate doubts about the reliability and mutual aspects of the treaty's stipulations.

Strauss mistrusted Kohl to the end and wrote a letter to him and the other minister-presidents of CDU-governed *Länder* in which he pleaded with them to take into consideration his ideas in the forthcoming deliberations in the *Bundestag* parliamentary party. Kohl wanted to reject the agree-

During deliberations concerning the Union's position on the Poland treaties, March 10, 1976. The minister-president of Lower Saxony, Ernst Albrecht, General Secretary Biedenkopf, and party chairman Kohl.

ment on the part of the government of Rhineland-Palatinate, but at the same time reckoned with only a slim majority in the *Bundesrat*, having correctly assumed that the CDU-led Saarland would be in favor of the agreement. Helmut Schmidt commented on Kohl's speech in the *Bundestag* rejecting the Warsaw treaty: "Do you think that you'll be able to visit Warsaw as federal chancellor after today's speech?"

It was during the domestic debates on the controversial agreement with Poland that the Union's chancellor candidate announced he would visit the country in 1976. At the same time, he said he would not make any more public statements about the treaty until after the final deliberations on it in the *Bundestag* parliamentary party on November 4. Kohl hinted that after that he would have "something fundamental" to say about how he thought the CDU/CSU should run the *Bundestag* election campaign. The "leadership issue" would also have to be solved and a way found which would give him, even as a candidate, a mandate to forge guidelines within the party on all key issues, in anticipation of possibly becoming chancellor. Franz Josef Strauss rejected this out of hand, pointing out that his party, despite its smaller regional base, would "never give up" its aspirations of an "overall federal role." He said Kohl had "misinformed him at least and possibly betrayed him" on the Poland issue.

A Stage in the War on Two Fronts

> The CSU does not intend to expand throughout the Federal Republic. At the same time, both party chairpersons believe emphatically that there is no room for an additional political party in the Federal Republic of Germany if both Union parties jointly represent the exact same view in all decisive political problems. I will exert my full authority as party chairperson and chancellor candidate in this regard.
>
> The leaders of the Union parties consisted of chairperson of the CDU and chancellor candidate Helmut Kohl; the chairperson of the CSU, Franz Josef Strauss; the chairperson of the CDU/CSU parliamentary party; the chairperson of the CSU *Land* group, Richard Stücklen; Hans Katzer; Gerhard Stoltenberg; Alfred Dregger; and Rainer Barzel. This circle also included the general secretaries, Kurt Biedenkopf and Gerold Tandler, who were charged with running the election campaign.

Kohl's communiqué, issued after a meeting of the CDU and CSU boards in Bonn, was designed to stop rumors about the expansion of the Christian Democratic Union of Bavaria to all of West Germany. At the same time, a dispute on November 17, 1975, between Kohl and Strauss made Kohl want to ensure once again that his candidacy for chancellor was safe. Kohl's dual role as chairperson and chancellor candidate was mentioned twice in the eighteen-line-long declaration. The Konrad-Adenauer-Haus staff were smart enough to make sure that everything was in order. At any rate, Kohl wanted to make sure he was protected against any nasty surprises after the partial victory at this stage.

The confrontation with the ruling SPD/FDP coalition then took priority again and well-meaning papers even talked about Kohl's unexpected decisiveness vis-à-vis Strauss. This was not really necessary, since the attacks by the Bavarian mostly collapsed as soon as he left Munich and reached Bonn. Naturally he allowed his well-known sarcasm free rein during meetings over meals with Kohl, heaping scorn on his "leftist" colleague and still looking the "black giant" in the face. Otherwise Strauss avoided direct confrontation with Kohl at these meetings, which became increasingly common, time consuming and nerve wracking.

Opinion polls in the winter of 1975–76 seemed to confirm the upward trend of Kohl and his party. The Allensbacher Institute, founded by Elisabeth Noelle-Neumann, the famous opinion pollster for the Union parties,

On March 12, 1976, the Bundesrat *ratified unanimously the treaties with Poland. The Rhineland-Palatinate minister-president spoke directly to Chancellor Helmut Schmidt several times during his speech.*

seemed to show that Kohl had just about caught up to Helmut Schmidt in popularity. The chancellor, who could deliver trick-filled and smooth speeches, chided Kohl in the *Bundestag* about an "indiscretion" from a confidential discussion about Poland with his challenger. He then cited the hardly indiscreet thought processes of the chancellor candidate, who revealed that the CDU/CSU would, according to his investigations, allow the Poland treaties to be passed in the *Bundesrat*, which Schmidt cleverly mentioned at another point.

Typically, another opinion poll by Infratest in the spring of 1976 showed Kohl to be further behind. It documented Schmidt as "continuing to be much more popular" than his challenger Kohl. However, the CDU chairperson had clearly gained in status in his own party.

Kohl was strongly applauded by his party friends after his speech commemorating the one hundredth birthday of Konrad Adenauer, the party founder who had died nine years earlier. However, the *Frankfurter Allgemeine Zeitung* correspondent Karl Feldmeyer was less impressed with the speech. This conservative journalist believed it revealed insufficient commitment to the basic issues of national concern: "It was evident that Kohl's speech did not touch upon the importance of the division of Germany for Adenauer. Kohl did not mention reunification at all. He talked about 'the German people' several times, although he obviously only meant those in the Federal Republic of Germany."

Since Kohl usually did not leave anything to chance, it can be assumed that there was a method, or at least a tactical move, behind the omission of this once-essential part of classical CDU politics. Since *Ostpolitik* did not remind people of reunification as much as it once had, Kohl was not trying to ignore the issue of nationality completely, but to circumvent it from the outset. It seemed plausible to him that the Union right-wingers

At a press conference on May 21, 1976, in Bonn, the chancellor candidate outlines the CDU and CSU common platform for the coming Bundestag *elections. Kurt Biedenkopf, Kohl's general secretary, sits next to him.*

were vociferous enough about the issue and he believed that toning down his semantics would help steer his party to the desired middle position. A fair description of his tactics might be: "No confrontation with broad or entrenched views; it is better to have something for everyone." Many critics in the press saw this tack as a danger signal about the strength of his campaign. However, this strategy, which some regarded as half-hearted and lacking in profile, and others saw as being clever and nonbinding, gained Kohl voters primarily from the left-middle. The potential on the right wing seemed to be exhausted; making political concessions to it seemed to the CDU chairperson to be only pandering to the Dreggers and Filbingers of the party. It was not that he could not work with them—he was a friend of Filbinger—Kohl just did not believe that he could mobilize anything for the Union from this side.

Freedom or/instead of Socialism

The 1976 campaign, a tour de force of exemplary proportions, overshadowed the summer. Kohl undertook some trips, as chancellor candidates had become accustomed to doing. For the first time he was concerned about his image, and got a new pair of glasses. No stylists or fashion advisers helped him choose: it was one of his sons who Kohl trusted to have good taste and an eye for appearance. The glasses were rimless and gave him a rather intellectual look; his hair was cut a little shorter and some strands were combed loosely over his forehead. The first posters which were to show the candidate during the pre-election period gave the CDU chairperson a Peter Pasetti look. This disappeared in the next series of posters.

Two weeks before the party conference in Hanover, Kohl traveled to the United States, again in keeping with his model, Konrad Adenauer. "*Der Alte*" was thus present in spirit on the trip. The chancellor candidate did not waste any opportunity to recall the first chancellor of the Federal Republic of Germany, in whose footsteps he believed he was following: "Just before he died, Konrad Adenauer had told me that if I had the chance I should speak to George Meany." This was said for the benefit of the journalists accompanying him; in actual fact Kohl was not especially interested in meeting Meany.

Above all, he wanted to be received by the American president, which was understandable in his role: the Union leader felt the photos from the one-minute session were absolutely necessary for the German election campaign. Before that Kohl had told Gerald Ford, who had kept him waiting for a few minutes in the reception area, about the preparations for

America's two hundredth anniversary by the U.S. troops stationed in Rhineland-Palatinate. The Christian Democrat Helmut Kohl was pretty much on the same lines in his assessment of current political issues as the thick-set Republican Gerald Ford.

In addition to securing his growing internal political image, trips became a top priority because the chancellor candidate was held to be colorless and lacking in profile in foreign policy. And Adenauer traveled with him in spirit. The CDU expert on foreign relations, Heinrich Böx, former ambassador to Warsaw and one of the first government spokespersons under Adenauer, recalled an incident during a visit to the Spanish court. When Kohl called himself "Adenauer's grandson" in a conversation with King Juan Carlos, the monarch, used to thinking in terms of dynasties, asked him with surprise whether he was related to Adenauer. Böx said that the interpreter solved the generation problem caused by Kohl's figure of speech so elegantly that the king then looked upon his German guest "with complete satisfaction and recognition."

The party conference in Hanover, conceived as the internal party kick-off to the election and carefully prepared by General Secretary Kurt Biedenkopf, had as its motto the controversial slogan "Out of love for Germany: Freedom instead of socialism." The original version, "Freedom or socialism," which the Bavarian sister party had preferred, was thought to be too strong by elements of the CDU and the media; it was finally abandoned in favor of a "softer" formulation. In the *Landtag* campaign in Baden-Würtemburg, however, a very clear-cut "or" was evident, as if it were a matter of life and death, of victory or defeat. Nevertheless, the CDU strategists in the Konrad-Adenauer-Haus did not insist vehemently that it was a matter of freedom *or* socialism. People such as Peter Radunski, the head of public relations, and the manager Karl-Heinz Bilke proposed a "less hard" slogan. This "Freedom instead of socialism" became a real hit "in the longest and most extensive election campaign in the history of the Federal Republic of Germany." It was with obvious pleasure that Margaret Thatcher, guest speaker at the Niedersachsenhalle, ended her greeting with "Freedom instead of socialism." The speech on which General Secretary Kurt Biedenkopf had worked into the small hours of the night contained practically incontrovertible proof that democratic socialism acutely endangered the consistent striving for freedom.

Whether "instead of" or "or" should stand between freedom and socialism, the party conference in Hanover had to accomplish one thing above all: it had to close the ideological gap between the CDU and the CSU, or at least disguise it in such a way that it would not undermine the campaign for the upcoming elections. Thus Kohl and Biedenkopf, each in his own

At the CDU election convention in Hanover, May 25, 1976.

way, hammered home the need for close cooperation between the Christian parties and for a fighting spirit in order to ensure victory. According to Biedenkopf, "This program (forged in Hanover) is the basis of the election campaign we are facing, the basis of the battle with our political adversary, but it is also a demonstration of the unity of the Union parties. It shows that the rumors about the supposed differences between the two parties are nonsense. In the coming months . . . and in the future, both parties, the CDU and the CSU, will be inseparable, however hard our political opponent tries."[56]

The words "battle" and "victory" appear most frequently in Kohl's speech, which ended, "We continue in certainty that we have laid the foundation for victory on October 3. The hysterical reaction to our slogan 'Freedom instead of socialism' shows us how right we were with this clear statement. And our political opponents all over the country know this too. . . . My friends, let us leave Hanover today to start working together. Everyone is important. We'll fight for every vote. We're fighting for a turning point in German politics. We can see the goal just ahead. We will win."

Helmut Kohl had even more reason to be confident in the meantime: in spring, the CDU candidate for minister-president of Lower Saxony, Ernst Albrecht, was elected in an upset caused by the extreme weakness of the *Landtag* SPD parliamentary party and with some votes from the opposing party. This augured well, thought those in the Konrad-Adenauer-Haus in Bonn. Albrecht swiftly sent some signals along the lines of Kohl's sentiments to the Free Democrats. Kohl was certain that sooner or later the Liberals would consider returning to a coalition with the Union. The head of the FDP, Foreign Minister Hans Dietrich Genscher, was often heard to joke—though of course surreptitiously—that "Socialism is progress—in the wrong direction."

Lower Saxony's "beaming" Albrecht appointed CDU treasurer Walther Leisler Kiep as finance minister because of his qualifications for the job and his good contacts with the FDP. Kiep indeed knew a lot about finance, which was proven by the fact that he had been an entrepreneur and had also raised millions of marks for the party. The Union party man from Hesse served as a lure for drawing the Liberals back to the CDU—a move which was not immediately successful. The CSU fossil Hermann Höcherl called the advances of the CDU "an invitation with a gilded edge to the FDP." And the right-wing CDU man Alfred Dregger was still angry with Kohl about his dual strategy on Poland, saying openly that the party chairperson was a "circus horse who ran around and around in a circle." Kohl was loath to let that sort of comment go, so that *Stern* quoted him as saying about Dregger, "I can't stand people who think that the goose step is a sign of authority."

One thing, however, was clear from the unexpected coup in Hanover: Helmut Kohl gained ground—temporarily—against Strauss. Even Conrad Ahlers of the SPD, former head of the government's press and information office and member of parliament in the Rhineland-Palatinate constituency Bad Kreuznach, was perplexed about the "new Kohl." He had the impression that Kohl "had had a session with a psychiatrist." Kohl was only nine points behind Schmidt in popular-opinion polls, a truly great achievement. Social Democratic candidates had never been able to reduce the gap between themselves and the incumbent CDU chancellor to less than twenty percent. Rainer Barzel had been happy to be only seventeen points behind Willy Brandt.

Kohl was again optimistic and said in semipublic circles that "Schmidt is afraid of me."[57] He knew of course that that was not true, but he did not know that he would have to pay for his statement a few days before the election.

The Tiger, on Loan from Vienna

Willi Weiskirch, who had been a reliable but not terribly resourceful press spokesperson for Helmut Kohl, was replaced in the spring of 1976 by Wolfgang Wiedemeyer, deputy head of the Bonn *Südwestfunk* studio. Weiskirch campaigned in the district of Olpe/Meschede for election to the *Bundestag*, which took up all his energy. The *Südwestfunk* correspondent had written a book about the chancellor candidate which some papers misunderstood to be a "critical biography."

Even before the change in the CDU press office, Kohl had looked at other possibilities and approached Gerd Bacher, who had just left a job as director of Austrian state television (ORF). Bacher had been in line for a top position at German Television Channel Two, but did not get it because he was not a German citizen, as was clearly required by the government contract for such jobs. He had to be placed and Kohl again had an idea to save the situation: he would appoint him his "personal" campaign adviser. When the announcement was made about the experienced radio broadcaster, who, along with Bruno Kreisky was one of the most well-known radio personalities—the media nicknamed him "tiger" because of his direct approach—Friedrich Nowottny, head of the Standing Conference of Public Broadcasting Corporations, called the CDU headquarters press office and asked brusquely "whether *one* Austrian was not enough for us."

Bacher was an unusual person and tried in vain to modify his boss's language and image. He gave Kohl notes for press conferences with friendly admonitions, suggested phrases, and all sorts of tips from the audience, because the CDU speaker held sway over the podium. Bacher carefully observed the meetings of the media coordinating committee of the CDU and the CSU led by the staff of Konrad-Adenauer-Haus. He seemed to have an endless source of practical experience, gesticulating and coming up with ideas in the meetings. The Austrian Willibald Hilf, the head of the state chancery in Mainz and Kohl's friend and confidant, ran out of patience and called Bacher a "radio Stalinist." Hilf had been acting like a self-appointed guardian of the grail of Western values in German media politics, which played an important role in those years when there was growing debate about possible private competition with the government-owned system. Bacher favored more diversity in television and radio, but ended up again in the well-upholstered armchair of the director of the ORF. There is nothing like security.

Bacher eagerly followed everything in the house on two legs. He had the intelligence of a quick thinker but became completely disinterested in something if he encountered it a second time. He did not feel himself tied at all, even though he commanded an extremely high salary and worked directly for the chairperson. The fifty-year-old was not a man of sorrow, but of wit. Once when a snowfall in the Rhineland was followed by the type of traffic snarls known to every Bonn resident, Bacher went on for half an hour about the "flatland Tiroleans." After a forty-five-minute telephone call to Kohl in which he tried to get the minister-president and chancellor candidate to agree to a cleverly formulated press release, the eloquent Salzburg journalist and Viennese director slammed down the phone in aggravation: "The man has the feeling for language of a high-school student!"

Had Kohl heard such remarks from his chief adviser he probably would not have gotten angry with him. Despite his suspicion of critics, Kohl has a well-developed sense of humor which spares neither himself nor others. When a political poster caused a scandal, Kohl knew how to take care of the situation. This was a caricature of the chancellor candidate as a baroque cherub with fat arms and thighs; the "little bit" had also been included. The head of Kohl's office, Wolfgang Bergsdorf, and the department head of the government manager's office considered a public protest and even legal action. However, the boss had to see the corpus delicti first and give his opinion. The well-designed poster was unrolled in the reception area and tacked onto Kohl's door for demonstration purposes. When the "black giant" came into the office on Monday morning and was asked his opinion, he grumbled good-naturedly to himself: "Obviously that's not meant to be me: mine isn't so little!" That put an end to the matter, with the faces of Kohl's entourage several centimeters longer and the CDU central office one "case" down.

Attention was now turned to daily business, which seemed to be very promising for the CDU in the weeks of the hot pre-election summer of 1976. Also, as a party organization, the CDU was professionally geared up to issue press statements of all kinds or to react correctly to any campaigns on the home front or from Kohl's vacation spot on the Wolfgangsee in Austria. A dedicated telephone line in the chairperson's office connected every authorized caller directly to the prominent vacationer in Austria. Kohl had invited the editor in chief of the daily newspaper *Die Welt* to the Wolfgangsee to approve the text of an interview which Herbert Kremp, with his good command of language and other talents, had composed himself and which contained pithy statements by Kohl. The Springer publication devoted a full page to it, a service which only a few publications in Germany were willing to give the challenger in the 1976 *Bundestag* elections. The chancellor candidate could not complain about lack of media exposure. Before he left on vacation, Karl Schiller (SPD), the former finance minister, approached Kohl with a proposal: "I, Schiller, will join the CDU on the condition that you, Kohl, will give me the economics ministry if you win the election." Kohl thanked him politely but rejected the offer firmly. He could not make any promises over the heads of his fellow Christian Democrats, and certainly not to a Social Democrat. Karl Schiller had also supported Ludwig Erhard in the Springer press years ago in a campaign involving the so-called German economic miracle. But Kohl recalled the failed Barzel strategy with those who changed party affiliations in 1972–73, and at any rate he was skeptical about such an offer. He seemed to be more intrigued by Schiller's escapades between all the parties than happy about the offer.

I Was Good at Hölderlin

Kohl should have known better than to have gotten caught up with such matters, but the man from Rhineland-Palatinate laughed off all warnings about intellectual traps. Discussing art, books, and music competently is not one of the things he likes to do and is not to his taste. But he did agree to an interview in *Die Zeit* which "would not be an interview in the usual sense."

It cannot be said that the Hamburg newspaper did not stick to the agreement. On the contrary: the result of the meeting between Helmut Kohl and the author Walther Kempowski was certainly out of the ordinary. Kohl did not notice at first that he had been led. When the interview was published in mid-August all the telephone lines at the Konrad-Adenauer-Haus glowed red. The German intellectuals were worried that "the election was lost." Upset CDU members said that Kohl had "disgraced himself and the party," that "he should never allow himself such exposure," and worse.

What had Kohl said that caused the weeks-long upset, led to articles in response, and resulted in a serious dispute between the government management office and the influential Hamburg publishing house?

"I read a lot," Kohl said, puffing his pipe, looking around contentedly at the books lining the shelves of his study in the bungalow in Ludwigshafen-Oggersheim. And the first book "was the new Adenauer volume," he said, looking at his friendly interviewer Kempowski with his eyebrows slightly knitted, "which I consider to be very good." At the same time, he had "started Golda Meir." Asked whether he could name five books which meant a lot to him, Kohl lost his composure for a moment, although it is always hard to tell with him whether the annoyance is feigned or genuine. Five books? "When I read, I try to read something outside of my field." All right, Adenauer and Golda Meir of Israel were in his field, at least in the broadest sense. The city library which he had just been to seemed to interest Kohl more. He gave replies that anyone could have given; the man or woman on the street went through his mind—making himself popular was uppermost in his thoughts. Thus he mentioned "three Joseph Conrads" which he had taken out of the library; Conrad was practically "a person like you or me." Carl Zuckmayer he was rereading; after all, he was not one of those people who read a book once and put it away.

The ensuing conversation with the well-known author, which was disorganized and in many instances improvised, provided insight into Kohl's pysche, his temperament, and his tactics for making himself popular, but less so into his intellectual powers, the ostensible lack of which in this interview in *Die Zeit* many readers were exceedingly quick to point out. Nevertheless, in this relaxed conversation with Kempowski, Kohl himself named twenty authors whose work he had read or to whom he often had recourse. He discussed classicists Goethe and Schiller only when asked: "I'm not someone who has a direct connection with poetry." That is an honest reply, for which one should be grateful, especially coming from a politician. At this point Kohl recalled an incident from his trip to China. The foreign minister, who had studied in Tübingen, had quoted from Hölderlin's "Song of Fate." When Kohl pointed out that he had finished the verse "in the middle of the stanza," the minister had become very cross. At this point the voice of the high-school student came out of the mouth of a man in his middle forties: "I was good at Hölderlin; no one else had had this passion, not even the teachers." Hölderlin as a subject: is that so impossible? As a student Helmut Kohl had loved the poet, and the adult was still attached to him, as attested to by his naive form of introspection.

It is easy to laugh at the man from the Palatinate, thinking oneself superior in education, depending on one's mood or disposition. However, this was one of the few instances in which the private citizen Helmut Kohl revealed himself in the process of projecting a public image.

Nevertheless, the leftist-liberal paper, which Kohl did not like but did respect because it appeals to a large portion of the middle-class elite, put him into a projected book by Kempowski on the "founding generation." The paper did not intend to cause him trouble; Kohl's comments themselves, which were not elicited by leading questions, continued to disturb well-educated people and tickle his political opponents. But the somewhat prissy protests worried the aesthetes, who shook their heads vigorously about the ostensibly unforgivable gaffes of the CDU chancellor candidate.

But these concerns died out in the end in the hurly-burly of the election which soon dominated day-to-day concerns. Nevertheless, the CDU campaign managers took the public reaction to the *Zeit* "affair" seriously, and considered a response. Kohl had not known about the tape recording, it was said. Naturally the editors in Hamburg were not about to let this assertion go unchallenged: it had been agreed ahead of time that chunks of the statements would be published, they responded. "Much which could have put Kohl in an unfavorable light had been left out," the editor in chief replied sanguinely after yet another intervention by the CDU management office. An emissary from Bonn listened to the tape in Hamburg, and after that things quieted down, although the "Hölderlin" statement became a well-known saying, thus closing the circle to the classicists.

Duel of the Pedants

The press department at the CDU management office had dreamed up a special campaign in the early summer of the election year. Office head Peter Radunski and his colleagues were extremely proud it: a sticker with "Schmidtchen Kneifer" (Schmidt the Shirker) tickled the imagination of the "infantry" of the party. The public-relations ploy was a reference to the supposed fear of Chancellor Schmidt to agree to a television debate with his challenger Kohl. "An insidious misstatement," said government spokesman Klaus Böllinger, probably rightly so. Böllinger said, "The chancellor may be afraid of a lot of things, but certainly not of Kohl." The man from the Hanseatic city had been nicknamed "*Schnauze*" (the mouth) early on, and with good reason.

The overzealous CDU propagandists had speculated that the voters would not understand the point of the campaign. It was designed to keep the thought in the voter's minds that Schmidt was avoiding a direct confrontation with Kohl, even though anybody with any sense knew that an American-style campaign television interview was not possible in a democracy with several parties and a ruling coalition. Chancellor Schmidt had extracted a promise from the FDP, the coalition partner, and especially from its leader Hans Dietrich Genscher, that he would not appear alone on television with Kohl.

This idea had been the brainchild of Reinhard Appel, the director of German Television Channel Two. He was a man of considerable talent and was always on the lookout for anything that would appeal to television audiences. Kohl dubbed the incumbent "the candidate of the coalition," and although this was not strictly true, it corresponded to the facts if the petty jealousies between the SPD and FDP were disregarded. However, the Liberals could not afford to be left out of the television game if they were not to disappear from the media scene and the public eye altogether, and to avoid giving the (false) impression of a sort of federal presidential election. The party's coalition partner was thus not terribly pleased about Appel's proposed "duel of the giants" even though Schmidt would love to have "nailed the pudding to the wall." In the end, Genscher threatened to under-

Elections in autumn 1976: Kohl makes an appearance in Herne, Westphalia.

With journalists and co-workers in the "election train."

The two "election locomotives" of the Union in the Westphalia Hall in Dortmund.

mine the peaceful relations between the two parties and even withdraw from government. This put an end to everything: "If Schmidt goes on television alone, I'll have my party nominate me as a chancellor candidate."

The television producers had to be content with representatives from the four parties in the government and the opposition and their chairmen.

Schmidt himself was to be an exception, since he was only deputy chairperson of the SPD; but without him, the "whole thing wouldn't really take off," according to Appel. He viewed the "elephant parade" as a sort of "ersatz duel" because the incumbent chancellor would indeed meet Kohl face to face, even though this show "was actually only for the party chairmen," according to Appel. For this reason Kohl had his press people ask publicly a number of times why Schmidt would be taking part, since he was not party chairperson. The answer came back: who was afraid of whom? Schmidt of Kohl, or Kohl of Schmidt?

The CDU chairperson soon put two and two together and told his colleagues that he suspected that people "certainly wouldn't believe that Schmidt was avoiding a debate with him because he was afraid, but only due to his respect for the party politics in the coalition." Radunski quickly stopped further production of "Schmidtchen Kneifer" stickers. They may not have been such a great idea anyway, since they referred to a popular but fairly silly hit record, "Schmidtschen Schleischer," which denigrated a federal chancellor who was well respected in many ranks of the CDU.

Hence, on September 30, three days before the election, there was an "open-ended discussion" which drew national attention. It started at 8:15 P.M. and was broadcast jointly by German Television Channels One and Two. Those who did not care for politics had only the third programs of the various *Land* broadcasts as an alternative, if they were not already inclined

Shortly before the start of the legendary televised debate of September 30, 1976. For the social-liberal coalition are Schmidt and FDP chairman Genscher, and for the opposition, the chairmen of the CDU and CSU, Kohl and Strauss.

to read a book instead. The program was directed by German Television Channel Two editor in chief Reinhard Appel and *Westdeutsches Rundfunk* (WDR) program director Heinz Werner Hübner (for ARD, the governing body for West German television). The program lasted until 12:30 A.M. In the makeup room the adversaries, Kohl, Strauss, Genscher, and Schmidt, met with icy coldness. Appel recalled that "the chief prophets seemed to be afraid of an encounter. The 'religious war' of *Ostpolitik* had affected all of them deeply. In the past they all had a glass of wine together. On this evening however, the atmosphere was really poisonous." While the program was being prepared the fighting roosters in the internal political ring were suspicious and mistrustful of one another, demanding attention for little things here and there because of reservations about this and that. The organizers were compelled to comply with their pedantic wishes and set up a complicated electrical mechanism which triggered a red light every two minutes, after which another speaker was to have the floor; it was a discussion with a stopwatch.

Around midnight Kohl lost his composure and yelled at the chancellor: "You, with your arrogance!" Schmidt only answered this with a charming wave of his hand and took yet another of many pinches of snuff, which he inhaled in a relaxed manner; it almost drove Kohl crazy.

If ever a television program determined a German election, it was the one on this auspicious evening. Kohl afterward told Reinhard Appel, who had done a total of thirty-five television programs with the "black giant," "I would have won the election without television." Elisabeth Noelle-Neumann soon provided the statistical evidence of this.

I Want to Become Chancellor

On the evening of October 3, everyone was present in the executive suite of the CDU government management office—all those who hoped to profit by an election win by Kohl and with Kohl. The Saturday issue of the *Frankfurter Rundschau* devoted a fifteen-line article to the wishes of a number of influential Union politicians who would rather have seen the "black giant" stay on in Mainz than in Bonn if he did not win the election. However, the outcome was still not certain for Bonn or for Mainz.

Helmut Kohl was in a good mood and sat down at his desk at 6:00 P.M., from where he had a good view of the television. Hannelore Kohl was on one of the two leather sofas; next to her were Juliane Weber, who had been Kohl's executive secretary for many years; Willi Weiskirch; party spokesman Wiedemeyer; and head of the office, Wolfgang Bergsdorf. The door to the office, which was only twenty meters square, was left open and it was very stuffy because the heating was turned up too high. Even though the papers had written that he was the "more human" of the two candidates, nothing could help the "giant" now. At this point the only things which mattered were numbers and facts. The tension mounted from minute to minute as the tallies flickered across the screen, but now and again there was also half-suppressed joy with reports of the increasingly favorable prognoses. The fact that the chancellor and the party chairmen of the coalition had already commented on the election did not bother the challenger. He said, "I want to know the results to the last decimal point," and beckoned to the deputy press spokesman, who wanted to get him in front of the dozens of cameras and microphones that had been set up in the auditorium on the first floor.

When the sensational figure of 48.6 percent was reached—just under an absolute majority—even Kohl could not keep away from the television screen. Now he had to appear before the cameras. Before that, though, he wanted to confer with Eugen Gerstenmaier, his political role model, and Richard von Weizsäcker, the theoretician he respected highly, in Bergdorf's small office. The three men needed only eight minutes for this meeting, after which a not exactly relaxed looking Kohl allowed himself to be questioned by the journalists. When asked what he was now going to do after this increased vote, which was good for the CDU but which had still not given him a partner for forming a government, Kohl answered with mock earnestness, "I want to become chancellor." Even references to the constitutional situation and the political fact that the Union parties had just lost the majority were not enough to deter the "victor," as Kohl viewed himself, from repeating his assertion. Alfred Dregger went one better, without actually giving a cogent reason for his statement: "We are the victors, and we will govern."

After that Kohl went back into his office for a while to do some phoning around. Hans Katzer, with his Rhenish good temperament, who was former social minister in the Grand Coalition and was loyal to Kohl, maintained that Kohl "walked around in his office and thought." That statement was thought up for the curious, because Kohl actually did not waste any time with superfluous cogitation. Strauss soon called and extracted a promise from Kohl that they would have to look very closely at why there was an increase of votes in some areas and a decrease in others. The analysis would soon show what was to be done.

The election results were the second best in the history of the Union, and a success Kohl himself had not dreamed of. Since he was always inclined toward a coalition with the Liberals he would have been satisfied even with two percent less. However, he had misjudged the FDP's willingness to change, as he soon learned.

There were parties on at least five floors going on into the night. The beer literally flowed, and many people ended up slipping on the wet floors. The so-called permanent representative of the GDR to the Federal Republic, Michael Kohl ("the red Kohl"), very much the worse for wear and asking to be allowed in at the main entrance (the thick-set man had just come from the SPD "barracks"), was not recognized by the security guards and was turned away because he did not have an invitation. This Kohl too wanted to see the thwarted chancellor. The *Junge Union* was waiting enthusiastically for their "Helmut, Helmut!" in the street. A woman called to him out of the dark, saying that he should not give up, that he was needed. He replied in Rhenish dialect, "Of course not, we'll do it."

He was not going to do anything for the moment, at least not what he had hoped. The former government partners got together that same night and reinstated the old coalition. Helmut Schmidt called federal president Walther Scheel just after 11:00 P.M. and informed him officially about the results of the vote, which had re-elected the governing coalition by a majority. The SPD and FDP decided to continue their work and the challenger was left with the role of opposition.

The "bitter laurel wreath," as a chronicler remarked, was worn by Kohl in the pose of a hero who had been cheated of victory. The Union parties had performed exceedingly well, but it was no encouragement, as might have been expected. They wanted to regain power and had been thwarted by the lack of a partner whom they had wanted to win back. Outwardly, however, Kohl continued to act as if he were still well on his way to wooing the FDP. On the Monday after the election he wrote Genscher a letter in which he again repeated the coalition offer he had made on television. "The confidence the voters showed in the Union must now be converted into politics which are realistic and promising for the future." Kohl also made an appointment to visit the federal president the same afternoon to hear his interpretation of the election results.

Scheel proved himself to be the former party chairperson of the Liberals. With a friendly smile, but also with the coldest precision which his happy temperament could muster, he explained the incontrovertible fact that the coalition's parliamentary majority, which was after all by eight votes, had convinced them to continue it. He would have to respect that and thus it was good-bye until (perhaps) next time.

With the support of the Union leaders and his colleagues in the Konrad-Adenauer-Haus, Kohl felt confident in continuing his tactics against the

SPD's junior partner. This was misunderstood by some in the CSU as "wooing" of the FDP without critical judgment. Kohl stated publicly—seemingly unruffled, but in reality very irritated by the stubbornness of the Free Democrats—that it was his intention "to form a government with the FDP."

Kohl's decision for Bonn or Mainz became the object of public speculation right after the final election results. Since he was honestly undecided, and had faced the election completely unprepared in this regard, he now had to achieve some success in negotiations. The CSU was also breathing down his neck, because newspapers were reporting that Franz Josef Strauss had already threatened on election night that anyone in the CDU/CSU who did not realize what was important "should go their separate way."

The General Has to Go to the Front

Almost six weeks to the day after the election there was an explosion. At their closed party conference in Kreuth, in Upper Bavaria, the CSU *Land* group voted by a clear majority to dissolve the association with the CDU in the *Bundestag*. The CDU/CSU association had lasted for decades and was now to be changed, with unpredictable consequences for the German party political system.

A long road going back to the 1960s had led to this painful episode, but now it was serious: the Bavarians in the Union rehearsed the uprising. Even before the sensational announcement was put out over all the news wires and landed on Kohl's desk in Mainz, Kohl got a phone call from Gerhard Reddemann, former journalist and now parliamentary leader of the *Bundestag* party. He had heard the news about the decision in Kreuth from his colleague in the *Bundestag* party, Richard Jäger, and had called Kohl immediately after the vote in the CSU *Land* group. Thus Eduard Ackermann was wrong in saying that Kohl's reliable friend Werner Dollinger had been the first to tell the CDU leader and still incumbent minister-president of Rhineland-Palatinate about the sensational decision in Kreuth. Reddemann got Juliane Weber to call Kohl to the phone at once. "We have a cabinet meeting," Juliane said, always ready to deflect problems from her boss. "That doesn't matter, he's got to come to the phone immediately. It's extremely important!" When Kohl finally answered the phone and listened to Reddemann's story, he was silent, and then said, "Terrible. Is the news accurate?" Reddemann said it was and Kohl could only thank him for informing him so quickly. Up to that time he had had no idea or even a suspicion that the CSU had wanted to split off. The CSU *Land* leader, Friedrich Zimmermann, described in his memoirs the procedure used to inform the joint chancellor candidate—which Kohl was, despite his lack of

Happiness—just five weeks before the Kreuther debacle—still reigns: Greeting at the first meeting of the CDU/CSU Fraktion *after the Bundestag elections, October 8, 1976. From left: CSU chairman Strauss, CDU chairman Kohl,* Fraktion *leader Karl Carstens, and* Fraktion *general manager Phillip Jenninger.*

success in the election. After the session at the CSU's Hanns Seidel Foundation in Kreuth there was a long line of people waiting to use the one and only telephone, so it was not possible to make a call with the news immediately. When Zimmermann finally reached Kohl an hour later, the man from the Palatinate reacted sourly. Even on the night of November 20, the day after the separation decision at Kreuth, Kohl assured friends in Mainz that he considered the incident "serious and grave, but still reparable."

Before the Kreuth decision, Kohl had gone through some emotional ups and downs. In trying hard to come to terms with the events after October 3, he had reached a turning point in his life that was laden with heavy personal pressure. Even as late as the fourteenth there were rumors that, contrary to earlier indications, Kohl wanted to stay in Mainz after all and continue in his office as minister-president. Kohl's social minister, Heiner Geissler, recommended "opposition from the benches of the *Bundesrat*."

But already the next day the CDU leader said in a German Press Agency interview that he was aiming for the chairmanship of the CDU/CSU party in the *Bundestag*. Why he hesitated so long is difficult to pinpoint. At any rate, the man from the Palatinate took longer than usual to recognize that he no longer had the power of decision, because returning to Rhineland-Palatinate would have put an immediate end to all of his ambitious dreams. The ostensible regret in the Mainz state chancery about his imminent departure for Bonn was shown to be hypocrisy on the part of those who hoped that the inevitable change at the top of the *Land* government would be to their advantage. No, most of Kohl's friends knew that "the general had to go to the front" if anything was to change in politics at the federal level. The major newspapers supported him in their own ways. Georg Schröder ("Sir George"), a journalist whose career had started in the Weimar Republic, wrote in *Die Welt*, "Now it's time for Kohl to lead." Alfred Rapp seconded this in the *Frankfurter Allgemeine Zeitung* with the headline, "A Good Stand in Front of High Hurdles." And the *Süddeutsche Zeitung* wrote, "Someone has to finally defy Strauss."

And when it came to the crunch, Kohl took the initiative himself and paid back Strauss's daily taunts ("Whoever enters the FDP by the back door is in reality in a hot air balloon") in kind: "And by the way, I don't go through anybody's back door." The Bavarian lion bellowed louder than ever and he was already thinking about the much-coveted expansion of the

The two longtime archenemies still publicly demonstrated unity: Kohl and Strauss at a CSU event in the late 1970s.

CSU to the north: "Now [after the election] is the critical time. We have to swim free. We have to push through. There is no more piety, now there will be death."[58]

Kohl had to change his daily routine completely. Most especially, he was continually in Bonn; his job in the *Bundestag* demanded this. This also meant a change in his family life, which he was obviously unhappy about. By nature home-loving and firmly established, he now had to be exposed to the much rougher climate of government-level politics. What sort of pleasure this is he would soon learn on a day-to-day basis. Hannelore Kohl, who had been greatly affected by the events of the past few weeks, was bedridden with a fever in Ludwigshafen-Oggersheim. She did not want to give up their beautiful home, but said that "If it has to be, however, I'll join him in Bonn, or wherever."

Before the Kreuth decision to split the parties there were personnel decisions to be made in Bonn, some of which were quite significant. Thus the selection of the president of the *Bundesrat* had to be postponed, since under a rota system the minister-president from the Rhineland-Palatinate would have been in line for this. Since the CDU/CSU was the largest parliamentary party in the *Bundestag,* it was to determine the candidate for the parliamentary president. Kohl recommended Karl Carstens, who would then allow him to take over the position of opposition leader. A previous commitment to Rainer Barzel was completely forgotten, and even Franz Josef Strauss dropped his former Franconian colleague, Richard Stücklen. The CSU man, who had been a member of the *Bundestag* since 1949, had to be content with the job of deputy. This was hard on Stücklen, who had been suggested for a number of offices, some quite senior, for many weeks: parliamentary president, minister of post (which he had already held in the 1960s), and even the next federal president.

There were also changes on the horizon in the party hierarchy. For the first time Heiner Geissler's name was mentioned in connection with the possible appointment of a new general secretary. Kurt Biedenkopf carefully crossed off "general secretary" after "profession" on the galley for his resume for the new *Bundestag* handbook. In the spring of 1977, Biedenkopf, bitterly disappointed by Kohl, said that the chairperson had not yet told him that he did not want him to have his post any longer, but that he, Biedenkopf, was considering giving it up soon, and it made sense to do so before the party conference in Düsseldorf on March 7–9. Kohl does not make public announcements about personnel "decisions" of this stature. He instinctively avoids being the bearer of bad tidings. "He leaves you hanging on for so long," Biedenkopf summed up, "or to starve to death on an outstretched arm until you finally realize that it's better to leave voluntarily."

This analysis is correct and could be confirmed by many of those whose careers were linked with that of the "black giant."

On the opposite side in the Social Democratic party, there was also a change in the chair of the manager at the federal level, from Holger Börner to Brandt's close associate, Egon Bahr. This position corresponded to that of general secretary. Bahr said after Biedenkopf's departure in the spring of 1977, which seems to have been a surprise to him, that had he known, he never would have taken on the job of manager. It was only the possibility of an intellectual duel with the "brilliant" Biedenkopf that had tempted him to become the SPD manager.

Reorganization of the internal party scene was in full swing by the beginning of November. A "secret meeting" took place between Kohl and Strauss in which the chairmen of the two Union parties wanted primarily to discuss the future strategy of the party in the *Bundestag* and its role in fighting the governing socialist-liberal coalition, and this meeting could not be stopped by the run-in of November 19. On the television show *Bericht aus Bonn* (Report from Bonn) it was obvious that the Kreuth decision had affected Helmut Kohl, who said, "I was not informed about the reasons for this decision." However, he also reacted calmly to journalists' questions and did not commit any blunders. Kohl considered the situation very serious and said so, because he wanted to use television to influence the more thoughtful people in the CSU sister party: "This is an important moment in the history of postwar Germany."

The schism of Kreuth demanded a clear-cut answer and Kohl gave it directly to the media in three paragraphs, each beginning with "I."

> "I have taken note of the decision of the CSU *Land* group to terminate the union with the CDU in the *Bundestag*. This decision was made without consultation or previous announcement. This is a step by the CSU *Land* group toward separation after twenty-seven years of successful cooperation as a parliamentary party. This is a step in the wrong direction. The election results of October 3 of this year showed that the CDU and CSU together have a good chance of obtaining a majority in the government of the Federal Republic of Germany. I would like to add a personal word: in this situation I believe that it is a given that my place is at the head of the CDU party in the *Bundestag*.

Although Kohl had been determined for some time to move to Bonn, he derived some political gain from this decision, which had been made quite a while before. If there were still any doubters in the sister party, he wanted to tell them, "I will be the chairperson." The minister-president finally left his post in Mainz on December 2 . The characteristic vertical lines of worry and anger contrasted even more with the "horizontal lines of the happy

Palatinate temperament—a real drama for every physiognomist." Kohl's face began to take on characteristics which made it unmistakable; this included his forehead, the oval head, and an energetic, prominent chin. The election fight was followed by one between brothers and it exacted its tribute in every regard.

The CDU party committees went to the front only a few days after the decision of Kreuth. The chairperson formulated his demands a week after this historic date. "For the CDU it is of importance that the joint parliamentary party be reinstated with a constitutionally binding commitment on the

With former chancellor Ludwig Erhard during a meeting of the CDU/CSU Bundestag Fraktion, *November 1976.*

part of the CSU not to expand into the rest of the Federal Republic—and connections of the CSU with other parties or political groups outside of Bavaria, unless agreed by us—and then we will not be compelled to campaign in Bavaria."

Kohl had had posters designed in case the conflict with the CSU continued, and he wanted to campaign for the CDU in Bavaria. Surveys showed that Kohl's party would have achieved about twenty-five percent of the votes in Bavaria, a deadly threat to the Strauss party's claim of being the only one. The posters stayed in the cellar. When unauthorized reports about such a measure appeared in the press, they were removed from the Konrad-Adenauer-Haus and their existence was "strongly" denied.

A man like Kohl does not give up hope easily that things will go back to being like they were. But there was a new source of trouble in the house, and it too had the dreaded name of Franz Josef Strauss.

On the same evening that Kohl listed his demands of the Bavarian sister party, there were news reports which grabbed immediate attention. In a speech in the Wienerwald restaurant in Munich that the news magazine *Der Spiegel* was going to publish, Franz Josef Strauss said that Helmut Kohl "would never be chancellor. He is completely incapable of it. He lacks the qualifications in character, intellect, and politics. He lacks everything for it." The abusive speech in the Wienerwald, given in an obviously drunken state in front of the *Land* committee of the Bavarian *Junge Union*, showed the highly talented politician Strauss in a state of complete abandon. The speech had been recorded and played for the *Spiegel* correspondent. In it, Strauss played all the registers of his colorful and unrestrained rhetoric, saying that the larger Union party had "pygmy ideology" and "dwarf mentality."

> The Christian Democratic parties have failed all over Europe, in Italy, Holland, Belgium, and France, but least in Germany. The crisis in Italy is yet to come. The popular front will come from the south and the west; perhaps we could have stopped it. And the same men in the CDU who have supported the treaties with the East, à la Leisler Kiep, will say now that we have to adjust to this unstoppable development. And whoever opposes this—I know that this is like carrying the earth's sphere on one's shoulders like Hercules—he has to talk for thousands of hours about why breaking out of this pygmy ideology, out of this dwarf mentality, is not criminal, not a sin against the community."

Then the Bavarian lion attacked the "friends of the CDU" more directly. "Consider me a megalomaniac, but I'll say now what I think: the political pygmies of the CDU who are only afraid of losing their electorates, these dwarves in vest-pocket format, this Reclam edition of politicians, why are they upset about the action of the *Land* group [Strauss was referring to the decision of Kreuth], when the opponent we mean reacts by being very hurt and says, 'Now the hunting down of us will start'?"

After this verbal beating Strauss got to the real point: "I tell you, I can only warn you: forget the extraordinary party conference, forget that with all the to-ing and fro-ing. At the end of this special party conference, after heated debate, I will call for a free 'German People's Party' in the north of this republic. Then you can forget me as well as chairperson of the *Land*; I've been prepared for that for a long time." Before that, and without going into more detail about the contradictions in his extemporized speech in the Wienerwald restaurant, Strauss repeated again that he himself "never wanted to become chancellor." What did he want? How did he propose to introduce the radical cure in Germany which he obviously believed was urgently required if he was not to head the government? Even those constructive critics of the Union expressed grave doubts about the judgment or the solidarity of the CSU leader. The *Spiegel* article on the Wienerwald speech went on to quote him as saying that he had "supported Mr. Kohl as a chancellor candidate, despite my knowledge of his inadequacy, for the sake of peace." The press department of the CDU commented on the terrible insults of the chairperson partly with defiant objectivity and partly with genuine worry. "Strauss is clearly contradicted by the excellent election results (of October 3) which the Union parties achieved under their joint chancellor candidate, Helmut Kohl. If what Strauss is said to have stated about the call for a 'German People's Party' is true, then all the fears of the CDU since the dissolution of the joint parliamentary party are completely justified."

But the specter soon had a well-deserved end. On November 28, 1976, the CSU *Land* executive—consisting of fifty political dignitaries from this self-confident party—met in Munich to deal with the consequences of the Kreuth decision. After a meeting lasting four hours, the 111 county chairmen joined them. The meeting had a decidedly appeasing character. In a four-point declaration which the CSU *Landtag* parliamentary party had prepared, the Christian Socialists wanted to make it clear to the CDU that they intended to tame the Bavarian lion. The declaration of this representative committee of the CSU was formulated with only one vote against and two abstentions, a truly rare show of unity among the Bavarian Union politicians who were ostensibly so ready for a separation. Rumor had it that after an encroachment by the CDU into their home territory, the CSU would be forced in regional elections into a coalition party, and that about one-third of all *Landräte* held by the CSU would lose their posts. The Munich correspondent of the *Neue Zürcher Zeitung* noted that the most recent CSU decision reflected "the growing dissatisfaction with Strauss and the strong determination to put an end to a Bavarian CDU." Nobody in the CSU—it was said everywhere—had intended to dissolve the joint work in the parliamentary party "without the agreement of the CDU." The key sentences of the final communiqué were definitely directed toward the overwhelming necessity for internal party harmony. The CSU wanted to sit down with the top committees of the larger sister party and find a way to satisfy all sides. "The party chairperson and other participants in the coming meeting are asked to negotiate on all issues regarding ways of ensuring further successful cooperation of the Union parties and to include in these discussions the question of the most effective form of organization of the CSU members of parliament in the *Bundestag* for the fulfillment of their task." These issues were covered in a dramatic meeting between the CDU/CSU presidia in the representation of Baden-Württemburg in Bonn. "It was difficult," Kohl said about the meeting. Strauss seconded that sentiment in his own way: "We were honest with each other." Further discussions followed in the second part of the "never-ending story." After that Kohl was more confident. "Clarification in the second round of discussions of questions which were raised but not finally settled have shown there is a possibility of continuing a joint parliamentary party." Strauss observed, "That also showed it may not be possible." *Spiegel* publisher Rudolf Augstein was also far off the mark when he wrote, "Admittedly, Kohl's chances of surviving the Kreuth decision are not very high."

Kohl told all his friends who sought to comfort him after the politically denigrating attacks (Kreuth) and assaults on his honor (the Wienerwald speech) that "that's what he's like." The man from Rhineland-Palatinate knew after this gray November day that after Kreuth and the Wienerwald there was no getting around the fact that he would have to live with Strauss's outbursts. The concept of friendship between men, which Kohl repeatedly used as an analogy to help explain the crisis-ridden relationship between the CDU and the CSU, stemmed from his own self-concept. Men—they often can and do tell other men their opinions with no holds barred. Kohl always avoided publicly attacking his internal party rival. This did not mean, though, that he did not take Strauss to task when, for example, he visited Kohl's office in the Bundeshaus. During these "shouting matches" (as they were referred to by Eduard Ackerman, Kohl's press spokesman in the *Bundestag*), Kohl's executive secretary, Juliane Weber, always carefully closed the padded door. When it got very quiet, Kohl's loyal assistant came in with a bottle of wine. The two fighting roosters would drink it in reconciliation, sometimes two bottles, and would discuss things quietly, until the next time.

The Eating-and-Drinking Working Group

Kohl now had to settle in Bonn, both domestically and politically. His "kitchen cabinet" consisted of Juliane Weber, his executive secretary and confidante going back to the days in Mainz; Horst Teltschik, political adviser and speech writer; and last but not least, Eduard "Edi" Ackermann, his press chief. Kohl had hesitated somewhat in the case of the latter because he did not know him and did not want to take him on. However, Edi's lobbying bore fruit. Kohl sought advice from other colleagues such as Wolfgang Bergsdorf, and Kohl's predecessor, Karl Carstens, praised him highly ("he was invaluable in many difficult situations"). Thus Edi held onto his office.

Kohl moved into a two-hundred-square-meter bungalow in Wachberg-Pech, near Bad Godesberg, in early December. Hannelore looked after decorating and furnishing the place herself. Juliane Weber and Kohl's driver, Eckart Seeber, also moved in, as well as two security guards. The kitchen cabinet was ready to start work.

The first thing on the agenda was good food, paid for from parliamen-

With Eduard "Edi" Ackermann, 1984.

Constituent assembly of the eighth German Bundestag, *December 14, 1976. A friendly encounter of the two chairmen of the major* fraktions. *The* "alte Fuhrmann" *and the* "Neuling" *Helmut Kohl.*

tary party funds. Kohl favored "a good Chinese dinner," Ackermann a good Italian one. The "eating-and-drinking" working group often ended up at Bruno's, on the Cäcilienhöhe, a restaurant known for good food and parliamentary oeuvre. It was a meeting place for "*tout Bonn*," primarily of the middle classes. Strauss also liked to frequent the restaurant when he was looking for a good meal and a place to talk with his friends. Kohl later changed his favorite restaurant to Isola d' Ischia, very close to the studio of German Television Channel Two. Edi managed to get his boss to stop eating pig's stomach for a while and earned the nickname "Dr. Carbonara." Sometimes Kohl left off the title: "Carbonara, please pour me some coffee."

People in the *Bundestag* were awaiting with interest Kohl's first appearance there, which was to occur before Christmas. It would be difficult for him, with his rather comfortable way of speaking, to pit himself against the gifted orations of Helmut Schmidt or Herbert Wehner's "contorted dialectic." Walter Henkels, with the *Frankfurter Allgemeine Zeitung,* is said to have remarked that Kohl kept his left hand in his pocket when speaking, just like his most famous predecessor. What he did not say was that Kohl refined his style of delivery in these first years in the Bonn parliament. "This is the hour" or "This is not the hour" in which we "in this our country. . . ." There was a lot of "country," a saying he often repeated, and often in rather strange contexts: "In the reality of the life in this country. . . ."

Kohl was coquettish with the phrase, "I'm old-fashioned in this respect," and in trying to introduce a note of seriousness in a debate would say, "this is not the hour."

The key issues Kohl would address in his future work as opposition leader all had to do with money: government finance, the pension, and health-care systems, all of which urgently required revamping. These were followed by energy policy and unemployment. Less pressing but still important issues were readiness in defense against the background of arms limitations in East and West; the future of the younger generation; reworking of policies regarding the middle class; and, finally, the concerns of the self-employed. For a long time no one had wanted to subject themselves to trying to make a living through self-employment. The new leader of the powerful opposition had learned his lesson: those who make up the majority generally are right. A survey by the Allensbach Institute in late January 1977 showed that the "black giant" was already logging a forty-six percent rate of satisfaction as leader of the opposition. Chancellor Helmut Schmidt achieved the same rating as his parliamentary challenger.

Even though not everything was all right at Konrad-Adenauer-Haus, Kohl was able to gain the reputation of being an achiever in a number of provincial newspapers. "As a Mainz nonconformist he has a leadership style with a thrust-out chin," exaggerated Helmut "Knüller" Müller ("Smash Hit" Müller) in the *Westfälische Nachrichten*, which was inclined toward the CDU. The man from the Palatinate's style was hardly that of a commando, even though he was inclined to give orders to his colleagues in a decisive tone. He was happiest to have things presented to him verbally: scrabbling around in files was not his way. His manner in the parliamentary party was to be a good colleague. He introduced a new weekly situation meeting with the chiefs, the CSU *Land* group chairperson Friedrich Zimmermann, and managers Willi Rawe, Philipp Jenninger, Walter Wallmann, and Paul Röhner.

Kohl's top priority was the *Bundestag*, and the party central organization was thus neglected somewhat. This created a vacuum at the top which no one dared fill. On the contrary, General Secretary Kurt Biedenkopf began to show clear signs of leaving. The press started to report that the chairperson had let his "first colleague" go, while others said that the "general" had wanted to leave his post prematurely. When the Bonn correspondent of the *Westdeutsche Allgemeine Zeitung*, Willy Zirngibl, wrote that Biedenkopf was leaving, Kohl directed his press department not only to deny this immediately, but also to add that he would "again be recommending him for re-election as general secretary at the party conference in Düsseldorf." But he knew better; denying a report makes it news.

Meeting of the CDU presidium, January 1977. From front left: Heinrich Köppler, Helga Wex, Hans Katzer, Karl Carstens, Ludwig Erhard, Gerhard Stoltenberg, Ernst Albrecht, Kai-Uwe von Hassel, and Party Chairman Kohl.

The display of harmony did not last long and Kohl had to recognize this bitter truth. Reissmüller, of the *Frankfurter Allgemeine Zeitung*, believed he had detected "a stirring in the Union," an observation which was absolutely true of the heart of the party, and was understated if anything. The "generalist" Kohl caused difficulty for the high-ranking experts in the *Bundestag* parliamentary party and the purists were annoyed at his stereotyped rhetoric. Conrad Ahlers, the former government spokesman and journalist who had a good feel for language, called the CDU press department to say that he had looked in all the dictionaries he could get his hands on, but could not find the word "generalist." He did not know what to do with it. In fact, what the CDU management office did not know was that there is a store in Paris called *Le Generaliste* that sells small items for the house and garden. Sooner or later, there is an explanation for everything.

However, the Union's worries were much more serious. For the third time the CDU and CSU had failed to wrest power from their rivals in government. No day went by without the media asking whether there would be a palace revolution: "When will Biedenkopf be ready to jump?" He hesitated for a long time, at first retreating to his *Bundestag* mandate and founding on the side the Institute for Economics and Society. It was mentioned in the press under the rubric "think tank," making Strauss react by poking fun in a short dialogue: "Where do you get thinking done? At Biedenkopf's." Dregger also came under scrutiny: Was he only waiting for the right moment? Would Barzel make a comeback? How many wanted Carstens back?

Good-bye to the Little Professor

The party said farewell to its most efficient general secretary to date at the spring party conference in Düsseldorf. The "little professor," which Kohl liked to call his friend when he wanted to tease him, left his post a disillusioned man, resigned and full of suppressed anger. Kurt Hans Biedenkopf, who had helped his party achieve success and respect from its political rival, bade a rather cool farewell to the party conference. His successor, Heiner Geissler, made a hesitant start in his new job. Geissler was a second choice for Kohl, who would have preferred his friend and confidant Walter Wallmann, but Wallmann turned down the position to pursue a career in Hesse. Geissler could be roughly classified as leftist in his social-political orientation, and tended toward the social committees and the women's organizations. Geissler gave preference to his Bonn "outposts" from his days in Mainz, especially the young Ulf Fink. Former Biedenkopf confidants, such as Meinhard Miegel—his closest colleague in the party central organization—and Fred J. Heidemann, either followed him to the new institute in the Bonn Economics Center, or looked for other jobs in organizations close to the CDU. The latter group included people such as Rüdiger von Voss, who achieved a successful career in the Economics Advisory Department.

A declaration on German politics was a highlight of the party conference. Kohl intended this as a message to the Free Democrats: the conservatives were capable of an "offensive intellectual" policy on Germany—whatever that meant. Werner Marx, one of the CDU/CSU parliamentary party hardliners, drafted the message for presentation at the congress. This was a clever move on the part of the chairperson in order to satisfy the right-wingers in the party and parliamentary party group. Later "corrections" were intended to come from the heart of the party and be supported by the nominees. Kohl numbered among these Richard von Weizsäcker and Heiner Geissler. Although they understood little of the subject matter, they would be able to aid in making at least cosmetic changes to any supposed right-wing tendencies of the Union. Mindful of the fact that he could achieve power only with the FDP, Kohl began to seriously consider the issue of double nationality in Germany. Naturally Marx and his friends rejected this out of hand. The main argument of those who wanted to reform policy regarding Germany was based on the experiment with the long-lived but politically dead Hallstein Doctrine. Bonn's claim to represent all of Germany had isolated the country internationally; this would continue if the Federal Republic insisted that the GDR could not grant citizenship. This led to Kohl's replying to Helmut Schmidt's government declaration with wonderful ambiguity about the "absolutely necessary policy of recognizing the reality in the GDR."

Kohl invited Karl Dietrich Erdmann, a history professor from Kiel, to Düsseldorf as an economic witness to a more "relaxed" German policy. Erdmann was to discuss a number of theses about this controversial topic in a small working group at the party conference at the beginning of March. Gebhardt's *Handbuch der deutschen Geschichte* (Handbook of German History) cites Erdmann's seminal thoughts at the beginning: "In the Federal Republic a specific feeling of belonging to the country has arisen, furthered

Carnival festivities in Mainz, 1977. Kohl with Hannelore and the Rhineland-Palatinate minister-president Bernhard Vogel.

especially by the Basic Law. Compared to this, German reunification represents a nebulous future without clear contours over the long term, and is usually referred to only in the context of the existing cultural unity." Aside from a few vagaries, this text is of great importance. Those in the Union who inclined to the right (*Rechtsausleger*, the pejorative name for the constitutional theorists who stuck to the principles) did not want to have anything to do with these attempts to placate the Liberals. And they most certainly wanted to disassociate themselves from the views of Professor Erdmann, such as: "The degree of hope we have that we in this divided Germany will be able to again talk to one another is matched exactly by the dialectic unity of the nation, despite our separation into two states. . . . The dialectic unity of the nation which depends on the willingness of both to listen to each other without denying the differences: that is the conceivable way of achieving this at this time."

The Hostages of Terror

For the Federal Republic of Germany, 1977 became the year of terror by the Red Army Faction (RAF). In May a federal lawyer, Siegfried Buback, was murdered by the RAF commando "Ulricke Meinhof," and in late July an RAF commando killed the Frankfurt banker Jürgen Ponto after a failed kidnapping attempt. In September the wave of terror reached its temporary zenith with the abduction of the president of the Employers' Organization, Hanns-Martin Schleyer, who was one of Kohl's very closest friends. The commando "Siegfried Hausner" claimed responsibility for the ruthless killing and the RAF demanded the release of eleven jailed terrorists.

But this was not the end of the wave of terror. On October 13, Arab terrorists held a Lufthansa aircraft hostage on a flight from Majorca to Frankfurt am Main, also demanding the release of RAF prisoners. With international assistance a special group of the Federal German Border Guard stormed the aircraft in an operation which has since become legend, and freed the hostages five days later at the airport in Mogadishu, Somalia. The German terrorists Baader, Ensslin, and Raspe committed suicide in their cells on the same day in sympathy with the failed attempt at coercion by their Arab comrades. Twenty-four hours later Schleyer's body was found. The country was deeply shocked. As opposition leader, Kohl, spoke repeatedly of the "hostages" of the terrorism that shook Germany to its foundations. The concept of internal security became a concern from this year onward, continuing to dominate the political scene.

Schleyer's kidnappers used audio and video recordings of their hapless

On the same evening that Hanns Martin Schleyer, president of the Employers' Organization, was kidnapped, Schmidt called an emergency crisis meeting. Opposition leader Kohl on his way to the chancellor's office, September 6, 1977, 11 P.M.

victim to blackmail the government and try to force it to its knees. Schleyer's family asked and even begged for the government to give in, but the Schmidt/Kohl regime held firm. The scenes of hand-wringing that prevailed during the Peter Lorenz kidnapping were not repeated. Kohl, who was involved in all the government crisis meetings in Bonn because of the national significance of the case, went along with all the painful decisions of the highest government security officials for reasons of internal harmony. Colleagues saw the CDU politician, usually so lively but now deeply moved, watching the videos of his friend. It was evident that Hanns Martin Schleyer's will had not been broken, but his great distress could also be seen. The government crisis force's decision to storm the highjacked Lufthansa plane necessarily carried with it the direct threat that Schleyer could be murdered. The decision was unanimous.

At a dinner at the Roma restaurant in Bonn eight days before the beginning of the kidnapping drama, Schleyer and Kohl had talked about what each would do in case the other were kidnapped. They both agreed that no concessions should ever be made to blackmailers. Despite Kohl's good relationship with Schleyer's family, he did not accede to an urgent request for a meeting with Schleyer's widow. Hans-Eberhard Schleyer, one of the sons of

With the chairman of the Junge Union, *Mathias Wissmann, at the CDU conference with the slogan "Future Chances for Youth" in Hamburg, October 1977.*

the Employers' Organization president, later became the representative of the *Land* government of Rhineland-Palatinate on Kohl's recommendation. Otherwise the sad chapter was closed. The present demands its tribute, and Kohl wanted to make this tribute vigorously, even though the times were not favorable. The complaints of the *Bundestag* parliamentary party about his supposed lack of charisma were getting on his nerves. His near miss in the election was already forgotten; the notorious critics and the unhappy circumstances made the man from the Palatinate think that his days might be numbered. Kohl said "possibly" more and more frequently about this assumption, since even with political enemies it is possible to get along very well politically if one has a strong enough will to survive. Kohl confided to a small circle of friendly journalists that he "was actually glad to have not only one, but four or five rivals of equal stature," who were after his job. "One alone could possibly be dangerous, but all five together cancel out their effect on the public," Kohl said with a good sense of realism.

Unlike his predecessors as party chairperson, Kohl appeared to be irreplaceable for the foreseeable future. He thus held the reins of power firmly in his hands by virtue of this identification with the party, a situation new to the CDU. "Kohl is the first CDU chairperson with whom the party identifies—a reforming social party which is vainly trying to couch its positive goals in a steamy prose, but which instinctively knows what it does not want, namely communist terror, socialist planning, and the dissolution of the all too free-thinking," wrote Johannes Gross in the *Frankfurter Allgemeine Zeitung* on March 29, 1978.

The World of the Two Helmuts

The peace that descended around the end of 1978 was rudely broken by Kurt Hans Biedenkopf, who was obviously dissatisfied with the post of CDU *Land* chairperson in Westphalia.

The clever professor had written a memo—others called it a letter—to the party leaders which contained a first-class political bomb: the former CDU general secretary suggested splitting the position of party chairperson and chairperson of the parliamentary party, meaning that Kohl should turn the leadership of the parliamentary party over to another Union politician. Should Kohl refuse to do this, Biedenkopf stated in an ultimatum, he, Biedenkopf, would nominate a rival candidate for the post at the Kiel party conference on March 26–27.

The memorandum hit the press like a bomb. Wilfried Hasselmann, the clever but somewhat talkative boss of the CDU in Lower Saxony, had leaked the story intentionally to journalists from *Die Welt* and the *Bonner Rundschau* at a fireside chat during the traditional press trip to the Harz Mountains at the beginning of the year.

Biedenkopf expressed in his memos—there were actually two of them—what most of the CDU board members thought: the party was not being led properly, if at all. The little professor became more pointed: ". . . weaknesses in the party leadership. These are interpreted by the CDU functionaries and increasingly by the voters to be a leadership crisis." Biedenkopf was even more candid with his friends: "The man is absolutely impossible."

The key statements of the anti-Kohl paper struck the party chairperson like hammer blows: "The institution of a de facto chancellor candidate during the entire legislative period has not proven viable." And, "If the leadership continues in this form, there is little hope of winning the *Bundestag* elections in 1980."

In a second memo, which could be regarded as a modification of the views in the first, Biedenkopf proposed "a debate about the principles" of party leadership in case his ideas were rejected. Biedenkopf knew he could count on the support of the CSU, though this was more of a tactical backing, because Strauss's party would want to support anything that would damage Kohl.

The "Kohl twilight," as *Der Spiegel* called it, pitted shifting factions against each other; Kohl himself could not always distinguish between friend and foe, comrade and rival. Even the foreign media picked up on the internal party wrangling; personality clashes have their own charm. With mild irony, the London *Guardian* spoke of "the world of the two Helmuts," setting Kohl's struggles beside the public perception (according to every poll) that there was no alternative to the other Helmut—Schmidt—as chancellor. Those who saw themselves as possible successors to the "black giant"—Ernst Albrecht in Hanover, Lothar Späth in Stuttgart, and Bernhard Vogel in Mainz—kept well out of the violent debates about party leadership. Hypocritically, Vogel and Albrecht "defended" their boss with stereotyped, empty words. Späth stayed on neutral territory—namely, the Canary Islands, where he did not allow his vacation to be disturbed.

Alarmed, Kohl immediately activated procedures planned for just such contingencies. Prominent critics of Kohl such as Hasselmann and Albrecht showed their loyalty to the chairperson in news-agency stories and interviews; others had their colleagues deny criticism. The CSU party leaders in Munich acted as if the matter had nothing to do with them, even though Kohl was "their" parliamentary party chairperson.

Biedenkopf, who had caused the huge commotion in the first place, told the *Bild Zeitung* with sincerity that he "did not want to topple Kohl at all," he "just wanted to make work easier for him." However, in a different place he styled himself as Kohl's "successor as chairperson of the parliamentary party." The chairperson could not help smiling grimly when he read this. Kohl fought with every possible means. He could not believe what was being said, especially by his former friend Biedenkopf, whose impossible attack had finally broken his solidarity with his chairperson, driving him to despair. "I'm finished with the man," he said candidly to a friend. Biedenkopf had Heinrich Köppler, the top candidate from North Rhine–Westphalia. He also believed that Kohl's workload should be "lightened": "Even just one of the two jobs (party or parliamentary party) is ruinous."

Basically, Biedenkopf was not offering anything new in his memo. He was merely calling to mind that Kohl himself had said that combining several important CDU offices was dangerous, and was thus trying to further his career on the government level. In the early 1970s the minister-president of the Rhineland-Palatinate had asked the founding rector of Ruhr University at Bochum, Kurt H. Biedenkopf, to support the idea of separating offices in order to remove his hated rival, Rainer Barzel, from the stage. The arguments which Barzel rejected at that time were the same ones Kohl logically—that is, in keeping with the consistency of power—was now unwilling to accept.

The well-organized Biedenkopf arranged two or three committee meetings and announced ex cathedra how he planned to "lead": with a carefully agreed division of roles in the small circle of top CDU politicians and "reduced (*gestrafft*) work in the parliamentary party." A joke quickly made the rounds of the *Bundestag* lobby: Kohl announces, "I want to reduce the work in the parliamentary party." The parliamentary party answers: "Leave it, Helmut, we're punished (*gestraft*) with you as it is."

The declaration of confidence in their boss by the presidium, government board, and parliamentary party was not meant to be long term. Life for Helmut Kohl was made difficult primarily by right-wingers such as Alfred Dregger and Franz Josef Strauss, supported by groups led by Werner Marx, the foreign and security politician, or Haimo George, the head of the CDU economics advisory. Efforts to dismantle the combination of CDU chairperson and chancellor candidate continued. The phrase thought up for the media was only a "reprieve from the gallows," according to *Der Spiegel*, and nothing more. But Kohl knew how to fight, at least when his back was to the wall. The most painful point that Biedenkopf raised in his warmed-over memo called to mind the procedure for determining the chancellor

The CDU chairman speaks at a freedom demonstration on the "Zone" Border in Phillipsthal, Hersfeld County/Rotenburg, June 17, 1978.

candidate. Biedenkopf reminded people that this candidate "could not be elected by the party conference, but only by a committee in which the CSU was suitably represented; that is, one in which the number of voters is the same proportion as in the parliamentary party."

Carstens: Helmut Kohl Wavered

The candidacy of Karl Carstens, Kohl's predecessor as head of the parliamentary party, for the office of federal president was not a success story in Helmut Kohl's life. Because of promises made to him in the fall of 1978 by some in the Union, Carstens assumed that he would be welcome as a candidate to succeed Walter Scheel as head of the state. But there were a few people who were happier with the idea of a second term by the former FDP chairperson, possibly in the vague hope that Scheel would lend his aid in a later agreement with the Liberals.

But nobody was more zealous in supporting the North German Carstens than the CSU. Friedrich Zimmermann led the pack in his usual brash way. However, as frequently happens in the candidacy for high government office, the envious people end up trailing the lucky ones. Carstens's supposed membership in the Nazi party in the final years of the war became the subject of public debate. With few exceptions, the press heaped scorn on Carstens ("arch-conservative, reactionary politician" was the thrust). Furthermore, Carstens was still involved in a civil court case which he had initiated against a former SPD member of parliament for slander. To the public, the case seemed to be just the opposite: many unsuspecting people believed Carstens had been persecuted by the law because of unsavory stories.

This CDU man from Bremen was concerned about the accusations about his NSDAP membership. However, Hans Neusel, the head of Carstens's office, offered to show the official membership files to anyone who was interested. Only a few people actually took advantage of the offer: it was easier to cultivate one's own prejudices! Zimmermann, of the CSU, who was worried that Carstens would step back from becoming a candidate because of the issue, immediately made an appointment for a confidential discussion with the incumbent federal president. Zimmermann learned that during Carstens's time as a legal adviser he had actually been more involved in the resistance movement than in serving the Nazis as a party member. At any rate, the publicly defamed Carstens was able to line up important evidence for his innocence. As he wrote in his memoirs, Carstens had "applied for membership in the NSDAP only because of massive pressure on the part of my boss, the president of the *Land* court in Bremen." Carstens had intentionally submitted his application too late, so that a decision could be made only at a time when he was already a soldier. This meant that his membership never became active. Proceedings by the *Spruchkammer* of Bremen charged with denazification ascertained this after the war and stated that "the man in question had offered active resistance to the Nazi regime and had also suffered disadvantages because of this."

This did not help, however, because the mechanism of public defamation had already had its effect, even in the ranks of the Union. The head of the CSU *Land* group, Zimmermann, who had arranged a meeting with Carstens on November 10, 1978, was relieved to learn that he still had every intention of becoming a candidate. Even as late as November 19, Kohl said that Carstens was "a really outstanding candidate," although this was generally understood to mean that he could also imagine others as candidates. Edward Ackermann, Kohl's loyal press officer in the chancellery, ameliorated his own role and that of his former boss in his memoirs, *Mit feinem Gehöhr* (With Good Hearing), when he wrote about ". . . how Carstens suffered as a result of these attacks, and even seriously considered whether he should give up the candidacy for federal president." The CDU and the CSU "had been united in their support of Carstens," he

The opposition leader during a speech by Chancellor Schmidt in a plenary session of the Bundestag.

wrote, contravening the facts. The support of many people in Germany and other countries and witnesses to Carstens's unsullied actions did not change the fact that the CDU leadership had been deeply shaken. Carstens wrote succinctly in his book *Erinnerungen und Erfahrungen* (Recollections and Experiences): "Helmut Kohl wavered." The leader of the CDU and the opposition, who should have been the one to drum up the necessary majority for the "really outstanding candidate," instead dispatched Gerhard Stoltenberg, a member of the presidium, in a semi-secret mission to see Carstens in the federal government office to try to dissuade him from trying to become federal president. In his memoirs Carstens was enough of a gentleman not to mention the name of his friend.

In the end, Carstens, who usually had such a North German approach to personal issues in politics, caved in, knowing that he would meet Kohl at the right juncture. Carstens asked Kohl's emissary whether he was aware that Federal President Walter Scheel had been accepted by the NSDAP in 1942. The latter could hardly disguise his embarrassment and could scarcely stand the painfulness of the encounter. Stoltenberg "was terribly taken aback," Carstens noted, and recommended that this disclosure "should be made public immediately." Carstens replied that it was not really his job. Stoltenberg understood his meaning and returned to Kohl with a conflicting message. The internal party process of clarification ended in triumph for the controversial candidate, who was "controversial" only because the Union parties in those months were not being led but only half-heartedly moderated. Biedenkopf's memorandum, Carstens's candidacy, and Franz Josef Strauss's greater inroads toward becoming a chancellor candidate—which led to the first decision on May 23, 1979, the day of the presidential election—made Kohl only too aware of the vulnerability of his political career. How he managed to get out of such situations and even triumph in the process are part of the phenomenon of Helmut Kohl.

Citizens Ask, Politicians Answer—Not!

Three months before May 23, Constitution Day in the Federal Republic of Germany, and also by tradition the day the federal president is elected, Kohl met his television Waterloo in The Hague.

Reinhard Appel was running a second series of his highly respected program *Bürger fragen—Politiker antworten* (Citizens Ask, Politicians Answer) for German Television Channel Two. In the live broadcast, the leader of the German opposition party became the target of provocative questions from a mostly extremely leftist Dutch audience. Before the well-meaning moderator could intervene, the "ugly German" had become the subject of this extreme television discussion. Although a representative of the opposition in the neighboring country, Kohl was inadvertently forced into having to defend to a few exceptionally angry Dutch citizens policies for which the Social Democrats and Liberals were responsible.

The most radical of the circle Appel had assembled presented a picture of a Germany full of Nazi murderers, solitary confinement, Baader-Meinhof groups, "extremist directive," and the disintegrating of the liberal legal state. The effects of the "fiasco," as the press almost unanimously termed the incident, would be felt for a long time. The group which Appel had assembled, hoping it would be a "proportional" representation of the Dutch view, turned out to be overwhelmingly socialist. Kohl was scarcely able to conceal his anger at some of the brain-wracking questions. The day before he had called Appel in The Hague and asked who the panelists were and what he could expect. The television director could only tell him what he had observed: "Two are wearing ties and two are women." One of the latter, it turned out later, had been fired from her job because of her notorious leftist agitation. The television moderator had indeed planned "something with more temperament than in the previous program with Federal Chancellor Helmut Schmidt," who had answered questions from Parisians.

"It is certain that the selection of the public was very unequal," said Francis Boreel, the cultural attaché in the embassy of the Netherlands in Bonn. "We have to consider what is to be done now to improve the image of the Netherlands in Germany. This television program has been very damaging to our country."

Kohl's confrontation with the Dutch public brought to light the dilemma in the two neighboring states' relations, more than three decades after the end of the war. The Dutch newspaper, the *Volkskrant*, wrote, "Despite all the efforts and pretty phrases of the politicians, a unified Europe is still a long, long way off. There are still great abysses which cannot be crossed between the peoples of this old part of the world."

Kohl made a few remarks on television which would have been better left unsaid. At that time, he was still unused to facing the yawning cavern of an auditorium. Thus the newspapers were able to point out that he had called for a tough stance against communists but had pleaded for mild treatment of former Nazis, "because they had only made the mistakes of youth." The *Frankfurter Allgemeine Zeitung* quoted the *Volkskrant*: "That is not only unacceptable to every Dutch man and woman, but also incomprehensible. Kohl's great fear of communism and the Soviet Union is just as alienating to many Dutch people as it is unfathomable to Kohl that the Dutch people are often more afraid of the Germans than the Russians."

In the internal political aftermath, Kohl could not think of anything better to do than accuse the German government of having neglected to explain the German situation sufficiently to its neighbor. Government spokesman Klaus Bölling's dismissal of the claim was couched in elegant rhetoric, but put the blame—incorrectly—on France and Great Britain. Recent surveys had shown that Germany's image in those countries had improved, and the leader of the opposition had acknowledged this completely in the last budget debates.

In the Valley of Humiliation

The signs were not exactly favorable for the man from the Palatinate in the spring of 1979. The fiasco of Strauss's nomination as chancellor candidate was about to happen, and this could have spelled the end of Kohl's political career. First, however, he had to pass through the cleansing fire, which would not only not purify him, but would almost destroy him. By summer Kohl spoke of "the valley of humiliation" through which he had to cross, deserted by all his friends and pointedly ignored by his fellow travelers.

The trail of bad luck first led to Kiel, where 123 party delegates refused to support his appointment as chairperson, his deputy Gerhard Stoltenberg garnering ninety more votes than he did. There was no more obvious expression of dissatisfaction with a party leader down on his luck than that. The party conference in general was under an unfavorable star: even Hannelore Kohl received only weak applause when she accepted the traditional bouquet of flowers from the conference.

Before the "accursed seventh year" of his office as chairperson Kohl plunged deeper and deeper into a crisis. The old master, Kurt Biedenkopf, reached deep into his bag of rhetorical tricks and was given more than just polite applause. Otherwise there were no high points at the Kiel conference, which ended with a pleasant evening during which the party manager, Radunski, presented a Parisian "topless ballet" to the delegates. Some of them were amused, others were angry, and yet others were completely dumbfounded. This faux pas committed by a party that had already shown signs of weakness in its organization remained a lasting blemish on the Kiel party conference.

Headlines about the CDU chairperson in the following weeks and months became more and more dramatic, boding ill for the future of a man who had seemed unshakable but who was now at the nadir of his career. Only the CDU-oriented *Die Welt* partially shielded him; though he was in a "nose-dive," he was "a good man down on his luck," the paper wrote. The party leftists had reason to celebrate when Ernst Albrecht, their own minister-president of Lower Saxony, became a member of the presidium. He had been considered the "crown prince" and chancellor-candidate-in-the-wings for some time. Manfred Schell put it succinctly: "Helmut Kohl is feeling that time is running out for him."[59] Not only *Die Welt*, but also the Springer publications in general become more and more partisan. There was probably a method in this: the previous candidate was to be a foil for the next. The Bavarian sister party was not only spared, but completely justified. It had "long held back." Germany needed "politics which did not just go for majorities." The last remark was indirectly aimed at Kohl: the man has done his duty, the man can now go.

There followed a tragicomedy which set the Union back years in its quest to return to power. Even while the votes that would make Karl Carstens the fifth president of Germany were being tallied, a rumor was making the rounds of CDU/CSU election delegate circles that the CDU presidium had just decided to designate Ernst Albrecht the chancellor candidate. Zimmermann, the *Land* leader of the CSU, was beside himself over this "surprise onslaught" of the sister party: "That simply can't be true. . . . They can't do that, after already having nominated Helmut Kohl behind our back as the Union candidate in the 1976 election, and now again not asking us and disregarding our wishes and slipping in a candidate they want." Zimmermann was not correct in this regard. The presidium had not yet met and did not plan to meet to make important decisions until after the election of the president.

The same afternoon there was a conspiratorial meeting of Union politicians of all levels in Strauss's apartment in Schäfferstrasse, close to the "Langer Eugen." Even Biedenkopf crossed the threshold of the Strauss villa. More and more champagne glasses covered the brocade cloth on the coffee table. However, it was not unbridled joy that had brought the men together, but acute fear of "being run over roughshod again," as one of the conspirators expressed it. Some of the people still had the words running through their minds that Kohl had been putting about: "I'll be freer the day after the presidential elections." Naturally they knew the rumor of the CDU plans to put Albrecht in the chancellor's office.

Zimmermann suggested that the red-hot issue should be discussed in the "Klopfstuben" in Bad Godesberg. There the wine flowed freely and after a few hours the time had come: Strauss admitted "defeat" and agreed to the candidacy which he had been talked into. It still had to be approved by the entire parliamentary party, that much was clear. But for the almost sixty-five-year-old it was the last chance, Zimmermann reckoned with what turned out to be an ulterior motive. "As open to influence as the CSU chairperson is, the demonstration of unanimity by the electors that led to the seizure of power must have greatly impressed him," wrote Klaus Dreher in the *Süddeutsche Zeitung*.

Norbert Schäfer, press spokesman of the CSU *Land* group in the *Bundestag*, was to officially announce the next day Strauss's willingness to become a chancellor candidate. The only problem was that Schäfer did not know anything about it, since he had not been present during the carousing at the "Klopfstuben," which Zimmermann completely forgot about. There was an excited phone call to Bonn by the CSU general secretary, Edmund Stoiber, asking where the announcement about Franz Josef was. In view of the constantly paraded self-assurance of the regional party "with federal government aspirations," leaving the announcement of the bombshell to a lower-ranking person in the *Land* group made it look like the CSU was making a veiled attempt to leave a back door open for itself.

The CDU reacted almost immediately: after a meeting of the board on May 28, Ernst Albrecht, the new "star" and "favorite son" of the party, was proposed as a candidate for chancellor if the election was won. This recommendation was to be presented by the CDU in the upcoming discussions with the CSU about their joint future. The CSU continued to back Strauss as their nominee for the next *Bundestag* elections. After the closed CDU board meeting, Albrecht felt that he had been privy to higher inner circles and said almost patronizingly, "Helmut Kohl naturally remains the chairperson of the party and the parliamentary group."

On the same day as the board meeting Kohl sent a telex to Strauss expressing his amazement about the CSU leader's unilateral declaration on his chancellor candidacy. Strauss felt that he had been insulted and sent a somewhat hypercritical telex in return. It showed that the "Klopfstuben" circle on Constitution Day had wanted to keep the door open for a tactical retreat. For this reason, Zimmermann wrote in his memoirs that he had given Schäfer the task of announcing Strauss's candidacy, even though the press spokesman had not been present at the "Klopfstuben." In his telex from the CSU head office in Munich, Strauss wrote:

> Dear Helmut,
>
> I have received your telex of May 28, 1979. I am sorry to have to inform you that your depiction of the events is completely incorrect. Neither the CSU general secretary, nor the chairperson of the CSU *Land* group, nor any other CSU politician had thought of making such a declaration, namely, that I was available to become a chancellor candidate.
>
> On the contrary, after our discussion in the spring, which lasted several hours, and based on your letter in which you proposed three dates for the next strategy commission and the agreement on June 22,

we assumed that up until June 10 all efforts would be directed toward the European elections, and that the discussions in the strategy commission would continue after June 22. To our great astonishment we learned on the day of the election for the federal president that the presidium of the CDU was to meet, already on election day, and then on the following Thursday, and finally—as has occurred—today, Monday, with the aim of nominating Ernst Albrecht as chancellor candidate after your decision not to become such. This was an open secret in Bonn. This breaks the previous agreements and makes it necessary that we not accept a fait accompli again, in even more drastic form than in 1975.

The CSU presidium has today discussed the situation resulting from the CDU's unilateral actions and has unanimously decided:

1. The CSU presidium unanimously approves that the chairperson of the CSU, Franz Josef Strauss, has declared his availability as a candidate for chancellor of the Union parties for 1980.
2. The CSU would deeply regret it if premature decisions on personnel, lack of understanding of strategy, and tactical rigidity were to prevent the best possible conditions for the 1980 elections.
3. The CSU thus deems it necessary to lead the strategy debate by determining deadlines and topics.
4. The CSU thus continues to adhere to the agreements, which have been reconfirmed several times, to bring this debate to a conclusion. Only after agreement in this debate is it sensible for the CDU and CSU to discuss the consequences in terms of personnel. Moreover, the presidium of the CSU has unanimously drawn attention to the need to concentrate all political energies on the European elections. All other matters must be shelved in the meantime.

Sincerely yours,
Franz Josef Strauss[60]

In the summer it became clear that the CSU was not prepared to accept Albrecht, who Strauss deeply mistrusted because he proceeded on his own in the ratification of the treaties with Poland. There was a suspicion that Helmut Kohl, who was not much inclined to talk a lot about strategy, but who acted strategically, had been depending on this "challenge." This thought was indirectly substantiated by Biedenkopf's subsequent criticism of Kohl's maneuvering on the candidacy: the CDU was put in "a terribly difficult position" by the fact that Kohl had "directly and inseparably" linked his candidacy with the "Albrecht proposal." The former general secretary complained that no relevant party committee had looked at this question. Friends had become intimate enemies; the bond between him and Kohl had been cut irrevocably. Kohl reacted to Biedenkopf's criticism only by commenting that it was "completely absurd." Kohl's obviously "conditional" adherence to the Albrecht proposal could mean that a different CDU nomination—for example, that of Gerhard Stoltenberg, who was also ready to become a candidate—could have forced CSU leader Franz Josef Strauss to intervene and in the long run give up his candidacy. Strauss respected Stoltenberg and believed he could win. This could be deduced from various comments by Strauss which can no longer be documented. In Kohl's view this meant that Stoltenberg had to be stopped. His intention of doing this can be read from his early and obviously irrevocable support for Albrecht.

In the spring of 1980 Kohl explained to a small group of friends at the Bundeshaus that he had been convinced for a long time that the Union under Strauss would lose in a *Bundestag* election. He explained that his

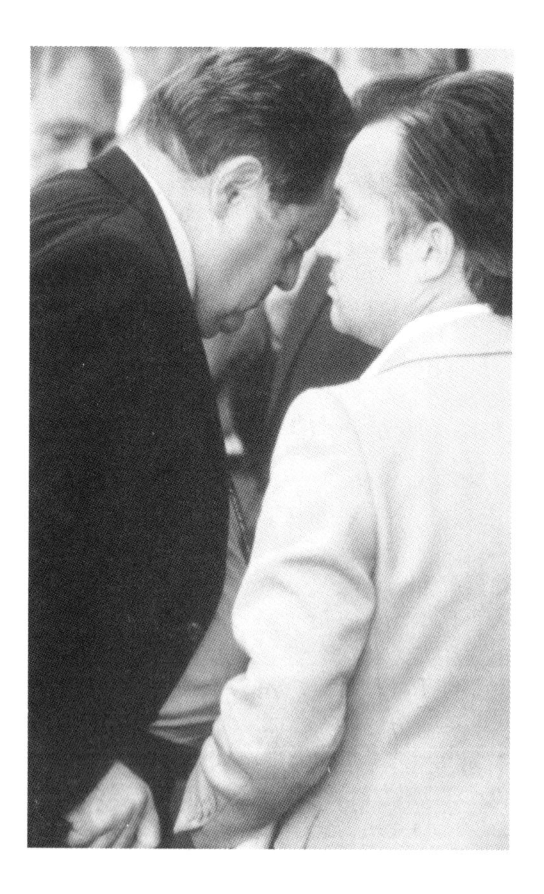

Karl Hugo Pruys and "FJS" (Franz Josef Strauss), late 1970s.

reasons "are known to everyone, and are due mostly to the fact that Strauss is capable of polarizing the German voters but never integrating them." At this time Kohl appeared confident and certain that his days were by no means numbered. Despite the loyal support for Strauss as a candidate, the election was doomed; this was not only the view of the "northern lights" of the CDU, who were determined to tame the Bavarian lion once and for all. Even Friedrich Zimmerman commented *post festum* about Strauss's candidacy as "an episode in the history of postwar Germany, though an interesting one." It is tempting to suspect that he too did not wish to see Strauss win.

7

The Contender (II)

1980–1982

Up the Outside Staircase into the Chancellery

The *Bundestag* elections ended with depressing results for the Union parties. Strauss had cost them more than four percent. Now even the greatest skeptic had to know that no victory could by won with the Bavarian. With the renewed confirmation of the parliamentary party it was already evident that the "spirit of Kreuth" had fled. The top man was undeniably Helmut Kohl, who gained 210 out of a possible 214 votes. The time had come when he could afford to be generous without being accused of being a snob: "We need the great competence of Franz Josef Strauss," the chairperson said at the first meeting. He hoped that his fellow members in the party and parliamentary group would desist from personal quarrels and political battles for the sake of unity.

Otherwise Kohl operated according to a maxim that looked easy on the surface: waiting instead of opposing. It became more obvious with every passing month that the crisis in the Social Democratic party had begun to affect the coalition as a whole. All over, people were talking about the "long, tortured deterioration" of the Schmidt/Genscher government. Though there was generally a consensus between the partners on foreign and security issues, there were serious divisions on social and economic ones in the coalition which had governed for almost twelve years. The coffers were empty and the government's debts stood at 230 billion marks. Schmidt rejected the idea of financing make-work programs by going into greater debt. The pressure from the party grew, and the Free Democrats, who continued undeterred in their belief in the principles of a market economy, made obvious moves toward disengagement. In view of the new ideological trench warfare between the coalition partners, the temptation was very great to try to form an alliance with those who swapped parliamentary party alliances, as had been done in the Barzel era. But Kohl stubbornly and successfully resisted such pressures because he had a different con-

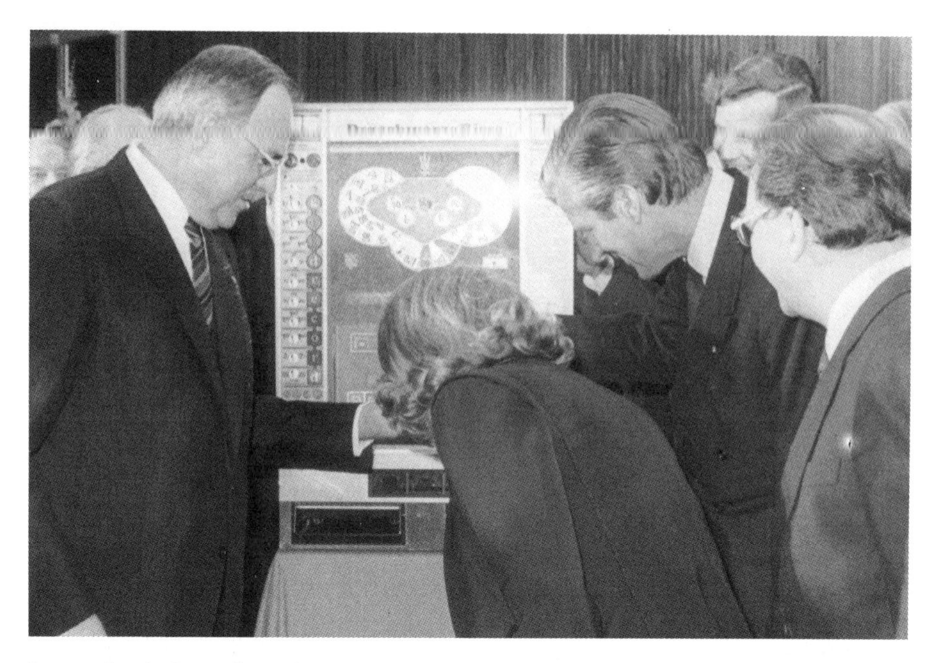

A reception in Bonn for Helmut Kohl's fiftieth birthday. CDU treasurer Walter Leisler Kiep gave Kohl a slot machine called "the black giant," a name laden with meaning.

cept. He did not want to get power by going through the back door. He wanted to enter the chancellery "via the outside staircase"[61] or not at all, the "black giant" told his friends in the Union leadership.

However, that also meant that Kohl would have to adopt a different tack and speak softly rather than loudly. Dealing with the fragile SPD/FDP coalition required flexibility; he must not kick the one who was stumbling yet again. Sometimes criticism was needed, sometimes a veiled offer to cooperate, depending on mood and feeling. Reissmüller said, "Kohl is making it difficult for the coalition to talk about the Union's inability to govern, as they had done during the election."[62] In spite of the obvious loss of face by the Liberals, which caused outbursts, by Strauss in particular ("The FDP acts like a flirt who gets into bed with anyone," the *Bild* quoted), Kohl continued to count on a partnership with the FDP. "The FDP has to know itself what it wants. It has decided now in Hesse and must make a decision in Bonn in the foreseeable future."[63] The man from the Palatinate obviously knew more than he was saying. Since the complete collapse of the coalition was only four months away, these words in the summer of 1982 sound almost prophetic. Hans Dietrich Genscher had sent him signals which he knew how to interpret. Kohl was becoming increasingly confident about more and more things, and his office in the "parliamentary party wing" became increasingly a center of the opposition. Despite the fact that Kohl had had a new suite of offices done up on the ninth floor of the CDU government management office, with a sumptuous reception area for filming television programs and interviews, the chairperson was seen there less and less. While Kohl's office as head of the CDU in the party central facility was almost impersonal and functional, his office as the parliamentary party chief was decorated with pictures of Ludwig Erhard drawn by Hansing; the Oskar Kokoschka study of Konrad Adenauer; and on permanent loan from the city of Koblenz, the famous Görres portrait. He discovered that very few visitors could identify the latter, which rightly embarrassed them, Kohl thought. A small collection of rock crystal, books, and coins made the room almost like home. Kohl played jazz or baroque music on the stereo, depending on his mood. He commented almost coquettishly to the *Bunte* correspondent Gerhard Krüger and star photographer Jupp Darchinger about the obvious wrinkles in his forehead: "A politician's face shouldn't be smooth. He is more believable if he has the marks of experience and the runes of mistakes."

Nina Grunenberg was certainly correct when she said that Kohl's victories in the past were "not overwhelming," but felt that his ability to overcome hard knocks was all the more astonishing. A master in the art of suppressing negative thoughts, however, Kohl did not want to acknowledge

Meeting with U.N. general secretary Kurt Waldheim in New York, October 1981.

that his party's problems could not be solved merely by pinpointing them. For example, he was unsuccessful in getting the parliamentary party to implement his reform concepts. The reason for this was that the board members who led the ungovernable parliamentary party with him only reflected the opposition and tensions in the CDU and CSU. When asked how he had managed to survive the last few years, with Strauss's candidacy and the march through the "valley of humiliation," he merely said, "Water under the bridge." The fact that he can shake off things that would break people with more sensitive natures is perhaps his biggest talent: "I wasn't killed off. Naturally I risked everything, I know that."[64] This statement can probably be taken as a confirmation that he never gave up but was always ready to risk everything.

The Letter of Divorce

Kohl was kept informed about the rumors circulating in Bonn during his summer vacation by phone calls from press spokesman Eduard Ackermann. Edi was also fed information by a small intimate circle of correspondents that came together in Genscher's house in Wachtberg-Pech, outside Bonn. These included the head of the WDR television and radio studio, Friedrich Nowottny, and the newspaper journalists Jürgen Merschmeier (later CDU spokesman) and Jürgen Lorenz.

Unlike his ministers, Genscher spent his vacation in the capital and took the opportunity of such meetings to speculate in some detail about the possible demise of the coalition during the upcoming budget debates. Such speculation was then always passed along as news to Ackermann, mostly by Merschmeier. When he started hearing "the fleas coughing" after that, the chief frequently advised that skepticism was needed. Hadn't Kohl, who had not seen Genscher the whole year, told journalists just before his vacation that he considered Genscher "to be an unusually bad party leader"? Kohl was not yet aware of how close the coalition was to being dissolved for good. Indeed, he did not trust his friend of many years. In retrospect he said, "The man who made the political change in Bonn possible is certainly Hans Dietrich Genscher. That is his contribution to history." That statement may have been made for the history books—for example in Manfred Schell's 1986 book *Die Kanzlermacher* (The Chancellor Makers)—but events in the early fall of 1982 pointed more toward Otto Graf Lambsdorff. In a spectacular interview in *Bild* with the Bonn correspondents Michael H. Spring and Friedemann Weckbach-Mara, the count had already said that in the *Landtag* election on September 26, the voter in Hesse must decide "what he thinks about a change to a different coalition." Weckbach-Mara, the editor of *Bild*, showed the hot interview to Lambsdorff's press spokesman, Dieter Vogel. He did not want to have sole responsibility for clearing its publication, and showed it to the economics minister for approval during a confidential meeting of the coalition at the chancellery. The cat was out of the bag: chancellor adviser Bruns (nicknamed "Kugelblitz" [bullet flash]), passed a note to his boss when he saw the journalist, letting him know that the meeting was no longer a secret. Schmidt broke up the meeting brusquely; his secretary, Mariane Duden, normally almost unflappable, was startled to see the editor of a Springer publication in the reception area, and at that particular moment.

After the SPD Munich party conference, at which wide-ranging decisions were made about an explicitly socialist "modification" of the market economy, leading Liberals had been ready for a return to a more middle-class direction. Chancellor Schmidt acknowledged in an SPD presidium meeting, "The FDP is growing increasingly ready for a change." Many of his party colleagues were surprised to hear Schmidt echo the sentiment that was prevalent among Social Democratic leaders, such as Hans Jochen Vogel, the SPD opposition leader in the Berlin parliament: "The situation has reached a breaking point."

On the other hand, like Kohl, CSU leader Franz Josef Strauss was not a true believer in the Liberals' readiness to make a change: "I've been hearing and reading for a year and a half that this coalition is finished, that it will not be able to continue. Mr. Genscher promised a change and Count Lambsdorff did too the following weekend—I take all that with a grain of salt, with a yawn or a smile."

The calendar showed the day as September 7. The *Bild Zeitung* published attention-grabbing proposals by Lambsdorff for improving the economic slump which had been causing the coalition grief: reducing unemployment compensation, a freeze on wage increases, limiting government debt to 28 billion marks, and drastic savings in personnel and social expenditures. This interview contained excerpts from the thirty-two-page document "Concept for a Policy to Overcome Economic Weakness and Reduce Unemployment." It went down in history as a "letter of divorce." When Lambsdorff presented the paper officially to the chancellor two days later, he already knew about it in detail and spoke of a "manifesto of secession." The similarities of this coalition, which Schmidt had to lead largely against the will of his party, had come to an end. The only ones disappointed were those who believed in miracles or who had been always wrong in their assessment of the way in which cooperation with the Liberals worked.

On September 17 the break was finally made official: it was finalized before the plenum of the *Bundestag*. The chancellor, visibly exhausted and with his nerves stretched to the limit, said he "had lost trust in some leaders of the FDP after the events of the last few days." Further cooperation could no longer be expected of the Social Democratic ministers nor of him as chancellor. Shortly before, Schmidt had informed FDP leader Genscher—his actual partner in the coalition and his deputy as leader of the government—as well as the head of the FDP parliamentary party, Wolfgang Mischnick.

Genscher's answer in parliament was clear. He pointed out the "special respect" of "the partners of yesterday": "The coalition of SPD and FDP has ended. They, like us, now have the freedom to make decisions on their own responsibility." Government spokesman Klaus Bölling, documenting the final thirty days of Chancellor Helmut Schmidt, characterized former coalition partner Hans Dietrich Genscher as having "an extraordinary understanding like a lawyer." Even years afterward, Genscher was at great pains to assure anyone who asked about the circumstances of the "change" that it had involved "neither betrayal nor stratagems."

8

The Turning Point

1982–1983

Freed from the Babylonian Captivity

The coalition had been torn apart, and in its final fourteen days in office some of the SPD ministers had to jointly manage departments with their FDP colleagues who were leaving. Chancellor Schmidt also served as foreign minister for two weeks, having the files brought to his office from the Foreign Office. Each day brought all sorts of novelties to Bonn, often such a drearily sleepy city. Once again, Strauss fired all guns from Munich against the hated man from the Palatinate who in his opinion was still doing things all wrong. The Bavarian wanted new elections right away to defeat the Liberals once and for all, even if a minority SPD government had to be put up with temporarily. The CDU continued with its plan of not putting the test to the voters until the spring of 1983 when the preliminary clearing out would have been finished. Kohl's thinking on this was that after the last few weeks, the FDP first needed to be put on a more secure footing. The SPD's campaign of treachery in Hesse after the FDP left the Bonn coalition had had a drastic effect on the latter.

However, in the FDP itself there were doubts about the choice of Kohl as chancellor. Nevertheless, the constructive vote of no-confidence was decided on; Kohl lacked only two votes from his own party for nomination as chancellor candidate; it was a great victory under the circumstances. Naturally enough, the Free Democrats were divided about the change: thirty-three agreed to a coalition with the CDU/CSU and eighteen were against. That was not overwhelming, but it was sufficient. Genscher, in a panic that his party might not survive the change, fought for every vote. Some of those who stuck with him at this early stage were later rewarded, among them Irmgard Adam-Schwaetzer. The FDP leader had promised his friend Kohl that he would "make him chancellor." General Secretary Günther Verheugen, who had switched in the meantime to the SPD, was more

Immediately after the successful constructive vote of no-confidence: The defeated chancellor congratulates his successor, Helmut Kohl, October 1, 1982.

than willing to speak freely about this. His opinion of his former boss, who had "raised" him politically, had hit an all-time low: "The man is simply impossible, I can't keep on going with him."

October 1 brought a real and not just temporary change in government. Helmut Kohl proved that he was not only the right man for the orphaned central government, but also that he had the nerve to tackle his new job as if it had been tailor-made for him. Even while the votes that would decide whether he would be chancellor were being counted, Kohl was discussing the change of chairmanship of the parliamentary party with

Alfred Dregger in a window niche in the lobby of the *Bundestag*. The leading Union politician of Hesse representing the right wing of the party was happy to take over the position from Kohl. Dregger was soon proudly calling himself "the chancellor's right-hand man."

On the day of his triumph, Kohl assembled his family in Bonn, happily allowing himself to be photographed with his sons and his wife. On the way from the plenum to the parliamentary party building he was accompanied by his closest colleagues: Juliane Weber, Philipp ("Don Filippo") Jenninger, Eduard Ackermann, Alfred Dregger, Rudolf Seiters, Peter Radunski from the party central office, and, naturally, Heiner Geissler. "Don Filippo" was beside himself with happiness and had taken Juliane Weber's arm, talking all the while, saying that they had "finally been freed from the Babylonian captivity." This was a reference by the parliamentary party manager to the long period of being in the opposition, now part of the Union's past, even if only for ten minutes.

October 1 was unforgettable for many in the CDU/CSU; the day saw a spontaneous meeting of the entire parliamentary party and its friends. One of Kohl's undeniable strengths is his ability to elevate such events to the

Overjoyed, the new chancellor hugs his son Peter in the lobby of the Bundestag.

level of a solemn festival. The elected chancellor of the Federal Republic of Germany called to mind the thirteen years of being the opposition, the highs and lows, strife and solidarity, times of pride and times of humiliation. He delved into history, saying that "it is not an accident, but an honor and a duty, that we can count among our ranks names such as von Stauffenberg, who so staunchly defied tyranny in the Third Reich." The CSU member of parliament Franz Ludwig Graf Stauffenberg, to whom Kohl was referring, was not present at the parliamentary party "mass," and had to be told about the respectful allusion to his family's name.

Kohl showed no more signs of stress after the election. He beamed at photographers who wanted a smile as if it were the most natural thing in the world. "He always knew it," said Jürgen Leinemann in *Der Spiegel* about the great moment. "There was no sense of relief because there was no longer any possibility of tension in this man who had a firm belief in his mission that was unshakable almost to the point of absurdity."

Decisions on staffing were made quickly. Waldemar Schreckenberger, Kohl's old school friend and head of the state chancery in Rhineland-Palatinate, was to become head of the chancellery office. "Schrecki," as the lovable and absent-minded professor came to be known, was soon completely overworked. The Westphalian Friedrich Vogel and Philipp Jenninger were also promoted to the central organization as state ministers, Jenninger to work closely with Kohl.

The cabinet was assigned strictly according to party proportions of CDU, CSU, and FDP. Hans Dietrich Genscher became foreign minister and deputy chancellor; Otto Graf Lambsdorff remained economics minister; Josef Ertl was agriculture minister; Hans Engelhard became minister of justice instead of Hans-Günther Hoppe, who had to resign for health reasons. Strauss had said of Engelhard that he was "so slow that his shoes could be resoled while he was still walking." Kohl assigned four posts to the CSU: Friedrich Zimmermann, as chairperson of the *Land* group, was next in line after Strauss for a ministry post and was given the interior ministry. Werner Dollinger became minister for transport; Oscar Schneider minister of housing; and Jürgen Warnke minister of development. The remaining jobs were distributed among CDU politicians, led by Gerhard Stoltenberg, who became the all-important minister of finance. Norbert Blüm became minister of social affairs; Manfred Wörner minister of defense; Christian Schwarz-Schilling minister of post and telecommunications; Heiner Geissler minister of family and youth; Rainer Barzel minister of intra-German relations; Heinz Riesenhuber minister of research and technology; and Dorthee Wilms minister of education and science.

Kohl, immediately after receiving the certificate of appointment from Federal President Carstens, Villa Hammerschmidt, October 2, 1982.

It was a cabinet based on reason and visual judgment. It included tried-and-true Liberals, over whom Kohl had no influence, as well as Union politicians who had already held ministerial posts in the 1960s: Dollinger, Stoltenberg, and Barzel. For the hundredth time the newly elected chancellor answered the incorrectly termed "Gretchen question." The "Gretchen question," an allusion to the issue of religion in *Faust*, was intended to provide insight into Kohl's attitude toward power. With almost careless directness, Kohl responded, "For me, power is not a problem which would cause my morals to be shaken." Indeed, Kohl was not shaken at all at the beginning, but only much later in the second and third legislative periods, although then it was not for moral reasons.

In Pursuit of the Spiritual Change

Helmut Kohl made the physical adjustment with "dignity," one of his favorite expressions. He would affirm this "spiritual" adjustment ten days hence before the *Bundestag*. Hannelore ("Loki") and Helmut Schmidt attended the formal farewell ceremony in the hallowed halls, surrounded by colleagues, journalists, and press photographers. Schmidt had called "Loki" on her botanical trip to Brazil and asked her not to cut the trip short for the ceremony, saying, "you can't help here." But she returned to Bonn in order to leave the bungalow they still occupied right on the dot of 3:00 P.M. on October 4, crossing the lawn to the chancellery for the final time; it was time for a change.

Helmut Schmidt, who smiled frozenly with his rattling charm one last time, became somewhat elegiac: "Democracy, as Theodor Heuss remarked, is power for a limited time. Mine has run out." His secretaries, Marianne Duden and Lilo Schmarsow, had tears in their eyes. Schmidt introduced Kohl as the first representative of the postwar generation to hold office in Germany by saying, "that can also mean opportunities." Kohl thanked his predecessor almost shyly. Whether or not Kohl wanted to admit it, Schmidt had always been a feared rival who had ridiculed him and whose ridicule Kohl returned frequently and with pleasure. Now, however, he became melancholy and attempted to align himself with his respected chancellor "colleagues": "Respect for their patriotic accomplishments; this change of office implies dignity and democracy and I thank you for that."[65] They had never been so close as at this time, after which they were to be separated forever.

The ceremony continued with almost anxious, or at least confusing, routine. In his government declaration the new man at the top tried to assure foreign countries in particular that German policy would continue to be reliable. Kohl hinted at significant cuts in domestic policies: the first cabinet meeting dealt with salary cuts of five percent for ministers and state secretaries by the end of 1984. In only a few months Finance Minister Gerhard Stoltenberg became a noteworthy federal politician, followed closely in public opinion by Hans Dietrich Genscher.

Public discussion continued outside the routine, and behind-the-scenes talk about the early new elections that Kohl was hoping to hold on March 6, 1983, was even more secretive. He had already set the date because he was confident that the federal president would agree to this and dissolve the *Bundestag* on time in accordance with Article 68 of the Basic Law.

"It was a typical situation in which Kohl the power politician came to the fore; he had no advisers who could have told him that he could not simply set a date for new elections and disregard the federal president's constitutional role," recalled Hans Neusel, head of the president's office, and an excellent adviser to Federal President Karl Carstens, who was always meticulous in following procedures when it came to the nation's well-being. It was, as "the best civil servant in the Bonn administration" said afterward, indeed a "highly unworthy procedure, with dubious concepts based on shaky grounds." Neusel was concerned that Karlsruhe could overrule the procedure if a court case based on Article 68 ensued on the vote of no-confidence needed for dissolving parliament.

Carstens said his decision of January 6, 1983, to dissolve the *Bundestag* in order to pave the way for new elections was "the most difficult decision" he had to make as federal president. He was afraid of losing his reputation as a nationally and internationally respected professor of law. He was a member of the German law professors organization as well as of the highly regarded law faculty of the University of Cologne. Making a significant legal error because he was put under pressure by a high-ranking politician was something he could not tolerate. In one of the earliest internal memos about this extremely embarrassing situation, Neusel warned on November 8, 1982, "The federal president is thus supposed to honor the change which was initiated without his approval and clarification of the legal implications. Thus the federal president, whose position is to a great extent dedicated to protecting the constitution, is given a great responsibility."

In one of the many discussions on this issue between Neusel and Carstens, Neusel said, "It just won't work at all." The federal president agreed completely with his adviser and head of office. Neusel thus had to look for arguments that could dissolve the *Bundestag* nevertheless; the federal president was able to decide on dissolving the *Bundestag* only if the reason would stand up in court. Neusel and Carstens, both experienced lawyers, wanted to stick only with this approach. Kohl on the other hand acted only as a power merchant, and Neusel and Carstens did respect his attempt to seek confirmation from the voters of the governing coalition of the Union and Free Democrats after only five months. It was courageous, because it meant postponing the promised breakthrough in economic and social issues until the spring. The chances of industry and commerce making large investments before the change to a liberal–middle-class coalition were not thought to be very high. As Christian Democrats, the two high-ranking men in the president's office did not believe this would hinder economic recovery.

However, the legal issues soon came to the fore. Aside from a defeat in the vote on the question of confidence, Carstens argued to Kohl on November 10 that there must be "elements which made the course already taken plausible." Stated plainly, before he could make a decision, the federal president had to be convinced that the government did not have a majority in parliament on key issues of domestic and foreign policy.

Cunningly, Kohl said in the mid-October debate about his first government declaration that he did not object to the opposition's term "transition government," but added, "but the chancellor standing before you is not a transition chancellor." In the ensuing debate Kohl announced drastic cuts in public spending, including cuts in the Federal Education Promotion Act and in family subsidies. On new elections he said, "The coalition parties FDP, CSU, and CDU have agreed to put themselves to the vote on March 6, 1983. This is also the view of the government. I know that it is constitutionally not simple to accomplish this. Since the opposition also regarded new elections as being the right course, it should assist as much as possible in achieving this plan."

Carstens and Neusel stuck to their view that the only way in accordance with Article 68 was to find additional reasons which would make a parliamentary vote of no-confidence plausible. Carstens wrote in his memoirs: "I said to Kohl (in one of the seventeen discussions on this topic in four weeks) that I had to be convinced that the government did not have a majority in important domestic and foreign issues." Strauss, who in the meantime had endorsed Kohl's view about the elections on March 6, accused Neusel of wanting to block new elections in a meeting with Carstens. It came to a dispute in which Carstens pointed out to Strauss that Neusel had only reminded him, the federal president, about "concerns, as was his duty."

On the flight to Moscow to attend the funeral of Leonid Brezhnev, leader of the Soviet Union and communist party, Carstens told Foreign Minister Hans Dietrich Genscher that if the route of Article 68 were pursued, it must be clear that the government did not have a majority for its important tasks. Discussions were also held with the minister-president of North Rhine–Westphalia, Johannes Rau, who supported the March 6 idea, even though he believed that Kohl's tack was wrong. After the Christmas recess there were final meetings with SPD leader Willy Brandt and the legal expert and member of parliament Gerhard Jahn, followed again by discussions with Kohl and coalition party members. All of these men gave Carstens the impression—according to him—that they were serious about new elections.

The decisive point—this was Neusel's suggestion—was that the heads of the parliamentary groups, Dregger (CDU) and Wolfgang Mischnick (SPD), should make a public statement "with great certainty" that they would no longer have a government majority after a vote of no-confidence. Dregger read the decisive sentences and the viewers got the impression that it had been rehearsed; mistakes in details could no longer be tolerated. The federal president dissolved parliament effective January 7, 1983, and called elections for March 6.

Before this happened, the president's office received fifteen hundred letters about dissolving parliament, the majority against. This was a party-political watershed, as Carstens said to his colleagues, because primarily SPD sympathizers and members of the FDP had written him before parliamentary elections in Hamburg on December 19. After the SPD's resounding victory and a crushing defeat of the Liberals, who plunged to 2.6 percent, comments came mostly from the Union and the FDP.

The reasons against using Article 68, which Carstens and Neusel had expounded in all party meetings, seemed under the circumstances to be justified. The coalition voted on the required budget and associated laws—it was still able to do this. But three days before that Kohl had posed the question of no-confidence which was to be voted on again one day after debates on the budget. As a result, the *Bundestag* withdrew its confidence in the chancellor. Thus he officially no longer had the required parliamentary majority. The coalition parties themselves had wanted it that way, which led people to suspect that in future the dates of new elections could be made to depend on this if it promised good results for a particular majority. However, the federal president had no other choice than to order the dissolution of parliament. The coalition had been successful in making its decision, "based on good reasons," "irreversible," or incapable of being put to the test of the vote before any further political action.

German law professors were generally sharply critical, as Carstens had feared. "Evil game with the constitution," and "self-disenfranchisement of the parliament" were the comments made by the Berlin professor Hans Reif, one of the fathers of the constitution. Theodor Eschenburg spoke of "evil manipulation." Carstens trotted out all of those who were respected in politics and law—Ernst-Wolfgang Böckenförde, Karl-Dietrich Bracher, Wilhelm Schlaich and Hans-Peter Schneider—to justify after the fact his warnings about a constitutional crisis which had been dismissed as petty legalism. Only then did he cite those who had favored the use of Article 68 under certain circumstances—although those circumstances did not exist in the autumn of 1982—among them the CDU politicians Roman Herzog, Hans-Hugo Klein, and Rupert Scholz.

The chancellor during the Bundestag *budget debate in December 1982: German Press Agency's caption: "Symbolic figure for coolness, confidence, and self-assuredness."*

"I was said to have dissolved the *Bundestag* because all the parties wanted it," Carstens wrote. "That is not correct. The agreement of all the parties on this issue was for me only an indication that no party thought that the dissolving (of parliament) would hurt their vital interests."[66]

The federal president acted in accordance with the law, which was the most important thing to him. His procedures were confirmed by the Federal Constitutional Court on February 16, 1983. Members of parliament Hans Lagershausen (CDU), Friedhelm Rentrop (FDP), Hansheinrich Schmidt

(FDP), and Karl Hofmann (originally SPD, then without a party) had tried to initiate a suit against the federal president in this court. The complaint was dismissed and everyone breathed a sigh of relief, although for different reasons. Carstens praised the "wise self-limitation of the court." In his concluding remarks, he said that "based on the unanimous action of the other high constitutional organs [the federal president, the chancellor, and the *Bundestag*], the court had recognized that in such a situation only extremely important reasons could have justified a different decision."

In the Shadow of the Missile Campaign

Kohl undertook more in those months than a man could do by himself in his position. The FDP partner party mostly looked to its own affairs, and also had more than enough to do. Thus the "black giant" had to marshal his energies for a two-front war. On the domestic front, he needed to muster elegance and wit for the spring vote on the much-desired constitutional security. He also needed to create a positive image abroad, since a chancellor, especially a new one, needs demonstrated recognition by foreign countries.

The first person of consequence Kohl received was French president François Mitterrand, in a far-from-routine meeting on the framework of European unification. When Kohl's predecessor, Helmut Schmidt, left the *Bundestag* in the next legislative period, he praised in his speech the "great and remarkable successes" of his successor in German-French relations.

A "noteworthy change" was noted by the *Neue Züricher Zeitung*, when Helmut Kohl visited the United States. President Reagan and his secretary of defense, Caspar Weinberger, had "expressed enormous satisfaction with the presence and views of the new German leader." Kohl's spokesman, Diether Stolze, former editor of *Die Zeit*, noted elegantly that Kohl and Reagan "spoke and thought in the same images." In his discussions, Kohl was at pains to let the president know that he intended to continue his predecessor's basic foreign and security policies. By 1982, discussions on the "dual-track decision" formulated by Schmidt and adopted by NATO had reached a peak, thereby placing the pre-election campaign in Germany under the shadow of the "missiles." Even though Kohl had not sought a "missile" campaign, he decided that whoever wanted it could have it. This issue—now only of historical relevance—was at the time highly controversial in both domestic and foreign politics, and showed the man from the Palatinate's real class. He surprised friends and foes alike. Kohl assured Washington that Germany would permit the stationing of intermediate-range missiles on its soil if all diplomatic efforts with the

Soviet Union failed to halt the positioning of Soviet SS-20 missiles and their next generation.

Because it was an election, *Der Spiegel* took aim with "missiles instead of socialism" but could not deny the fact that the Kohl government's strongest anchor was the politics of Helmut Schmidt, who had defined and formulated the NATO dual-track decision. The *Washington Post* rightly assessed that Kohl was campaigning in the United States for the West German elections in the spring. But it would be completely wrong to assume anything further than that the positioning of missiles in Germany was not as popular as many thought.

Fear of the Russians, which had persisted for decades, seemed to continue unabated; Germans were still plagued by the suspicion that an invasion from the east would wipe out their hard-won prosperity.

It is difficult to fathom the domestic proportions which seemed to promise victory for the new coalition, although almost all public-opinion institutions persisted in their (incorrect) assessment of an interim government. The commitment to save money probably made the biggest impression on millions of people, as well as the feeling of being governed again, whereas an orator as gifted as Helmut Schmidt had been ground down by the "trench warfare" with the SPD party wings. Thus March 6, 1983, and the "theater of the absurd," as *Der Spiegel* called it, became a triumph for a man who most chroniclers—friends included, but most especially his opponents—had always underrated. Now, even the skeptical *Times* of London championed the "everyman" chancellor against his cabaret critics.

With 48.8 percent of the vote, the CDU/CSU attained its best election results since Konrad Adenauer's days. "*Der Alte von Rhöndorf*," the old man of Rhöndorf, had only once managed to achieve an absolute majority, during a period of unusual circumstances in domestic and foreign relations. Kohl had obviously not even wanted to achieve an absolute majority, as he involuntarily admitted in a television interview on German Television Channel Two, broadcast from the large auditorium in the Konrad-Adenauer-Haus. An interim tally had shown a CDU/CSU majority for the chancellor of 249 seats in the *Bundestag* and a reporter asked Kohl his opinion. He dismissed this almost rudely, remarking that he would not comment until he knew the final results. How was that possible? A party leader, and chancellor to boot, was not happy about his party's absolute majority? Damn it, it was not only "his" party, but also that of Franz Josef Strauss! Kohl had the choice of governing with the Liberals or with the CSU alone, but in that case with an internal party opposition which would have caused him far more trouble than the FDP would have. The man from the Palatinate had always wanted only a government coalition with the FDP, and thus favored it at this first juncture, which was so important for his chancellorship. If the CSU decided to make trouble, he could always reclaim the enforced respect for the FDP. In this regard, Kohl showed himself to be a politician with long-term vision: governments with an absolute majority, at least those supported by the middle class, tend not to stay in power very long. The Liberals were in the same boat and the bill would be settled if the victor on March 6 did not forget who sought to put obstacles in his path. For example, Hans Neusel, Carstens's intelligent and stubborn adviser who bravely resisted Kohl's unfettered attempt to wrest power, and who did end up as kingmaker in new elections, did not escape retribution. When the interior minister Zimmermann (CSU) wanted to appoint the highly competent civil servant as state secretary in his department, Kohl and Strauss—in a rare display of unity—tried unsuccessfully to block it. Zimmermann did not want to do without Neusel, and he got his way. During the farewell celebration for the state secretary in the president's office, Neusel was presented—unlike the usual case—not with a book of contemporary history, but with an antiquarian volume of Brentano's fairy tale "*Gockel, Hinkel, und Gackeleia.*"

Apocalypse Now!

> The foreign policy of our nation is at stake. The Soviet Union must not succeed in intimidating us Western Europeans with its enormous armament which cannot be justified by any recognizable defense and security requirement, limiting our freedom of political action and drawing a dividing line between ourselves and the United States. Only by preventing this can the door be kept open to peace in Europe based on justice and not might."[67]

These were the opening remarks of one of the tensest *Bundestag* sessions of the 1980s. On this auspicious day, November 21, 1983, the chancellor was more serious than usual. The atmosphere in the forum, in which the Greens were sitting for the first time since the March elections, was highly charged. The Greens hoped to gain a higher profile in the debate on the NATO dual-track decision. This party had had notable support from the media due to its rejection of anything having to do with armaments, even when this was put in a context designed specifically to prevent a further turn of the spiral. In television talk shows especially there were more and more proponents of the peace movement and/or Green alternatives who offered almost clown-like solutions and slogans about the end of the world, such as "Apocalypse Now!" This slogan was ostensibly a consequence of the decision by NATO to station intermediate nuclear missiles in Western

Constituent meeting of the newly elected Bundestag, *March 30, 1983. The Green party entered the* Bundestag *for the first time. Kohl is shown here with the Green delegate Walter Schwenninger, a teacher from Tübingen. Caption: "With their demonstrative, laid-back leisure look, the Greens attracted undivided attention."*

Europe. "Why are we talking about this so long, let's be relaxed and happy. We'll all be meeting in Heaven next summer anyway," one of them laughed grimly on one such television show, slapping himself on the thigh. The television host Franz Alt made a lucrative business out of publishing a superficial pamphlet aimed at the Christian Democrats, who were supposedly trying to cheat humanity of immediate world peace. The booklet was enormously successful because it quoted irrefutable passages from the Sermon on the Mount aimed at the desires of simple minds, thereby ignoring the fact that the Soviet Union was endangering this same peace by its unilateral arms build-up.

Quite a few Bonn journalists recall a tea with Helmut Schmidt, the onetime host of Brezhnev in Bonn. Bending over a map, Schmidt told the Moscow potentate, "Mr. General Secretary, your weapons are an unacceptable threat to us!" If the public were not prepared to believe Helmut Kohl, then they should have looked to Schmidt, his predecessor, for advice.

The situation in autumn, a first test for the new coalition, was worse than confusing, because proponents took matters to the streets and reason was regarded as being no longer historically relevant. During the armament debates, at any rate, a protective zone around the *Bundestag* had to be cordoned off and protected against intruders, especially the ones who wanted to violate parliament with marches and demonstrations. After one dramatic debate in the *Bundestag* ended at midnight, the Greens left the forum singing, which was a blatant affront against every parliamentary custom. According to one middle-class member of parliament, it was a "fatal reminder of the remarkable behavior of the first NSDAP parliamentarians in the *Reichstag*." But Kohl reassured America (in an interview with the *Washington Post*) that violence and terror would not dictate public policy in his country. During the vote on the arms package the coalition of CDU/CSU and FDP achieved an impressive victory and a year of unpleasantness neared an end.

Summarizing the sometimes serious, sometimes even hysterical politics of peace practiced by powers inside and outside of parliament, Kohl said aptly that "no one should be allowed to privatize the longing for peace." This warning was aimed at his own ranks, in which there were heralds of the "pure" lesson of peace in politics and the media who did not want to accept the slick phrase "*Frieden schaffen mit weniger Waffen*" (make peace with fewer weapons).

Weapons played a role on other fronts, namely in the Middle East. Ill-considered statements by Israel's president Menachem Begin made it impossible for Bonn to continue long-planned negotiations on a deal with the Saudis to sell German-produced Leopard 2 tanks. The project had already been planned when Schmidt was in office; his government had been in debt to the Saudis for twenty million dollars. Riyadh's ambassador on the Rhine, confided to the CSU *Land* group chairperson Friedrich Zimmermann that he was staking his diplomatic career on the desired supply of the unique tank to his country. This put Bonn in a dilemma: an arms deal with a defense-oriented desert country appeared to be an industrial coup almost without parallel. On the other hand, Israel had legitimate security concerns which Germany especially had to respect. Moreover, in those summer months of 1983, the bourgeois-liberal coalition committed its first sin against the holy spirit of German-Israeli relations: the chancellery cut the usual words "special relationship" from a press release about a high-ranking Israeli visit after the fact (and thus noticeably). Begin, who had lost many of his family in the Holocaust, had taken Schmidt to task two years earlier, in connection with the planned sale of tanks to Riyadh, for having been a soldier in the *Wehrmacht*. Begin had directly connected the *Wehrmacht* with the pogroms of the Jews: "Wherever the *Wehrmacht* went there was an orgy of destruction of the Jews." Even the Israeli ambassador at the time, Johanon Meroz, thought his leader's comment "very unfortunate," though he did not express this openly.

Begin attacked the new coalition, although it did not necessarily have to put up with these specific accusations. German visitors to Israel, whose

In a plenary session of the Bundestag, *December 1983.*

numbers were increasing, had to listen to Begin and others saying that German authorities had acted disloyally during the October war against Egypt in 1973 by holding up supply shipments from the United States in Bremerhaven. Israel wanted to know nothing about the "German balance between Arab and Israeli interests." The Israeli side was supported by Alfred Dregger, who found it unsatisfactory "that the field had been left open for the Soviets in Saudi Arabia." On the other hand, Dregger did not overlook the fact that in German-Israeli relations, "feelings too were of political significance."

9

The Chancellorship (I)

1983–1987

The Billion-Mark Deal with Honecker

In the summer of 1983 Helmut Kohl and Franz Josef Strauss arranged a strictly private meeting by phone at Salzburg Airport. Its purpose was to discuss Strauss's fervently championed proposal that the federal German government should give its assent to lending over a billion marks to the East German regime of Erich Honecker. A Bavarian bank was ready to lend the money at the usual interest rate, and Bonn was to guarantee this loan by transferring the transit visit money and other intra-German financial transactions by the GDR. The taxpayer would thus not have to pay anything.

Strauss became a hot topic of discussion, especially among his own people, for supposed generosity to the rigid communists of the Socialist Unity Party. The CSU party conference became an unplanned tribune to the "great chairman": over four hundred of eleven hundred delegates did not vote for Strauss, an almost unheard of occurrence for the usually unified CSU. Strauss tried to put down the critics in his party by accusing them collectively of "ignorance" and "provincialism." They "didn't have a clue," the Bavarian lion roared angrily. But Strauss himself was ignorant: without any warning he had fallen into a trap laid for him by Kohl. In the spring, Alexander Schalck-Golodkowski, Erich Honecker's financial advisor—actually only his money procurer—had asked the chancellor's office whether it would be possible to "do something short-term" with a credit for a billion marks. Kohl asked his friend and minister of state Philipp Jenninger to carry out the secret task; "Don Filippo" knew right away how best to interpret his boss's wishes. He recommended Strauss to Schalck, because the former could easily do something via Bavarian banks. Paul Pucher, editor in chief of the *Münchener Merkur*, whose only fun in life was taunting Franz Josef Strauss, followed up the story, recounting it in great detail in his unfortunately quickly forgotten book, *Der letzte Preusse* (The Last Prussian).

Strauss, who had quickly written a strictly private letter to Kohl about the "secret," had an unusually warm reception from his chancellor, who immediately approved the credit, because he had long since considered the matter closed. His cabinet would make a decision, he informed Strauss, but it would be good if he, Strauss, as CSU chairperson, would explain it to the public if necessary. Thus Strauss became the "initiator" of the credit deal which Kohl himself had wanted and planned. "In Kohl's presence it was puzzling that the tricked CSU chairperson had made such a big deal about his role as initiator of the credit deal, but he was satisfied with this," according to Pucher.[68]

Kohl pulled off an ingenious trick that would keep the Bavarian occupied for a long time, entangling him in a matter which he would not have supported had Kohl "invented" it. At the same time, his standing among CSU friends sank visibly, which was of course to the good of peace in the Union as a whole.

After the party conference in Salzburg Strauss saw the light. The real responsibility for the credit deal was the chancellor's, and he defiantly told all those who maliciously criticized him that "whoever rejects this policy has to attack Helmut Kohl. Kohl made the decision on the credit, not me." He was sick of it, he complained bitterly to Manfred Schell, "being forced into the role of a bully. Where was there any resistance to the criminal credit for Poland?"[69] Strauss was not wrong in this, but the rebellious CSU chairperson had had a hand in the billion-mark credit for the GDR, it had to be said, which was after all quite strange given his strong resistance to the SED clique up to that point.

In order to improve his damaged image, Strauss requested—verbally via Schalck and in writing to the SED leaders—"binding reports about relaxation in procedures for transiting the border between the countries." Thus some good came out of this: Schalck discreetly reported how and what he had told Honecker about Strauss's requests. It transpired that the reports of "success" on the relaxation of border checks were true to description. Thus each side gained something. It was not until many years later that the broken Schalck-Golodkowski told the West German administration that the billion-mark credit in the early 1980s had probably saved the ruined GDR from bankruptcy. The chancellor also admitted this after the fact. In an unpublished manuscript which originated in the chancellery, Kohl had outlined the complicated situation in an almost irrefutable way:

> We agreed that the loan [to the GDR] could pose a risk to stabilization. People are always wise after the fact, and after 1989 it would be easy to say that had it not been for this first billion and then the second, the GDR would have become destabilized a lot more quickly,

> which would have unified the two countries sooner. I do not believe this for a very important reason: the Soviet Union was in a completely different situation. At that time it was still very strong militarily and diplomatically. And the decision would have been very different under Brezhnev and Andropov."

Significantly, the chancellor added, "It is possible that the military-political element could have been manifested in a completely different way."

He and his political friends had been well aware of the watershed in allowing the billion-mark credit, Kohl said. The (indirect) guarantee of the federal German government (in fact, the GDR pledged its outstanding transfer payments if it defaulted on repayment) in 1983 had been one of the more difficult decisions, as well as the determination to go ahead and invite Honecker to Bonn in 1987. "But today [1995] I am still of the opinion that both were right. It could not have been in our interest to stop our humanitarian efforts and thus contribute to massive destabilization."[70]

Rendezvous in the Bermuda Triangle

He still enjoyed being chancellor, the newspapers quoted Kohl as saying one year after the "change." That is one of the typical understatements of a rather laconic person: Helmut Kohl was only really starting to govern. The day-to-day routine, of course, was not as exciting as those first days and months after the change from Schmidt/Genscher to Kohl/Genscher. Kohl's leadership style in the chancellery and elsewhere in the party and parliamentary group was pretty much as it had always been: improvised, unsystematic, somewhat erratic, but always goal-oriented, designed to preserve and, where possible, extend his power.

The chancellor presided over the morning situation meeting in his own office, and whoever missed it did not know what was going on that day. Aside from his two state secretaries, Schreckenberger and Jenninger, the meeting was attended by department heads Ackermann and Teltschik. Others were government spokesman Diether Stolze (until the first *Bundestag* election on March 6), Peter ("Pepe") Boenisch, and Kohl's efficient office manager, Wolfgang Burr. The previously regular department-head meetings were generally not continued or occurred only at irregular intervals and obviously did not have the same weight in decision making in the chancellery as could be expected. Though some leading civil servants were quickly replaced by new ones loyal to the coalition, Kohl mostly governed with the personnel he had inherited from Schmidt. "Thus the new leadership looked like a small squad from the old team," Carl-Christian Kaiser wrote in *Die Zeit*. This was unlike the situation in Washington, in which three to four thousand government appointees were replaced at the same time. A newly elected German chancellor has to find his way with the existing arrangement.

Schmidt tended to study files closely, but Kohl more frequently reached for the phone. At short notice he would call Schreckenberger or Juliane Weber into his office to discuss current problems, appointments, or tasks for the various departments. At such times he usually pulled out of his pocket a note which was to be turned into official procedure. Face-to-face discussion remained his hallmark of governing, along with allowing whoever he entrusted to carry out the details of his policies. "People play an important role for him, and not just the strict procedures which his predecessor mentioned frequently, though with a sigh," said Kaiser. Many people thought his style of governing "ingenious,'" among them his friend "Schrecki," who cracked jokes about it. Even though discussions with the chancellor were fairly informal, they were usually effective, despite a few serious mishaps. These meetings were frequently joined by Horst Teltschik, head of the department of foreign and security policy, who soon became the chancellor's "little Kissinger." He was made fun of by no less a personality than Franz Josef Strauss, who had once been invited to the chancellery for a discussion on basic foreign policy. Kohl was obviously speaking from a text prepared by Teltschik. Strauss later said about the meeting, "I had a lot of trouble staying awake." The Bavarian, never one to mince words, became more cutting about his rival Kohl: "What Genscher's doing to Kohl . . . . It's impossible. If a middle-sized business were run like Kohl does the chancellery, it would have been bankrupt a long time ago."

Kohl, Jenninger, Schreckenberger, Teltschik, Ackermann, and the government spokesman formed the "kitchen cabinet," as it was disparagingly called, but it meant in the long run that the cooking was done by a group that was of a manageable size for what needed to be done. Tortuous and long-winded bureaucratic procedures seemed to Kohl "completely unacceptable," as he frequently said in a tone typical of the Palatinate. Since, unlike his predecessors, he valued unconventional methods of governing and delegating, people who wanted something from him tended to adopt the same methods: the word got around the ministries that "routine things had to be done with the usual procedures, but for really important issues, you called Juliane."

Things had pretty much settled down into a daily routine and even those of Kohl's critics who were involved by virtue of their office, such as the Social Democrat Peter Glotz, found that Germany was now "being ruled from the right by a Helmut Kohl who acted like he had never done anything else in his life." This was perplexing most of all to the leftist politicians and media, who compared Kohl to Schmidt and wondered why Schmidt's successor did not want to be one of those people who "run around day after day and want to look stressed out," according to Kohl.[71] Indeed, Kohl, unlike Schmidt, gave his ministers free rein in accordance with the management procedures of the federal government: "The coalition parties argue unashamedly, and there is little evidence of guidelines being imposed."

It was only one year after the transition that CDU politicians took their boss to court in his two functions as chancellor and party chairperson. They accused him of mismanagement and coordination problems; one of his critics stated that he lacked a Wischnewski, referring to the man who had aided Helmut Schmidt. That is, "Schrecki" was hardly the same sort of professional politician as "Ben Wisch." The professor of law loved and preferred "the bureaucratic method" in all situations and regarded his friend the chancellor as a genius, considering that for himself there was only "the office and no opinion," loosely following Schiller's Wallenstein. As absent-minded as the man was, there were more files lost than could be tolerated, so that investigations into certain legal proceedings occasionally were like a rendezvous in the Bermuda Triangle in which everything threatened to disappear forever into a black hole. The CSU and in particular its chairperson, Theo Waigel, were quick to pin the responsibility for some of the small disasters in government functions on its leader. The finger was pointed at Waldemar Schreckenberger as the one mainly responsible, which was probably not incorrect. He was the classic case of a wrong appointment par excellence: with no experience of Bonn and no knowledge of the personalities in national politics it is very difficult to manage a complicated office such as the chancellery. Furthermore, Schreckenberger had successfully covered up a serious health problem for years, which under normal circumstances—that is, if he had not been Kohl's school friend and had not already worked for him—would have almost certainly disqualified him from working in the chancellery. Schreckenberger was obviously well hooked on pills: during a move to a new house within Bonn the moving company used drugs to pack the boxes. He obviously needed them in order to stand up to his difficult job, and they led him to say things which outsiders found incomprehensible. Parliamentary investigation committees naturally quizzed the head of the chancellery on his relationship with the head of government. Some of his answers were very strange or puzzling, such as those given to the correspondent of the *Münchner Abendzeitung*, Sönke Petersen, who recorded them for personal reasons and not for publication. *Der Spiegel* borrowed the tape from its colleague and published the original recording of Schreckenberger, which is excerpted here: "I don't have any problem with Dr. Kohl. And the criticism is always leveled that Mr. Kohl will always provide a shield. . . . Yes, there's no other way for it to work. We have all sorts of shields, that's the only way a group which has to meet the challenge of making important decisions for the public can act at all. . . . It works. So, I don't know, don't know."

The chancellor slowly began to suspect that his school friend was starting to fail miserably and could embarrass him on the next occasion when Kohl so desperately needed a coordinator, or, more accurately, a crisis manager. As Klaus Dreher reported, experts felt that "with this sort of drifting, no company in a market economy could survive for any length of time."

The assertion that Kohl had an unerring instinct for choosing suitable people was disproven in this instance, if not for the first time. Schreckenberger continued in office for a while, but was replaced as head of the chancellery in November 1984 by parliamentary manager Wolfgang Schäuble in the first change in cabinet to take place during the first two years of government. Schäuble demanded the title of federal minister for special assignments, which was to clear up any existing confusion about the all-encompassing responsibility of the head of the chancellery.

"Schrecki" held on to the title of state secretary; his responsibilities—the supervision of the secret services and issues of European cooperation—were only pro forma. From then on, Schäuble kept a tight rein on power. Even the head of the intelligence service, Hans-Georg Wieck—formerly ambassador to NATO and to Moscow—refused to talk to Schreckenberger. He wanted to be received personally by the chancellor in the government office. Even in the two years before that, Horst Teltschik knew how to get around "Schrecki" and have reports by department heads, which he as office manager was supposed to see, go directly to Kohl. Within twenty-four hours of assuming his position and taking over his new, massive desk, Schäuble, in his quiet but effective way, put a radical end to the unorthodox procedures that Schreckenberger had made necessary because of his arbitrariness. A new era was launched in the house of Kohl with the advent of the parliamentarian from Baden-Baden, now head of the chancellery and eager to rise further.

Liaison Dangereuse?

Without Juliane Weber practically nothing would function in the Bonn central government office, and the same is true of the chancellor's close staff. Juliane monitors access to her boss; her career has been linked directly with the political one of Helmut Kohl for over three decades, just like that of the wife of a career-minded husband striving for the top. Whoever phones Kohl or wants to see him in person has to pass through the "gateway of her senses."

The relationship between Weber and Kohl will be described in more detail later on. Nine years younger than her boss, Juliane Weber started working with him in 1963 in the parliamentary office of the chairperson of the CDU in the *Landtag* in Rhineland-Palatinate. From then on she followed every step of Kohl's career. Not implying a "*liaison dangereuse*," it can be said that their relationship became far more than the usual boss/assistant one. In more romantic eras than our own, people might have speculated that it was a love relationship—without any untoward thoughts—though an exceptional one. The degree of trust between them has led to rumors, mostly way off course, which "Jule," as she is called by friends, decided to scotch once and for all in a statement to a journalist friend in Bonn: "I'll say it for the last time: I'm not involved with him, except for the way in which you all are. But no one is interested in that." She made this remark with its bitter undertone in the late 1980s during a party put on by the chancellor in the park of the Palais Schaumburg. She meant that she did not deserve to be plagued by suspicions. *Leute*, an illustrated magazine along the lines of some American ones, had published a scandal story, but disappeared soon after the first issue. Juliane and Kohl's wife Hannelore have been good friends since they first met, which ought to place the idea of a "relationship" of any sort between boss and assistant firmly in the realm of the fairy tale.

As wrong as it is to equate other industrial nations' societies to that of Germany, it is equally incorrect to describe the relationship between Helmut Kohl and Juliane Weber as a mundane story about a secretary. Kohl and Weber are like an old married couple who only need to look at each other to understand a situation. They have probably worked several thousand hours together, separated only by an oak door, and their desks are only about ten paces apart. Weber knows from Kohl's walk, body language, and tone of voice what is going on with him. Furthermore, in Bonn, which has never been home to Kohl, she lends an atmosphere of Rhineland-Palatinate, of the familiar, which he could not do without.

This small person, still attractive in her mid-fifties, played a role which should not be underestimated right from the beginning of Kohl's Bonn era. She has been described as having a nature similar to Kohl's. It is probably true to say that both are fighters with a well-developed sense of what is possible and of power. Weber never tries to directly influence her boss, but still is the most influential person among those closest to Kohl. To describe her as "competent," as did the gossip columnist Almut Hauenschild, is a woeful understatement. It is equally incorrect, considering her key position in the reception area of the power center, to say that there is no "up" or "down" for her. Deciding who is valued and welcome "at the court" is for the most part up to Helmut Kohl's powerful assistant and the head of his reception area.

Weber has a quick-thinking and precise mind. "See what needs to be done—and do it," is her motto at work. When this extremely clever person moved from the parliamentary party office to the chancellor's office and was promoted to the position of section head with the salary of a government director, there was an outcry from those people who obviously had no idea what was involved in being the closest colleague of Federal

Benefit ball for the handicapped in Bonn, May 1986. The chancellor and his assistant Juliane Weber.

During a visit to Bonn in April 1984, Teddy Kollek, mayor of Jerusalem, presents Helmut Kohl with a souvenir photo taken during Kohl's trip to Israel in January of the same year.

Chancellor Helmut Kohl. Weber, who has been married since the 1960s to an administrator with German Television Channel Two, is able to happily confine her private life to the weekends, but not all the time. Kohl values her ability to keep confidences and fend off those with too much curiosity with her feminine charm. Her working day is usually over twelve hours long; she stays fit with decaffeinated coffee and a mixture of peppermint and chamomile tea. Illness never keeps her away from the office. She supplies her boss with sweet things when he wants them—though she does not like him to eat them because of his weight—and keeps a large stock on the shelf. His photograph is on her desk, and when he travels they are in touch by phone daily.

Taking Care of the Bonn Landscape

It was Kohl's bad luck that his first year in office was overshadowed by scandals which for the most part were not the fault of the new coalition, but stemmed from the early 1970s. The major one involved party financing and was inextricably linked with the Flick business group, though more than one hundred contributors from industry and commerce supported political parties for decades, and some parties believe they have been kept afloat by such financing.

In the Flick group these machinations sailed close to the winds of legality or went beyond and were referred to as "taking care of the Bonn landscape"—an unsurpassed expression of the arrogance of money. As Helmut Schmidt's eloquent press spokesperson Klaus Bölling once said in a different context, "money makes one impudent." This expression could apply equally to Flick and his helpers' helpers.

Kohl too had already been questioned by a public prosecutor, because Eberhardt von Brauchitsch, a senior Flick company official, had kept accountant-like notes on his various attempts at corruption; among others, there were references to payments "because of Kohl." These actually only meant contributions to the CDU as a party organization; the use of Kohl's name was in this instance a shorthand for the party itself, of which he had been chairperson since 1973. The matter was extremely embarrassing for the incumbent chancellor, especially since *Der Spiegel* published an excerpt of the examination by the public prosecutor. However, the accused did not have to blame himself for anything. "Helmut Kohl's image was not damaged in the long run," Maser wrote correctly. And "what remained for the

Bundestag *president for 20 months: The chancellor and Rainer Barzel in the* Bundestag *plenum a few days before Barzel's resignation as a result of the Flick-contribution affair, October 1984.*

observer who was not directly involved was less the memory of the affair than incontrovertible proof that almost from the beginning, Kohl sat more firmly in the saddle than all other chancellors."

Before the parties—all of them were involved in some way or another except the Greens—could recover from the consequences of the Flick and party-financing affairs for themselves and the *Bundestag*, the Kiessling affair came on top of it, just one year after the start of the Christian Democratic–Liberal coalition. Unlike the party-financing affair, the "Kiessling affair" was home brewed. It stemmed from the most serious mistake ever made by Defense Minister Manfred (Manni) Wörner in his political career. Kohl rejected the malefactor's resignation twice—when the sad affair had just reached its zenith—only because he feared that Wörner's vacating the position at the defense ministry on the Hardthöhe would inadvertently lead to a change in the cabinet. This in turn could mean that Franz Josef Strauss's desire for a ministerial post in the Kohl/Genscher government would be fulfilled, even though Strauss had warned his party friend Zimmermann against taking the job of defense minister as a career move when the cabinet was formed in 1983 ("What do you want with that ejection seat? You'd ruin your whole career."). In the meantime, however, the CSU leader seemed not disinclined to meddle in foreign affairs from the chair of defense minister. Kohl had to prevent that at almost any cost.

In late 1983 or early 1984, Wörner's press spokesperson, Jürgen Reichardt, told a small group of journalists who he had invited to his apartment "in confidence," at first with hints, and then outright, that the seniormost German NATO general, Günther Kiessling, was a homosexual and was, in the view of the defense minister, no longer to be tolerated. High-ranking U.S. authorities had already commented negatively about this officer (in the U.S. Army homosexuality was considered grounds for discharge). Thus the supreme Allied commander in Europe, General Bernard Rogers, had refused to receive his German "colleague," especially since he would have had to "shake his hand," which he should not have had to do. For many weeks and months at the defense ministry on the Hardthöhe, secret notes and files were passed around conspiratorially, which in the end led to the condemnation of the still unsuspecting General Kiessling.

From military toilet graffiti a movement gained momentum which could have had fatal consequences for the government and soon became a crisis echoed in all the media for weeks and months. Wörner, who had been alerted to this internally early on, gave General Kiessling early retirement as of December 31, 1983. A small newspaper item brought this to public attention, and it surprised everyone who had anything to do with the Hardthöhe—and there are a lot of people who do—that there was no military ceremony to mark the occasion. There were inquiries from the media and the reports as to why the general had been forcibly and abruptly retired became more and more confused from hour to hour and day to day. Wörner, who was making all sorts of excuses as to why he had decided to retire him, continued to maintain that he had had to categorize Kiessling as a security risk because of his homosexuality and his susceptibility to blackmail. The matter ended for Wörner, and for the government led by Kohl, as an "unmitigated disaster."[72] Wörner and chancellor office chief Waldemar Schreckenberger received Alexander Ziegler, the prominent editor of a Swiss homosexual illustrated magazine, who was well known to the European gay scene and who was to provide information about Kiessling. Ziegler quickly proved to be a fake and a slanderer who had publicly accused the Austrian ambassador to the Federal Republic, former foreign minister Parr, among others, of homosexuality.

When the chancellor's reputation had really begun to suffer he sprang into action. This was initiated, according to recollection by good sources, by the spokesperson of the CDU/CSU parliamentary party, Hans (Johnny) Klein. When Klein detected that even his CSU friends were beginning to distance themselves from Wörner, he wanted to help his *Fraktion* colleague and close minister friend from the CDU. Backed by higher authority, he offered Kiessling a confrontation with his opponent on the Hardthöhe, to which the trapped general agreed surprisingly quickly. The deal initiated by Kohl was implemented by Paul Mikat, an attorney well chosen for such a delicate mission. It was settled via lawyers that the general should be reinstated in office so that he could be retired with full military honors. Manfred Wörner continued on the Hardthöhe after ruefully admitting "credulity" after questioning a "male prostitute" (*Der Spiegel*). A "Catholic solution," according to government spokesperson Boenisch, was "reward for penitence and good intentions."

The Mood Was Really Bad

It was no accident that in view of the threatened court cases on past unauthorized party funding the chancellor tried in his first year to achieve a general amnesty by a special law with the aid in particular of the parliamentary manager in the *Fraktion*. Unpleasant matters are best taken care of early in a legislative period. At first Kohl had his friend Hans Dietrich Genscher completely on his side; the Liberals too are large beneficiaries of funding from industry and commerce.

At the CDU party conference in Stuttgart in May 1984 Kohl once again pulled out all the stops in his rhetoric: the delegates should know that what was at stake was not just the issues of right and wrong, but also protection after the fact for those who contribute heavily to the parties. It was a matter of "the good reputation of the citizens who give to the democratic parties, also the CDU." For this they had gotten "tax receipts which are recognized by the finance offices." The CDU chief expressly rejected the idea of tax evasion in the planned bill which had not yet been passed by parliament. Kohl "passionately protected" the unsuspecting contributor, of course. Ernst Benda, who had recently left his post as president of the Federal Constitutional Court, and was a former federal minister of the interior, parliamentarian, and legal expert, was of a different opinion. Here too, he showed himself to be a critic of Kohl par excellence, by describing on television the "broad discretion" of the lawmaker in granting an amnesty in terms of the people and the circumstances. Benda then concluded that this should only hold true in exceptional cases: "I consider it completely unacceptable to grant a blanket presumption of innocence to people of a larger or smaller number who are not innocent, but guilty, instead of an individual judgment based on justice and the law."[73]

Logically enough, the coalition had difficulty coping with these bad marks. The CSU member of parliament Erich Riedl called the mood in the coalition "really bad." The press attacked it, which caused the Liberals to waver again. Just before the final attempt at agreement the Free Democrats pulled out of the fairly loose amnesty law, gravely endangering the coalition's cohesiveness. The chancellery openly admitted defeat; Kohl expressed "deep disappointment" to Genscher, Lambsdorff, and Mishnick about the lack of cohesiveness between the coalition parties. Some CDU members of parliament, supported by elements of the CSU, tried to pin the blame on the "evil tactician" Schäuble. Otherwise there was agreement in the coalition that there should be no further disruptions before the upcoming meeting of the federal convention which was to elect the federal president on May 23. The coalition candidate, Richard von Weizsäcker, was elected as expected by an overwhelming majority. The next day the chancellor told the *Bundestag* that the plan to grant amnesty to any tax evaders in the case of party contributions had been dropped and would not be reinstated.

An opinion poll showed that two-thirds of the population were against an amnesty for tax evaders in the party-funding affair, but no one asked whether a deep-seated antiparliamentary feeling was at the root of this. Commentators from the right and the left are seldom in agreement. Robert Leicht wrote in the *Süddeutsche Zeitung* that it was "a breathtaking reversal of the concept of amnesty . . . that the one granting the amnesty was in reality granting it to himself." Friedrich Karl Fromme, who colleagues made fun of as "*Tillman Riemenschreiber*" (Tillman, writer of reams) because of his lengthy columns, wrote in the *Frankfurter Allgemeine Zeitung* in his own inimitable and carefully critical tone that the coalition demonstrated "traits of the uncontrolled, even of misuse." The *Süddeutsche Zeitung*, which thought the issue presaged a "Bonn Watergate," was exaggerating. At most, it was possible to talk about villainy, but because it was never implemented there could not be any comparison with the criminal actions of high officials in the Watergate affair.

State of the Nation

"It is remarkable that in a country with two million horseback riders the term '*aussitzen*,' meaning 'not rising to the trot or posting,' should be applied to a man who never sat on a horse and who would scarcely know the difference between a posting trot and a gallop." Iring Fetscher's guess was actually incorrect, since as a schoolboy Kohl did sit on a horse on the farm in Franconia, and there is even a photo to prove it. But his explanation of the term "sitting trot" is illuminating and probably would be new to the chancellor. "Sitting trot" applies only, Fetscher said, when "a rider sits as tightly as possible in the saddle and allows himself to be carried by the regular movements of the horse, instead of standing up in the stirrups at a trot along with the horse's rhythm." This very carefully thought-out comparison hit the proverbial nail on the head: Kohl, as is widely noted, sits out political problems, firmly in the saddle. Despite all the unpleasantness, the man from the Palatinate could not be seriously shaken from his position at the head of the federal government, at least not then. The economic data were promising, many sectors of industry and commerce were booming, the growth rate satisfied even the greatest skeptics, and the tariff front was surprisingly quiet and balanced. These factors alone can prop up a chancellor in the opinion of the people and even carry him for quite a while. "Helmut Kohl is seated more firmly in the saddle than even his closest friends had expected. The office obviously suits him well. His 'provincial image' at least has faded. . . . At the moment there is no alternative to Kohl," wrote Walter Bajohr in the *Rheinischer Merkur*. The Kohl cabinet had set itself a rigid savings program since assuming power. In the eyes of most Germans, Gerhard Stoltenberg appeared to be a "good house father"—solid, frugal, and cautious—who ensured that there was order in the budget, with no experiments.

Kohl summarized his two years in office since March 1983 in an interview in *Die Zeit*. He had a ready answer for the accusation that he tended to "sit out" problems. "I have been used to the fact for years that people give me certain labels. I have nothing against this, as long as the voters retain their discretion." It is true that Kohl did not know a great deal about the functioning of the economy of such an important industrial country as Germany. Most of the heads of the Bonn industry lobby tend to have pained expressions on their faces when listening to the head of government speaking on relevant issues at meetings at the chancellery. On the other hand, no one in the 1980s had reasonable cause to doubt that the economy was on the upsurge after a decade of slump. Industry obviously had more confidence in the new bourgeois-liberal coalition than in the preceding one under Helmut Schmidt, whom Kohl still enjoyed calling the "world economist."

The chancellor and his party took advantage of the favorable atmosphere in the election campaigns in the various *Landtage* that year. Former CDU chief of public relations Radunski, who had in the meantime risen to being Heiner Geissler's federal manager, had had a look at American electioneering techniques and applied what fit to German campaigns. This consisted mostly of the psychological principle of telling people that they felt good, thus making it true. In crowded auditoriums the chancellor made statements that the people liked to hear, statements which appealed to the emotions but which did not necessarily provoke reflection. "Where is there any other country like this one in which the carol singers of ten to twelve years old have collected eighteen million marks to help stamp out hunger in Africa?" Or, "Whatever the Fatherland must have, it must grow." Whoever thinks that these phrases were from the *Gartenlaube* or worse in terms of thought or speech has never attended such meetings with their worshipful audiences. Such statements were received gratefully by several thousand listeners; it is documented that no one laughed. "'*Heimat*' (homeland) is a German word which cannot be translated. Wherever I am in the world, when someone comes along and says, 'I'm from the Rhineland-Palatinate too,' that's *Heimat* which suddenly appears."[74] The public relations people in the central office of the CDU know what this man considers important: addressing the people "not with the ear, but with the stomach."

In this phase of the internal political scene, one critic who made himself heard from time to time was Richard von Weizsäcker, who even as federal president obviously had not forgotten that he had made his career in the Union by being one of the "fundamental thinkers." "What has become important is clear guidelines for the future, without sugarcoating of the true situation and with the capability for close cooperation. It would be both wrong and unintelligent to offer patent solutions and castles in the air in the hopes of popularity with the people." Whether this criticism of the situation in regard to the public that Weizsäcker leveled at the chancellor from the sterile atmosphere of the Villa Hammerschmidt actually applied was questionable considering the rapidly growing economy. Many people contradicted Weizsäcker's theory directly, others said that the *Freiherr* was incompetent. Aside from having been the lord mayor of Berlin, Weizsäcker had never held public office at the government level, and when he was at Rathaus Schöneberg his senators called him the "*ayatollah*," in reference to his sharp intellect. In any case, no significant practical initiatives were initiated by this Union politician, who some people said was "born to be president."

The Union made an official midterm assessment at the party conference in Essen. This meeting was not a particularly stellar one, but did set some favorable accents in the annals of the CDU. In his speech to the delegates, the federal-level CDU chairperson expressed the "hope" that it had been possible under his chancellorship so far "to create the preconditions for reducing unemployment." Tax reform at the level of twenty million marks would be the highest in the history of the Federal Republic. Kohl sternly warned the social reformers of his own party against "demanding things which now cannot be solidly financed." Kohl was able to claim credit for the increase in the number of apprenticeships which had been made available in the previous few years to the people born during the baby-boom years.

The "black giant" had worries about the economy after 1985, but fate and the slipshod management of his own house held other, more delicate problems for him. These involved a political area which increasingly drew Kohl's attention: German policy and, above all, Germany's relationship with the United States. It was not until spring that Kohl delivered his state-of-the-nation report to the *Bundestag*. He said that despite all the misinterpretations, "the statement in the Warsaw Pact continues to be valid," according to which "the Federal Republic of Germany and Poland do not claim any territory of each other." This might have been very painful to a man like Herbert Hupka, who fiercely defended the aggressive slogan "Silesia is ours" against all critics in Germany and abroad. But the sentence from the state-of-the-nation report is, according to the chancellor's words, "legally and politically clear." As he explained many times during those weeks, this was the basis of the "German question which was in principle still open." People reminded the chancellor and CDU politician later on that he had referred to the preamble of the Basic Law in this context, which was for him "not just any text, but a precondition for German policy." Kohl wanted to repeat this to the GDR leader Erich Honecker when he paid an

Kohl and Gorbachev meet for the first time in Moscow, March 1985, at the funeral of General Secretary Chernenko. The chancellor offers condolences to the newly designated Soviet leader.

official visit to Bonn, which the chancellor wanted, though he met with strong internal party opposition.

Kohl and Honecker met in Moscow in March for two and a half hours when both were attending the funeral of Konstantin Chernenko. Walter Schäuble, head of the chancellor's office, also took part. The meeting occurred at a significant and—as it later turned out—auspicious point: Chernenko was succeeded by Mikhail Gorbachev, whose rise in Soviet politics became the event of the century.

The Bitburg Syndrome

Helmut Kohl's tendency to revel in historical symbolism grew with his term in office. Konrad Adenauer, who he called his role model, increasingly drew his heart and mind for historical things. Kohl had shaken hands with his "friend" François Mitterrand on the battlefields of Verdun as a sign of reconciliation between these two peoples, which had taken on semiofficial status with the German-French friendship treaty signed by Adenauer and Charles de Gaulle in 1963. The high mass in Reims cathedral which sealed the Adenauer–de Gaulle pact was one of those historical events which the chancellor still enthused about in the 1980s. It was the first step in creating understanding between former enemies. Kohl wanted to continue this process and selected the Americans, since there was little else "historical" to do in German-French relations. He believed he could gain fame in other ways, leading him to think of the military cemetery in the small town of Bitburg, in the Eifel mountains. The idea for a screenplay for a drama with declared and involuntary heroes was conceived in the house of Kohl. Often the only thing his partners could do with a decision that was already made was to react.

However, Kohl first had to keep a lot of domestic appointments, because the calendar in the spring of 1985 was dotted with commemorations, most of which brought to mind the unpardonable crimes of the National Socialists. Others applied to the end of the war itself and to the unconditional surrender; the liberation of the concentration camp at Bergen-Belsen became a ceremony of "reconciliation with the victims of the Nazi terror." Kohl's speech was authentic. In this case, to use a typical expression of his, he indeed had no need to "refresh his memory." Even as a youngster he had been active in a Christian-Jewish initiative in Worms whose purpose was reconciliation between the two religions. Even his internal party opponents could be satisfied with what he said at the ceremony of the Central Council of Jews in Germany.

> Reconciliation with the survivors and the descendants of the victims is possible only if we accept our history as it is, if we as Germans recognize, to our shame, and to our responsibility for history. . . . We have—even forty years afterward—a duty to ask ourselves how it could have happened that a culture collapsed to which German Jews in particular had made such an outstanding contribution. Many showed themselves consciously to be German patriots. They were witnesses to the whole world, ambassadors to German and Western thinking. When the evil took over in Germany their rights were taken away and they were driven out. The party officially declared them "subhuman" and they were subjected to the "final solution." . . . We will not permit anything to be falsified and ameliorated. It is exactly the knowledge of this guilty entanglement, of this lack of conscience, also of cowardice and failure, that puts us in a position to recognize the first symptoms of destruction and to resist them, since totalitarianism, which was able to take root in Germany after January 30, 1933, is not an unrepeatable aberration, not an "accident of history."[75]

On a visit to the memorial for the victims of the Holocaust at Yad Vashem, in Jerusalem, Kohl said that he could not forget the words of a Jewish mystic of the early eighteenth century: "Wanting to forget makes exile longer, and the secret of salvation is remembering." At a different place Kohl had once said that the question about how many victims there had been was irrelevant: even if the Nazis had murdered only one Jew they deserved God's punishment. Kohl was not always clear-cut and binding about German-Jewish relations. However, he was a far cry from his CSU party friend Theo Waigel, who had taken over as leader of the *Land* group from Friedrich Zimmermann after the change in 1982. Waigel once made some remarks not intended for publication—which does not detract from their relevance—about the so-called "Auschwitz lie." He uttered the terrible sentence, "We will not change our laws because of a few Jews in the world." This remark was in answer to a question about the CSU *Land* group's attitude toward the critical statements of the World Council of Jews on the still undecided legal issue of the "Auschwitz lie." When Waigel's remark was quoted in *Der Spiegel*, it was repudiated not by the CSU *Land* chief himself, but by his press spokesperson, Ida Aschenbrenner, in a reader's letter to the magazine which did not say anything about the matter itself, but merely stated that the words quoted had never been said. This can be believed or not. Kohl was morally a lot more secure than Theo Waigel, who repeatedly became excited about the fact that "one cannot always confront young people with the past." A positive image of Germany was needed, according to the Bavarian Swabian from the Catholic town of Oberrohr, near Augsburg. The chancellor, who had become much more a master of international affairs, was always cognizant of Konrad Adenauer's idea that maintaining a good relationship with Israel was a "moral duty" of a German politician which required "political reason." Kohl may not have uniformly condemned anyone who did not think as he did, but for the man from Rhineland-Palatinate there are some fixed principles.

One of these was called Konrad Adenauer, and anything "*der Alte*" had done or said was therefore not wrong because he was the first chancellor of the republic. He was thus to an extent Kohl's "ancestor." Kohl was the "grandchild," not in the biological sense, but in a sort of *unio mystica*.

The dates for the highly charged events of 1985 had been arranged a long time in advance, but with some uncertainty. Both Kohl and President Ronald Reagan realized too late that they had trusted their colleagues too blindly. Helmut Kohl found again that this proved the statement by the poet Gottfried Benn that "the opposite of art is not kitsch, but good intentions." And what the chancellor had planned with the embellishment and addition to the world economic summit in Bonn was really "well meant," as even

At the CDU Land *party conference in Oldenburg, April 1985. The original caption read, "Who spit in the chancellor's soup?"*

the SPD opposition leader Hans Jochen Vogel said in parliament. However, the way in which it was done lacked the necessary tact. Kohl had asked Reagan to pay an official visit after the summit, and during the course of that visit to go with him to the military cemetery in Bitburg in a gesture of reconciliation between former enemies for all the world to see.

Horst Teltschik, department head of foreign and security policy in the chancellery, and Michael Deaver, Reagan's chief of staff, were responsible for detailed preparations. Between April 4 and 14, during a stay at his ranch, Reagan noted in his diary:

> . . . the press has had a field day assailing me because I'd accepted Helmut Kohl's invitation to visit a German military cemetery during our visit to Bonn. I had turned down a not-official invite from a West German politician to visit Dachau in his district. All of this was portrayed as being willing to honor former Nazis but trying to forget the Holocaust. Helmut had in mind observing the end of World War II anniversary as the end of hatred and the beginning of friendship and peace that has lasted 40 years. I have repeatedly said we must never forget the Holocaust . . . so it will never happen again. . . . There is no way I'll back down and run for cover. However, Helmut is upset and thinks this may become such an uproar it will color the whole Economic Summit. He may change the program. We'll wait and see. I still think we are right.[76]

The entry in Reagan's diary offers an unusual opportunity to compare the events in Germany with his reaction at the time. Ignoring the Foreign Office and not even informing it afterwards, even briefly, Teltschick discussed the operational details of the visit directly with his American counterpart, Michael Deaver, on the phone. Reagan recorded remarks in his diary about it which were somewhat worried and somewhat encouraging:

> . . . a cable arrived from Helmut Kohl and Mike Deaver took off to Germany. Helmut may very well have solved our problem re the Holocaust. The invite I turned down about a visit to Dachau was a private thing. Helmut is making it official. He'll invite me to visit the camp as well as the cemetery. I can accept both now that it's official.[77]

Starting in the third week in April, the Bitburg drama culminated in press campaigns, calls, and diplomatic contacts at all levels. Mike Deaver talked to Teltschik in the chancellery office and Ambassador Arthur Burns had a meeting for several hours with Chancellor Kohl which started to resemble crisis management. On April 19 Reagan noted:

> A brief signing ceremony opened the day, then we got back to my "Dreyfus" case—the trip to a German cemetery. I told our people . . . there was no way I could back away in the face of the criticism which grows more shrill as the press continues to clamor. Mike Deaver is back and said Kohl was going to phone me. Our ambassador Arthur Burns met several hours with Kohl. Our people want me to suggest a national German war memorial as a substitute for the military cemetery. I said only if it presented no problems for Kohl.[78]

On the same day, Kohl called Washington and informed Reagan that they would visit Bergen-Belsen instead of Dachau, as the president noted in his diary.[79] The shots were called by the man from the Palatinate, and with trust like that of the Nibelungs, the most powerful man in the world acceded to the decision of the head of the Bonn government. Kohl emphasized in his phone call with "Ron," which he called his friend almost lovingly, "that calling off the visit to the cemetery would be a catastrophe at this point and, aside from that, an insult to the German people." Reagan promised that he would not call it off.

Ten days before the Bitburg visit Kohl made a speech before the *Bundestag* on the state of the government, in which he gave a midterm assessment of his performance as chancellor since the spring of 1983. Separately, Kohl discussed the controversial program of the visit during the upcoming world economic summit and the official visit afterward by the U.S. president. Kohl made a point of mentioning his meeting in the fall of 1984 with the French president at Verdun, thus officially drawing the intended parallels between the German-French and German-American reconciliations.

They had shaken hands "over the graves of the First World War" as a token of understanding and peace, and the visit of the U.S. president on the eve of May 8 had also been viewed as a gesture of reconciliation of former enemies. Kohl stated proudly that Reagan would give a "speech to the youth of Germany" during his visit at Schloss Hambach in the Palatinate, which had played a significant role in the nineteenth-century freedom movement.

The opposition tried to adopt a tone of moderation in the debate; they could not help but blame the chancellor in general for the worsening of German-American relations due to obvious mistakes in planning the presidential visit. In his entry for April 29, just before his flight to Germany, Reagan noted optimistically in his diary that there were "a few signs that the Bitburg issue may be turning. . . ."[80]

He Suffered as Seldom Before

Reagan's assumption was proven false, unless the circumstances surrounding the visit are not considered as important as they should actually be. Reporters from *Newsweek* sent a guard at the cemetery to the town hall in Bitburg to get a few black, red, and gold German flags and used them to cover a number of gravestones which were clearly marked with the SS symbol. This perfidious collage was used as a cover photo by the magazine, which, like other American ones, wrote about "Nazi graves." This is naturally a pernicious exaggeration, aside from the fact that the dead had been very young men who had more or less been pressed into service with the SS. *Stern* reported that a French television crew had also placed flowers at undecorated gravestones for filming.

There had been a similar instance of journalistic "documentation" of alleged living Nazi past in Munich in the 1960s. Reporters from *Paris Match* had rented Nazi uniforms from a costume supplier and paid young men to wear them for a regular SS orgy that they staged in the back room of a Bavarian bar. The dreamed-up story was published as an original story by the magazine and naturally damaged German-French relations. In the Paris illustrated magazine and in the Bitburg falsifications, the Germans were confronted with the old resentments about "unreformable" Nazis even when they did not exist. On the other hand, it suited the baldly commercial interests of the CDU *Ratsherr* and managing director of the Bitburg brewery that his beer had already gained notoriety in the United States as "SS beer." As he said, "If that's what makes our beer better known, then we're happy about that."

The chancellor did not take all this with equanimity—the myth has long since been exploded that he does not take press reports seriously. He told *Time* magazine: "I suffered as I seldom had before in these hours, these days." He was referring directly to his relationship with Ronald Reagan, who the man from the Palatinate genuinely regarded as a friend. He was seriously worried that the image of the world economic summit had been damaged in the eyes of the media by the Bitburg incident, and the official visit was viewed almost completely in the light of these unpleasant peripheral circumstances. He praised the American's "very unusual charm" at every opportunity: "We can get along together; we understand each other and are on the same wavelength."

Reagan documented May 5 in the diary he kept on his German visit for his memoirs: "Dawns the day the world has been hearing about for weeks. By 9 A.M. we were on our way to Konrad Adenauer [sic] grave site with the Kohls. Our wives put flowers on the grave. The press had only been given an hour's notice on this. We didn't want them claiming we were doing it to soften the criticism on Bitburg."[81] That had been Kohl's idea, but Reagan had been prepared to go along with it.

Finally, there was a ceremony at Bergen-Belsen:

> This was an emotional experience. We went through the small museum with the enlarged photos of the horrors there. Then we walked past the mounds planted with heather each being a mass grave for 5,000 or more. . . . Here I made a speech I hoped would

Shortly before he met with President Reagan, Helmut Kohl spoke at Bergen-Belsen to commemorate the fortieth anniversary of the liberation of the concentration camp.

May 5, 1985, Helmut and Hannelore Kohl, Ronald and Nancy Reagan, and the minister-president of Lower Saxony, Ernst Albrecht, visit Bergen-Belsen.

> refute the phony charges that had been made. I declared we must *not* forget and we must pledge "never again." Before the day was out there were reports that my talk had been effective.[82]

Bitburg "occurred," as it should be described, in the afternoon, with taps, after which the guests of honor, General Matthew Ridgeway (United States) and General Johannes Steinhoff (Germany) "shook hands in a truly dramatic moment." The faces of Reagan and Kohl show how much the two men were moved, which the American president wanted to note in his diary.

> We went to the cemetery and met General [Matthew] Ridgeway, 91 years old, last surviving top World War II leader in America and Gen. Steinhoff, a German general who had been shot down in flames and whose face had been rebuilt by an American army doctor. . . . Kohl and I and the generals walked through the tiny cemetery . . . the generals placed wreaths. The German "Taps" was played and then in a truly dramatic moment, the two generals clasped hands. . . . My speech was sort of a sequel to the one at Belsen. It was enthusiastically received and our people thought it turned the issue around. I felt very good.[83]

Kohl told American soldiers at the air force base at Bitburg after his visit to the cemetery, "the walk with President Reagan past the soldiers' graves was not an easy one. It must have called to mind many deep-seated emotions. For me it meant a great sadness and dismay at the extreme amount of suffering caused to people by war and a totalitarian regime—sadness and dismay, which will never cease."

Star Wars

For Helmut Kohl, the "great organizer," it was already evident in April or May, and especially in June, that it would be a "summer of discontent." Bitburg, the international economic summit, and the elections in North Rhine–Westphalia were followed by the controversy of Germany's participation in the American Strategic Defense Initiative (SDI) as the hottest German domestic issue. Already forgotten several years later, "Star Wars" became in those months the pretext for an unparalleled war of words. The Reagan administration planned a gigantic project of space-based ballistic missile defense, militarily and financially the most ambitious project in the history of civilization.

Conservatives, foreign-policy makers, and the notorious skeptics—in regard to the Soviet communists and their satellite states—supported German participation in this project for the obvious reason that it would benefit research and industry. Chancellor Kohl pledged Germany's participation on April 18, 1985, before the issue became a bone of contention in the coalition. No one in the Federal Republic of Germany really knows the crux of the matter; the SDI papers which were to form the basis of a technical decision by Germany were kept under lock and key for a whole year. However, at the height of the public debate about the space-based defense program, a German cabinet member leaked the text of the German-American government agreement to the *Express* newspaper in Bonn. The paper, which Eastern and Western intelligence services were chasing in vain, was published in six pages of a special issue. Even now it is not known exactly what it was about; the technological details are still incomprehensible to the layperson. The editor of the *Express*, Friedemann Weckbach-Mara, had the success of his career. On the day after publication, the general federal attorney, Kurt Rebmann, called the editorial office to congratulate Weckbach on his "coup," and at the same time to learn that he—naturally—would not reveal his sources. However, the *Express* had gotten a look at the SDI paper—it had been photographed by a Minox camera—from a government minister, a man in high office. Other than that nothing else is known about the informant. The uproar "at the court" about this unseemly behavior was of course in keeping with its seriousness. The *Bundestag* debated for a whole week about the details of the top-secret paper which could now be read in a newspaper.

Kohl considered this a breach since the American president's visit in the spring of 1985 was imminent: "In my opinion there is not a shadow of a doubt about the decisiveness and moral right of the American president on this issue. The American research program [SDI had been initially presented as such, and only later as a strategic project in easily comprehensible terms] is in our view justifiable, politically necessary, and in the security interests of the West in general. Therefore we in the Federal Republic of Germany support in principle the American program for strategic defense."

Even Heiner Geissler, who had already begun to steer a course contrary to that of his chancellor, supported him on the SDI issue: "Naturally the government will participate. To do anything else would be idiotic. And if no one else in Europe participates, we still will." Peter Radunski, the CDU manager at the government level who had studied U.S. election campaigns, interpreted the spirit of the times which had reached Europe from abroad in glowing terms: "Somehow or other man will transcend the earth. We, the party of the future, want to be a part of this. That is a philosophical and conceptual process."[84]

Newspapers commented or reported that SDI would "bring the apocalypse nearer," was "an unfinanceable project of gigantic proportions of megalomaniacs out to conquer the world," was "completely cut off from reality," and worse. The Russians came into play again, warning by every means possible that the United States was well on its way to someday becoming strategically invulnerable. Critics summarized the German position by saying, "Bonn is isolating itself and becoming a toy of the superpowers." Egon Bahr jibed that it was "the most grotesque dilettantism that had existed since the war." When nothing else did any good, Soviet diplomats and communist central-party members such as Michael Semyanin started threatening, which also accomplished nothing: "If the Federal Republic of Germany wants to take responsibility for SDI, it must also suffer the consequences."

Germany did not suffer the consequences in the end, in part because the Americans started work on the project only half-heartedly due to lack of funding and German industry did not participate. Moreover, given the complexity of technology in this program, the Americans were not inclined to pass on technical know-how in the face of increasing industrial espionage by the Eastern bloc. This also affected the ability of Western nations to develop technology. A few years later, the world had changed completely, but this was something nobody could have predicted in the mid-1980s. "Star Wars" never came to be.

This narrow focus also had a negative effect on German-French relations, in which Kohl had made great strides as chancellor. His predecessor,

Helmut Schmidt, at least recognized this, reminding listeners in his farewell speech to the *Bundestag* about the zeal with which Kohl had pursued this goal. However, it was now this predecessor who was greatly concerned about the supposed decline in relations between Bonn and Paris. Schmidt warned his successor in a letter about any false steps in relations with France as well as with the United States. In Schmidt's opinion, participation in the SDI program was not advisable in terms of alliance politics. The former chancellor, with his good rhetoric and proclivity for hitting the nail on the head, used the expression "of American developments," by which he may have meant that other things should also be taken into consideration which were more general than the SDI project, perhaps Washington's political intentions and other things. Finally, Schmidt wrote: "The Federal Republic can represent Germany's interests successfully only if and to the extent that we have the necessary backing through close relations with France. Should cooperation with Paris stagnate or be reduced to mere lip service, the standing of our government within Europe and in the world will automatically be reduced."

Friendship between Men Put to the Test

"I'll tell you how the next *Bundestag* elections will turn out. The Greens will no longer have seats in the *Bundestag* and my coalition will be just as strong in the elections."[85] Kohl was completely wrong in both predictions that he made to a reporter, since the bourgeois-liberal coalition suffered a noticeable setback in the 1987 election and the Greens entered the *Bundestag* stronger than ever because of it. But it was not only Kohl who was wrong about the Greens. The Social Democrat Peter Glotz, a first-class party and political theoretician who wrote extensively in his books about the future of the republic, was also wrong.

It had already become evident in 1985 that there would be a strong backlash in the coming years. However, Kohl overlooked realities and did himself a disservice by making incorrect assessments of the situation. Naturally he had other problems in those months than the fate of the Greens. There were just as many stirrings in the coalition as in the CDU/CSU. In the middle of the legislative period the middle class began to feel uneasy and even worried about soon losing power. Comparing Kohl to Ludwig Erhard in this situation, however, was not only premature and thoughtless, but was completely wide of the mark in regard to a personality such as Helmut Kohl, even at that time. One of the faults of middle-class rule which cannot be eradicated is that it is difficult to underpin by appealing to solidarity. Criticism of the chancellor, whether veiled and spiteful or open, seemed to never end. Often this was in the form of naming his presumed successors and other political heirs, such as Stoltenberg, Albrecht, and Späth, the latter more and more frequently. "Picking at the person," as Kohl's adviser called it, soon became something he was constantly subjected to, and thus somewhat reduced. However, there was concern in the *Bundestag* parliamentary party that the Union's cohesion was again endangered, as it had been previously in the breakaway attempt at Kreuth, because the relationship between the two Union party leaders, Kohl and Strauss—who were linked in a "friendship between men"—was being put to an even more severe test. If Kohl's government spokesman, Peter Boenisch, is to be believed, the "friendship between Helmut Kohl and Franz Josef Strauss existed only in the wishes of the man from the Palatinate." The Bavarian had never wanted it. Paul Pucher described the situation well when he said, "The unasked-for good advice which Strauss publicly offered his rival is meant as a slap in the face and is understood to be such. The man from Upper Bavaria is concerned only with a different type of politics. Primarily, he wants a different chancellor. He will always want a different one from the one at a given moment. He cannot do anything else."[86]

For this reason the CSU minister stated more or less openly that he intended to resign from the ostensibly unsuccessful cabinet. The guessing game in Bonn began again after a short break: What did Franz Josef Strauss want? His analysis was correct: it was not the economic statistics which had gotten worse, it was the Union parties' election results. For the *n*th time the CSU demanded long-winded, nerve-wracking strategy meetings about how better to coordinate government work and to "sell" its successes better through the press office. Hans Dietrich Genscher, who had in the meantime given up party leadership to Martin Bangemann, was able to express sympathy almost patronizingly for the first time: "I feel sorry for Kohl."

There was another person who suffered under Strauss's attacks on Kohl: Heinz Schwarz, Kohl's long-time political colleague and minister in his Mainz cabinet, and parliamentary party expert on domestic politics. He was piqued by a headline in a popular newspaper and wrote a letter to Strauss about a certain remark regarding the possible break-up of the parliamentary party which drew public attention for days and weeks. Schwarz wrote,

> Dear Dr. Strauss, yesterday someone drew my attention to a headline in the *Bild am Sonntag* saying "Kohl and Strauss: the Chancellor Won on Points." My answer to this headline was, "It is not relevant that one of them won over the other on points; what does matter is that both together beat the Sozis in 1987." . . . I am slowly coming to the opinion that it is more important to you to be right than for the Union

> to win. . . . Your behavior is slowly damaging the Union. I was a proponent of the unity of the Union in the form which had developed traditionally in the Federal Republic after 1945. If you persist in knowing better about everything instead of continuing others, it would be useful . . . to found a CDU *Land* organization in order to allow voters in Bavaria the chance to vote CDU. This would prove whether the hundred percent Union voters in Bavaria really ascribe to your thinking or support the politics of reason, as practiced by Chancellor Helmut Kohl and Finance Minister Dr. Gerhard Stoltenberg.[87]

These were the words of one of the staunchest allies of the man from the Palatinate; on the other hand, they also reflect the loneliness which surrounded him. Not one of his friends in the top party leadership took up the cudgels for him; only a colleague from the old days who no longer had any political ambitions and therefore ran no risk when he publicly went on the offensive against Strauss. The letter soon gained notoriety. A few days before that, Kohl and Strauss were both at a strategy meeting of the CDU and CSU lasting several hours in the chancellor's office, the CSU's intention

Together with Franz Josef Strauss (bottom, partially hidden), Helmut Kohl appeared in May 1986 as the government leader at the traditional Sudeten German Day festivities in Munich.

being to gain greater influence in the government. When Schwarz's letter arrived a few days later, it had already been featured in newspaper reports. The *Neue Revue* named Heinz Schwarz "Man of the Week" because of his "courageous action." Even the *Tagesschau* (the leading television evening news program) reported on it. The cause of the excitement was the concept of a Bavarian CDU *Land* organization.

Strauss did not reply until seven weeks later, and then it was via his department head Christian Hegemer and with his letterhead paper (Dr. h.c. Franz Josef Strauss). Strauss had him answer the CDU member of parliament that he considered the results of the *Landtag* elections in North Rhine–Westphalia to be a "catastrophe" for the CDU affiliate, and that he, Schwarz, was "blind to problems" considering that. That was the way things were with the two sister parties which did not exactly like each other, but who knew that they were linked for better or worse.

In one respect, the usually irrelevant comparison with Erhard might actually have a bearing. Kohl showed weakness, but could not successfully head off a political collapse because as the manager of the coalition his hands were tied. When Interior Minister Friedrich Zimmermann, who was traditionally more on Kohl's side than Strauss's, openly and almost aggressively accused Kohl of "weak leadership" in a program on German Television Channel Two, the accused tried to react to the intended insult with silence, which only made the painful episode even worse. Lothar Späth, perhaps the most serious party rival to Kohl, tried to imagine how he would have reacted to such strong accusations. "If a reporter had asked me as chancellor how I would have reacted to such an action [by Zimmermann], I would have said, 'I was not yet sitting at my desk, but Zimmermann's resignation will certainly be lying on it.'"

At the same time Späth, like Kohl himself in such a case, would have risked the CSU minister's leaving the cabinet.

Stern and *Der Spiegel* started writing prematurely about the threatened demise of the chancellor. The *Süddeutsche Zeitung* appeasingly headlined a feature on Kohl's mistakes with "Reviving Blows to the Neck." The issue in these months was not at all just about Kohl's position as head of the federal government; there were also heated disputes in the parliamentary party about the way forward in German domestic and foreign policy. The contenders were the so-called "steel-helmet group" and the "Genscherites," the latter referring to a group of CDU members of parliament who supposedly adhered too closely to the course proposed by the FDP and its foreign minister.

Deputy parliamentary party leader Volker Rühe was an adherent of the "Genscherites." The CSU had decided to make him their internal party rival, particularly because he had coined the phrase "binding effect" in regard to the Oder-Neisse border and staunchly defended it, to the annoyance of the Bavarians. The "steel-helmet group" was led by parliamentary party leader Alfred Dregger and the *Vertriebenenpolitiker* (politicians of the expellees) Hupka and Czaja. Kohl left little doubt in his public speeches as to which group he belonged to, without referring to them by their official names: "We, the Federal Republic of Germany and the People's Republic of Poland, have no territorial claims against each other now and in the future. I call upon Poland not to interpret these clear statements as a proviso to block any peace treaty made by a united Germany." Kohl avoided using the term "binding effect" in order to avoid annoying the CSU unnecessarily. However, he was on the side of Rühe, whose "great talent" the CDU chairperson had already spotted in the late 1970s. Although no one spoke openly about it, Kohl had confided to friends that he viewed the competent man from the Hanseatic city as a possible ("sometime later") successor.

The constant theme of "How do I best sell my 'really unusually good' (to quote Kohl) policy?" became an acute issue again in the summer, after Peter Boenisch was forced to leave his position in the press office due to accusations of tax evasion. The high-spirited former editor in chief of *Bild* had been an asset for the bourgeois-liberal coalition and many journalists, even some of those who were not close to the government, felt that his departure had been a loss. He was replaced by Friedhelm von Ost, a successful journalist with German Television Channel Two, who had moderated the economics program "WiSo" in a popular fashion. Ost was not as outgoing as his predecessor, but was competent and cleverly protected his chancellor against "insinuations," "speculations," and assertions in dry Westphalian manner. Kohl still had not reached the nadir of the season: 1986 still held many tests of his strength. The closer it came to the end of the legislative period, the more inflamed and tense the internal conflicts became in the coalition and CDU/CSU parliamentary party.

Is Kohl a Handicap?

Optimism was the trump suit again. The majority of German citizens regarded 1986 positively. It was difficult to say whether this was the result of the successful "optimism campaign" by the Bonn coalition, as *Der Spiegel* contended. At any rate, fifty-six percent of those polled by Infas answered positively the question, "Do you believe that the next ten years in the Federal Republic will be secure?" This "yes" could not have been imposed by whispers from the government press office. Economic indicators also led to optimism, and—surprise, surprise—the new government spokesperson, Friedhelm Ost, who was well versed in economic statistics as a professional journalist, turned the new optimism to the advantage of the dented image of the coalition. The chancellor himself referred to the "economic upswing" in his New Year speech: "Hopelessness and pessimism have been defeated. Hope and optimism are to be found everywhere."

The next *Bundestag* elections would occur in just over twelve months, and time was of the essence. The laurel wreaths doled out ahead of time were already wilted and new green was needed all over. Heiner Geissler, the CDU general secretary, who normally led the party in such a way that the chairman was superfluous, wrote a letter to the 251 chairmen of the CDU county organizations extolling the economic-political successes of the coalition and the new optimism of the citizens. Since there were no favorable data to be reported about the chancellor himself—more the opposite—Geissler did not even mention his name in the six-page letter to the Union party functionaries. Renewed public-opinion polls about the chancellor showed him to be sometimes in a better, sometimes in a worse, position than his challenger, the Social Democratic minister-president of North Rhine–Westphalia, Johnnes Rau. This confirmed the fears of the CDU central office that an election could be won by Kohl only by a tiny margin, if at all. "No chancellor before him had had to put up with such a lack of political support," wrote Rüdiger Altmann, a former advisor of Ludwig Erhard, advocating that Kohl give up his office. Rau's campaign manager, Bodo Hombach, rejoiced that "Helmut Kohl is a handicap for the CDU," saying that that was a real advantage for the candidacy of "Father Johannes," as the SPD was wont to half-jokingly, half-lovingly, call its "father of the *Land*."

Nevertheless, Kohl had done almost everything that he had to do after taking over as chancellor, even in the eyes of his critics: with equanimity Kohl had regained control over "foreign and security policy which had been in the grip of demonstrations." The coalition had beaten the depression under his leadership, propped up of course by the favorable U.S. economic climate. Germany's debt had been reduced by stringent savings. The one person who had profited from all this was not Helmut Kohl, the helmsman of the ship of state, but Finance Minister Gerhard Stoltenberg. More than once the "cool blond from the far north" let his ambitions for the highest office be known, more quietly than openly. But whenever the media called him a possible successor to the chancellor, Stoltenberg, embarrassed, had these rumors categorically denied, as if he had been caught in wrongdoing.

Even in late summer there were speculations about Kohl's role in the party and coalition: "The only thing left to the Union is to change chancellors," Altmeier wrote. Naturally the experienced journalist and political adviser was right when he stated that many people (in the Union) were talking about a supposedly inevitable "regicide," though if only in whispers. But neither did Kohl's rivals come up with any convincing suggestions for a change at the top.

Kohl had only one real option in this tight situation: to breathe some new life into the cabinet through new ministerial appointments. He knew that this was nothing more than a diversion, but it was something. The chancellor appointed his trusted friend Walter Wallmann to the new post of environmental minister, but with only limited powers. He also greatly expanded the role of Rita Süssmuth on women's issues in the cabinet. These appointments demonstrated the chancellor's ability to act, even in the face of surprises, completely disproving the frequently made assertion that Kohl is incapable of decision making or is an inveterate procrastinator. The list of his decisions during only four years as chancellor—even if they were disputed or controversial—is really fairly long. It includes the intermediate-range missile decision, budget reductions, discernible cuts in the social security system, significant environmental progress, opening borders within the European Community, defeating attempts by the Socialist Unity Party of the GDR to have the "two nations" of Germany recognized as the status quo, and extending conscription and alternative service. The chancellor had protected some of his ministers in times of difficulty, even when he had been advised to dismiss one or the other of them. Kohl truly did not shirk decision making, though he did surprise friends and opponents alike with tactical dodges which bucked trends in popular opinion.

Only After Political Power?

"Politics is only a question of character," Kohl often told his colleagues. They were supposed to subscribe to this motto and act on it. The widespread political-moral change in Germany had hardly gained Kohl any new friends—more the opposite. The media used this phrase to remind Helmut Kohl at every possible opportunity of the yardsticks by which he wished to measure himself and others. What sort of morality does Kohl have, Dirk Koch of *Der Spiegel* asked, if he could relativize a statement by the CSU member of parliament Hermann Fellner about alleged Jewish characteristics? During an evening party for journalists with cold cuts from Rhineland Palatinate, wine, and beer he speculated vaguely—perhaps intentionally—that Fellner had echoed the sentiments of the majority of people in the republic.

The Christian Democrat had said in regard to restitution for enforced laborers in the Third Reich that "the Jews were quick in coming forward whenever they spotted gold in German coffers," an extremely stupid and nasty comment. The matter became a temporary public embarrassment to the chancellor when sharp journalists noted that he did not clearly contradict the back-bencher. Fellner was a complete idiot, a lot of people knew that, and that could scarcely have escaped the keenly observing Kohl. But should he end up in a fight with the sister party because of it? Fellner's unfortunate remark was obviously not a "one-shot"; he was already well known for his singular behavior. The Israeli ambassador, Itzak Ben-Ari, when questioned about the incident, produced a letter from 1979 which associated the parliamentarian with the same ideas.

What did Kohl have to do with this? Could the incident have been brought to a close perhaps if the Austrian journalist Werner A. Perger had not grimly persisted, to his amusement, in making Kohl explain the background to the embarrassing misunderstanding about anti-Semitism or the lack of it. Kohl's many critics in the media ensured that it became a political issue. It also touched on the position of his rival Strauss, who was quoted as saying, "The worst thing about Fellner's remarks was not the *lapsus linguae*, and not the psychological misinterpretation, but the fact that more people were proven right than was evident to outsiders." That could only have been speculation, because the Bavarian himself meant "that is was not obvious to outsiders." Other statements could be quoted here which made speculation superfluous.

The "new impudence" also became evident, along with many other instances, in the thoughtless comment by the CDU mayor, Wilderich Freiherr von Mirbach Graf von Spee, during the budget debates of his Lower Rhine community of Korschenbroich: "Several rich Jews would have to be killed in order to balance the 1986 budget." Around the same time, the newsletter of the *Junge Union* in Nürtingen referred to the "arrogance of Israel to make our democratic nation responsible for murdering the Jews in the Third Reich." The article ended with an appeal: "Let's stop all this complexity, I say! Let us be true to ourselves again."[88] That sentiment is not typical for CDU publications or members. But the fact that by the mid-1980s there was this frequency in such racist and anti-Semitic verbal aberrations seems to be sufficient proof that virulent radical-right tendencies did not just start with the reunification of Germany. It would be wrong and factually incorrect to make Kohl responsible, considering the sources of such impudent comments. But Kohl did make it too easy for himself with the oversimplification that these statements were not anti-Semitism, and his attempt at the same time to get the Federal Republic to pay restitution to Israel lacked a certain amount of sensitivity.

"Keep a lower profile," seemed to be Kohl's motto in cases when peripheral political figures drew attention to themselves for undesirable behavior, disturbing—God punish them!—the chancellor's circle. That is how the problem was approached by the man from the Palatinate, who was legitimately concerned about keeping his power. His attitude sometimes made others bitter: don't look too closely, otherwise it could be unbearable. A spirited woman in Kohl's life told him what she thought: Helga von Brauchitsch wrote a letter to him after members of the security forces put the suspicion in the public mind that her husband, Eberhard von Brauchitsch, could be considered an "Eastern influence agent" because of his machinations in the Flick group. "How is it possible that, behind the back of a man whose talents and energy you often called upon for the good of the public and the state, suspicions could be raised that he was an agent of a foreign intelligence service? You must allow me to say that for my part I am suspicious that in all this your only concern was political power, and that you have not respected the constitution of our republic and its Basic Law to the degree expected of you."

The Chancellor Has a "Blackout"

Yes, the chancellor was concerned with power: how else should it be? And to hold onto this power was not always easy. Kohl was now fifty-six years old and had gained a lot of weight, his hair was thinning and streaked with gray, and the lines in his forehead were more deeply etched than ever. He was not able to be at his peak every day, with the pressures of work in the office, foreign trips, and appearances in parliament. But above all, there were the numerous phone calls to keep colleagues in the government center and at the party management office moving in the right direction. All this was too much for one person.

Alarm bells rang on every floor and in every office of the widely spread CDU personnel in the chancellor's office and party central office when the media reported that a preliminary investigation had been launched against the chancellor on suspicion of making a false statement to the Mainz committee on party contributions. This had not occurred, despite Flick and the amnesty law, Brauchitsch's secret contributions list, and Lambsdorff's resignation as a result of the ensuing legal proceedings. The CDU general secretary tried to "explain" the reports with a desperate and helpless reference to a "possible blackout" of the chancellor during that ominous hearing of witnesses before the end of the year in the capital of the Rhineland-Palatinate. Otto Schily, a prominent member of the Greens, a forensically trained trial lawyer, and the self-appointed public representative of the prosecution, could only laugh gently. At the time, Kohl had been asked whether he knew that the Citizens Organization in Koblenz had served as an agency for procuring money and contributions; he answered with a clear-cut and obviously incorrect "no." Geissler made the matter worse by attempting to explain the matter in a television discussion with Schily. At that time he was especially garrulous, nervous, and ready to protest, and he lacked concentration. "The chancellor," Geissler tried to explain in sweeping terms, "had answered 'no' to a complicated and imprecise question" and later corrected it. Such a blackout "was possible during such a long hearing." The chancellor had a "blackout"? Was this just one instance, or could it happen more frequently? Geissler was confronted with a lot of uncomfortable questions. One person did not ask first, but reacted, authorized by Kohl himself, with a sharp comment for the CDU general secretary: "Total nonsense," said the head of the chancellor's office, Walter Schäuble, about the "blackout" explanation. Kohl's "no" had occurred at the beginning of the hearings

With the head of the chancellery, Wolfgang Schäuble, at a cabinet meeting in November 1986.

by the Mainz investigation committee, because the committee chairman had lumped several questions together and given them one value. That's how it had happened—obviously erroneously. Schily picked up on the second attempt at an explanation for the "blackout no," by considering "a possible further denunciation" because a money-laundering apparatus implied the "evidence of aiding tax evasion."

According to *Duden's*, a blackout is "a short-term loss of memory," and this is what Geissler meant. This dictionary also has another definition which was even more relevant to the incident: "a smaller sketch which ends with a sharp point and sudden darkness." The CDU was in an uproar for weeks over the "blackout" statement. At any other time party officials would have long since hammered out detailed plans for an effective election campaign which could have brought the already dented Union, and along with it the coalition, back up to snuff, thereby preventing a disastrous vote in January 1987. Gerhard Stoltenberg, the *Land* chairman of Kiel, and possibly Kohl's most serious rival for the top post, was generally very restrained, but this time he threw all caution to the winds. At an informal meeting with journalists in the beer cellar of the *Land* representation of Schleswig-Holstein, Stoltenberg said, "It's really very, very serious."[89] Other top CDU leaders also began to distance themselves from Kohl, or attempted to give explanations about the possible actions of the "old aunt CDU" in such crises as this one. For instance, Hans Katzer, once the powerful chairperson of the CDU social committees and minister for labor and social affairs in the Great Coalition of 1966–69, with his Rhenish quick way with words and cleverness, warned his friends that "in the party the comfort and patience come to an end when the first parliamentarians say, 'We've done worse at the polls because of this incident.'"

Helmut Kohl, who had been publicly subjected in these weeks and months to almost nothing but hatred and spite, acted more naively than he should have in the controversy about the party contributions. Thus the chancellor, pressured on all fronts, attempted on a television program moderated by Reinhard Appel, who was predisposed to him, to depict his encirclement by the media, with its vehement attacks against him increasing daily as a preliminary to the election campaign of 1986–87. He called it "the beginning of an unparalleled mud-slinging campaign." The man who should have known his Machiavelli backward and forward (Kohl had read him as a student) lost his temper almost like a schoolboy in front of such experienced journalists as Theo Sommer. It was power that was at stake; what else? Kohl's opponents thought that they had finally cornered the hated man from the Palatinate after having pursued him so long. A chancellor in front of a court? He'd really have to give it up. The opposition and its media contacts were not interested primarily in getting to the bottom of the confusion about party contributions. (Had they been, they would have had an enormous swamp of their own to drain during the 1970s.) The only witness who could have been cross-examined as a representative for the Social Democrats and who could have given factual answers was Treasurer Alfred Nau, and he was dead. The natural end of the person responsible had put a stop to the legal side of the spending issue for the opposition.

Kohl fought because he was determined to survive politically. The chancellor presented the situation initially in such a way that "a magazine" (*Der Spiegel*) made accusations against him which had not yet been noted in the courts: "I am being asked by millions of the German public about an incident in which one person [Schily] has made an accusation which puts the authorities on the spot, and I have yet to have an opportunity to make a statement about it. I don't know what has been said in detail which is provable. I know about it . . . only through newspaper reports."

Der Spiegel planted the suspicion that Kohl "could not exactly remember" certain events because he wanted to cover up the discreet role which his confidante Juliane Weber had played in this. He was not supposed to have been able to know that his close friend Eberhard von Brauchitsch was able to reveal something about Juliane Weber to the Bonn *Land* court in December 1985: "She had already received money for Mr. Kohl in the past." Kohl himself told the parliamentary investigation committee that he had received such party contributions "mostly in cash personally from von Brauchitsch." Schily, who viewed this case as a good way to promote himself and used it extensively as such, made the insinuation that Kohl's suppression of the complicity of his colleague Juliane Weber in the party contribution affair leads to the conclusion that it was premeditated. Only Schily himself knew what that sort of legal stratagem was supposed to achieve. His sole vote on the final report of the Flick investigatory committee comprised three hundred pages. Protests by the coalition resulted in the fact that Schily's accusation of Kohl was not mentioned in the text. The chairperson of the committee, Manfred Langner (CDU), reported categorically, though completely impartially, that the opinion of the majority of the committee held that Schily's sole vote "could not be harmonized" to a large extent with the investigatory committee's task in the Flick affair. Moreover, the reproduction of a criminal declaration in a parliamentary judgment was "inadmissible," since a possible court action against the accused was exclusively the domain of the prosecution authorities.

Is Germany to Continue on This Course?

The year 1986 showed Kohl continuing to walk through a vale of tears in the wake of the Flick affair and created a new Heiner Geissler, the CDU general secretary. Kohl had to be on his toes, since his "general" was well on his way to severing relations with his boss after ten years in office in order to go his own way and pursue his own politics. That could have become dangerous, as Geissler's unhappy attempt at explaining the chancellor's "blackout" demonstrated. After the Flick affair, Kohl began thinking ahead about replacing Geissler in three years. The general secretary, who was appointed for four years at the recommendation of the party chairperson (who served for only two years), had been confirmed in office for only one year. Party statutes deem that the general secretary cannot be dismissed during his term of office and may leave only at his own wish. Just before a general federal election this could be a catastrophe, and Geissler had no intention of retiring. Kohl, on the other hand, already had every intention of getting rid of him at the next opportunity. Geissler was an increasing encumbrance and was far too wont to act on his own accord, expressing views publicly about things which were no concern of his. Kohl was not the only one in the party with this opinion, although the circle Geissler had assembled was very presentable. Party cohesion had loosened noticeably in the past few years, and political research showed a significant growth in voters who switched party allegiance. This had the effect in the parties themselves of greater openness and flexibility in self-presentation and of changes in social aims.

In Kohl's view, Heiner Geissler's independence in programmatic thinking was shown by his turning away from general politics. The next party conference in Mainz demonstrated that Geissler was much too smart to "throw the baby out with the bath water," as the expression goes. He was well aware that, especially in a crisis year such as 1986, the chancellor would want quiet on the political front more than ever. But the increasingly strong suspicions about the "leftist tendencies" of Geissler's party apparatus, which started to turn into an emancipation movement, began to poison the atmosphere between the CDU and the Bavarian affiliate to an extent which had been hitherto unknown between the government wing and the party center. In the meantime the feeling had come over the CDU of being a party once used to power that had returned after a long absence. At the top of the party, Alfred Dregger termed himself "the chancellor's top colleague," which caused amazement or complete lack of understanding among the department and section heads. "The party has a completely different job than that of the government, even when its people are leading it," said his press spokesperson Jürgen Merschmeier. The same was true for the parliamentary party in the *Bundestag*, it was contended, which drafts laws and should not just applaud the decisions of the government without criticism. The party central organization, which was represented for the most part by politically independent thinkers such as Geissler himself, Peter Radunski, Wilhelm Staudacher, Ulf Fink, Warnfried Dettling, and Wulf Schönbohm, threatened to slip from Kohl's day-to-day control. The chairman was able to "set up a type of spy network" via confidential phone calls to obtain detailed information about the actions of his colleagues who were now on Geissler's side. This was not done to subordinate them; the CDU strategists who were after their own advantage were smart enough to know that once again it was necessary to "really promote" the party chairperson and federal chancellor at the congress in Mainz in October in order to create the "right" preconditions for the *Bundestag* elections on January 25, 1987. With careful preparation and almost perfect management of the party conference, Geissler achieved this in the city of Kohl's former residence in Rhineland-Palatinate. For a brief moment it looked as if peace prevailed once again in the party. Geissler, the talented "lateral thinker," blew the impending decision on the future manifesto into a rhetorically pleasing hot-air balloon, which at least managed to encourage for a while those delegates whom Kohl had disappointed.

> Our great task is securing the future of the Federal Republic of Germany. Aside from coal, Germany is a country with practically no raw materials. Our capital is based on industriousness, the willingness to work, the inventiveness of our fellow men and women, the employee as well as the employer. In future, too, we must be able to sell our high-technology products on the international market in competition with Japan, the United States, and newly emerging industrial countries. In a word: Germany must continue to be first class; we must not become second or even third class. "Made in Germany" must be a sign of quality of the German industry in the future.

The protocol noted applause forty-seven times, applause lasting a long time, laughter, or both together. Geissler's speech carried the plenum along, primarily due to its pointed comments, as well as some well-aimed malicious shots at the "valued opposition and its voting opportunism." The chancellor and the imminent *Bundestag* were placed in the middle again and again, which corresponded to traditional CDU ritual. It was present as the chancellor's party and, many thought, as the chancellor's "voting organization," and would remain so for the foreseeable future. Tribute had to be paid to this situation, which was not lost on Geissler, the experienced party man: "Our fate depends on which powers determine the future of this country—and for this reason the *Bundestag* elections are of great importance. It is clear: in view of the profound changes and the far-reaching social and political processes which must be shaped, these *Bundestag* elections will determine the future of our land. For this reason we are right in saying that it is also a vote on our course. I have nothing against saying that it is a fateful vote. . . . I would say that it is a vote on our direction with fateful significance." The speaker flattered Kohl, although he was becoming increasingly aware that he was secretly starting to write him off: "I believe we are not exaggerating when we say that we are better off today than we were four years ago. The Germans are stronger than they were four years ago. In a word: the Germans are a great people when they have the right political leadership." Kohl wanted to hear that, and he appeared to be grateful once again to Geissler, who he smiled at from the podium, for these sentences uttered for party political reasons. Geissler concluded by saying: "Carry on like this, Germany; like this, Helmut Kohl; like this, Christian Democratic Union!"

The coalition was confirmed once again at the *Bundestag* elections on January 25, 1987, with over fifty-three percent of the vote. The Union parties, of course, had a noticeable loss, their percentage of votes having sunk to 44.3 percent, representing a drop of 4.5 percent compared to 1983. The chancellor rightly considered the government majority to be still comfortable, since the Free Democrats had made slight gains, which made him, the declared friend of the bourgeois-liberal coalition, view it "with deep satisfaction."

We Would Welcome Honecker

"We would welcome Honecker." Kohl stated the invitation in this way for the first time on August 31, 1984, at a government press conference. On almost the same day, three years later, the SED general secretary paid a visit to the Federal Republic of Germany which had been prepared a long time in advance. The invitation to the head of state from East Berlin had been made during the term of office of Kohl's predecessor, Helmut Schmidt. The new coalition had postponed it many times, as one would neglect to resubmit an uncomfortable file for review, in the vague hope that it would take care of itself.

But that was not Kohl's intention. Basically he hated things which seem never to come to a conclusion. Instinctively he knew that the relationship between the Federal Republic of Germany and the German Democratic Republic was becoming a problem that he would definitely have to master. The number of visitors between the two countries had shot up dramatically.

Never before had Germans on both sides of the Wall and the barbed wire seen so much of each other and for so long. This also increased the knowledge that the people had of each other; more and more West Germans were becoming aware of the dissatisfaction of the people in the GDR. The relatively easily obtained visitor's permits in the divided country were gradually creating a movement which culminated in the "peaceful revolution." In the beginning, Bonn treated the phenomenon of the large numbers of visitors as a matter to be documented in each report on the state of the nation. The federal government presented this as evidence of the "success of its policies," even though as the heir to the socialist-liberal coalition it had taken over German policy in almost unchanged form. The SPD could not do anything other than emphasize "the high degree of continuity in the political decisions regarding Germany by the Kohl/Genscher coalition," according to Egon Franke. The chancellor's position, like that of his predecessor, was not especially clear, but was pragmatic.

> The leaders of the GDR know that we are bound by principles stemming from the constitution and the Federal Constitutional Court. These we cannot and will not place at anyone's disposition. The leaders of the GDR know, however, that we are always willing to meet with them and look for solutions to practical problems. I am convinced that the differences of opinion in fundamental issues do not need to be a barrier to increased cooperation and to allowing the people in divided Germany to see each other more often.[90]

Policy on Germany as a type of government concessionary togetherness? Fifteen years before that, Salvador de Madariaga wrote about the "basic agreement" between the Federal Republic and the GDR that no more progress had been made except agreement on a "general visitor's permit in the state prison." The differences of opinion refer primarily to Honecker's demands for recognition of two separate states in Germany and for GDR citizenship. No one in the Union seriously considered tackling this. Nevertheless, Honecker's visit drew attention to a wing of the party which wanted to strike the precept of reunification from the CDU's program. Even in 1994, Rainer Barzel, Kohl's predecessor as party chairperson, accused the man from the Palatinate of "having gone along with this disgusting situation."[91] In an unpublished manuscript, Kohl sidestepped a binding answer to the question of whether the precept of reunification should no longer be in the party program, which was a hot issue at the time.

> It cannot be expressed like that. In essence, the crux of the matter was whether European integration policy should have precedence over German reunification policy. My position was clear: there is no

> contradiction there, both were equally important to our understanding of ourselves as the CDU. Name me one CDU politician, who, like Jürgen Schmude of the SPD, had demanded that the precept of reunification should be stricken from the preamble of the Basic Law. I do not know any.

Kohl's dialectics, which tend toward a decisive "not only, . . . but also," committed him to answer unasked questions. For this reason he could easily answer the question of whether there were Union politicians who wanted to see the reunification precept stricken from the party program with the sentence which did not apply, that the preamble of the Basic Law was sacred.

This notwithstanding, developments moved apace and Bonn saw itself more and more in the role of at least having to react, even if it did not want to act. Horst Sindermann, the president of the East Berlin sham parliament which called itself the "*Volkskammer*"(People's Parliament), had journeyed to the Rhein at the behest of his top boss, Erich Honecker, in order to meet with real parliamentarians and prepare for the general secretary's visit. Sindermann, a friendly man with dark-rimmed glasses and silver-gray hair, was the number three person in the apparatus of the "Workers' and Peasants' State," courteous in manner and precise in speech. Members of the SPD were more inclined to open up to the emissary from the GDR than were the middle-class politicians. They spoke agreeably about "Mr. President" and gave the old communist from Dresden an almost cordial reception. Official protocol allowed the guest only three instead of the usual five motorcycle escorts, exactly as the chancellor's office wanted.

The intent was that all top officials of the GDR were to be respected not "as" president or minister-president or whatever function, but in each case as analagous to, that is, "*like* a president," etc., a fine distinction which would escape notice. The main thing was that no one in the chancellor's office gave away anything. Relationships, even in private meetings, were documented; no opportunity was to be given for any long-term consequences, such as a boost to the prestige of the GDR communists.

Bundestag president Jenninger received Sindermann politely, but put on a serious expression whenever photographers turned the cameras on him. The chancellor met for over two hours with Sindermann, who was undoubtedly the most approachable of the SED leadership, and therefore almost cut out for the delicate mission. The *Volkskammer* president was able to speak gently to his hosts, who were even more tense about the formalities of the visit: "We Germans must learn how to live together. We have a lot to catch up on." Meetings between SED functionaries and government and parliamentary representatives did not achieve much. However, they demonstrated that meetings between officials on both sides of the German demarcation line did not necessarily have to get bogged down in mutual accusations of guilt. Naturally the SPD got above itself when its member of parliament, Rudi Walther, said during a walk around the Bundeshaus that Mr. Sindermann had given the man from Rhineland-Palatinate a two-hour-long coaching session in policies on Germany. To which *Der Spiegel* quoted Hans Dietrich Genscher as saying, "You shouldn't take that so seriously: the interpreter took up an hour."

In the CDU/CSU parliamentary party, once decidedly anticommunist, fewer and fewer opposed Honecker's planned visit. However, members of parliament Manfred Abelein, Jürgen Todenhöfer, and even Rainer Barzel and some of his friends quietly expressed doubts about the logic of an official visit by the SED leader, who only wanted to improve his international image. Honecker might regard a visit to Bonn as the crowning glory of his career, but he would bring no discernible advantage to democracy in the Federal Republic of Germany. That was the gist of statements by parliamentary party leader Alfred Dregger, who refrained, however, from making more pointed comments.

Many of those privately or publicly opposed to Honecker's visit feared that it could possibly mark the end of efforts toward reunification. It is perhaps significant that it was a little-known delegate who set in motion a discussion of the German question which parliamentarians and the public had been wanting for years. This was sparked by Bernard Friedemann, a "back-bencher," as it was termed in Bonn, a stubborn and punctilious person when it came to things that moved him emotionally and intellectually. In the late 1980s he moved from the *Bundestag* to become chairperson of the European financial oversight authority. He made reference to the connection between disarmament and policy on Germany for the first time at a meeting of the CDU/CSU parliamentary group on November 4, 1986. This was triggered by a report by the chancellor on his recent meeting with U.S. president Reagan, who had informed the German leader about his disarmament talks with Soviet general secretary Gorbachev in Reykjavik. Friedmann, who not only the chancellor considered fairly naive, had spectacularly drawn attention to himself and his ideas in a "position paper" on the German question. Kohl was even more annoyed about this, since he had declared policy on Germany to be a "matter for the chief." Thus he stated canonically once again to the Union parliamentarians that although the German question was still open, "its solution was not yet on the agenda of world history." Friedmann retorted that he had at his disposal "indications that Moscow was thinking about a possible German reunification." Those present at the session reported that Kohl shouted at the back-bencher that he should stop making such wild speculations, which were "complete nonsense."

The chancellor's violent reaction froze the parliamentary party into inaction, robbing the speaker of effect. But Friedmann was soon cast in the role of the lonely knight. About one year after that there was a real confrontation, when Kohl was questioned about Friedmann's theses at the forty-ninth Franco-German meeting in France. After that the chancellor exploded on television and referred to it as "absolute nonsense." This outburst is not easy to understand, because only a few weeks later he himself said in a report on the state of the nation, in much the same terms as his denigrated party colleague, "German and security policies cannot be separated." The fact that Friedmann inadvertently ended up being a visionary with his stubborn insistence on this point which was supposedly not "on the agenda of world history," became known only in 1991 with the publication of the memoirs of Eduard Shevardnadze, the former Soviet foreign minister.

In the seventh chapter Shevardnadze writes:

> "When did you come to the conclusion that German reunification was unavoidable?" Hans Dietrich Genscher asked me. The meeting took place in my apartment in Moscow after my resignation. Not being bound by any government or political restrictions, I was able to say to him completely openly, due to the fact that all agreements had been ratified, "As early as 1986. At that time, in a meeting with one of our leading experts on Germany, I said that I suspected that this problem would come up soon. At that time, I said that the German question would very soon become one of the key issues for Europe. For more than half a century, with a people divided, this had been a national question. A question of the unity of a nation which did not want to be separated by the walls of ideology, weapons, and steel and concrete."[92]

Several sentences after that, Shevardnadze came to some conclusions which the CDU back-bencher Friedmann was trying to get his chancellor to accept at the very same time: "The existence of two German states at the heart of our continent had become an anomaly under the current circumstances, which was a serious threat to the security of Europe. It was a matter of thinking about how best to avoid a dangerous and unruly situation with political means." At that time, the former Soviet foreign minister continued, it would have been impossible to openly express such a view. Obviously, it was just as impossible—under completely different conditions—for the German member of parliament.

Mr. Gorbachev, Tear Down This Wall!

Looking back to 1985, Soviet president Mikhail Gorbachev viewed the developments much more coolly than his prophetic friend and foreign minister, Eduard Shevardnadze. "Of course Moscow viewed the German question differently in 1985 from the way it does now. The GDR was our ally. The Federal Republic, though our number-one trade partner in the West, was considered a potential enemy."

In the summer of 1987, Ronald Reagan again visited the Federal Republic and in a dramatic gesture at the end of a speech at the Brandenburg Gate, he called to mind the former actor: "Mr. Gorbachev, tear down this wall!" Pictures of Reagan and Helmut Kohl at this historic spot were published all around the world. Reagan uttered these words having no idea that his vision would become reality in only a few years.

In his next report on the state of the nation on October 17, the chancellor drew the consequences of this: "We have the hope that the German question will once again be on the agenda of world history, at whatever point that may be." Kohl summed up by saying, "The German question

Ronald Reagan during his speech at the west side of the Brandenburg Gate in Berlin, July 12, 1987: "Mr. Gorbachev, tear down this wall!"

Two weeks before the fall of the Berlin Wall, Helmut Kohl greets the Hungarian foreign minister Gyula Horn, October 25, 1989.

remains open, historically, legally, and politically." This acknowledgment is rhetorical; it was addressed to the "hawks" on German policy in his own parliamentary party, as there were more skeptics in the cabinet, and in particular, Wolfgang Schäuble. The proven pragmatist Helmut Kohl did not appear to be convinced about the feasibility of achieving the larger goal in the near future. As late as the early summer of 1989, only a few weeks before Foreign Minister Guyla Horn opened the Hungarian-Austrian border, Kohl abruptly stopped television moderator Gerhard Löwenthal in mid-rhapsody on policy on Germany. In one of the few instances in which the two very different men actually had a conversation, he said, "Oh, forget that, the German question is not on the political agenda."

It does not take a visionary to practice solid politics, which Kohl was successful at more frequently than his critics would have liked. Thus he presented the official visit to Bonn by the SED general secretary in a way in which he could get kudos from all sides, including the opposition. The five days in September were officially treated as "a working visit by the general secretary and chairman of the government council of the GDR." The details were worked out by Schäuble, the chief of the chancellor's office. Kohl put on a dinner for his guest at the Redoute in Bad Godesberg, not at Schloss

Gymnich, where only "genuine" heads of state were received. In his dinner speech, Kohl spared no rhetorical flourish in reference to Pan-German policy, as Honecker looked on grimly: "The feeling about unification is higher than ever, and the will to maintain it is unbroken. . . . Many people have difficulty with their feelings and with the idea of how this meeting fits in with the continuity of German history." And in order to make sure that none of the East Berlin leaders had any false expectations, Kohl said at a different point, "This visit cannot and will not change anything in regard to the different concepts of the two states on fundamental issues, among them

The unpleasant reality at the Redoute in Bad Godesberg: The chancellor speaks at the dinner honoring GDR leader Erich Honecker, September 9, 1987.

the question of nationality. For the Federal Republic I reiterate: the preamble of our constitution is not at disposition, because it reflects our convictions. It wishes a unified Europe and challenges the people of both Germanys to bring about the unity and freedom of Germany through free self-determination." The ceremonies and the dinner speeches were televised live. The cameras played upon Honecker's face, which was lifeless and frozen; he seemed to be pained by some of the things Kohl said: "A person must never be a pawn for political means. Peace starts with the respect for the unlimited and absolute dignity of the individual in all facets of his life. Each person must be able to determine his or her own life. The people in Germany are suffering from the separation. They are suffering from the Wall, which literally stands in their way and which throws them back. If we tear down that which separates people, we do justice to the longing of the German people which cannot be ignored: they want to come together because they belong together."

The wooden Honecker answered with a speech that detailed every conceivable subject of agreements between the two countries, including the "joint declarations," with SED footnotes and raised his glass in the usual toast, not forgetting to mention "valued friends and comrades."

Kohl recalled the meal in his honor hosted by comrade Honecker on the second day of the visit.

> It was long, too long. . . . I sat between Honecker and Günter Mittag, and next to him sat the president of the *Bundesrat*, Bernhard Vogel. . . . I would have liked to have talked to him, but wasn't able to! Once the very few topics of conversation were exhausted, I asked Honecker who his successor might be. It was a group in which you could ask such a question. Honecker was no longer young, and therefore it was not wrong to pose this question. It was amazing how really amused Honecker himself and Günter Mittag were in answering. The fact that his era could be ending was for Honecker not light years hence, but at least a long way off. That showed me more clearly than a whole library full of books on political science how much these people had already lost contact with reality."[93]

During this visit two agreements were signed, and Honecker also had the opportunity to meet in Munich with Foreign Minister Franz Josef Strauss, who gave a reception for him. One of the agreements was aimed at scientific and technical cooperation. The minister responsible, Heinz Riesenhuber, gave a declaration. An agreement on environmental protection with an appropriate declaration by Minister Klaus Töpfer, as well as an agreement on protection against radiation, gave the SED delegation the feeling of being involved in international top-level meetings. The protocol gave the guests everything which SED functionaries hungry for recognition could

After the signing of the Agreement for Scientific and Technological Cooperation. From left: Honecker, Research Minister Heinz Riesenhuber, Kohl, and Environment Minister Klaus Töpfer.

want: dinners and meetings with Federal President Richard von Weizsäcker, red carpets, anthems, and honor guards (though only in front of the chancellor's office, not at Villa Hammerschmidt). Honecker, along with his foreign minister Oskar Fischer, GDR ministers Gerhard Beil and Kurt Nier, GDR state secretary Frank-Joachim Herrmann, and the chief of the permanent representation of the GDR in Bonn, Ewald Moldt, met with Dorothee Wilms, Wolfgang Schäuble, Klaus Töpfer, Heinz Riesenhuber, and Martin Bangemann. Always present were the federal deputy state secretary for intra-German relations, Ludwig Rehlinger; the secretary for economics, Dieter von Würzen; press office secretary Friedhelm Ost; and finally the chief of the Bonn representation in East Berlin, Hans Otto Bräutigam. Oskar Fischer and Foreign Minister Franz Josef Strauss met outside of the official delegation meetings due to the special relationship between the two German states.

During a private visit after the official part of his stay in the Federal Republic, Honecker traveled to his childhood home in Wiebelskirchen in Saarland to see his very old sister. The general secretary, who had acted so woodenly, made an astonishing comment which referred in his view to a time long in the future: "I believe, if we act jointly in accordance with the communiqué which we agreed on in Bonn and work together peacefully, the day will come in which the borders will no longer separate us, but will unite us, just as the border unites the German Democratic Republic and the People's Republic of Poland."

Dorothee Wilms reacted for the most part positively to Honecker's statement, which could have been interpreted a number of ways. She talked about a remarkable perspective: "General Secretary Honecker has recognized that the border between the two states of Germany is not as it should be. His expectation, that through peaceful cooperation in accordance with the joint communiqué the day will come in which the border will no longer separate us, but bring us together, is of great importance and enormous political significance."

The Federal Republic could already claim as a success the fact that none of the SED functionaries at any level took offence during the visit to Dorothee Wilms as intra-German minister. The SED had previously refused to acknowledge the existence of the Ministry for Intra-German Relations. Now ideas were exchanged freely during a walk through "her" building and the discussion held little dissension. For the first time, the minister told friends, she "took real pleasure" in her section, whereas normally her political task gave very little reward.

The GDR was already starting to crumble in the year of Honecker's visit, though the SED leadership gave no sign of it either at home or abroad. At the same time, the political leaders in Bonn were not fully aware of the real circumstances in the GDR. But Dorothee Wilms suggested in meetings closed to the public that there were "circles in Dresden and elsewhere which took a lively interest in a change in the domestic situation, and, as a consequence, in a shift in the GDR's foreign relations." The federal government regarded this information only as vague and unconfirmed speculation, the consequences of which no one was prepared to draw. Quite the contrary; exactly thirteen months after Honecker's visit to Bonn, at the prompting of the chief of the chancellor's office, the transit fees were raised by more than fifty percent to about 860 million marks per year, and were fixed at that rate for ten years! This was not exactly a sign that the Bonn coalition believed the situation would change in the short term; on the contrary, it seemed prepared to settle on the status quo, and for the long term.

10

The Chancellorship (II)

1987–1990

The GDR Becomes Insolvent

There is fair reason to suspect that there was a direct connection between the drastically higher transit fees in October 1988 and a secret note by Alexander Schalck-Golodkowski, the man responsible for getting currency for the GDR. This note was among the secret documents which the politburo was either unable to destroy after the peaceful revolution or which had already been moved elsewhere. Schalck's comment about the situation in nonsocialist currency was extremely enlightening, because this close confidant of Honecker was a frequent guest of the chief of the chancellor's office, Wolfgang Schäuble, who later expressed his opinion that as the procurer of currency Schalck "played a large role in unification."[94]

In the meantime, however, by reporting on the disastrous financial situation in the GDR to Schäuble, who was of course acting for the chancellor, Schalck had gotten Bonn to be more generous in transfer payments to the GDR than it had been in the past. Schalck's comment to "comrade Günter Mittag" exactly one month after Honecker's visit depicted the hopeless currency situation in the GDR for the coming years. Solvency, or, the imminent insolvency, "was a question of survival for our republic." Should developments in the nonsocialist currency reserves continue as before against the background of runaway debt, "the country's ability to meet payments in 1990 . . . could no longer be guaranteed." To stave off the bankruptcy of the government, the transit fees and other credits from Bonn would not only be greatly increased, but at the same time a preliminary ten-year guarantee would be applied. That meant that the bourgeois-liberal coalition, just like its socialist-liberal predecessor, did not trust historical developments, but looked for its salvation to a purposeful stabilization of the domestic conditions of the tired old Workers and Peasants' State. There was a certain logic to this, especially since the chancellor and his first dependable steward knew exactly what they were doing. Naturally they knew the contents of the Schalck paper, or at least its general outline. The pertinent authorities in the federal government noted "growing discontent among the population of the GDR," which Schäuble and Wilms wanted to counter with additional funding. In this context reference was made directly and publicly to the GDR's lack of currency reserves. The Bonn negotiators had not allowed themselves to be "dragged across the table," as some media reported, in the agreement about the transit fees. Quite the contrary: the results were what the chancellor was after, and Schäuble

A. Schalck
H. König

Berlin, den 16.10.1987

Anlage 1

Mitglied des Politbüros
und Sekretär des ZK der SED

Genossen Günter Mittag

Lieber Genosse Mittag !

Beiliegend übermitteln wir Dir einen

Standpunkt zur voraussichtlichen Entwicklung der Zahlungsbilanz NSW 1988 - 1990 und der NSW-Verschuldung

mit der Bitte um Kenntnisnahme.

Mit kommunistischem Gruß

Anlage

The cover page of the secret "Schalk paper" of October 1987.

Geheim

Nur zur persönlichen Information

S t a n d p u n k t

zur voraussichtlichen Entwicklung der Zahlungsbilanz NSW 1988 - 1990 und der NSW-Verschuldung

Im Zusammenhang mit den Arbeiten am Plan 1988 und der Einschätzung der voraussichtlichen Erfüllung der Außenwirtschaftsaufgaben 1987 haben wir Berechnungen zur Zahlungsfähigkeit der DDR gegenüber dem nichtsozialistischen Wirtschaftsgebiet bis 1990 und danach vorgenommen.

Ausgehend von der uns von Dir übertragenen Verantwortung zur Sicherung der ständigen Zahlungsfähigkeit unserer Republik müssen wir Dich im Ergebnis unserer Berechnungen darüber informieren, daß die Zahlungsfähigkeit der DDR bis 1990 nur noch gesichert werden kann, wenn

- der von der Staatlichen Plankommission vorgelegte Plan 1988 zum NSW-Ex- und -Import vollständig eingehalten wird und
- in den Jahren 1989 und 1990 mindestens die gleichen NSW-Exportsteigerungsraten, wie für 1988 geplant, erreicht werden.

Die Sicherung der Zahlungsfähigkeit nach 1990 stellt noch wesentlich höhere Anforderungen an die Steigerung des NSW-Exports und damit an die Verteilungsproportionen des produzierten Nationaleinkommens.

The GDR is in fact bankrupt: Schalk's proposed rates of increase in the "NSW-Exports" (export into nonsocialist areas) to guarantee solvency are pure illusion. On page 5 of the document Schalk states, "If this is not guaranteed after 1991, then the solvency of our republic in 1991 will not be certain under any circumstances."

acted cleverly and effectively. He was negotiating with the knowledge that at that time not much could be done in the long term. Schäuble clearly told journalists that "in the German question, which for us is still open, we were unable to achieve any movement in talks with the GDR or the Soviet Union."

Operative reunification politics were thus shelved, perhaps forever. For Heinz Teltschik, the chancellor's foreign and security advisor, there was "no reason" anyway. Nevertheless, he still found "interesting" the thoughts of one of the authors who was at that time more strongly gripped by the idea of reunification. Hermann von Berg, a former official at the Federal Office for the Protection of the Constitution in Cologne, published his *Conversations about Germany* in November 1988. He discussed an interview with Kohl which had been published several months before in *Le Monde*; his questioners had been the paper's Bonn correspondents Luc Rosenzweig and Daniel Vernet. The chapter in Berg's book was entitled "Freedom Is More Important than German Unification," a comment which the editor did not especially like. However, Hermann von Berg showed political imagination, while on the other side, in the intra-German ministry, at least as could be determined as late as 1989–90, there was not even a sketchy type of crisis planning in case the two parts of Germany should be reunited. The author had made a list of questions in the mid-1980s which could be regarded as an operative plan of action for unified German politics.

> What can we do on a practical level? Let us take a secret popular poll in 1990 on the following questions:
>
> - Are you in favor of a peace agreement with Germany on the fiftieth anniversary of the end of the Second World War, yes or no?
> - Are you in favor of a pluralistic-democratic constitution in Germany which would come into effect with this peace treaty, yes or no?
> - Are you in favor of a five-year transitional regulation effective January 1990, which must be prepared immediately, in the form of a customs, economic, currency, passport, and political union between the two states of Germany and between East and West Berlin, yes or no?
> - Are you in favor of a first vote in the *Bundestag* in January 1990 aimed at creating a constitution for Germany, representing the political union of Germany on an international level, and preparing a peace treaty with the victors, yes or no?
> - Are you in favor of Berlin as the seat of the *Reichstag* and the *Reichs* government, yes or no?

Leaving aside the restorative tone of some passages, it contains—almost prophetically, at least in parts—later events in Germany. The chancellor's comments in this book about unification were almost defensive: "being anchored in the West is one of the bases of our state. Freedom is more important than unity, than the borders." Kohl also categorically rejected Stalin's "offer" in the early 1950s of a retrospective unification of the divided countries, which had been coupled with the unconditional neutrality of Germany. Kohl was right about everything, but did not show any imagination. No one in the Bonn administration in those years was seriously interested in the topic "unification." It belonged to the realm of exotic dreams and illusions; instead, museums should be built for German history, one in Bonn and another in Berlin, as temples of remembrance of the past which would never return. Kohl had propounded this in government declarations and the coalition adhered to it.

The federal government was decidedly restrained in this phase of intra-German relations in protesting human-rights violations at the Wall. When an eighteen-year-old fleeing the GDR had been shot by troops of the *Nationale Volksarmee* on the west bank of the Elbe river, which he had swum across, Friedhelm Ost reported formally that the permanent representative of the GDR had been summoned to the chancellor's office to receive an official protest. Such occurrences in the meantime scarcely raised any questions by the press. The public had become inured, and media interest in stories of this sort had waned. One had to look hard in the papers to find headlines such as the one in the *Aachener Volkszeitung*: "Mild Protest against Arbitrary Action." The headline is justified, because a week later the public prosecutor's office in Lüneburg declared that though the young man could have been saved by quick medical treatment, he was shot by the GDR border guards "with the clear intention to kill." When questioned, Schäuble, the chief of the chancellor's office, made the excuse that "We cannot say with absolute certainty who fired, because we did not find the bullet which penetrated the man's chest."

Gorbachev and Kohl: An Attempted Approach

October 1, 1987, marked five years of the Kohl/Genscher government. Governing was not getting any easier for Kohl, though pressures by the opposition Social Democrats and the Greens in the *Bundestag* did not seriously threaten his position. In times of difficulty, the man from the Palatinate kept in mind the adage which has held true for decades, that a coalition cannot be voted out of office, but can only give up on itself.

But Kohl did not waste much time thinking about this; on the contrary, whenever the internal party situation dominated and his party friends gave him a hard time, he oriented himself more and more toward the Free Democrats, whose continued support had become crucial for governing. Unexpectedly, the issue of the Pershing 1A missiles, which were to be excluded from the United States–Soviet disarmament agreement, took on existential significance. Some members of the CDU/CSU, most especially the *Fraktion* leader, Alfred Dregger, supported it. Exercising his powers as chancellor to establish guidelines, Kohl reached a decision in late August on this very confusing debate about the seventy-two missiles that hard-liners regarded as the final possibility of defending Western Europe with intermediate-range weapons.

Kohl announced at a press conference that he was ready to forgo the planned modernization of the seventy-two Pershing missiles (with American warheads) in the German air force if an agreement could be reached and implemented quickly to scrap the intermediate-range weapons. Foreign Minister Genscher had already strongly supported such a move, arguing convincingly that a United States–Soviet agreement of such magnitude could hardly fail because of the Pershing 1A missiles. This decision, which Kohl presented unilaterally at a government press conference, was still meeting with resistance five weeks later from his party friend and former state secretary in the chancellor's office, Philipp Jenninger. During a debate on parliamentary reform, *Bundestag* president Jenninger criticized Kohl for having used the press conference as a forum for announcing such an important decision: "It is impossible that a parliamentarian has to read the newspaper" to learn about such a decision. "Obviously it is possible," Kohl joked in the chancellor's meeting the next morning when he read the headlines.

Following a sure instinct, Kohl had placed himself with the Pershing decision at the forefront of a movement, and did not have to wait long for a favorable echo from the Soviet capital. In early October, the secretary of the central committee, Dobrynin, gave Kohl a letter from Gorbachev, who expressed approval that the German decision specifically had contributed to achieving a basic agreement between America and the Soviet Union on reduction of intermediate-range nuclear missiles in Europe. Kohl took almost three hours for a detailed discussion of a meeting between himself and Gorbachev, which both sides obviously wanted. Even in the spring of 1988, the Soviet president was well aware that the Germans were probably seriously worried about the planned meeting between him and Kohl because of Moscow's sharp reaction to "the blatant attempt by the German government to exclude the Pershing 1A missiles from the INF [Intercontinental Nuclear Forces] agreement." In the meantime Gorbachev had issued a formal invitation via his foreign secretary, Eduard Shevardnadze, for the chancellor to visit him in Moscow in May of 1988. The minister-president of Baden-Württemberg, Lothar Späth, paid an initial visit in early February. Späth became nervous and stubborn when he broached the subject of Kohl's visit. Gorbachev said, "I had the feeling that people in Bonn were afraid of missing out on the new developments in Europe." Discussion of this point served to dispel any remaining tensions between Bonn and Moscow.

Späth said, "Chancellor Kohl thinks it is absolutely necessary that he meet you. He doesn't care whether he travels to Moscow or you come to Bonn, but if you're planning a trip to Western Europe, he feels it's imperative that Germany be on the program. This is psychologically significant. Speaking candidly, the chancellor would be disappointed if, having already visited France and Great Britain, you traveled to other Western European countries and left out Germany."

Gorbachev replied, "We agree on this point. The chancellor is right, it's time to make a firm date so preparations can be made. Therefore I have invited the chancellor to Moscow via Shevardnadze." Späth said he was certain that the question could be resolved quickly. Gorbachev said, "We can resolve this this evening."

Späth said, "The chancellor is being advised by everyone to meet with you quickly and without complications." "Then let's make firm plans for the summit. We've already held discussions with West German politicians. Now we should meet at the highest level," Gorbachev said.[95]

Nine months were to pass before Kohl's Moscow visit. Federal president Richard von Weizsäcker, who paid a state visit to the Soviet Union in June of 1987, heard only the old orthodox line of the Communist Party from Gorbachev, that "the two German states are a reality." But reality was also the Moscow treaty, the treaties of the Federal Republic with Poland and Czechoslovakia, with the GDR and other Eastern-bloc countries. Gorbachev assured his German visitor that he had addressed "the unity of the German nation very carefully and tactfully." At the same time, he, Gorbachev, had not had cause to make any more binding statements than these: "We must assume . . . that things will not change very quickly." His foreign minister, Shevardnadze, who had already been secretly working on more far-reaching plans, had apparently not agreed with his boss in the Kremlin on politics in this time of great change.

Gorbachev was open about a suspicion that he seemed to have had about Kohl even as late as the spring of 1988.

> Bonn officials were imitating the Reagan administration's zigzag course with German pedantry. In Moscow we often had the impression that we were hearing a good translation of familiar texts from English into German from the shores of the Rhine. The German government obviously lacked the imagination or political courage to react appropriately to the changes in the Soviet Union.

> When Chancellor Kohl finally took a public stance [in a 1986 interview in *Newsweek*] and said that the statements about reforms in the Soviet Union and the new thinking were merely demagoguery along the lines of Goebbels's propaganda, I had doubts whether the German leaders were capable of adequately assessing the events.[96]

In fact, during a Washington visit the chancellor had told a *Newsweek* reporter that "Gorbachev is a modern communist leader who is good at public relations. Goebbels, one of those who was responsible for the crimes of the Hitler era, was an expert in public relations." The quote proves, at this point at least, that *Kohl* was no expert in gaining confidence, another way of looking at public relations.

Just before leaving for Moscow on October 23, 1988, Kohl responded vigorously to a question by the German Television Channel Two moderator Wolfgang Herles on whether he had "stage fright": on the contrary, he saw the Moscow visit as a "chance," he replied. That is no contradiction, but Kohl correctly says of himself that he is a person "who approaches people directly." Therefore he was successful in reversing the damage done by his infamous Goebbels reference in this first meeting, which Gorbachev, according to his memoirs, was looking forward to as much as his guest from Germany.

After the formalities, Gorbachev said that "we want to base our relationship on trust and on the realities. . . . It should reflect the spirit of the times and their demands. We are counting on an honest and serious dialogue about basic problems which directly affect both our countries. I believe that we should open a new chapter in Soviet-German relations."

Kohl answered, "I agree with you completely. I've seriously considered everything and have come to Moscow with precisely these intentions. . . . I consider my personal contact with you to be of extreme importance. I have come to Moscow as the chancellor, but also as citizen Kohl. We are about the same age and belong to a generation which has lived through the war." Kohl described in detail his family background and his extreme aversion to war and oppression. "Our personal contacts must be on a radically new basis of openness." Kohl addressed the human-rights issue in Germany far more emphatically than his predecessors, with vivid references to "the Wall, which one should try to imagine here in Moscow."

Also mentioned were the more than two million people who had felt themselves to be Germans in the 1979 census, a great number of whom wanted to leave the Soviet Union and return to "the land of their fathers"—Germany. Kohl made the issue of the "Russian Germans" a personal one when he returned to Bonn, having in the meantime given his party friend and parliamentary state secretary in the Ministry of the Interior, Horst

Waffenschmidt, the task of organizing the technical details of the orderly return of the Russian Germans. Kohl could hardly have chosen anyone better than this Protestant parliamentarian from the Bergisches *Land* for this delicate and nerve-wracking job. Waffenschmidt's slogan, despite all the difficulties, was "Are you all happy?"

Whether consciously or unconsciously, Kohl spoke to his host from his soul and his humanity impressed the Kremlin leader. Accompanied by Raissa Gorbachev and Hannelore Kohl, the German and Russian delegations listened to Beethoven and Mussorgski played by the Munich Symphony Orchestra. The man from the Palatinate was impressed by the Danilov monastery, the sanctuary of the Russian Orthodox Church. The ice was broken, as both sides and the people representing them made very clear in words and actions. If Brandt, Scheel, and Genscher opened the doors of Moscow, Kohl brought light and warmth to the relations between Moscow and Bonn. "We said good-bye," Gorbachev wrote for posterity, "with what I felt to be cordial feelings."[97]

With the exception of Germany, the media in the West began to express doubts and criticism of the country's reliability as a NATO ally. The British thought Kohl was on the wrong track, but less so than some writers in the French press, particularly *Quotidien de Paris* and *Figaro*. Both papers' editorials cast strong doubt on Germany's loyalty to the principles of the community. American papers also joined the chorus; diplomats of Western countries insinuated that Bonn could be turning away from Western values and toward the Soviet Union, an inaccurate and insulting sentiment. Looking back at the events of late 1988, Gorbachev remarked that "our partners emerged only with difficulty from the jungle of the Cold War." And what about the Soviet Union itself? It has not been proven one hundred percent, but all indications seem to be that Gorbachev made the first offer to reunite Germany in a private conversation with Kohl attended only by the chief interpreter of the Soviet administration, Ivan A. Kurpakov. The offer was probably made on the condition—which Kohl completely rejected—that Germany leave NATO. Even during the visit there were rumors via the official Moscow protocol that Gorbachev and Kohl disagreed on this point. In retrospect it seems remarkable that these rumors did not reach the press delegation and were only to be found in semiofficial circles.

The following facts prove that these rumors were not merely a mystification or an invention *post festum*. In the spring of 1995, Andrei Ivanov from the Russian Federation Embassy in Bonn was asked if these events of 1988 were true. He said that he "had heard of them, but could not confirm them from his perspective and from having heard them." However, he added that the matter was "extremely sensitive." Ivanov said that his predecessor, embassy advisor Kurpakov, now in the German section of the Moscow Foreign Ministry, would be able to give an official statement. Kurpakov stated that "he was not authorized to speak about it." The only witness to this conversation aside from Kohl and Gorbachev did not refute the issue in a written request for information, but referred to his duty to maintain confidentiality; the content of the conversation had "not yet been released." Gorbachev published the conversation with the German chancellor, which ended on the question of unification, in mid-June of 1990, three years after the protocol.

He Does Not Allow Himself to Be Blown Over

Even before Kohl was able to bring home his "Moscow visit" trophy, there were a number of emergencies and setbacks to be dealt with. He took his time in appointing his cabinet after the *Bundestag* elections in January 1987, not letting himself be pressured. "The impression that the chancellor has been degraded to being the choir director of politics for which Franz Josef Strauss has written the chorale book is blatantly false," wrote Eghard Mörbitz in a commentary in the *Frankfurter Rundschau*, normally critical of the government. Others, not Kohl, had lost standing over the years, which obviously increased the desire of the "black giant's" internal party rivals to bring him down. That was true of highly respected or feared men such as Gerhard Stoltenberg and Strauss. After a cabinet meeting on personnel, Strauss bragged to journalists that Kohl had given him the choice of any cabinet post, including finance minister. Should Kohl have actually said that—and there is no proof—this would have been an insult to his old friend Stoltenberg. The Bavarian lion was probably exaggerating, as he so frequently did. When he was told that no one in CDU circles took his cabinet aspirations seriously, he told Detlef Peters of the Bavarian *Land* representation playfully, "Reply, reply!"

There were not too many appointments: Hans (Johnny) Klein (CSU) became minister for economic cooperation; Dorothee Wilms moved from education to intra-German relations; Jürgen Möllemann, one of the brightest stars of the Liberals, took over education from Wilms, having been responsible for "foreign cultural policy" for the previous five years as state minister in the Foreign Office. Jürgen Warnke (CSU) took over as transport minister. These new appointments and reappointments meant no radical changes or voices in the cabinet, the changes having been confined to the expected limits. Kohl stabilized his position of power by forgoing spectacular appointments, which he was advised to do at irregular intervals by unasked advisers. Like his predecessor, Kohl had to maintain a balance in his appointments, which primarily meant avoiding getting mixed up in matters pertaining to the CSU affiliate or the Liberals. Thus he lent stability to his policies from within and from without. Kohl's position also avoided any abrupt end; he hates changes. He wanted to convey the message, "We're doing what we've always done. No need to get excited."

But Hans Jochen Vogel was skeptical about a swift replacement for the chancellor, who was not popular in his own ranks but was more and more feared by the opposition: "In regard to being 'blown over' [an expression of Vogel's party friends], I believe that Kohl will leave the chancellor's office only when his own party elects a successor with the required majority against his will; that was not so certain with other chancellors." The controversy over the Strategic Defense Initiative, the reduction of the top tax rate, the spending policy, and the start-up of the Buschhaus coal power station for which the government regulations on the filter system had been completely forgotten—these were all issues of the day or had been suppressed.

When the chancellor was again vacationing at the Wolfgangsee, Strauss sounded off in *Bild*: "Problems cannot be solved by sitting them out, ignoring them, or sweating them out." The columnist Meinhardt Graf Nayhauss told a story from ancient China: there was once an Emperor Wanli who ruled by doing nothing. He called this principle "Wu Wei," and it worked for thirty years, after which Wanli and his empire were at an end. A lesson for Helmut Kohl?

Kohl does not like such jokes; his sense of humor is to be able laugh about other people. And so what? The serious newspapers were well satisfied with Kohl in 1987–88, as a look at the headlines of the editorials shows: "Why Kohl Feels Secure" (*Süddeutsche*, Hans Heigert); "The Chancellor's Fortune" (*Rheinische Post*, Joachim Sobotta); "Finally a Pilot in the Airplane Again" (*Die Zeit*, Nina Grunenberg); and "A Chancellor Like an Oak Chest" (*Die Zeit*, Rolf Zundel). *Der Spiegel* too assured Kohl that he was a "Chancellor in Luck."

But the affair of Kiel minister-president Uwe Barschel in the fall of 1987 caused more than just a setback for the CDU, though its effects were quickly dispersed. On September 12 *Der Spiegel* published a cover story on the CDU politician that shook the Union to its foundations. The accusations against the leader of the northernmost *Land* seemed so appalling that officials prematurely suspected that the facts had been manipulated, though this soon proved unfounded. The magazine reported that Barschel had engaged the "media adviser" Reiner Pfeiffer to investigate his Social Democratic rival, Björn Engholm, and look into his tax situation, his lifestyle, his personal circle, any failings, and more.

During a cabinet meeting in Bonn, September 1988.

Barschel had personally dictated the text of an anonymous advertisement against the opposition leader and finally had Pfeiffer bug his, Barschel's, office to incriminate Engholm.

A month after the sensational *Der Spiegel* story Barschel was found dead in the Beau Rivage Hotel in Geneva, after which the drama reached its temporary climax. Kohl, who usually is inclined to talk a lot about such things, kept it short in his television report: "We all feel the tragedy of these hours which make one silent. And I think that everyone—above all those

Kohl receives an honorary doctorate from the University of Toronto, Canada, June 1988.

people who worked most closely with him, who can still picture and recall his conversation when he was able to talk again after the serious accident a few months ago in which he was almost killed—everyone will understand that this is not the hour for great speeches. We thank Uwe Barzel for that which he did for us and our community, the CDU of Germany."

Inaugural visit of the new NATO general secretary to Bonn. Kohl warmly greets his former defense minister, Manfred Wörner.

Barschel was not one of the party members who Kohl had particularly liked. What the CDU chairperson said was obligatory in the face of having to say something publicly about the death of a CDU "*Land* prince." The distance Kohl had always kept between himself and the younger man was mutual. As minister of a *Land*, Barschel had always fought whenever he could on the Bonn scene for Gerhard Stoltenberg, his minister-president, to be top leader, putting Kohl down in an extremely spiteful way. Barschel's tack was clear: the sooner Stoltenberg left for Bonn, the sooner he would become the top leader in Kiel. Fate fulfilled his strongest desire for power in a very different way. It cursed the power-hungry and lying man in such a way that his desire to destroy others turned into self-destruction. Hence Wolfram Bickerich's statement that the rumors about arms dealing and a violent death, possibly by Stasi agents, were "complete nonsense" was probably true. Barschel's death was planned "with clever and despairing intelligence, and garnished with references to a supposed meeting with an unknown person" exactly out of a scene from the "German Society for Humane Death."

The Fish Starts to Stink at the Head

Whether or not the economic indicators and the measures of success in foreign policy were favorable to Kohl, he still faced a strong headwind on the internal party front. In the *Bundestag* people still talked about the "weak and unenergetic" chancellor, and it was not Heiner Geissler, the main critic who was on the firing line from the those who were dissatisfied, but Kohl himself who was blamed for everything wrong. "The fish starts to stink at the head" and other cruel phrases were circulated like secret orders of the day. A former government official recalled Kohl's appearance at a parliamentary party meeting on March 15: "Kohl rattled off without emotion a general report on government performance and at the end lamented about the threat to tropical rain forests."[98] Leading CDU men and women who set the tone in the party and the *Fraktion* seemed to have given up on Kohl and his chances of leading the Union to victory once again. Not so Theo Waigel, of the CSU *Land* group: "Kohl is without an alternative."

In the meantime things had become restless and confused in the camp of Kohl's opponents, as Lothar Späth, often considered his "successor," harshly replied, "I want to remain minister-president of Baden-Württemberg." Kohl had already decided the battle for himself almost before it began. The new constellation in the cabinet in the spring could be interpreted as a reaction to "putsch rumors." Likewise his energetic appearance after a long break at the party presidium, where he warned sternly that the

With performer Marlene Charell at the Sport Ball in the Rheingoldhalle in Mainz, 1988.

"grumbling and the defeatism" would have to stop so they could get on with the work of the government and the *Fraktion*. It seemed appropriate when Dieter Weirich, media spokesperson for the *Fraktion*, sprang to the defense of his chancellor, saying that "Kohl should not be taken apart, he's got to be helped."[99] But when Kohl's rival Späth said at the same time in Karlsruhe that he should "stop all the complaining," the chancellor had already half won. It is probable that Späth never really wanted Kohl's position and Geissler reined in his zeal because he could not be sure of the support of the Bavarians. Geissler saw himself at best as a kingmaker, and never seriously as an ersatz chancellor or successor to Kohl. Späth also calculated quite coolly and therefore fairly accurately. Mindful of his friend Kurt Biedenkopf's analysis of an election which did not promise the CDU success after the failures in Berlin and Hesse, Späth told Kohl's biographer Maser, "Why should I have challenged the party chairman and chancellor? The average party member would have been put in a terrible quandary."

The dice had already been thrown for Kohl on the internal party front. The opposition of his general secretary was no longer tolerable, even though his once close friend was pursuing policies which Kohl himself could have formulated. The "black giant" wanted to draw a balance and make some personnel changes in the party central organization. Kohl expressed his deep-seated anger on the phone to party spokesperson Jürgen

Kohl declares war on critics in his own ranks. At the small party conference in Bonn, Kohl challenged the Union to go after those among them who "grumble and cause trouble."

Merschmeier. He yelled, "Are all of you crazy?" his spokesman recalled. "No, I'm not," Merschmeier answered, annoyed. There was half a minute of silence. Then Kohl asked, "Aren't you speaking to me anymore?" "Of course. I answered your question truthfully." The chancellor could not contain himself any longer, he was fed up. "One of you ought to be reasonable, that's what you're here for. You make a mess from morning to night. . . .

You'd think you were all mentally ill. At the moment people are saying I'm surrounded by crazy people. . . . Why don't you all go to the Pacific, to the Fiji Islands, that would be something useful for the party."[100]

According to party statutes, the general secretary is to assist the chairperson in the fulfillment of his duties. When Geissler was no longer prepared to do this he had to go. He had served during three legislative periods, a total of twelve years. In the end, Kohl tried to appoint his unloved "general" interior minister, but Geissler, almost obsessed with reform, turned the position down. He would continue to devote himself to party work even if not as its top manager; he was deeply suspicious of the cabinet post his clever friend was trying to tempt him with.

On August 21 things came to a head. Kohl informed Geissler in a private conversation during the lunch hour in his office that he had irrevocably decided that he would not propose him as general secretary at the party conference in September. The next day Geissler told a government press conference, "A party in government stands and falls with the image of its government and government leader." That is undoubtedly true, but the CDU leader himself, under pressure to succeed, was also looking to polish his image. Kohl had been preparing for a change in the post of general secretary for a long time. Although this was suspected by a number of observers, it was unnoticed by the public and was not predicted. He chose Volker Rühe, deputy chair of the *Fraktion* and an expert in foreign affairs. A native of Hamburg, Rühe had only a small political lobby but had long been Kohl's favorite for a top appointment. "Pay attention to Rühe, he will do great things," Kohl had said in the past when the Union was still in opposition. The forty-six-year-old was supposed to keep things quiet on the party front, but no one knew what surprises lay ahead in the next few months and the handsome man from the Hanseatic city who was a master of the quick retort was unable to cope with the difficult task. The expert appointed by Kohl was initially confident "that the CDU can clarify its foreign-policy competency through the person of the general secretary."[101] For a month Hans Dietrich Genscher pricked up his ears in the Foreign Office, but then went back to devoting himself to routine work. Rühe modified his assertion by saying that "a more clear-cut curtailment to the foreign minister's course was not necessary."

Times of trouble are for Kohl always times to prove himself and for surprising new achievements. He fights best with his back to the wall. This was true before and in part after the Bremen party conference. On September 11, Kohl ousted some of his closest rivals from the presidium with the help of the conference plenum. Lothar Späth and Ulf Fink—the manager of the CDU central office under Geissler—lost their seats in the top CDU committee. Rühe was elected general secretary on the chairman's suggestion and Kohl himself was confirmed in office for the eighth time with a vote of 571 to 147. That was the worst result in his sixteen years as head of the CDU, but being elected is being elected. Kohl took no notice of the damper by the conference. Quite the contrary: he elegantly attacked the critics who accused him of being an enemy of reform: "The CDU in Germany has become in the last few decades a party which discusses matters under this party chairman. . . . Why is everyone worrying that we have become an organization to elect a chancellor. That's what we were before 1969. . . . We have sailed to new shores. We're not a chancellor-electing organization. Don't believe a word of it!" Kohl was mindful of the presidium favorites, who surrounded him in top committees and staunchly defended their corners. He was overjoyed after the conference had confirmed him and trumpeted, "Dear people, I am naturally for teamwork. What sort of daily routine do you imagine I have if you think you have to suggest that to me? I'm happy to have anyone who takes over work, and I mean in all areas. That is true for the government as well of course for the office of the party chairperson."

The media had assessed Kohl's chances of success in Bremen to be pretty slim. Even *Der Spiegel* later had to admit "A Great Victory for Kohl: Now He Is the CDU."

Right after the party conference Helmut Kohl, now fifty-nine years old, had to go into the university clinic in Mainz to be treated for acute prostate problems. He had managed to get through the party convention only with strong painkillers, though only his closest colleagues, such as Ackermann and Juliane Weber, knew about this. People have heard the "black giant" complain about a lot of things, but not physical ailments.

German Politics on the Phone

A "don't rock the boat" attitude had seemed implicit in the CDU's election slogan two years before: *"Weiter so, Deutschland!"* (Keep on going in the same vein). But who could have forgotten that the Union was always concerned with Germany as a whole? The plight of the GDR had to be considered, even when open discussion was avoided. And the wish for a prosperous Germany to continue "*so*" could not leave this "other" Germany out of the calculation. The slogan, though suitably succinct for election posters, sent the wrong message. "*So*" was exactly the way things should *not* continue!

One person who always expressed this bravely and blatantly was touched until the very last days of Germany's division by the horrendous injustice to his fellow countrymen and women on the other side of the Wall and the barbed wire. He made these statements in light of the changes in the heart of Europe, after the besieging of the embassies in Prague, Warsaw, and Budapest, and especially the permanent representation in East Berlin: "The only person who is not going along with Ceausescu [the changes in Europe] is Erich Honecker. This is leading to growing despair in the GDR. If that continues it will lead to trouble." The approaching fortieth anniversary of the founding of the GDR, which was obviously going to be celebrated despite the unrest throughout Eastern Europe, brought criticism from the media.

Ulrich Schwarz, the East Berlin correspondent for *Der Spiegel*, wrote a moving essay on the forty years of the Workers' and Peasants' State. This journalist had been a victim of the GDR leadership ten years before when they ordered his office to be closed and he was forbidden to work after facilitating publication of an anonymous "manifesto" in the Hamburg-based news magazine. The authors of the "*Spiegel* manifesto" were later to be in the New Forum.

But that left a lot of people unaffected. Even as late as the early summer of 1989, a few weeks before the Hungarian-Austrian border was opened by Foreign Minister Gyula Horn, even Kohl said that "the German question is not on the agenda of history."[102] Was this tactical consideration for former wartime allies whom one did not want to bring out of their reserve with pan-German aspirations? It had to remain open until the chancellor made a final statement about his innermost thoughts and feelings about those memorable weeks. His general secretary, Volker Rühe, made a more strongly accented statement on the German question, probably as a result of carefully agreed work sharing. Responding to journalists' questions about how he viewed Henry Kissinger's warning about the "illusory" pressure by the Germans for reunification, Rühe answered, "For us there is nothing else but unity in freedom. . . . There is no Western politician who could deny the Germans the claim to freedom. If the Germans exercise their right to self-determination, then it is clear that a reunified Germany would be anchored in a European house." Nevertheless, Italian prime minister Guilio Andreotti continued to warn about the threat of a supposed "pan-Germanism" even during the days of change, a remarkably nasty anti-German sentiment. Only a few people agreed with Andreotti and none echoed the sharpness of his words.

What was unthinkable for many people happened on October 18, 1989, when the SED apparatchiks toppled their long-serving leader, Erich

Honecker. The one who comes last is punished by life. The Springer publication *Bild* obviously knew about it a week before, with the headline "Wednesday, October 18: Honi's Last Day at Work!" The central committee, which did not just consist of dunderheads but had some people who supported reform, elected Honecker's long-standing deputy, Egon Krenz, to succeed him. A week later Krenz had himself elected chairman of the government council (*Staatsrat*) by the *Volkskammer*, with twenty-six votes against and twenty-six abstentions. This alone shows what sort of changes were going on in the once almost ossified state apparatus. Krenz told the top committee: "The way of working in the *Volkskammer* and *Staatsrat* is to be changed; GDR citizens should not turn their backs on the GDR; social dialogue is to continue; changes are being introduced in the election laws." After his rapid loss of power Krenz admitted that he himself had not believed that this could have saved the GDR.

In the meantime, Honecker's heir tried vainly to smooth the waves of public unrest with soothing phrases. While the people in the street shouted abuse at Krenz, Kohl had a telephone conversation with the new top GDR leader on October 26, between 8:30 and 8:44. The chancellor offered Krenz the chance to talk "at all levels," by which he meant the telephone in particular, his preferred medium.

After brief formalities Kohl got right to the point: "My first wish, to state it from the beginning, is to maintain regular contact by phone, and on my part, although it has been somewhat different this first time, I don't necessarily wish to have it publicized every time." Krenz only answered, "Aha." After that the conversation went as follows.

> Kohl: "If we believe it makes sense, then we'll reach for the phone and simply talk to each other."
>
> Krenz: "That's a good idea. I'm open to this approach. Talking with one another is always better than about one another."
>
> Kohl: "It's now possible for me to pick up the phone, for example, and talk to the general secretary in Moscow in the same way, or he calls me. And I hope that it will be the same way with us."
>
> Krenz: "I agree, Mr. Chancellor. When you have problems, pick up the phone and I'll do the same and we will surely find a way of being better informed by our advisers about what we're talking about."
>
> Kohl: "Yes, the subject of contacts. I believe that it would be useful if Federal Minister Seiters were to come and see you in late November, the second half of November."

> **Krenz:** "Yes, I'd agree to that. I assume, Mr. Chancellor, that you have been informed about the content of my two speeches. I spoke about a change and I sincerely mean that."

After that Kohl and Krenz discussed travel restrictions, indiscriminate arrests of demonstrators, the fate of the embassy refugees in the GDR's neighboring countries, and the amnesty of people arrested for trying to leave the republic. Kohl then became pointed: "Speaking openly, if people here can associate a great step forward with your name—and I am consciously saying your name—it will have a great effect not only here, but I am certain, also in the GDR."

After that Krenz could only be heard to mumble, "Hm, hm . . . ." After a pause he continued, "You are completely right, these things have to be arranged to be in the best interests of the people." Kohl answered, "Yes. So, Mr. General Secretary, let us do what we have promised!"

The conversation between Kohl and Krenz, the first ever between the two, followed by only one other on November 11, 1989, was not yet over, although Kohl's last sentence sounded like a conclusion. Kohl proposed that the talk be "publicly confirmed," to which Krenz said only "yes." Kohl made a few more remarks about procedures and rounded them off with a statement which is typical for him: "No details at this point, I don't put any stock in them. . . . We don't want to publicize a time frame, only the broad statement."

At the very end the tone became almost familiar, with a personal involvement, especially from Krenz: "Thank you, Mr. Chancellor. I give you my very best wishes, also for all the problems you will have to deal with as you said at the beginning, a good hand, and much strength. I hope you are in good health."

> **Kohl:** "Yes, thank God, yes."
>
> **Krenz:** "I wish that everything may go well. I believe you just had an operation [for prostate problems, in September]. If everything has gone well, then I wish you continued strength, Mr. Chancellor."
>
> **Kohl:** "Yes, thank you. Good-bye."
>
> **Krenz:** "Good-bye and best wishes."
>
> **Kohl:** "Thank you."[103]

What remained of this conversation, at least in the ensuing weeks? Krenz had promised to do the best he could. He was "completely determined to achieve change." Naturally Krenz did not mean the same sort of change Kohl was thinking of, but a reformed GDR in whatever guise, which was, in the view of the so-called moderate communists, "also in the interests of stability in Europe." But that was out of the question, at least according to the perceptions of FDP *Fraktion* leader Wolfgang Mischnick, who met Krenz a while later in Dresden in order to learn more about his intentions. Mischnick had the impression, which he stated at a government press conference on his return, that "Egon Krenz's government would last some time."

11

The Way to Unity

1989–1990

Now World History Is Being Written

November 9, 1989. The day of all days had come: the Wall was open. Berlin celebrated and the rest of the world was astonished. The second day of debate on Helmut Kohl's speech on the state of the nation was interrupted in the early evening. Vice President Julius Cronenberg gave permission to speak to the CSU parliamentarian Karl-Heinz Spilker. The protocol noted the following exchange.

> **Spilker:** "Mr. President! Ladies and gentlemen! Before I come to my point, I would like to read you a report which has just been passed to me."
>
> **Comments from the SPD:** "We know about it already!"
>
> **Spilker:** "I didn't know it. Effective immediately, all citizens of the GDR are allowed to travel to the Federal Republic directly via all border points between the countries."
>
> Long applause from the CDU/CSU, the FDP, and the SPD.
>
> **Comments from the CDU/CSU:** "Thank God!"
>
> **Spilker:** "I believed that as an exception I should be allowed to report this outside the topic at hand."
>
> **Dr. Penner (SPD):** "You can!"
>
> **Spilker:** "I thank you very much."

The Union politicians Ernst Hinsken and Hermann Josef Unland started to sing the national anthem, joined by practically everybody; only a few Greens left the plenum, but not all. After the strains of "*Einigkeit und Recht und Freiheit*" (Unity and Right and Freedom) had faded, Vice President Annamarie Renger said, deeply moved, "It is difficult to simply return to the agenda," after which Gerhard Jahn, manager of the SPD parliamentary party, moved that the session should close at that point, since returning to the agenda "could not easily be imagined."

Helmut Herles had observed the scene.[104] He saw Willy Brandt, to whom many eyes were turned, sitting introspectively, appearing to wonder "whether he would still be proved right that reunification was the lie of the Federal Republic." Member of parliament Liesel Hartenstein hugged the honorary head of the SPD when the tearful people departed. Someone quoted Heine's poem, "When I think of Germany in the night I can sleep no more. No more can I close my eyes, and my hot tears flow." Not only Berlin, even little Bonn had never lived through such a day.

After the session had been declared closed at 9:10 P.M., some members of parliament got together in the bar of the press club to drink to "that which was inconceivable even a few weeks ago, and has now happened. The Wall has fallen and Honecker has been ousted from the SED."

Was it really so "inconceivable"? the parliamentarians and journalists asked themselves in the bar on this dramatic evening. Someone knew the answer.

> It was just as inconceivable as it is now for the preamble of the Basic Law to have been fulfilled: Conscious of their responsibility before God and humankind, animated by the resolve to serve world peace as an equal partner of a united Europe, the German people have adopted, by virtue of their constituent power, this Basic Law. It had also acted for those Germans who were unable to act for themselves. All Germans are therefore called upon in free self-determination to ensure the unity and freedom of Germany."

Herles was right: "Revolution begins in people's heads." The philosopher says that the conceivable is always possible. Or, to quote the Austrian satirist Nestroy, "Reality is always the most beautiful proof of the possible."

Around noontime the chancellor left on a flight to Warsaw. His adviser, Teltschik, noted in his "Internal Views of Unification" for November 9, "The chancellor was obviously uneasy in the last few days that he was leaving for his first official visit to Poland when the situation in the GDR was becoming more and more dramatic." After initial discussions with Prime Minister Tadeusz Mazowiecki, Lech Walesa, and Bronislaw Geremek, leader of Solidarity in the Polish parliament, Kohl's small circle met in the Polish government guest house before leaving for the official dinner. Kohl learned about the recent events in Germany via a hotline. Teltschik described Kohl's reactions to the events in the center of Berlin: "It is always difficult to tell what Helmut Kohl is feeling; the only way you know he is uneasy and tense is by the rapid-fire orders and quick movements. He had just learned something which hardly anyone could believe and which immediately relegated the talks in Poland to the background: the Berlin Wall had just fallen."

Kohl immediately contacted Rudolf Seiters, head of the chancellor's office in Bonn, instructing him to keep in touch constantly, and directing him to get in touch with General Secretary Egon Krenz to set up a meeting as soon as possible. Kohl himself recalled the reception and dinner which followed this: "There was a big dispute when I told my hosts that I would be going to talk in Berlin the next day [November 10]. I insisted to President Jaruzelski that the reception and dinner planned for the next day would have to be cancelled. I definitely had to leave, but promised to return."[105]

Lech Walesa expressed his concern to Kohl about the possible consequences for Poland of German reunification, which Walesa considered inevitable, and that very quickly. "I am surprised," he told Kohl, "that the Wall is still standing." It was to be torn down in two to three weeks. Thereafter, he said, the situation could become dangerous and he was "very fearful that there could be revolutionary chaos." At the Marriott Hotel, where the journalists who had come to Poland were staying, Kohl was asked after the official Polish government reception whether he would terminate his trip. He answered truthfully, in order not to offend his Polish hosts, that he was not terminating, but rather interrupting his visit to the country. Kohl called it "cutting it in half." Probably like the journalists, he had the feeling of being "in the wrong place at the wrong time." He said that he was all too aware that Germans in the East and West were being very closely watched to see "whether they had learned from history." Kohl was in his element, but still was more tense than usual, although he was carefully suppressing very high spirits. Moreover, despite his own admonition to carefully watch what was said, the chancellor cried in view of the coming triumph, "World history is now being written!"[106] Even though no one could name the exact time of German reunification, "the wheel of history turns much more quickly." How quickly would only be discovered in the spring of 1990.

Kohl's premonitions were right: the opening of the Wall very quickly caused problems for Germany as a whole which could only be solved by reunification. Hundreds of placards with the slogan "One Fatherland" on the streets of Berlin, Leipzig, and Dresden expressed this wish; another saying was "Either the mark will come to us, or we'll come to the mark."

The place for the chancellor of the Federal Republic of Germany in this unsettled time was Berlin. Ackermann found out that the chancellor had already been scheduled without his knowledge or approval for a major speech in front of the Rathaus Schöneberg on November 10. Kohl spent the morning in official discussions with, among others, General Jaruzelski, who felt it was important to meet the chancellor for substantive talks and not just a polite visit. His flight in the changed itinerary was at 2:30 P.M. The flight was already problematic because the *Bundeswehr* aircraft was not allowed to fly directly to Berlin. U.S. ambassador Vernon A. Walters solved this problem by offering the chancellor and his delegation a connecting American military flight from Hamburg to West Berlin. Hardly anyone said anything during the U.S. Air Force flight, not wanting to disturb the chancellor in his preparations for his major speech. As Teltschik recalled, it was only after the greeting by the organizer of the speech, the president of the Berlin parliament, Jürgen Wohlrabe, that Kohl learned that he was to make a second speech in the evening at the Memorial Church. Kohl lost his temper and yelled at Wohlrabe that everyone responsible in the Berlin CDU was "incompetent." The next day Kohl complained bitterly that during the improvised party event, which is how the media regarded this appearance of the chancellor in front of the Memorial Church, with no imagination about its significance, no television cameras were turned on him. It seemed that during these "days of change" everything was conspiring against him. First he was in the wrong place, and then when he reacted appropriately to the event of the century, nothing went right.

Kohl was to remember the evening of November 10 for all sorts of reasons, most of them negative. On the square in front of Rathaus Schöneberg he was greeted by an ear-splitting whistling from an assembly of leftists from Kreuzberg, most of them rabble-rousers and so-called "autonomists." By the time the speeches started it was already dark. The nearly five thousand people were relatively quiet during speeches made by the lord mayor of Berlin, Willy Momper, then Jürgen Wohlrabe, Willy Brandt, and Hans Dietrich Genscher from a small wooden podium. It was only when the chancellor spoke that the rabble-rousers started whistling again.

Horst Teltschik was called to the phone during Willy Brandt's address. On the other end of the line Julij Kwizinskij, the Soviet ambassador, gave the chancellor's adviser an urgent message from Gorbachev to his boss, which was to be communicated to him during the speeches. Major rallies were taking place in both parts of Berlin, and, said Kwizinskij, all efforts must be made to "prevent chaos." President Gorbachev asked the chancellor to calm the people. At this moment he could hardly have chosen a more unlikely politician to do this, since Kohl himself was being pressured by the rabble-rousers. Regarding the "chaos," Kohl remembers more accurately than Teltschik what was being communicated to him: "While I was stand-

The day the Wall fell, November 10, 1989: CDU speeches in front of the Memorial Church in Berlin. From left: Fraktion *leader Alfred Dregger (with hat), Foreign Minister Genscher, and Kohl.*

ing hemmed in on the balcony [of Rathaus Schöneberg], a colleague [Teltschik] told me that Mikhail Gorbachev had called Bonn and asked if it were true that an angry crowd was storming Soviet army facilities."[107]

Gorbachev's cause to worry can be seen only from this more accurate account: when military facilities are endangered, the military may have to be called on to defend them if necessary. Kohl himself learned about this in more detail only much later.

> . . . had learned that Gorbachev had been deliberately misinformed by the Stasi [secret police] and the KGB on this point so that he would order the tanks to roll. I told him via my colleagues that this was not the case, but that there was a happy, folk-festival-like atmosphere. . . . Gorbachev believed me more than he did the Eastern intelligence services, and in this way great damage was prevented. Our personal relationship built on trust—especially during his visit to Germany in June 1989—paid off. If I am grateful to Gorbachev for any one thing among many others, it is for the fact that he ignored the inciters and was open to reasonable arguments.[108]

From then on events happened one on top of the other and were difficult to follow, with many things at first overlooked and others understood only in retrospect. In Bonn, opposition leader Hans Jochen Vogel demanded "round tables" in both parts of Germany. The coalition was to take care of smooth coordination of logistics to channel the stream of people wanting to come to the West. In East Berlin, the SED and citizens'-rights proponents would meet to discuss new forms of governing. It would be shown that the stream of people would drop off sharply after the border through the center of Germany became more porous.

Since "world history" was being written, the screenplay of day-to-day political life also called for weekend working by order of the chancellor. On Saturday, November 11—every day could be significant—Kohl, dressed in his obligatory black cardigan and white exercise sandals, assembled his "kitchen cabinet" in the chancellor's office. Teltschik could not recall "when this kitchen cabinet last met on a Saturday." They discussed an interesting TASS report of the previous evening which said that the GDR "was a country open to the world and now, without the Berlin Wall, no longer cut off from the world in practice." Moscow spokesperson Gennady Gerassimov said in a further TASS report that the GDR's decision to open the border "had been a sovereign act" of the country and the new travel regulations was "wise." The "kitchen cabinet" was satisfied with itself and the world on this gray November weekend. There was still no concrete policy on Germany which could make the necessary steps to a possible reunification any easier, but as a born organizer, Kohl knew how to improvise. A week before the great events, CSU chief Theo Waigel had accused his chancellor of not having a concept about the reform process in the GDR. Waigel's general secretary, Erwin Huber, was even more direct in stating what the CSU wanted: lose no opportunity to galvanize policy on Germany, to increase pressure on the SED leaders, and to "mobilize world public opinion in order to drive the reform process in the GDR—even to the point of free elections."[109]

Scarcely a week had passed after the "fall" of the Wall when a number of reformers—unlike Waigel and Huber and others had imagined—began to be concerned that many people in the GDR had had "capitalist desires awakened, the consequences of which could make the selling of the GDR to the Federal Republic unavoidable." Sebastian Pflugbeil, speaker of the New Forum, was basically satisfied with the new freedom to travel, but was also concerned that "everything was coming too early."[110] This was the first statement of nostalgia, which was to be followed by a hundred thousand others, at a time when the exact date of German reunification was not even foreseeable.

The Ten-Point Plan

"The fate of the Helsinki process was riding on the plan," Soviet president Gorbachev wrote in his memoirs. He was referring to the fact that Chancellor Helmut Kohl had already presented a "ten-point program"—at other times it was called a "plan" or "catalog" in the *Bundestag*—to the public as early as November 28, 1989, much to the surprise not only of the Soviet Union and its leadership, but also of the British and the French. Gorbachev also noted that even Foreign Minister Genscher was taken by surprise by the ten points "to overcome the division of Germany and of Europe," as the chancellor's government declaration was called. Naturally the election played a role—with elections for the *Bundestag* due in 1990—and that meant gaining a good position. Moreover, Kohl could not risk having the reactionaries in the "changed" GDR turning the rudder of the sinking ship again.

The Kremlin leader hit a bull's eye when he noted Genscher's reservations, but missed the target entirely in his worry that Kohl would not give due consideration to the CSCE (Conference on Security and Cooperation in Europe) accords in Helsinki. In fact, a process had already begun in the GDR leading toward fulfillment of those principles of respect for human rights, freedom, and self-determination. It is interesting to note that Gorbachev took exception to another of Kohl's perceptions. In a later conversation, the chancellor intimated to the Soviet president that he had been convinced from the very beginning that Egon Krenz would not be able to control the situation in the GDR. Gorbachev was skeptical. "It is well known that our best thoughts naturally occur only in retrospect," he caustically observed.

He then continued with an assertion which should be kept in mind in light of later decisions in the process of German reunification. "For my part," Gorbachev said, in contrast to Kohl, "I have to honestly admit that I hoped that the new leadership of the party and country [the GDR] would be successful in channeling the events in the republic—given the fundamental internal political changes—toward a new relationship between the two German nations." The Kremlin did not want to entertain the idea of German reunification, and thus Gorbachev noted on November 11 that he was pleased when Chancellor Kohl assured him on the phone that the Federal Republic of Germany was aware of its responsibility in this dramatic situation and would act cautiously and circumspectly. Gorbachev complained bitterly to "Helmut," with whom he otherwise got along very well, that he had obviously forgotten to consult him before publication of the ten points.

Unlike Kohl, the Kremlin leader regarded the sweeping changes in Europe with suspicion. Though he himself was in the process of dismantling the enormous Soviet empire, he was considerably worried about the revolutionary changes in the West. From developments at that point it can be said with absolute certainty that Kohl had taken the initiative for reuniting the two German nations at a very early stage and obviously was not going to let anyone else take control. On the other hand, Gorbachev clearly warned the chancellor against making any changes in the situation, because change meant "instability in a certain sense." What a misinterpretation of the situation! The changes in the GDR were the basis for reunification, but one looked in vain in the autumn of 1989 for a gesture of support from Gorbachev. Nevertheless, the former Soviet president gives us an idea of Kohl's own assessment of the situation in a phone conversation: "A government meeting is just over, and if you'd been there you would probably have been amazed at how similar our assessments are. This historic hour requires an appropriate reaction, demands historic decisions. I would like to assure you that I am very conscious of my responsibility."[111]

Comparing Kohl's and Gorbachev's ideas reveals no trace of congruence. Kohl, on the other hand, appeared to be on the right track: as the German chancellor he was compelled to act in accordance with the constitution after the changes in the GDR. It is clear that the Kremlin leaders were afraid they would not be able to control this process and thus they repeatedly warned about "agreement and consultation" at all levels, to which Kohl did adhere in all future international meetings, even though he correctly opted to exercise his historical right to act. The man from the Palatinate was not one to start the process with reservations. It is interesting to see who was pressing whom, perhaps even pushing and braking, in this race toward German unification. Kohl emphasized repeatedly the invaluable role Gorbachev had played in marshaling international opinion in favor of reunification, graciously ignoring the billions (over the years it became one hundred billion) the German taxpayer had to pay to facilitate Russian military withdrawal from East Germany. A chancellor of the Federal Republic of Germany was not going to be stopped from doing what was necessary despite the Soviet leader's fundamentally different view at the time (and possibly now) of the progress and the goals of the revolutionary changes in Central Europe.

Perhaps that is Kohl's contribution to history. Call him "blunt" (Gorbachev used this expression in connection with "actions which could endanger the changes") or opportunistic; Kohl rarely has to chide himself for being afraid. He was courageous and decisive in preparing for German reunification, adopting an attitude that was radically different from that seen in his earlier pragmatic and hesitant statements on unification.

The ten-point plan was also controversial on the home front. At the FDP party conference in Celle the coalition partner gave the unfortunate impression that it was not plowing the same furrow on the ten-point plan as the Christian Democrats. FDP leader Otto Graf Lambsdorff, with whom Kohl had a nonrelationship, quickly began to backpedal after a disastrous reception from the media. "The refusal by the party conference to approve the ten-point plan has caused a crisis in the coalition," Lambsdorff said of the strange actions by the delegates at Celle. That was merely a criticism of procedures, and the party had only wanted to avoid having to rework its own paper on Germany, he said. "A nebulous excuse," the *Frankfurter Neue Presse* criticized. The decision of the "small party conference" was all the more confusing because the Liberals essentially agreed with the reunification processes. People in the CDU party central office were relaxed and there was even a great deal of pleasure taken in the "great chairman's" willingness to act. The CSU *Land* leadership in Munich bragged about the Liberals' not wanting to toe the line: "the chancellor will soon tell the count [Graf] what's what."[112]

Genscher felt the displeasure of his host during a visit to Moscow when Gorbachev dropped all the diplomatic niceties and blasted the foreign minister: "Such a document should really only be presented after consultation with partners, or doesn't the chancellor have to do things like that anymore?" That indeed was the Kremlin leader's worry, that the Germans could emancipate themselves from international control and guidance.

Even Kohl himself did not consider the ten-point plan a "master plan," but "only a guideline which enabled flexible action." It occupied people's attention for weeks and months but in the end was almost completely superfluous because the events in the spring and especially the summer of 1990 that were leading toward unification came thick and fast. Kohl was careful not to refer to it as a "German plan" out of astute consideration for the sensitivities of European and Eastern neighbors. He became convinced and let others know his conviction that reunification would come when the Germans wanted it, regardless of whoever else said "yes" or "no." In Kohl's opinion, unification could not be described and planned at the negotiating table or with a diary in hand.

The ten points contained a practical catalog of immediate humanitarian and economic measures for the people of the GDR, and ended with "There are today many hopeful signs that the 1990s will offer greater peace and freedom in Europe and Germany. The decisive factor—and

The chancellor receives the board members of the opposition GDR group, "Democratischer Aufbruch," Rector Rainer Eppelmann, and Attorney Wolfgang Schnur (who was revealed as a Stasi informer shortly afterward). Right: Minister of the Chancery Rudolf Seiters.

everyone feels this—is our German contribution to this. We all must meet this historic challenge."

The chancellor had already personally accepted this challenge and thereby erased the memory of many failures and half-hearted efforts of the recent past. He deliberately avoided speaking of a "confederation" when discussing the practicalities of German unification, as this was a legal concept which Geissler and others were unwise enough to mention. A confederation of the two states would be impossible not least because of their membership in two different security alliances. Only those states wanting to pursue a common foreign policy but which want to keep their different internal political organizations are able to form a confederation. The politicians—with Kohl at their head—who were aiming for a united Germany were striving for just the opposite.

Though he announced prophetically on December 12, 1989, before the government-level committee of the CDU in Berlin that "German reunification is a vision," he added, "We do not know the day on which this vision will become reality, but I am convinced that it will."[113] The tone of this conference prose with its mixture of circumspection and pathos was meant in the first instance to calm the fears of Germany's allies, who had followed the proceedings with great suspicion.

It's Happened

Egon Krenz was replaced by GDR prime minister Hans Modrow as sole leader. Modrow was a former first secretary of the SED district government organization in Dresden and had been recommended by his colleagues as being a "reformer." Helmut Kohl did not regard this as a new situation but felt himself confronted with a new "leadership figure" after the changes in the GDR. Modrow, who appeared to be somewhat petit bourgeois, had been a machinist and obtained his doctorate as a mature student. He awaited his prominent guest on December 19 for breakfast in the Hotel Bellevue in Dresden, in which Kohl had already stayed a number of times with his wife when visiting relatives.

The day was scarcely over when it was being called "historic" because it saw what was perhaps the most profound internal change in the still-tense relations between the GDR and the Federal Republic. When Kohl stepped off the bottom step of the gangway of the Challenger in which he and his small delegation had flown from Bonn to Dresden, crowds of people—some of them already waving black, red, and gold flags—waved to him from the roofs and windows. Kohl turned to his office chief, who was right behind him, and said somberly, "Seiters, it's happened."[114]

The ten-kilometer drive to the hotel was a triumphal procession for the chancellor, who silently enjoyed smiling and returning the waves of the people lining the streets. December 19 was the day that made up for the many disappointments and humiliations of the fifty-nine-year-old Christian Democrat's political career, which now spanned almost four decades. Several thousand people had assembled in front of the hotel and were joined by more once Kohl and Modrow went inside. They shouted "Helmut, Helmut" or "Helmut, come to the window without the ghosts." A young man carrying a stage sword with a black, red, and gold banner pointed it during the spectacle in front of the Bellevue in the direction of where he thought the politicians were, shouting almost angrily, "Helmut, you promised to speak to us and not with the Bolsheviks!"

A group of workers were clustered around a placard with the green and white of Saxony which said "The Land of Saxony Greets the Federal Chancellor." Some people had cut out the hammer-and-sickle emblem from the compass flag of the GDR and used the remainder like a coat. The atmosphere was like a folk festival with a few sharp tones in between directed at a small group of stubbornly unrepentant SED comrades who still carried "their" flag. The orderlies with their green armbands had feared incidents which fortunately never happened. It was like the old German adage of "revolution with tickets for entry."

They sat there in the Ludwig Richter Salon with cups of coffee, pastries, juice, and water. After Willy Brandt and Helmut Schmidt, Kohl was the third chancellor to pay an official visit the GDR. Modrow was physically the exact opposite of the "black giant," being of middle stature and thin; he gazed at his self-assured guest with some embarrassment, underlining his few hesitant words with nervous gestures. Two more different statesmen could hardly be imagined, even aside from their origins and political convictions. Kohl was able to break the ice in his expansive, jovial way, being able to feel completely superior. "The chemistry was right between them," Kohl's office chief, Seiters, said after the formalities were dispensed with, though with an expression which showed that he was not convinced of this: "Yes, they'll be able to get along." Pressed by journalists on the atmosphere between himself and the GDR leader, Kohl answered good-naturedly the question of whether he "could" get on with him, saying, "I believe so." That can hardly have been the case. During the press conference in the Palace of Culture, one of the horrible legacies of socialism, Kohl and Modrow gave the impression of a portly, rich uncle who was paying his undernourished nephew a patronizing visit.

Teltschik had observed the GDR prime minister in larger circles during the negotiations, sitting hunched up with his thin hair unruly, avoiding every look and studying the typewritten text of a government position for fifteen minutes. Modrow was concerned that the West German mark had become a second currency on the GDR "market." The Dresden SED leader was well informed about everything. Schalck-Golodkowski, who had procured Western currency, told Manfred Schell of *Die Welt* in 1990, "I instructed Prime Minister Modrow personally and before I left I gave him a handwritten letter dated December 3, 1989. Mr. Modrow is informed about details, including foreign accounts, the sums, etc. I withheld nothing, neither information nor money."

Who should be believed? Both were entangled in the GDR government with all the consequences of tricks of secrecy in addition to the well-known deceptions.

Dear Fellow Citizens

The "day in Dresden," which December 19, 1989, could be called without any false associations, reached its climax in the afternoon in front of the Church of Our Lady. Several thousand people assembled in front of a quickly cobbled-together wooden dais. In the twilight, Kohl and his small staff, led by government spokesperson Johnny Klein and adviser Horst Teltschik, made their way through the expectant crowd. When the chancellor ended his speech with "dear fellow citizens," the crowd started to cheer wildly, and the speaker himself was able to restore calm only by raising and lowering his hands, signifying how moved he was. Kohl spoke with admiration of "this peaceful revolution," and of the fact that "such a monumental change happened for the first time in history with so little violence, with such seriousness, and in the spirit of solidarity."

After only a few minutes the fervently awaited German chancellor held his audience's rapt attention without any false pathos, arguing simply and without ornamentation: "My goal remains—if this historic hour permits it—the unity of our nation. Dear friends, I know that we can achieve this goal if we work together and act rationally and circumspectly, keeping in mind what is possible. It is a difficult path, but at stake is our mutual future." Whoever did not feel the same emotion—Klein thought he saw tears in the eyes of Klaus Bresser, the hardened editor-in-chief of German Television Channel Two—put himself outside this spiritual band of those who hoped. Kohl used the words "mutual," "our," and "we" in every sentence. It was the best speech of his entire political career; moreover it was a good speech because it was authentic, had no intention of feigning, and made nothing better than it was. Even one of Kohl's keenest internal rivals, Oskar Lafontaine, minister-president of the Saarland, praised it highly in the *Bundestag*, although he found it most difficult to do so. Kohl's speech was imbued with political realism and moving warmth, two elements of eloquence which would deflect potential opposition.

The scene in front of the Church of Our Lady was completely and utterly German. The inwardly excited but outwardly disciplined crowd listened and cheered at the end, "God bless our German Fatherland!" For Kohl it was the confirmation of his cautious assumption that the peaceful changes in the GDR would gradually lead in an ordered way to unification. At this point he was unable to offer his fellow citizens, made almost drunk from the speech, anything other than this honest oratory, which ended nevertheless with pathos. Not even the hot-dog stand at the traditional Dresden market was open—it had had to close four days before Christmas because there was literally nothing for the guests to nibble on. The waffle bakers had to close before the Bonn media found out that they had completely run out of dough to make the sweet things. Kohl, who had not noticed that the market had closed, would have been sad. He had crossed it hastily and people had waved at him half-heartedly, as if they had been caught in the midst of their bare daily lives by a spoiled manager.

After his speech in front of the ruined Church of Our Lady, Kohl met representatives of the Protestant church and then had dinner with artists who had been invited from various districts in the GDR. Around midnight he returned to his retinue at the Bellevue, where most were still at a reception for the media and politicians. Teltschik was lucky: the chancellor gave him the handwritten manuscript of his speech at the Church of Our Lady "as a reminder of a day which none of us will forget."

The next day the newspapers ran lengthy and somewhat wooden reports and editorials on the events in Dresden as if the writers themselves did not rightly know if they could trust their eyes and ears. Constraint and lack of courage could still be felt all over. The headlines were strangely conventional and stiff compared to those in the West German press: "With Great Sensitivity for the Problems of Our Time" (*Die Union*), "Already a Lot Which Is Useful for the Germans and Does Not Hurt the Others" (*Sächsische Neueste Nachrichten*), "German-German Relations Get a New Basis" (*Nationalzeitung*), "So Many Voices, So Many Bitter Questions without Answers" (supplement to the *Sächsische Zeitung*), "On the Way to a Treaty Community in a Common House in Europe" (*Sächsische Zeitung*), "Working Visit with Emotions" (*Junge Welt*), "A Start is Made toward German-German Relations on a Completely New Footing" (*Neue Zeit*), and "German-German Summit on the Banks of the Elbe" (*Der Morgen*). These headlines and the accompanying reports and commentaries show that the East Germans were not yet terribly enthusiastic about the possibility of living in a unified Germany. But the West German media reaction, as Teltschik noted in his diary, was really "overwhelming." The chancellor was happier with the press than he had ever been before. The general theme was that Kohl's discussions and meetings in Dresden had "laid the foundation for German reunification."

Interestingly enough, Kohl said in retrospect about the day in Dresden that it was "a snapshot" that proved itself to be "very reliable."[115] That sounded like a clear-cut depreciation of what many observers had called the "inner revolution" in Dresden since the day the Wall came down. But more important for the head of the German government and chairperson of the CDU were the elections on March 18, 1990, and the *Landtag* elections in Saxony, Mecklenburg-Vorpommern, Brandenburg, Thuringia, and Saxony-Anhalt in the second half of the year which surprisingly—even for Kohl—gave the Germans unification. A skeptic who is usually not inclined to celebrate ahead of time, even on November 29, 1989, the day his ten-point program was discussed in parliament, Kohl had assumed that unification would take three or four years at least. Of course, after his meeting with Modrow the chancellor recognized that he would have to revise his original prognosis. "I was fully convinced that the European common market would be complete before German reunification," Kohl commented on his assumptions about the process of reunification at the time.

Kohl returned from Dresden with the distinct impression that all doubts about Germany's determination to reunify had been dispelled on the part of Western countries, which had followed the events with suspicion, and of the Soviet Union, which had tried to delay unification. He said, "The fact that the Americans carried the event [his speech in front of the ruined Church of Our Lady] on live television did more than anything else to contribute to the correct understanding of the situation and mood in Germany."[116]

One of the Happiest Hours of My Life

"Helmut Kohl handled things well in Dresden," *Der Spiegel* publisher Rudolf Augstein declared. Augstein counted himself among the "reunifiers," probably in contrast to most of the editors of his Hamburg-based news magazine. "Even though there was little that he could have done wrong, just a small slip could have broken a lot of the china from which people still had to eat." Helmut Kohl was followed by "historic moments," starting with his speech in front of the Church of Our Lady in Dresden. Two days before Christmas Kohl and Modrow opened the Brandenburg Gate in a ceremony which was perhaps not as moving as his Dresden appearance, but much more loaded with symbolism and probably more effective as a media event. "One of the happiest hours of my life," was what he was experiencing in the "old capital," Kohl told the cheering crowd on this damp, cold December day, joined by half the world watching it on television. Kohl, still under the influence of Dresden, tried to stifle his excitement rather than fan it. "Dear friends . . . let us be patient and circumspect in the steps which lead to a joint future."

The difficulties had already begun, aside from the fact that the openings in the Brandenburg Gate approved by Modrow were late. But since this happened just before the holidays the ceremony took on a special significance, an additional present, so to speak, for nationally minded Germans. Prime Minister Modrow and Chancellor Kohl shook hands under the gate in a display of the unity with which the future of a united Germany would be negotiated. The "premier," as the GDR called him, showed no emotion, except perhaps a slight stubbornness for which he had reason. On the morning of this eventful December 22, Modrow's close associate Karl-Heinz Arnold had reminded Teltschik about the fifteen billion marks "that the chancellor had promised in solidarity." Arnold and Teltschik were supposed to keep in close contact about this and as a first gesture Teltschik noted the phone and fax numbers of his East Berlin contact. At first nothing came of the fifteen billion marks, because Bonn had already begun to mistrust the

Modrow government's entirely different plans. Karl Otto Pöhl had warned the chancellor on the phone on the morning of December 22 against any rash and unconsidered moves on currency with the GDR.

The East Berlin regime was indeed almost finished and Kohl therefore rejected the equalization of burdens which Modrow had suggested at the meeting in Dresden. The chancellor did not expressly take up the demand for up to seventeen billion marks, but was conscious of the need for a "necessary act of solidarity."

All those involved, and Kohl in particular, had become aware in the meantime that anything which would keep alive the historically doomed SED regime was to be avoided, most especially in light of the changed indications and conditions.

On the other hand, Kohl was under pressure because of the incontrovertible fact that more and more people were streaming into the West every day, a situation which could not be allowed to go on. Kohl played for time with the inscrutable heirs of the Honecker regime. The first suspicions were about the people who he would probably have the most to do with, among them the GDR CDU leader Lothar de Maizière, who expressed support of socialism despite the changes, terming it "one of the most beautiful visions of human thought." That sounded like he wanted to tell his West German "party friend" Helmut Kohl that he could continue making himself comfortable on the Rhine, but "without me."

Such statements were difficult to assess, but the fact that de Mazière's staff, among them Angela Merkel, still spoke of "our comrades" who had not issued any directives on how to proceed was beginning to irritate Seiters and his colleagues during the now routine discussions with the future fellow campaigners of the Eastern CDU in Berlin. There were still signs all over that the past had not been overcome. But at the same time, Kohl was becoming convinced that much had changed and that the GDR party officials were willing to adjust to this only slowly. "The past year has brought us a great deal closer to the unification of our Fatherland," Kohl said in his New Year's speech, which he intentionally aimed at all Germans.

I Govern, Therefore I Am

Publications which were normally anti-Kohl praised him as an exception, but only because he had admitted in Dresden that the road to unification "would be difficult." Some of his critics hoped that he would fail. Others, such as Rainer Eppelmann of the group Democratic Breakthrough, wanted to postpone unification until after 1994. The *Demokratischer Aufbruch* (DA), which also numbered other demagogically talented people such as

Wolfgang Schnur, played a leading and tragic role in the fight to gain the favor of GDR citizens in the first free election in the *Volkskammer* on March 18 in the "Alliance for Germany." Those who hesitated and procrastinated became even more vociferous after the *Volkskammer* election.

That was not at all what Kohl had intended, but he tolerated outsiders astonishingly well in those days. Despite all the pressures he faced as chancellor, he had hardly ever seemed as self-confident and even jovial as in the spring of 1990. Only from time to time did he become extremely indignant, for example when Eduard Ackermann read out critical media reports in the morning meeting for longer than Kohl's nerves could stand. "Ah, leave me alone with all that junk," he exploded, which frequently drove poor Ackermann to despair and to think longingly about "finally looking for a respectable job." But by lunchtime his friends Teltschik, Johnny Klein, and above all, Juliane Weber, had cheered him up again. Otherwise, the daily routine became more tolerable; the atmosphere improved because there were decisions to be made and things to be done which would go down in the history books.

It was not until unification that Helmut Kohl found *the* great theme of his life. At the same time it is a persistent legend that he had dreamed for decades of having history single him out as the person to solve the problem. Only when unification seemed possible to the world and to himself did Kohl fearlessly take up the task, after which he finished it unhesitatingly and with single-mindedness, more so than any other German politician could have or would wanted to have done. Kohl knew instinctively that only unification with all its tumult would secure his position at the head of the federal German government and in future of *all* Germans within internationally respected borders. After the Bremen party conference in 1989 Kohl had become, in some respects, the "party personified," which did not speak well for the CDU's strength. But as the government head he was still the target of criticism and his strongest supporters feared that the coalition under his leadership would not be able to score the desired victory in the *Bundestag* elections which were probably going to be held in late 1990, since the *Landtag* elections in the previous years had brought nothing but defeat. The *Frankfurter Allgemeine* wrote concisely in late January that "the government has been running fairly successfully since 1982, but Kohl has not had much luck for a long time." With or without luck, he was determined about one thing: to keep on sitting in the chair he had been sitting in for the last seven years until better times came along. In the final analysis, he was only interested in extending the classic proof of existence to "I govern, therefore I am."

The GDR government had sealed its own doom twenty-five years before the actual event with an admission of its weakness: building the Wall in order to protect itself from "damaging" influences. The process of destruction from within had started that way and was perhaps historically unstoppable in any case. In retrospect—and it is tempting to say "naturally"—Helmut Kohl believes that change cannot be brought about without the strong guidance of influential people. He therefore believes in the role of the individual in history, but at the same time underestimates "the significance of structures and anonymous processes," as has been pointed out repeatedly. In the words of one of his press spokesmen, he is of "archaic simplicity." Though this can sometimes be doubted, Kohl the active politician and statesman sometimes leaves the observer no other choice but to assume this. The fact that he reads a lot and often rereads books was revealed in a rather unfortunate interview with the writer Walter Kempowski in the 1970s. While working on ideas and the practicalities of uniting Germany in the spring of 1990 he was reading Lothar Gall's *Bürgertum in Deutschland. Die Bassermanns* (Bourgeoisie in Germany: The Bassermanns). Who knows whether it had anything to do with the events which were completely occupying his attention. Kohl liked it and that was enough.

Starting immediately there was a much more clear-cut division of work between the party central organization and the chancellor's office. Naturally Kohl still controlled the tone and direction at the Konrad-Adenauer-Haus because he was the party leader after all. But Volker Rühe, who had only been general secretary for a few months, had more room to maneuver because Kohl trusted him more than he had his predecessors. He also entrusted him with more tasks, for example with pruning the Eastern-bloc CDU personnel, a delicate job, as Rühe discovered, but one which had to be done at the beginning of the new era. The Christian Democrats were weighed down with the shadows of the past when they tried to say that they were like their West German colleagues. They had not wanted to have anything to do with them in the past decades and they were still hesitating about joint action.

The Western CDU and especially its party leader, Helmut Kohl, took a big risk in forming an "Alliance for Germany," which combined past CDU members and self-professed reformers in the *Demokratischer Aufbruch*. Each day there was another Stasi spy uncovered, a CDU apparatchik unmasked as a secret SED party boss, but the other parties did not fare any better.

During the election campaign in February 1990 Kohl still stood on the platform in front of the cathedral in Erfurt with Lothar de Maizière for the CDU East and Wolfgang Schnur for the DA. The square was covered in black, red, and gold flags and a placard was unrolled in front of the platform that read "God protect our Chancellor Helmut Kohl." The event gave the impression of having been perfectly orchestrated, but aside from the technicalities, the CDU propagandists had not had to worry about anything. The people came in the thousands and aside from a few troublemakers, "Erfurt," one of the many stopovers on the East German campaign trail, went quietly and harmoniously.

On the periphery of the official program Lothar de Maizière warned his West German friends against expecting a large victory and the East German CDU chairperson told Wolfgang Bergsdorf, head of the domestic section of the government press office, that he had "serious doubts" that the alliance would get enough votes in the north of the republic. Bergsdorf advised them to concentrate more heavily on those areas in which the CDU had not had a good response, for example, in Brandenburg.

In other respects too the Union was not completely confident of victory and was spoiled by fortune, because Kohl's triumphal march through the provinces was soon overshadowed. In mid-March, Schnur, a small man with powerful rhetoric (Kohl called him a "lightweight") was uncovered as a so-called unofficial helper of the state security service, and was immediately ostracized by Kohl. Dirk Koch of *Der Spiegel* had tracked down the commanding officer of the lawyer and political dilettante and spent weeks

The last and most impressive appearance during the GDR elections, spring 1990: Helmut Kohl speaks in front of 300,000 people in the Leipzig Opernplatz on March 14. The banner in the foreground already proclaims the "Federal State of Saxony."

painstakingly researching Schnur's role in spying for the state security organization. The magazine journalist roared down the intra-zone highway in his Porsche between Bonn and Rostock twice in one week to convince himself of the DA chairman's guilt. The magazine commissioned two graphologists independently to decide whether Schnur's signature on the monthly receipts for five hundred marks for the Stasi was genuine. The result was clear: Schnur was lying when he defended himself against the accusations and denied his guilt.

Kohl sent his delegate on the East, Bernd Neumann, to listen to Schnur's confession on his sickbed, which the now-repentant sinner gave without resistance. A half hour before his important appearance in the Leipzig trade-fair halls four days before the *Volkskammer* elections Kohl announced Schnur's resignation from all his duties in the alliance. When Kohl was just getting into his car afterward a young woman grabbed his arm and tried to convince him of Schnur's "importance for about ten thousand people." What had he done that was so wrong? Kohl answered, "You are probably right, but consider it yourself: is that a question which I can answer now? Shouldn't it have been answered earlier?" The approximately three hundred thousand people of Leipzig who jammed the opera-house square regarded the Berlin lawyer who had just left the arena of "change" as a sad figure who had suffered a tragic fate, but nothing more. His departure did not affect the March 18 elections.

Battle on Several Fronts

With many unsolved problems in the background and the unclear battlefield with political adversaries between Mecklenburg and Saxony, Kohl was engaged on many fronts in the spring of 1990. His first meeting with French president François Mitterrand on January 4 at his country home Latché in Gascony, did not give Kohl any indication at all about France's stance on German reunification, which could not be achieved without the support of allies. In this regard the French president was closest to him for many reasons, especially regional ones. Whatever Mitterrand thought about unification could decide the war; the Russians would be more satisfied with currency.

As Kohl traveled from one marketplace to another in eastern Germany to speak to crowds of ten thousand or a hundred thousand, he always kept in mind the questions of his friend François: "In what way and under what conditions will the German people be reunified?" or "Will borders be guaranteed or not?" Teltschik noted that "It was always unclear whether Mitterrand meant the intra-German border, which he had once called a 'border with a special quality,' or whether he was referring to the Oder-Neisse border." That could have been cleared up by questioning him more closely, but the German side mostly stayed silent. The whole situation still had such fragile charm, with the dawn of unity sometimes shining directly into the eyes of the disciples and sometimes twinkling far off.

International affairs did not yet determine the daily routine and there was also the busy foreign minister, Genscher, for whom 1990 was the crowning achievement in his career. He was the one responsible for gaining the support of the allies, which demanded a shuttle diplomacy of unparalleled proportion.

Spring 1990 became a real challenge for Kohl, especially a physical one. For the almost sixty-year-old it became such a joy to be living and working that he frequently overtaxed his colleagues, but not himself. The descriptions of election campaign appearances recall the similarly dramatic times in the early 1970s in West Germany, but now everything was suddenly different. To many people in the GDR, Kohl seemed to be a sort of awakener or savior, or at least the embodiment of the German economic miracle, in which they could finally share. Just as the man from the Palatinate feared nothing, the people in the provinces also generally approached him directly and openly, "hunted down," in the best sense of the word, by the CDU crowd which was remotely directed from the Konrad-Adenauer-Haus in Bonn. That was campaigning as Kohl liked to have it. He made an unscheduled stop in Mecklenburg, between Wismar and Neubukow, when his car halted at a railroad crossing. The chancellor opened the door and at that moment an older woman raced toward him, embraced him, stroked his hair, kissed him on the cheek, and said, "Mr. Kohl, my good man." Hans Ulrich Kempski reported this in the *Süddeutsche Zeitung* with overtones of the "*Gartenlaube*" publication, present-day fairy tales, and occasional reports from the front: "New stop in Rostock. The broad boulevard on the harbor was swept clean. Neat red-brick buildings, slender warehouses, small pubs. The column halts because the major has to report that a large group of troublemakers has spread out on the edge of the assembly area. The major advises waiting. 'How many troublemakers?' Kohl asked. After discovering that there were about five thousand of them, he asked, 'How many people in total?' 'Well over a hundred thousand.' At which point the chancellor said, 'Let's proceed—we'll start on time.'"

The man of the hour, Helmut Kohl, never tried to further incite the emotions of his listeners, as a person of weaker character might have done. On the contrary, whenever he used the word "unity," which always brought cheers and the chanting of "Helmut, Helmut," he immediately made several factual statements aimed at calming emotions. The mood was often difficult to assess, but it was often electrified. Demagoguery could only do harm. Karl Feldmeyer observed that, "Kohl was very sparing of this fuel."

The people in the GDR were pressing for speed, not wanting to sit in second class after forty years in the slow train when an express train was on offer. This news had already reached Switzerland, as could be seen from what Helmut Schmidt's former press spokesman, Klaus Bölling, now a freelance journalist, wrote in the *Weltwoche*: "That was really not the mood of those Germans who, having been in an enormous training camp with relentless loving care, were determined to enter a new and better era."

And since the chancellor of the Federal Republic of Germany was sitting on the coffers, so to speak, he determined the course of action. Kohl's internal political rivals never neglected to add their comments on the unbelievable events: "Willy Brandt, who represented hope to them and to whom many people in the GDR looked, had political wisdom but no money."[117] From then on the internal political debate focused on whether it was all too understandable or offensive that the GDR citizens were chasing after the West German mark instead of the ideals of freedom.

There were still internal battles to be fought before the "Alliance for Germany," an artificial grouping of the Eastern CDU, *Demokratischer Aufbruch*, and the *Deutsche Soziale Union* (DSU), an Eastern formation of the Bavarian CSU, were ready to go before the voters on March 18. Kohl regarded the political dilettante organization centered on the Leipzig pastor Hans-Wilhelm Ebeling with some suspicion. He did not want to get too close to his CSU counterpart Theo Waigel, since the election could hardly be won without the national wing in the "Alliance."

Consequently Kohl put a good face on it, and Ebeling was not such a bad fellow after all. After Kohl's speech on the Leipzig Opernplatz, Stasi minions slashed the tires on the brand new car the CSU had donated to the pastor. The police did not interfere and left the matter to private initiative. The GDR had changed since March 18 and gave up on itself more and more. Understandably, the chancellor had one goal in mind: to keep the people there. The satisfaction which Kohl had felt after the first successful step toward unification had become a momentary pleasure because newer and even more urgent tasks awaited him. After the elections in the *Volkskammer* the next step toward unification was to be the amalgamation of currencies and economic and social systems. It was to occur "around the middle of the year," that is, in just over three months.

Before this Kohl visited Moscow to obtain the Russian seal of approval for unification. It had almost been forgotten that Gorbachev had once been one of those people who were not at all in agreement with Kohl's temperament and supposed haste in this question. Now, "Gorby" said affably, "There is no difference of opinion about the unification." Kohl and Gorbachev announced jointly at an international press conference that it "was the Germans' decision alone whether they wanted to live together in one country." Gorbachev had cleverly said the same thing to Modrow, knowing well how the game would turn out. The Moscow visit was a breakthrough for Kohl and Genscher; Helmut and Hans-Dieter, friends for three decades, shook hands under the table. Such an event can be "numbing" even without alcohol, Genscher muttered to himself late in the evening in the guest house on the Lenin Hills. It would be "unworthy" to open a bottle of champagne now, so they had soda and beer.

It is strange in the light of the "big brother" of the GDR which was doomed to die that hardly anyone in the West German media in those weeks posed the question of the material price of unification. It was clear to planners in Bonn with vision, and to the chancellor especially, that it would have to cost many billions. The final word had not yet been spoken. The points had been shifted, but the train which was to pass through them had not yet started on its way.

Up to that point, no ministerial official in Bonn, let alone a cabinet member, was willing to put a price tag on what the Russians would have to be paid for unification, that is, for withdrawal of military equipment and payment for facilities and land the Soviets had confiscated. Who could blame the Soviets for the fact that they would be leaving a poisoned landscape and an internally and externally disorientated army for whom the Germans would have to pay to have houses built in their homeland? The world is ruled by money and a lot can be accomplished with it: the Western capitalists did not have to be taught this.

In the spring of 1990, in which all the important preliminary decisions had to be made for unification, Kohl was right to consider that it was not sensible to support financially the rump-GDR, as he now thought of it. For this reason, his internal party challenger, Lafontaine, tried to make the chancellor appear to be "caught lying" on his travels through East Germany, implying that Kohl had promised help for the GDR which had hitherto not been forthcoming. A more incorrect argument could hardly be imagined. The man from the Saarland, who could not understand that the overwhelming majority of the people in the GDR would not go along with his negative views of unification, was fighting a long-dead battle. The people did not want Bonn to "give the old regime sugar." Rather, they wanted to starve it to death or make it ready for anything. Only unpolitical people could accuse the Bonn government's tactics during those months as being "completely without solidarity" (*Die Zeit*). Anyone arguing like that fails to

GDR minister-president Hans Modrow visits Bonn, February 14, 1990. The chancellor and his guest had to be led into the federal press room over the fire escape because hundreds of journalists were blocking the entrance.

understand politics as an attempt at harmony whose goal is primarily that everyone is as nice as possible to each other.

The suggestion by Hans Modrow, who some considered only a "destroyer of the *Reich*," of "cooperation and good-neighborliness between the German Democratic Republic and the Federal Republic of Germany," was regarded in Bonn not quite as a bad joke but as a transparent attempt to prolong an undesirable situation instead of terminating it forever after the first free election in the *Volkskammer*. For this reason Kohl was not at all inclined to take up the suggestion of the GDR prime minister, which was only geared toward propping up a rotten system against the interests of its citizens until its demise. It was later proven that this was the correct course of action, a decision which proved the long-range political vision of a statesman, even though it appeared cold-hearted and calculating to many observers in February and March of 1990.

Kohl, the driving force behind the "Alliance for Germany" election campaign, was correctly understood by the people of the GDR. The alliance scored a good victory in the first free *Volkskammer* election contrary to all demographic data, private and official prognoses, and speculations by the media and political parties. For many GDR citizens it was the first free election in seven decades, counting the brown and red dictatorships. With voter participation of over ninety-three percent, the alliance gained 192 votes to 88 for the SPD. No one in the chancellor's circle was disappointed that the FDP would have only twenty-one seats in the *Volkskammer*, Teltschik noted in his diary. It had been Helmut Kohl's election, and no one in the coalition or the alliance had to be unhappy that this was so. It seemed exaggerated when Gerhard von Glinski wrote that the GDR election had made "the chancellor the leader of the European scene," but it was not really that wrong either. Rudolf Augstein's magazine's cover lines read "Kohl's Triumph." Kohl had again proved his instinct for power, he had "represented the right thing." It was obvious at that time that Augstein belonged to the "reunifiers," which led to internal controversy at *Der Spiegel*, the opposite camp at the magazine being headed by Erich Böhme. Nevertheless, Kohl stuck to his decision not to read *Der Spiegel*, but to have it read to him, though a lot more thoroughly in future.

For Helmut Kohl the victory of March 18 was much more than a triumph of the will to achieve German unity with might. It bolstered his self-confidence, which had suffered as a consequence of the many doubts of strong forces in the CDU before and after the Bremen party conference. He was obviously pleased that this resounding victory was "especially good," looking back at the Bremen convention. At the same time, probably carried by the emotion of the moment, Kohl took a sideswipe at those who were already predicting a structural change in the party scene to the Union's disadvantage as a consequence of reunification, pointing to the broad spectrum of voter support. Whether this was "merely talk," or a nasty harbinger of a coming disaster remained to be seen.

Soli Deo Gloria

As chancellor of a united Germany Kohl was closely surrounded in the next few months by people who differed greatly from those in the past. The alliance had chalked up its great victory because Kohl had been a drawing card, but the leaders now had to form a government which was to be a transition between the dying SED state and the unified "Fatherland," which had become Kohl's favorite expression for it in public. The practicalities were left to the interior minister, Wolfgang Schäuble; the finance minister, Theo Waigel; the state secretary, Günther Krause; and the finance minister, Walther Romberg. The foreign relations details were the bailiwick of Foreign Minister Hans Dietrich Genscher and his East German colleague Markus Meckel. The apt expression "window of understanding," taken from satellite technology, was used in regard to securing foreign policy to allow internal political room to maneuver.

But in the meantime the GDR was still led by Lothar de Maizière, very secure in his position at the head of the last GDR government. When required, Kohl spoke directly to the Berlin lawyer and music-loving political dilettante, the "black giant" leaving the other cabinet members to his Bonn wire pullers. As in the case of Modrow, there could not have been two more different men than Kohl and de Maizière. The one embodied the German economic miracle, acting before others could draw breath, while "Premier" de Maizière, made fun of by conceited West Germans as "Notar de Misère," was thin and small, contemplative, and a chain smoker who was not prone to making decisions. It was typical of this man with a secret wish for "Christian Socialism" that he had graduated from the *Berlinisches Gymnasium zum Grauen Kloster*, and that, like his bigger brother from the West, he had joined the CDU when he was barely sixteen years old. The younger man tried as best he could to stand up to Kohl in the next few months, after becoming the first (and last) freely elected prime minister of the GDR on April 12, 1990. This was an almost impossible task for obvious reasons, but for an honest and open Christian Democrat, it was one which had to be done. "The renewal of our society stood under the motto of 'We are the People.' The people have become conscious of themselves. For the first time in many decades the people in the GDR have become a people. The election which created this parliament was an election of the people. For the first time the name of the *Volkskammer* truly applies," Lothar de Maizière said in forming his government. The speech was well formulated. Schäuble noted succinctly in the chronology of his book *Der Vertrag—Wie ich über die deutsche Einheit verhandelte* (The Treaty: How I Negotiated German Unification), "Government declaration by Prime Minister Lothar de

The chancellor and the first (and last) freely elected GDR minister president, Lothar de Mazière, at the CDU Unification Convention in Hamburg, October 1, 1990, two days before the official beginning of German unity.

Maizière. Acknowledgment of the unity of Germany." Four months later on August 31, 1990, when the unification treaty was signed at the Kronprinzenpalais, the Protestant de Maizière wrote on his copy the words used by all pious musicians since Johann Sebastian Bach: "*Soli Deo Gloria*" (to God alone the glory).

After the *Bundestag* elections Kohl intended to reward de Maizière with the high-ranking position of president of the *Bundestag*, but Rita Süssmuth already had a lot of strong supporters for this office and fended off all outside contenders. Lothar de Maizière thus became a cabinet member without portfolio. Unsuspecting, he felt flattered that the chancellor wanted to send him to universities to win students for the Union. Some people told him he should have done this, but things turned out differently in the end. Kohl had quickly recognized and honored the limited political potential of his East German partner in a cool manner, obviously thanking him, knowing full well that it looked good at party conferences and other large political functions to repeatedly express gratitude to Lothar de Maizière for "his significant role in the reunification of Germany." However, Kohl had discovered in the year of unification that de Maizière had hesitated in setting the date for the decisive accords and that Günther Krause was pursuing the event of the century quickly and single-mindedly.

From the very beginning Kohl appeared to be well disposed toward Angela Merkel. Born in 1954 in Hamburg, the daughter of a theologian, she had moved with her parents to Mecklenburg, joining the *Demokratischer Aufbruch* in late 1989. With a doctorate in physics (her dissertation was entitled, "Calculating Velocity Constants of Elementary Reactions Based on Simple Hydrocarbons"), she was working as a press officer before being appointed deputy government spokesperson for the de Maizière government in March. Angela Merkel appeared innocuous and reserved when she entered the political arena, but this changed when Kohl "discovered" her and secured for her the completely exaggerated position of temporary first deputy of the CDU government chairperson. But Angela knew how to cope with and adapt herself to the changed circumstances, becoming the first minister from the East with a guaranteed job, and six years after unification still holds the position.

Only a few others found a way to Kohl or Kohl to them. Rainer Eppelmann had become a friend in Bonn after Heinz Schwarz's family took in the wanderer between two worlds from time to time, followed by Norbert Blüm. Another person who ensconced himself on the Bonn scene was Günther Krause, the intelligent envoy who worked on the unification treaty; he became adept at having a good nose for the fleshpots of the Bonn jungle. This speaker of the East German CDU *Land* group resigned his ministerial post in the spring of 1993 in the wake of the "cleaning woman affair."

One Country, One Election

Since the events of March 18, there was in Kohl's view only one way to achieve unification, and that was in accordance with Article 23 of the Basic Law. This was a step to be decided by the GDR politicians, perhaps as one of their final acts of office: joining the Federal Republic of Germany. This act, constitutionally the only one possible, naturally went against the grain of a number of members in the East Berlin *Volkskammer*, the ugly word "*Anschluss*" having made the rounds since spring.

The Bonn coalition was practically unanimous in its view, but opinion was divided in the alliance and SPD in the GDR. Many people's illusions had been destroyed, especially those who retreated into nostalgia and wanted to save whatever possible of the GDR. These sentiments were found not only in the remains of socialist circles; the Christian Democrats also dreamed of the "oh so quiet SED times," as a *Volkskammer* member sighed. Some strong words were needed by the chancellor, as they had been in the deliberations on the way the voting would be run in the first all-German elections set for fall or winter. It would have been strange if the two eternally squabbling sisters, the CDU and the CSU, had been able to agree on this point. No, the CSU demanded a chance for the small *Deutsche Soziale Union* (DSU), which was campaigning only regionally, becoming the most obvious affiliate of the Bavarian CSU in Eastern Germany. In order to allow the DSU to survive the elections in the GDR, the chancellor favored reducing the parliamentary lower limit from five to three percent, consciously taking into the bargain saving the SED, which had renamed itself the *Partei der Demokratischen Sozialismus* (PDS). The Free Democrats opposed this, demanding a genuine all-German election with a uniform five percent lower limit. One of the FDP *Fraktion* legal experts, the former interior minister, Gerhart Rudolf Baum, formulated the Liberals' demands as "One country, one election."

For most people in Germany such theorizing about election procedures seemed to be useless and superfluous, but they were truly relevant to genuine political motives and power struggles. Indeed, there was also a more noble motive: to allow the people's movement representatives to be elected to the *Bundestag* via the *Bündnis 90/Die Grünen* (the Green party).

Most people were more concerned about how Eastern Germany was to be helped back on its feet. Moreover there is a principle in the Basic Law which demanded that similar conditions had to be created in the entire Federal Republic of Germany. That naturally meant the same buying power throughout the country which would soon be united. Some people might turn their noses up at that, believing that "higher" issues were more important for the approaching unification. But many people, especially in the Western part, had to be reminded that that was not right. "Money is a coinage of freedom," wrote Dostoevsky, who knew whereof he spoke. Kohl did not have to be taught this. He threw all of his prestige into the balance on the issue of currency union, forcing through an exchange rate for his Eastern German fellow citizens that *Bundesbank* chairman Karl Otto Pöhl

The CDU celebrated with a reception in the Beethovenhalle in Bonn on April 3, 1990, the sixtieth birthday of the party chairman. One of the first well-wishers was Federal President Richard von Weizsäcker.

was barely able to euphemistically describe as "political." The financial expert thought the situation was "quixotic." He then resigned from his position for personal reasons, but actually because his admonitions about the threat to financial stability had been ignored "by the top."

The time of trials and proving himself had only just begun for the sixty-year-old government leader and candidate to become the first chancellor in a united Germany. This also held true for his long friendship with Genscher, which, it could be said, was as often as not unilateral. In any case the FDP chairman and foreign minister seemed to take it more seriously than the Christian Democrat. Politically, Genscher was the only counterweight to Kohl, "bathed in all Rhenish and Saxon waters," as Klaus Harpprecht said, and "the only one able to master the chancellor's hardness and quick decisions." Unlike Kohl, Genscher is an expert who is good at details, whether as interior or—in the meantime—"longest-serving foreign minister in the world," which he is proud to be. Genscher does not have Kohl's hunger for power, which makes him immune to criticism in controversial questions. Friedrich Schorlemmer uses the slightly inapt metaphor and turns it neatly into a paradox: "He [Kohl] has such a firm stand that he can sit to anything. He is so sensitive that nothing can bother him."[118]

It was no surprise that with the confusing internal political situation, with deadlines coinciding, "ensuring the unification process through foreign policy" made the headlines daily and made Kohl sit and worry at his desk. When Rudolf Augstein wrote that "the chancellor and his favorite, Teltschik, do not understand foreign policy and do not even take notice of it," there was a suspicion that two Liberals were whispering to each other, one of whom would not be Genscher. He was rightfully considered to have an "exceedingly good" lawyer's mind and thus would not be one to speak without propriety. Nevertheless Genscher and his staff were not exactly overjoyed about the Two-Plus-Four negotiations, which dominated the foreign-policy work of the "little Kissinger" (Teltschik). For example, as soon

Authoritative credit for German unification: The chancellor and his foreign minister during a cabinet meeting, April 1990.

as Genscher advised accepting Moscow's offer for unification without insisting that the "alliance question" should be solved first, Teltschik, speaking on behalf of his top boss, let it be known that there had been strict warnings against "decoupling" this issue from the unification process. Kohl considered the Soviets' offer to be "negotiation poker" anyway, which turned out to be right.

Kohl obviously did not dream of protecting his friend in public appearances, but, whenever it seemed necessary or good for internal party politics or just playful interest, he left his close associate "standing in the rain." Unlike in the past, Kohl acted according to his own election slogan in the unification year, "many enemies, much honor." He took this upon himself so that he could say later, "you were not only brave, but most importantly you were right." Whether one worked with him closely or at a distance, mocked, mistrusted or tried to get around him, in the end, his presence could not be ignored.

Kohl usually reacted frostily to indiscretions against himself in 1990 and to one in particular which Prime Minister Margaret Thatcher, of all people, committed. In a *Der Spiegel* interview she said that Helmut Kohl had told her "in a confidential circle" during the Strasbourg summit in the spring that he could not necessarily guarantee the western border of Poland. Such suspicions sowed dissatisfaction between the Western allies and were naturally not well received in the East. Kohl knew that Germany did not have just friends and the climate became more tense over the course of unification. Whoever opens doors has to realize that they let in a strong draft. At that point Kohl was tempted to consider Thatcher a "subject," his standard expression for despicable people, but he was careful not to let this feeling go beyond his own office. The man from the Palatinate took revenge on the British leader when they again met in European Union circles and Kohl tried to avoid a private conversation with her, saying he had "appointments which could not be broken." As luck would have it, Maggie Thatcher saw her "friend Helmut" shortly afterward sitting at a café and happily eating cake with no sign at all of stress from the conference. This unplanned confrontation was said to have been the end of the friendship.

A Happy, Fulfilling Time

When the chancellor wanted to see himself portrayed according to his own wishes in a newspaper, he talked to Johann Georg Reissmüller of the *Frankfurter Allgemeine Zeitung*. He has a very close relationship with the co-publisher of the newspaper, which is why he disclosed his most intimate thoughts to Reissmüller. "It was a happy, fulfilled time for him," could be read a few days after the "conversation,"—Kohl would have said "a good conversation"—in the "newspaper for Germany." He said he had "more work to do than ever before in his life." The world was in order, the day of unification was approaching. Kohl asked his colleagues not to bother him with details, otherwise they would make him take his eyes off the main goal. The chancellor had to consider not only German unification, but its place within the European unification process. The German unification would occur with the approval of all of Germany's neighbors, "even though the 'yes' was said with varying degrees of warmth." As a political realist, Kohl knew only too well that it could not be any different. Kohl was particularly pleased that the Americans regarded German reunification with special favor; he had always known that the United States would cause him the fewest problems. In these moments he scanned the horizons and allowed himself to be briefed about internal events only cursorily. Almost everything was in a state of flux.

The first clearing operations in the massively confusing Eastern German bureaucracy brought the dawning of realization. It brought home to the West German authorities, especially Hans Neusel of the Bonn interior ministry, that here was a jungle to be hacked through before sowing and harvesting could be done. Up to that point he had been unsuccessful in getting GDR interior minister Peter-Michael Diestel, who played on his Christianity, but who in reality was as slippery as an eel and was misanthropic, to turn over Stasi documents about the implications of the GDR regime in past terrorist activities. When Neusel himself escaped an assassination attempt with a fright and slight injuries to his upper right arm, the usually phlegmatic Westphalian lost his temper. Screaming down the phone line, he demanded that Neusel turn over all papers relating to terrorist activities, whereupon the latter sent a Volkswagen bus around to the interior ministry and had several hundred pounds of documents loaded and sent to Bonn, where they were quickly copied.

This sort of thing happened in almost all departments which held onto their jurisdiction, defending it even during reunification in a good old-fashioned manner against all outsiders. Money, however, was an exception. It was accepted without discrimination by everyone since July 1, 1990, regardless of authority, whether or not one thought the country should have its own administration. Those people in the GDR who wanted to conserve it were the only ones who could afford feelings of nostalgia, in order to save it for the new era.

Prime Minister Lothar de Maizière was open to everything which was new, but even after the "change" he clung to his favorite GDR brand of cigarettes, "Club," an evil weed which burned the tongue but recalled the good old, less hectic days. The forensically trained lawyer countered accusations that he had been hired by the Stasi as an unofficial helper under the cover name "Czerni" with what de Maizière probably regarded as a rhetorical question: "Do you believe that they would have left me and my family to rot in a two-and-a-half-room apartment and stopped my daughter from getting her *Abitur* if I had been an informant for the Stasi?"[119]

Kohl was not bothered that his East German counterpart still smoked his Club cigarettes, or by whether or not he worked for the Stasi. Although de Maizière never seriously stood in the way of reunification, Kohl believed that he was not suited for politics. But he spoke almost endearingly of his love of music: "His spiritual dacha is music."[120] It was soon evident that Gorbachev shared Kohl's view that Lothar de Maizière would "prove to be a transitional figure."[121]

The Earth Is Round

On July 15, 1990, Helmut Kohl and his host Mikhail Gorbachev met at the Soviet government guest house on Alexei Tolstoy Street in Moscow, a turn-of-the-century neo-Gothic monstrosity, for a decisive talk about German unification. Gorbachev awaited his German guest and friend on the inside stairs of the huge building, greeting him with: "The earth is round and we are always flying around it." Kohl quickly responded: "My need has been fulfilled; I am looking forward to our discussions and hope that they will be successful."[122]

In later meetings in Stavropol, in the Caucasus, it became clear, as Gorbachev wrote in his memoirs, that unification was, "as one says, sealed." But the matter was not ready for signature until Moscow. In retrospect Kohl said that:

> The decisive discussions during my visit to the Soviet Union took place on July 15 and 16 in Moscow. In a private talk I asked Mikhail Gorbachev whether he would insist on Germany's neutrality, that is, that we would have to leave NATO. I told him it made no sense to leave that open, since if he were going to insist on that we did not have to fly to the Caucasus, that I would return home, since it was clear to me that the stream of time which led to German unity would prevail. He did not say yes or no, only "we should fly there." . . . Moreover, since the ten-point program of November 1989 I was certain that I would sooner or later convince Gorbachev.[123]

The "miracle of the Caucasus," which Horst Teltschik rightly called "of Moscow," described in detail by Kohl's government press spokesperson, Johnny Klein, did not take place. Klein had started to work even before joining the chancellor's official delegation on the trip to Moscow and the

The legendary meeting in the Caucasus, October 15, 1990: Kohl and Gorbachev (from left) with Information Minister Hans Klein, Finance Minister Theo Waigel, Raissa Gorbacheva, and Soviet Foreign Minister Schevardnadze.

Caucasus, which achieved "the German dream of reunification in peace and freedom with the assent of all friends and neighbors." This lasted only fifty-two hours: "the hours of the Germans. The hours which have changed Europe."[124]

The Caucasus had been chosen primarily to lend an attractive framework for the hearts and minds of the participants and for the historic occasion. Gorbachev devoted only two pages to the Caucasus in his memoirs; Moscow was more important to him, which is why three years later he personally had the transcription of the private conversation which he obviously regarded as decisive published in the West. Gorbachev greeted Kohl cordially, and the chancellor started the conversation.

> **Kohl:** "We live in a unique age. The first half of the 1990s are set to be full of significant events and tasks. The coming years will be etched deeply in history. And we can note with satisfaction that we have the possibility to assist in achieving these great tasks. Such an age happens only rarely. It would be unforgivable to act half-heartedly or indecisively. No one will be able to say that about us."
>
> **Gorbachev:** "Naturally the dynamics and the character of the events offer a unique opportunity to make decisions which could make the first half of the 1990s a historic milestone in

the development of the world and especially of Europe. The politicians of our generation have the responsibility for ensuring that this chance does not go to waste. I agree with you that the measure of our personal relationship and trust offer a good chance to achieve these goals. I believe that we will understand each other much better by the end of your visit in the Soviet Union."

Kohl: "I don't doubt that. I find something which Bismarck once said to be very good: 'You cannot do something yourself. You have to wait to hear the footsteps of God through the events, and then jump up and grab his coattails—that is all.' These words in particular are characteristic of our age, and above all, of the first half of the 1990s. Our generation in particular has a special responsibility. We did not directly experience war, our conscience is clear, but we remember war and have seen its horrors. That's the difference between us and the youth of today, which I see in the case of my two sons. I once spoke of 'the grace of a late birth' in regard to the people of our generation. We've had experiences that others haven't, and we should exploit these fully in the development of our civilization."

Gorbachev: "I'd like to emphasize this thought especially. We indeed are able to compare past and present. I was ten years old when the war started and fifteen when it ended, an especially sensitive age. The present generation is possibly better, but we have unique experiences. We have taken the chance which this offers. Our generation can still have something to say in history. Today there is less talk of who won and who lost—we have in the meantime discovered that we are of the same generation."

Kohl: ". . . I've been following developments in the Soviet Union with great interest. Above all, I would like to congratulate you on your success with the twenty-eighth Communist Party Congress. I could see it was not easy for you and I'm happy that everything ended as it should have. I'd call such a party congress 'riding an Amur tiger.'"

Gorbachev: "The goals had indeed been set very high. The conservatives wanted revenge and therefore it was really not easy. But we worked with the people and sometime or other on the fifth or sixth day the tide was turned."

Kohl: "All the Communist Party congresses have been called 'historic,' but I'm convinced that only four actually were: the last two during Lenin's life, the twentieth, after Stalin's death, and finally yours, the twenty-eighth."

Gorbachev: "It was indeed a historic Party Congress. The exchanges were open; ideas, positions, and views were thrown up against each other. . . . I'd like to raise an important issue. It has transpired that Germany and the Soviet Union have had and can have a lot to do with each other in the 1990s again in order to live harmoniously and to assist each other, to increase understanding and cooperation, which is to mutual advantage. When their ways separated, it had serious consequences for our people. We two can ensure that our people come together again. I regard our relationship as being equal to the Soviet-American one. They are equally important for our people and for history."

Kohl: ". . . The purpose of my visit is to give new impetus to relations between our two nations in order to be able to conclude a treaty between the Soviet Union and a united Germany within one year, which includes everything relevant in the existing treaties between the Soviet Union and the two German states and naturally a lot of new aspects. I can at least say that if everything goes normally, all-German elections will be held this December. I don't want to preempt this, but I assume that I will continue in office. Therefore in one year we will open a new chapter in Soviet-German relations and enter a new era. . . . After the all-German elections the question of unification will be answered. Then nothing can stop us and we can quickly achieve mutual success. The planned joint declaration of the two alliances will be significant. I hope that it will be in the form of a pact on nonaggression and not using force. Then all people would breathe easier. . . . Our own main task in the next few months will be solving the problems in the GDR. There the economic situation has proven to be far more serious than was at first thought, and the trend is for things to get more complicated and not simpler every day. We have to take that into consideration. In the past we had other ideas, we thought that everything would take its course, solidly and thoroughly. We did not want to force the process. But developments took a dramatic turn, which also affects you. We've been forced to take several steps at once and therefore we have to trust each other. In this regard the all-German elections on December 2 will be decisive."

Gorbachev: "It can be said that you are facing your own *perestroika*. The tasks are large and difficult."

Kohl: "We will help each other. We agreed to do that on your visit last year to the Federal Republic of Germany. We have kept our word about credits and the Soviet armed forces in the GDR. We are able to trust each other's word."

Gorbachev: "We appreciate your problems. In the present phase of relations we have to strictly adhere to the political context of the development of our states. What are needed are the same opinions, trust and mutual understanding, and cooperation. . . ."

Kohl: ". . . In my view the primary questions to be answered are the future of the Soviet armed forces in Germany, membership of a united Germany in NATO, and the future size of the armed forces in a united Germany. These are three hurdles we have to clear. They also play a role in concluding the Two-Plus-Four negotiations and achieving the full sovereignty of Germany; and the size of the German armed forces directly affects NATO. But naturally the most important thing is the relationship between the Soviet Union and a united Germany."

Gorbachev: ". . . We know and value the role which the federal chancellor and the German government are playing in the positive processes in Europe and it is followed closely in the Soviet Union. Our people are gradually coming to understand the choice of the German people in reunification. We cannot forget the past, and every family at that time was affected. But we must turn toward Europe and follow the path of cooperation with the great German nation. That is our contribution toward increasing stability in Europe and the world. Some of the military have accused us of having sold for German marks our victory which was won at such a high price and with such great sacrifice. We shouldn't simplify the context but we also have to see this reality. Nevertheless, the situation is getting better and we can make concrete plans with a view toward the future, without considering the emotional side, but not forgetting it either. You, as we, have to begin with the precept that we see the goal, the future, and we see that current problems must be solved as a package. Otherwise we won't achieve anything. It is therefore of overriding importance that we base our relationship on a new treaty and I would like to give you our ideas on a treaty between the Soviet Union and Germany, not as a draft, but only in the form of considerations. Perhaps you too will have had some ideas. We will then proceed with this. That is our goal."

Kohl: "I too have written down a few thoughts which I would like to give you. I would like to emphasize that these are my personal thoughts and have not yet been deliberated by the federal government. I have also not enlisted the aid of any ministers. The ministers have colleagues who talk to one another and then it's all over the papers. I have even left out the Foreign Office and the finance ministry. For the moment it is only a draft of thoughts and ideas. I would like to add that it has a lot in common with the Franco-German treaty. I would like to suggest that my close associate, Horst Teltschik, and someone you nominate look through this preliminary version and afterward we'll involve the two foreign ministries. Until then I would like to keep it under wraps because I don't want it to become an issue in the election."

Gorbachev: "I understand you and will do what's necessary. We have to consider each other in formulating the treaty and clarify the positions to prevent misunderstandings. One of the positions has already crystallized, the rest can be worked on. It is clear that the new Germany will encompass the Federal Republic, the GDR, and Berlin and that there will be no claims to change the borders. There are other issues on which we agree to a certain extent and which can be quickly harmonized."

Kohl: "Much of it does not pose any problems for us and we've made progress in many regards. Two resolutions with the same wording will be passed by the *Volkskammer* of the GDR and the *Bundestag*. That's a serious and fundamental step. I don't entirely understand the Poles. I suggested to [the Polish prime minister] Mazowiecki that we would conclude a treaty on the German-Polish border three months after unification, and that I would start negotiations on a comprehensive political treaty with two steps—first the borders and then the main treaty. The Poles are hesitating and avoiding answering. But if Germany and the Soviet Union sign a treaty,

> they'll wrinkle their noses, make a lot of noise, and think of history. We have to find a way to avoid this and get the Poles to see reason."[125]

Egon Bahr, who lost standing on the home front in the early 1970s for his role in the negotiation of a Moscow treaty (of the socialist-liberal coalition under Willy Brandt) and statements made to the Soviet Union with double meanings which came out only later, called the Gorbachev-Kohl discussion as documented by the Russian, "a lesson in politics." The transcript allows a rare look into what could be called "great politics," and "indeed at a moment of significant preparations for significant decisions." The old master of international negotiations even noticed that both men used the familiar pronouns with each other (Kohl used *du*, while the Russian transcript recorded the formal *Sie*). As Bahr points out, it is possible to imagine similar conversations with such a degree of trust between Nixon, Brandt, and Brezhnev, since "great success is not possible without some degree of intimacy."[126] For Wolfgang Herles, who commented on the publication of the transcript which had been kept secret for a number of years, the protocol showed a number of differences between Kohl's and Genscher's political views of unification. While "Genscher, from Halle, . . . would have been ready to sacrifice Germany's NATO membership for unification," Kohl "won back this position in Moscow."[127] Because unification happened without this first condition the assertion cannot be actually proven, but a few years later Helmut Kohl said, "as he was always wont to do," that unification was a present. On the other hand, Genscher continued to assert with more insight that "there had already been a concept behind it."

Triumph of Boldness

Suddenly Helmut Kohl, the politician who had been completely misjudged and grossly underestimated by colleagues and enemies alike, had nothing but friends. Rudolf Augstein said rightly that Kohl "was not a Bismarck, but also not a Ribbentrop." Nevertheless, "the statesman will not disappear off the map" (is there already a place or a battlefield which has been named after the man from the Palatinate?). Whenever his staff told the chancellor about the media's response, Ackermann and his staff began to feel like altar boys who fan incense in the direction of their prelate. Kohl himself began to wonder whether he had "done something wrong in the end." For two weeks publications from all over and of every leaning continued to give him hymn-like praise, including *Le Monde*, which normally was very negative about him, but which now ascribed to him "the triumph of boldness."

Le Monde diplomatique even said he had "the highest degree of skill," having conducted his business "the way de Gaulle did things."

However wonderful all this was, the daily work on the fronts between Bonn and Berlin, Hamburg and Leipzig, Paris and Strasbourg, was not made any easier by his recently gained fame. The dispute over the date for the first *Bundestag* elections in a united Germany ground on into the summer recess, which Kohl definitely wanted to have for his annual "weight-loss program" (to again lose seventeen kilograms) as well as to spend time with his family.

At a secret meeting at St. Gilgen on the Wolfgangsee, Lothar de Maizière and Helmut Kohl decided that the *Landtag* elections in Saxony, Saxony-Anhalt, Thuringia, Brandenburg, and Mecklenburg-Vorpommern would be held on October 14. The meeting was kept secret, the only other parties to it being the Chancellor's office manager, Walter Neuer, and his media adviser, Eduard Ackermann. Not even Kohl's government spokesperson, Johnny Klein, was informed. Schäuble listed July 31 as the date of this meeting in his "chronology" on unification; Ackermann had August 2. Lothar de Maizière was accompanied by the head of his chancery, State Secretary Günther Krause, on a special Interflug flight from Berlin to Salzburg, where they were both picked up by car.

President George Bush also counted as one of the architects of German unity. This photo for Helmut Kohl shows Bush at the White House enjoying a portion of genuine "Saumagen" *(pig stomach) with which the chancellor had honored him.*

Kohl had had to use all his persuasive powers to get the reluctant GDR prime minister to agree to this. De Maizière the next day immediately communicated the decision to the *Volkskammer* to prevent anyone else from announcing it as his own.

Kohl was able to note in his diary during his vacation in St. Gilgen that October 3 would be the day of German unification. The CDU East and CDU West were to merge the day before at the party conference in Hamburg. The die had been cast, the countdown was running. The CDU's chief organizer, Karl Schumacher, set up the Hamburg "unification party conference" like an opera, with dramatic interludes, some solos, and the well-known final chorus of "*Einigkeit und Recht und Freiheit*." Helmut Kohl was elected almost unanimously as the first chairperson of the newly merged Christian Democratic Union of Germany, and only a handful of people without a Fatherland dared to abstain. The almost unimaginable triumph allowed Kohl to manfully suppress criticism of the actions of the Eastern CDU after the SED had made it a bloc party in 1947. But those were past battles and should remain so. Those who had not been allowed to live in freedom (Kohl had once used the expression "the warm sofa of freedom," which would have worked well in a cabaret), should not now be allowed to sink back into an untimely Pharisee state. Contrary to his original skepticism of the GDR prime minister, who still ostensibly clung to the "ideals of socialism," Kohl told the party conference, still steeped in the atmosphere of unification, in reconciliation, "With courage and breadth of vision, Lothar de Maizière has returned the party to independence and at the same time put it on the road to the new unity." Lothar de Maizière received 97.4 percent of the votes for deputy chairperson of the party. It was a "GDR" result, but no one saw the slightest cause to smirk about it.

In an article in the *Frankfurter Allgemeine Zeitung* on October 2, the day before German unification, the federal chancellor reassured an international readership that "Germany would not tread a separate or a nationalistic path." Alluding to a well-known book title, Kohl wrote in this intelligently argued and very honest article that there would be no reason in future to speak of the "restless *Reich*." He did not neglect to mention—which probably cheered up his East German party colleagues—that even the election successes of a Konrad Adenauer or Ludwig Erhard had been preceded by "passionate debates with supporters of a planned economy."

Kohl and his close colleagues left immediately after the Hamburg party conference and flew in a German air force plane to Berlin-Templehof. The merger of the CDU of Germany and the serving "premier," Lothar de Maizière, had enabled a German chancellor to fly in a German plane directly to

Four days before October 3, 1990, German television presented a discussion of the questions raised by German unification, which was broadcast from Adenauer's former office in Schaumburg palace. The discussion included former Chancellor Willy Brandt.

Berlin for the first time since 1949 on the day before Germany was legally unified. On that evening, Helmut Kohl, his wife Hannelore, and all close associates from the chancellor's office, his coalition partner and friend Hans Dietrich Genscher, and numerous other representatives of the opposition party attended a concert at the Schauspielhaus at the Gendarmenmarkt. Kurt Masur directed the Leipzig Gewandhaus Orchestra in playing Beethoven's Ninth Symphony's final chorus, which left many with tears in their eyes. Lothar de Maizière had the final word in this hour, which was spoken in the GDR for official reasons. After that the chancellor's entourage traveled in convoy to the *Reichstag* where hundreds of thousands of people waited. The sky was clear and the Germans were granted a joyous night, which would not soon be repeated. There were fireworks, a choir sang, the bells of freedom rang out, and "Helmut, Helmut," was to be heard when the chancellor arrived.

When the federal German flag was raised at midnight and many thousands of people sang the third verse of the national anthem, the chancellor

The night of German unification, October 3, 1990. On the front steps of the Reichstag *building. From left: Foreign Minister Genscher, the chancellor with his wife, and Federal President von Weizsäcker.*

had tears in his eyes, which so many people thought would not be possible for such a hardened politician. A television camera showed Willy Brandt, honorary chairman of the SPD, openly crying.

After the fireworks started a day of inestimable joy, this historic day of October 3, 1990, Helmut Kohl and his wife and Lothar and Ilse de Maizière withdrew into the chancellor's office in the *Reich* chancery, followed by Kohl's close associates Wolfgang Bergsdorff, Norbert Prill, Juliane Weber, and Johannes Ludewig. Ackermann says that Kohl and de Maizière were "visibly moved" at this moment. Every time Kohl wanted to respond to the cries of "Helmut, Helmut," and go to the window he tried to bring de Maizière with him. But this fragile man declined, tired and shattered from the pressures of the last few months in which he had given his best. This gesture was symbolic: one had played out his role, he could do and wanted to do nothing more. The night of October 2–3 ended in the bar of the Hotel Kempinski, where the chancellor's crew bumped into Edzard Reuter of Daimler-Benz and Heinz Dürr of AEG (*Allgemeine Elektrizitäts-Gesellschaft*, or General Electric Company).

12

The Chancellor of Unity

1990–1994

That Is the Hour in Which One Learns to Pray

Ten days after the day of German unification, a mentally disturbed man fired a gun and injured Interior Minister Wolfgang Schäuble just after the party conference ended. After Kohl visited his friend on his sickbed, he said almost reverently, "That is the hour in which one learns to pray."[128] The CDU politician from the southwest, not even fifty years old, was in danger of being confined to a wheelchair for the rest of his life as a paraplegic. Kohl commented cautiously, but his meaning was understood by everyone: "In view of the serious injuries . . . questions remain open. . . . It is a terrible affliction."

Kohl, who is ostensibly cold about anything which does not directly affect him, suddenly discovered a weakness in himself: not only having sympathy as a private person, but showing it in public. But he quickly tried to turn this weakness into a strength by stepping into the role of protector of this small cabinet member who did not fit in with his image of a man, and to whom he sometimes ascribed "Baden craftiness." This was also a form of dependency into which Kohl is wont to thrust all those he tolerates in close proximity. And whoever rails against this dependency is punished by withdrawal of love.

Six months later on an election campaign trip Kohl gave the first hints of who might possibly succeed him: the person who was now tragically confined to a wheelchair. During a break at the traditional guest-house stop at the "Hexenbäcker" in Kaiserslautern, the chancellor, who had just spoken of a hopeful picture of coming economic prosperity in eastern Germany, was suddenly "overcome by autumnal thoughts" (Dreher). He surprised his listeners by saying that when he retired from office "everything would go to Wolfgang Schäuble." The CDU *Land* chairman Hans-Otto Wilhelm made reference to the chairmanship of the CDU/CSU *Bundestag* parliamentary party, but Kohl interrupted his confusion, saying "no, no, the other office." Kohl painted a picture of a person in the highest office who had at his disposal many means to get around, even with a physical handicap, almost like someone without one. In Bonn, Schäuble was already making ironic jokes about his handicap, according to the *Süddeutsche Zeitung*. Thus he told Otto Graf Lambsdorff, who had to use a walking stick due to severe war injuries (which is why he is sometimes called "Count Silver Crutch"), that he, Schäuble, was at a real advantage at stand-up parties.

Blooming Landscapes Are on Their Way

Forming the first all-German parliament was a real battle which did not last as long as the elections preceding it. On the other hand, the whole year had been one of controversy. Day-to-day life had the Germans again fully occupied, the currency union and day of unification having been given their sentimental due. The chancellor of unification, so recently lauded, was again given a frontal assault by Augstein and others. "The broken word is valid," came the taunts from Hamburg and other press strongholds.

The tactical and semantic mistakes the chancellor made at the many election meetings in this "year of unification" that was now ending were starting to come home to roost with a vengeance. Kohl's quotes indeed appeared highly insidious because they were made without due consideration out of necessity at the time and their intention to generally mollify any anger which might arise: "For the people in the Federal Republic of Germany"—spoken on July 1, 1990—it holds true that "no one will have to do without anything due to the reunification of Germany. Only some of what we produce as surplus in the coming years will be given to our fellow citizens in the GDR, as help for self-help." When his party and he himself began to meet strong resistance from internal political opponents four months later, Kohl became a casuist of a special class: "I did not say that there would not be any increases in tax and contributions; I said that there would be no tax increases in view of the problems of German unification." Kohl obviously misjudged the Germans' willingness to forgo part of their prosperity to ensure a smooth transition of the two parts of the country. But the taxpayer was not going to do that without objections and it was all the same to them whether they were being asked for "taxes," "contributions," or "fees": everything cost money.

The basic government propaganda for the next few years was formulated in those weeks. The billions needed to meet the ongoing costs of "rebuilding the east" had to be paid, whatever wild arguments the government used, some of which oddly enough had nothing to do with unification. The "landscapes in bloom" which the east was soon supposed to have and to which Kohl referred with too much haste were another example. Much later this campaign slogan in a television ad spot became one of Kohl's original sayings: "The blooming landscapes are on their way." But how could they be when they're not yet there?

It was shown once again in the case of the change to unification that the Kohl government had had highly inadequate public relations advisers. The chancellor should probably have listened to Johnny Klein, whose campaign motto was "Everything can be formulated, especially the truth." Obviously no one at "the court" had stuck to this motto, as the October opinion poll of Elisabeth Noelle-Neumann showed. She gave Kohl a "chancellor bonus," probably to make the man from the Palatinate happy in the year of unification, in which she had had a hand. If this assumption had actually corresponded to the opinion of the average German, the elections' results for the Union parties of December 2, 1990, would not have been so poor. At any rate, the results of 43.8 percent were less than the 1987 *Bundestag* election results of 44.3 percent.

A question can be raised about the "chancellor bonus." The CDU had not spared anything in the election campaign in accordance with the directions of its master of ceremonies, Karl Schumacher. It offered everything that was good and expensive and would make the people happy: impressively decorated speakers' platforms, spotlights, good loudspeakers, buses for transport, propaganda chit-chat, and big-band music. The background was an enormous dove-gray placard with the Union's campaign slogan, "Yes to Germany, yes to the future—together we'll do it." Nothing helped: the election results were disappointing even though the coalition was confirmed for the third time and for the first time there was a chancellor of a united Germany.

Don't Forget the Tomatoes and Eggs

The chancellor began a long political swing through eastern Germany at the beginning of 1991, the start of a new era. The purpose of the trip was to meet the people in the halls and the marketplaces as an expression of the new normality in Germany. The democratic framework which was to be set up in the eastern part of the republic required the public appearance of its governor. Aside from that, Kohl loved being surrounded by crowds, even if it was not always comfortable. Moreover, the Bonn leader intended to show the new citizens in the eastern part of the republic by his frequent appearances that it was better to stay at home and build it up than to "take off" for the west and intensify the fight for jobs.

A nasty incident happened in early May during Kohl's visit to Halle. A

With President Bush during the Conference on Security and Cooperation in Europe Summit in Paris, November 26, 1990. The thirty-four nations signed the Charter for a New Europe, which proclaimed the official end of the Cold War.

small but pugnacious group of radical leftist demonstrators threw tomatoes, eggs, and bags of dye at the chancellor standing in front of the city hall. A few young people called Kohl a "liar" and he was hit by projectiles on the head and shoulders. The "black giant" lost his temper momentarily, storming off in the direction of the troublemakers, not allowing his bodyguards to stop him from grabbing an approximately twenty-year-old man by the collar in the heaving crowd and holding on to him. People tried to stop Kohl and separate him from the crowd which was just barely under control. But he had never been so incensed and with an angry expression he again stormed the crowd. Kohl's bodyguards were finally able to stop the 1.93-meter-tall man and convince him grudgingly that it would be better to withdraw to the city hall. Pictures taken during the incident went all over the world.

This was supposed to be the chancellor of unity? Was this the new peace that was spreading across Germany? Some people understood his anger, others condemned his outburst. Friedrich Bohl, the manager of the CDU/CSU in the *Bundestag*, made an official protest to SPD chairperson Hans-Jochen Vogel. Bohl demanded an apology from the SPD because the local leader of the Young Socialists and his people had been among the troublemaking demonstrators, waving a flag and hardly to be overlooked. Rudolf Seiters, the minister in the chancellor's office, who had watched the images on television with shock, was extremely angry about "the use of force by radicals against the federal chancellor, who had pledged himself to unity and freedom for the people." That was "outrageous and cannot be accepted."[129]

The great internal political battle began along the usual parliamentary lines, everyone seeking to get one up on his political opponent and put a feather in his own cap. The echo was not clear in the SPD, however. While SPD leader Vogel's designated successor, Björn Engholm, said that Kohl's outburst in Halle was a "refreshing and sympathetic reaction," Bavaria's SPD leader and vice president of the *Bundestag*, Renate Schmidt, defended the radical demonstrators in Halle. She could understand "that people who are without jobs and hope could express their disappointment by throwing eggs." Volker Rühe, general secretary of the CDU, found everything "really bad." The question of Kohl's personal safety at public appearances in eastern Germany was already being seriously debated in Bonn.

After the recent outbreaks this security did not seem to be guaranteed any longer. At any rate, the incident in Halle, after which Kohl had absolutely peaceful visits to Schkopau and Bitterfeld, showed that the danger to his person could no longer be ignored. It was observed that in Halle his only protection had been his bodyguards, with no uniformed police visible. Was this only a disastrous mistake or was it a deliberate omission? A note by the man responsible for security in Saxony-Anhalt, Klaus-Dieter Matschke, dated November 16, 1990, shows that the drama in Halle could have been avoided. Six months before the event, the senior adviser on criminal activities in Frankfurt am Main had researched and documented the dangers to the top visitor from Bonn for the *Land* interior minister.

> The guest house Die Quelle in Halle on Hegel Street is the meeting place for a group of "autonomists" and Spartakists. The group comprises about forty to fifty people and has already had several confrontations with right wingers. Handbills and fliers were distributed which called on people to assemble for Kohl's visit and "not to forget the tomatoes and eggs." . . . That there will probably be trouble during the chancellor's visit must be reckoned with. The group's potential is considerable. It is strongly advised that this group be observed before and during the chancellor's visit.

Because Interior Minister Braun was eager to block Matschke's appointment as head of a *Land* Office for the Protection of the Constitution, he or one of his colleagues did not give their unpopular competitor from the west a chance. Matschke believes that the note was thrown into the wastebasket without being noticed. At any rate, no conclusions were drawn from the notes on security. This incident and many other less serious cases of incompetence or boycott show how difficult it was to achieve political and administrative unification of the two states of Germany. The chancellor of the unified Federal Republic of Germany became the first victim of an obviously planned breach of security. Because he had already been too successful in uncovering former Stasi helpers, the Frankfurt senior adviser was to be removed from office and summarily dismissed. Only a few months later the interior minister was unmasked as an "unofficial helper" of the Stasi and he immediately resigned. He was replaced by a man who was trusted by the chancellor, Hartmut Perschau, the top Hamburg CDU candidate, who was able to prove himself "on the front" for the first time. Incidents such as the one in Halle no longer occurred, although the chancellor paid visits to the new *Länder* in the years afterward which often made him feel like he was "running the gauntlet." But he always emerged unscathed.

Berlin Is Not a Village

"In June 1987 I stood with Ronald Reagan in front of the Brandenburg Gate when he cried, 'Mr. Gorbachev, open this gate!' If someone had asked me at that time—but no one asked me [laughter in the *Bundestag*]—what the German capital was, I would have said, 'Berlin.'"

Helmut Kohl appeared to be in top form when he made these remarks to a full *Bundestag* on the auspicious and memorable day of June 20, 1991. At that moment he even had those who were laughing on his side, as the protocol noted. But there was very little laughter during the highly charged debate touching the emotions of the members of parliament of all the *Fraktionen* on whether Bonn should remain the seat of the parliament and government or the move should be made to Berlin.

The CDU chairperson and federal chancellor, although by no means dissatisfied with Bonn, had long ago decided on Berlin, but was resolutely quiet about it, which made many of his colleagues feel insecure, annoyed, or even angry. However, Kohl was aware of his role in the state and he did not reveal until only a few days before the voting where he thought they were going. For him, Berlin had always been "a chance to overcome the separation." A debt of gratitude should be paid, putting Berlin in the center of the political work of a unified Germany. The federal interior minister, Wolfgang Schäuble, who had spoken ahead of Kohl, lambasted the Prussians. The man from the Baden area, much more inclined toward France by origin and intellect, had already joked before the end of the year that people "now had to learn: Mecklenburg-Vorpommern, Saxony-Anhalt, etc." Not a

In a good mood at the last cabinet meeting of the year, December 1991.

word of this surfaced in the debate on the capital—a ridiculous description for a bone of contention which had to be clarified as to whether the cosmopolitan Berlin or the quiet Rhenish town of civil servants was more suitable to be the seat of parliament and government. This was only a hypothetical question for Schäuble because he always supported paying due tribute to the "symbol of unity and freedom, of democracy and legality for all Germany." Schäuble ended on an almost embarrassing note of exaggeration, though his speech was rightly considered to have swayed the vote,

At the Otto-Hahn Peace Medal Award Ceremony for Nazi-hunter Simon Wiesenthal in Berlin, December 1991.

saying, "The issue today is not Bonn or Berlin, but our common future, our future in our united Germany, whose unity still has to be founded, and our future in a Europe, whose unity must be achieved it if is to fulfill its responsibility for peace, freedom, and social justice."[130]

Kohl could be well satisfied with this speech, although it ran contrary to his hatred of pathos; Schäuble had perhaps mobilized the final, missing votes for Berlin. That was all the man from the Palatinate cared about on that day, a day which, to be sure, left more sad faces than happy ones in the two people's parties, the CDU/CSU and the SPD.

The Autumn of the Dinosaur

Had the autumn of the dinosaur already come? Since 1992 the speculations about a successor were rife. The end of the protection of this great personage, seemingly larger than life, but in reality surrounded with the suspicions, disapproval, and cunning of potential competitors, seemed to have come.

Helmut Kohl at the zenith of his power and of the glitter surrounding it, had become, inevitably, overshadowed by the loneliness of all those in power. He had to bid farewell to some illusions, should he have had any, and also to two companions of differing origins and stature. After ten years of government, and for very different reasons, Hans Dietrich Genscher left the cabinet in the spring and Christian Schwarz-Schilling left in the winter of 1992. Both of them had been with Kohl since 1982. Genscher, the friend (to whom Kohl once wrote angrily, however, that he 'drove every truck into the wall!'), phoned the man from the Palatinate at home in Oggersheim between Christmas and New Year, as was customary: "I'd like to have a long talk with you about everything, including my future; you know about it." Kohl was surprised, but not surprised: it had to happen sometime. He said, "Come along to the press ball in Berlin in January. Bring Barbara; Hannelore is coming too. Then we can talk during breakfast at the hotel." Genscher agreed to this and told Kohl during this breakfast that he was resigning and that he would assume this was confidential. Kohl "kept his mouth shut," which did not surprise Genscher—he could be counted on for

Permanent topic: the state of the economy in the new federal states. Women's Minister Angela Merkel at one of the numerous chancellor "round tables" with business representatives.

that. He said later, "If I had told my FDP friends about it all of Bonn would have soon known it!" Kohl had become one of his best friends because he could be counted on, according to Genscher.

There must have been a great deal of trust between the two, to the extent that this can be believed in politics. Their trust survived all the storms and convinced Genscher in the early 1960s that "I'll achieve something with him!" In April 1992 Genscher finally turned in his resignation, effective the middle of May, as foreign minister, marking an internal political end to the ten-year team of Kohl/Genscher, now a thing of the past.

The resignation of the foreign minister showed Kohl "the limits of his power," Werner Perger wrote in *Die Zeit*, whatever that meant. Genscher's successor, Klaus Kinkel, gave signs of being a comfortable minister to head the coalition, comprehending fully the concept of "servant" (with pension) in the original sense of the word. Genscher's motives were speculated on at the government press conference in the traditional way. Genscher himself said later that thirteen years under Brandt and Schmidt and ten years with Kohl had been enough. And his health had played a role, probably a decisive one. He had decided that his heart attack in 1991 had been a warning.

The media speculated more than ever that there would be a major cabinet reshuffling in fall, and that Genscher's resignation had thrown a wrench in the works. This was not true for many reasons, as can be seen from looking back at the past years. Kohl had never reformed his government in a major reshuffling, and it could not be expected now. Even in 1987, the deputy chair of the *Fraktion*, Volker Rühe, had said he wished the chancellor would finally give the sign for "take off, and stop just making minor personnel changes." When questioned about this, Kohl said he "put no stock in such modern concepts." In the spring of 1992, Kohl again offered only a "small menu": four weeks before Genscher's resignation had become public, he made a change at the defense ministry on the Hardthöhe: Defense Minister Gerhard Stoltenberg, also a long-time companion (whom he had arrogantly called "*Stoltenzwerg*" (Stolten dwarf) in the early 1960s) was swapped for Volker Rühe, once possibly a reserve choice for chancellor, now put in the ejection seat without any prospect of gaining public favor from that post.

Each member in his or her way had Helmut Kohl to thank for their political career, otherwise they would not be in his cabinet. Whether Rühe now or Stoltenberg then—their careers were due to the man from the Palatinate's usually conscious efforts to make people dependent. Kohl avoided the other, far more difficult way like the devil avoids incense, just like all basically skeptical people. His "ancestor" Adenauer had had a different attitude: the patriarch could afford to be generous to small spirits who opposed him; they did him no harm, they did not disturb his circles.

One of those who had been happy to be appointed a minister, but who did not demonstrate the necessary dependence, was Christian Schwarz-Schilling, who threw in the towel in 1992. He was the only CDU head of department who left the cabinet of his own accord and without external pressure. As a representative of the middle class and the employers' wing, Schwarz-Schilling was a rarity in the Union parliamentary party in the *Bundestag,* and for that reason Kohl probably would not have fired him. Nevertheless, he had denigrated him for months as being "ready to be fired." In his letter of resignation of December 10, 1992, the minister felt himself to be insulted but heroically did not directly attack Kohl. His criticism was actually very mild: "It is not easy to have the media term you a candidate for being replaced without the chancellor giving some public sign of just how important the Postal Reform II is to him." Only two years before *Die Zeit* had taken Schwarz-Schilling to task during the formation of the new cabinet after the first all-German *Bundestag* election: "Whether Schwarz-Schilling should not have already gone of his own volition when deals where made and announced over his head and the *Bundespost* had been milked of two billion marks each year between 1991 and 1994 as a 'special contribution' to the government budget, that is another question."

Now that the minister for the post had resigned, he himself raised his leaving to a higher sphere for Kohl by bidding farewell to the chancellor in a letter that showed his devotion: "I would like to thank you for everything you have done for me in the past years, especially for the fact that I was able to work at your side in such a decisive role at such a decisive time."

The resignation, which had been given on short notice, did not fit in at all with the government leader's plans. In the first place he was just getting ready to leave for a trip abroad. When the head of the chancellor's office, Bohl, informed him about the irrevocable resignation of his cabinet member Kohl asked that it not be made public until he returned to Bonn. The circumstances of the resignation too are characteristic of Kohl's dealings even with colleagues at his level. When the resignation arrived at the chancellor's office, Juliane Weber called Schwarz-Schilling to try and make him change his mind: "Christian, think it over." A second attempt was made by Friedrich Bohl, who asked his party friend from Hesse whether he would be allowed to "tear up the letter and throw it in the wastepaper basket, then the matter would be over." Schwarz-Schilling stuck to his decision; he was the longest-serving member of the coalition and did not have any financial worries.

Dr. Christian Schwarz-Schilling
Bundesminister
für Post und Telekommunikation

Heinrich-von-Stephan-Straße 1 · 5300 Bonn 2
☎ (0228) 14-5500
den 10. Dezember 1992

Sehr geehrter Herr Bundeskanzler,

hiermit erkläre ich meinen Rücktritt und möchte Sie bitten, mich aus meinem Amt zu entlassen. In der letzten Kabinettssitzung kam der Krieg der serbischen Armee gegen die Bevölkerung in Bosnien-Herzegowina und die entsetzlichen Morde, Vergewaltigungen und Menschenrechtsverletzungen, die sich dort täglich ereignen zur Sprache. Ich habe bei dieser Gelegenheit von der Sitzung der CDU/CSU-Fraktion am letzten Dienstag berichtet. Die Schilderung der Augenzeugen war erschütternd und hat eine einmalige Betroffenheit in der Fraktion ausgelöst. Die Frage nach entsprechenden Maßnahmen der Bundesregierung konnte nicht beantwortet werden.
Ich habe dem Kabinett meine Einschätzung dargelegt und in diesem Zusammenhang geäußert, daß ich

Page 1 of the four-page letter from Post Minister Schwarz-Schilling to Kohl, December 10, 1992: "Dear Mr. Chancellor, I hereby declare my resignation, and request to be relieved from my office."

On Mondays I'd Love to Shoot Myself

This was not true for the beginning of every week, but there were too many Mondays on which Kohl had feelings that made him think of suicide. They were, for example, those Mondays on which the presidium and then the party board met. For years and years, the depressing election results were dissected. At press conferences, which he hated, he had to fend off questioners who were sometimes rude without losing his composure. Then friends and colleagues had to cheer him up with the hope of better days to come, when what he most wanted was to disappear to his vacation home at the Wolfgangsee.

Arrival ceremony for Japanese prime minister Miyazawa in front of the chancery, May 3, 1992.

With Provost Bernard Heinrich in front of Cologne Cathedral, before the start of a mass commemorating the twenty-fifth anniversary of the death of Konrad Adenauer, April 28, 1992.

At the signing of the German-Czech treaty in Prague, February 27, 1992. The chancellor raises glasses with Czech president Vaclav Havel.

"Completely unbearable"—another one of his usual expressions—were critical publications which dealt with him as a person but were mainly aimed at gaining the approval of the leftist intelligentsia. There was also the small volume published in the summer of 1992 about Weizsäcker's *Sorge um die deutsche Demokratie* (Worry about German Democracy). Gunter Hofmann and Werner A. Perger got the federal president to make strong public accusations of those responsible in the parties and the government—excepting himself: "I am convinced that our state is dominated by two things: the hunger for power to achieve election victory and the hunger for power in the political leadership task of implementing content and concept." A real slap in the face for the incumbent at the top of the bourgeois-liberal coalition! Kohl lost his temper when excerpts of the text that were published by the German Press Agency were read to him.

Conversation was impossible, because the chancellor had had a long love/hate relationship with Weizsäcker, who Kohl had got started in politics and had supported for over two decades, and had in the meantime sometimes "praised away." When the book with the *Freiherr's* quarrelsome statements hit the market people had the feeling that a bomb had gone off. At one time these two friends who used the familiar form of address were thought to be as inseparable as Castor and Pollux. Richard spoke, unlike his friend, almost tenderly about "Helmutle," while Kohl addressed him in a respectful tone, but not without warmth, as "Richard."

At functions such as receptions and banquets at which the two were unable to avoid each other, Kohl had only a limp handshake for his former friend while already looking at the person next to him. The book was followed by a similar one, an open declaration of war against the man who had helped him gain entrance to the party and achieve unparalleled success. Was he taking a form of revenge because he never became chancellor, a post for which some of his colleagues had recommended him, misjudging his capabilities? The reasons for this are still not clear even three years later.

A similar sort of thing happened to Kohl shortly afterward with his valued colleague and friend in parliament and government, Wolfgang Schäuble. The relationship between these two very different men is extremely difficult to describe. After Volker Rühe dropped out of the hypothetical race to succeed the chancellor and Schäuble, despite having been confined to a wheelchair by the assassination attempt by a mentally deranged man, was being touted as the "crown prince" by the media, Kohl gave a clear reprimand to the supposedly hasty office-seeker on his fiftieth birthday: "If the press does not have anything to write, it invents news of personalities, which always sounds good, doesn't it? Dear Wolfgang, we've had enough of that, haven't we?" And Wolfgang, who was actually supposed to be the honored guest, now had to listen in front of an invited audience at the Bonn Konrad Adenauer Haus to the man who was the boss and intended to remain so for a while, nodding in a half-tortured friendly way at the chancellor's rebuke.

Perhaps Kohl was overreacting at this time in his varied career, with its ups and downs. In the previous weeks—September of 1992—the media had heaped criticism on him. The presumed successor Schäuble had appeared far too frequently; that not only annoyed the incumbent, it hurt him. The tenth anniversary of the CDU/CSU/FDP coalition was just around the corner. The federal capital awaited a festival of superlatives, and the person celebrating his jubilee wanted to shine, even if it was to be for the last time. He wanted to be number one, with no doubts from any corner and no unnecessary criticisms from anyone. In the Maritim the party put on a "happening" for the great chairman with the motto "Ten Years of the Kohl Government," and the celebration exceeded even the trappings of a party conference in terms of the number of guests, personnel, and media coverage.

Kohl had his ten years in office presented in a large brochure—mentioning the Free Democrats, who had helped him gain power—celebrating his term as a "German decade": Kohl on forty-seven color pages, larger than life. It was primarily his foreign successes—which according to German reckoning were the least subject to criticism—that were honored through quotes, some florid, some succinct ("The politicians of the world are always our partners."). Domestic politics were viewed as being a little "more critical." To quote Kohl, "It's not as if I get up in the morning and think there are no problems in the world." On Kohl and the media: "He can bear criticism and take it seriously. He is relaxed about defamation. Ernst Moritz Arndt knew that 'whoever cannot do that should return to his tailor's workshop.'"

Byzantine speeches were made at this celebration in a packed room smelling of sausages and Kohl's beloved wines from the Palatinate. His friend Genscher allowed himself a joke and a nicely formulated note: "His [Kohl's] entry in the *Bundestag* as opposition leader always reminds me of a passage in Goethe's *Dichtung und Wahrheit*, which refers, by the way, to April 3, Helmut Kohl's birthday. . . . It was 1764, when Joseph II was crowned in Frankfurt. Goethe writes about this that: 'The *Kurfürst* of Mainz entered. The cannons were fired, which deafened us for a long time. This festivity was an important part of these ceremonies, since all the men who we had previously seen, however high ranking, were only subordinates. There appeared a sovereign, a true prince, the first after the *Kaiser*, led in and accompanied by a great man of his worthy retinue.'"

Kohl laughed heartily at this; he liked such jokes and loved such comparisons. Genscher, who had recited the story, grinned broadly.

Boris, the Friend in the Sauna

Boris Yeltsin entered the world stage in 1991, having stood as Russian Czar Number Two in the shadow of the charismatic Gorbachev. Yeltsin soon sought contact with Germany, primarily with its number-one politician, Helmut Kohl. He visited Bonn as early as November 1991. Soon a relationship of trust and mutual respect as well as personal empathy was built up between the two statesmen. The public soon got the impression that Kohl got along better with Yeltsin than he had with the more intellectual Gorbachev.

Yeltsin was the first democratically elected president of his country, and with his government began a new epoch in the development of the Russian Federation. However, German economic leaders were too trusting too early of Yeltsin's statements concerning a radical liberalization of the trade

Kohl greets Russian president Boris Yeltsin on an official visit to Bonn, November 1991.

Helmut Kohl accompanied Yeltsin to the farewell ceremonies of the Russian armed forces in Berlin, and to Yeltsin's meeting with Federal President Roman Herzog.

relations between Germany and Russia. At first Moscow needed help with capital, which Bonn had already given generously, always trusting in the smooth and punctual withdrawal of Soviet troops out of eastern Germany. After only five years the transfer of capital between Bonn and Moscow had reached one hundred billion marks. Kohl knew that he had to support "Czar Boris" because there was no other appreciable and trustworthy alternative to him, as Western Europe soon noted after Yeltsin came to power.

Kohl and Yeltsin soon got along, although their first meeting on the Rhine was rocky. Yeltsin did not want to answer any of the urgent questions about Honecker, which the hosts, and Kohl especially, took to be an insult. The former GDR leader had been able to flee to Moscow and obviously enjoyed political asylum. The Russian administration reacted coolly to extradition attempts and Yeltsin tried to pin responsibility for this on Gorbachev, who was still in office. Yeltsin did that under the chancellor's mild pressure at a press conference at which Kohl used his rough but often successful diplomacy. Kohl insisted on legal proceedings against Honecker. Yeltsin would now say something about this, said Kohl, guiding him in a friendly, firm manner. He had no intention of doing any such thing and made as if he wanted to leave the room. "Practically using physical force"

(*Süddeutsche Zeitung*) Kohl blocked the Russian president's retreat from the microphone. Kohl found his Russian friend's attitude toward the Russian Germans disappointing, to say the least. Yeltsin, the symbol of hope, proved not to be strong on this point. He was obviously ducking out when his ostensibly strong hand was supposed to be bringing order to the Russian system. Kohl's designate on emigration, Horst Waffenschmidt, had great difficulty with the fact that Moscow was offering ethnic Germans three thousand square kilometers of unusable land for settlement—a former missile test ground without natural water outflow to the Volga. "An unheard-of insult," said the press, and not just the conservative papers in Germany, which was supporting a project to reinstate the former Volga Republic. The incident remained in the public eye for a long time, because on the German side, lots of new variations on policies regarding minorities were created with a great deal of imagination and were supported with millions, far from the "Land of the Fathers." Yeltsin was often all too reticent on this question or approved decisions with slim prospects.

At the same time, Yeltsin and Kohl seemed to be cut from the same cloth, which is why both men basically understood each other and got along tolerably well on the phone, at the conference table, and in the sauna. In the latter case it was impossible not to be close when Russian robustness sat sweating next to Palatinate strength. At some point or other Kohl and Yeltsin had discovered that they both loved the sauna and the rest was taken care of by protocol, with a break in the official programs or by the supreme will of "Czar Boris" himself. Kohl once took Theo Waigel along. Waigel was quite flattered to be sweating next to the naked great of this world, and he regaled his friends at his regular table in Bonn with stories about Moscow nights. Once a colleague of the president, "in a suit, shirt, tie, and socks" joined the prominent guests on the wooden benches of the sauna to hand over a message ("The president is always on duty"). Another massaged Yeltsin's back with a rough brush. Kohl and Waigel had to do this for themselves.

Even when Kohl had only a little time on a visit to Moscow, his friend Boris said the sauna could not wait. Kohl recalled, "Once when I was in a real hurry, actually only on a stopover, I really didn't want to go to the sauna at all. It was an ice-cold evening and I met Yeltsin at his dacha near the airport. Boris greeted me, 'Let's go right to the sauna.' I answered, 'Just a minute, I'm not in the mood for it now.' He really wanted to go and so we went to the sauna, did our three or four courses, swam, and had a serious discussion."

The sauna created a climate for discussion between the two experienced politicians which other statesmen found by the fireside or over two or three glasses of port. Kohl worked harder on the relationship with Yeltsin than he had on that with his predecessor. He appreciated Yeltsin's character, which was typical of others who were close to Kohl: both feet on the ground, open, and uncomplicated. The man from the Palatinate admired his courage, which Yeltsin had proved to him "in several dramatic situations since 1991 in an extraordinary way." In 1994 Yeltsin visited Germany twice

With Employment Minister Norbert Blüm before the start of the sixteenth chancellor round on the state of the economy in the new federal states, April 1993.

At the "CeBit" in Hanover, March 1993. The chancellor watches a three-dimensional presentation of the planned governmental buildings in Berlin .

at the chancellor's invitation, in May and in late August for the farewell ceremony of the Russian armed forces. Kohl was not suspicious of the Russian because he had become certain in the meantime that he would not try to get the better of him. Even the war in Chechnya did not change the fact that Kohl followed his friend in Moscow with benevolence as long as there

Taking their places at the press conference at the end of the sixty-second German-French consultation at the Bonn chancery, December 1993.

With Foreign Minister Klaus Kinkel in the Bundestag, *January 1993.*

was no proof that he could not be trusted. Aside from that, Yeltsin probably told him that this horrible action against a rebellious regime in the Caucasus was a sort of duty for the Russians. Should they not halt that rebellion, they would fail elsewhere in the fight against the mafia, organized crime, and corruption. Democracy is good, Yeltsin seemed to want to say, but only as long as there is a strong state to back it up.

13

Chancellor Without End

1994– ?

The Family Man

The archetypal prosaic person, Kohl hides a lyrical side behind his scarcely penetrable facade. His marriage of three and a half decades to an interpreter who has become a respected second lady (the position of number one is reserved for the spouse of the federal president) has been long and harmonious, a rarity in political circles. Hannelore and Helmut have tried to keep their two sons out of the spotlight. This has not always been possible, especially when their son Peter was badly injured in a car accident in Milan. The press swarmed around the hospital to which Peter Kohl had been brought by ambulance and pictures of the completely destroyed car were published in all the newspapers.

On this gray November day in 1991 there was also agitation in Bonn because Kohl himself was unable to go because of an appointment he could not postpone. His wife Hannelore quickly decided to fly to Italy, accompanied by Kohl's office manager Neuer and a doctor. Not suspecting how expensive it was, the Kohls chartered an aircraft from the defense ministry's flight. The *Bundeswehr* pilots chose an already old VFW 614 Fokker, which was to transport the small group to Milan—to be sure, as the chancellor found out to his horror, at the fat price of seventy-two thousand marks! This invoice was actually submitted and paid by the Kohls without objection.

Even *Stern*, not terribly inclined toward the chancellor, joked about the remarkable "luxury flight," because with a privately chartered Lear jet the flight would have cost at most fifteen thousand marks. The *Hardthöhe* responded to the magazine's question that the defense ministry cannot be compared to a charter service, since it cannot simply transport the chancellor and his wife from A to B, but has "a military service to perform." What these were in regard to Frau Kohl's flight the spokesperson was unable to say. It was true in general that "military facilities do not apply commercial criteria." The American or the French president, as chief executives having government functions comparable to Kohl's, would probably have shaken their heads at such practices.

Kohl has an unreflecting and natural pride in his children, who are now grown up and have good careers, one as an economist and the other as an information technologist and economist—they obviously were not eager to follow in their father's footsteps. After having studied in the United States and Britain, both are now working in Germany, Peter for a bank and Walter, who finished his studies at Harvard, in the management of a department-store chain.

Is Kohl a real family man? There are many indications of that, even when he hardly has time today for long conversations with his wife and sons. Deep inside, he has to stop himself from drifting into sentimentality when it comes to his emotions about his family. Mostly he phones them on longer car trips, when he has time to relax momentarily. At such times his friends have seen him beaming all over when he hears some good news from a family member. He can also empathize with other people, particularly old friends. Hanns Schreiner, his press spokesman in Mainz for many years, told Klaus Dreher that Kohl had spontaneously called in the mid-1980s and offered help after Schreiner's son was killed in a car crash in Germany and the devastated parents were on vacation and stranded in Mexico by an air strike. "On the day of the funeral he was standing at our

With Hannelore at a festival in the Bonn chancery park, September 1992. Kohl bites into his favorite apple, a Cox Orange.

The Kohl family home in Oggersheim, Rhineland-Palatinate, 1990.

front door in the afternoon. He had come from Bonn and spoke to us for a long time. We will always remember that."[131]

That is the one side of Kohl. The other had to bid farewell, whether he wanted to or not, to his beloved family life because of the office he has held since 1982. Hannelore Kohl said, "with due consideration," as she told Barbara Friedrichs in a television interview, that she "had learned to hide her tears in a dog's fur," referring to the German shepherd Igo, who her husband liked to take with him occasionally to the Mainz *Landtag*. On a different occasion, Kohl's wife said jokingly in response to an apt psychological description of her prominent husband that he "was able to completely relax and even sleep on nights with a full moon."

Even in his eleventh and twelfth years as head of government of one of the greatest industrial nations, Kohl is still basically a domestic person, with middle-class and no urbane or extravagant habits. He often chooses the menus himself and he is no stranger to the kitchen, washing dishes when he is only entertaining family, only balking at doing the drying. His small bedroom in the Palais Schaumburg park is always neat. A guest, Mattias Wissman, was once allowed to see the bedroom, with pajamas neatly pressed and on hangers.

All this is to say that the world of Helmut Kohl is subject to an unshakable symmetry. The tidiness of the bedroom—perfect, germ-free, and dust-

A benefit dinner for the Hannelore Kohl Foundation for the Rehabilitation of Brain Damaged Patients, January 1995. The chancellor toasts the donors.

free—the chairs in the dining room arranged exactly, the flowers in the opulent vases appearing to have been numbered. The small kitchen is as clean as an operating theater and the refrigerator is always full. Therefore it is not surprising that Kohl was not as distressed by the conflict in the former Yugoslavia and the devastating battles as he was by the news of starving children and old people: "I experienced hunger as a fifteen-year-old." It was for that reason in particular that the chancellor said during the two-day meeting of the Conference on Security and Cooperation in Europe (CSCE) in December 1994 in Budapest that "it would be barbarous if the joint declaration of the CSCE nations on the situation in Bosnia were not made." Whether it was out of pure stubbornness or whether the other statesmen in the Hungarian capital had not had experiences similar to those of the German chancellor, the resolution failed due to vetoes by Russia and the Bosnian government.

A Friend, A Good Friend

It was at that point that Kohl really needed friends, but they had made themselves scarce. Wolfgang Schäuble was more and more keen to challenge his sole power to govern and determine tactics, and the *Bundestag's* parliamentary party, always restless, tried to meddle in coalition affairs more than ever. Within the party it was still not certain whether Helmut Kohl would still be the top candidate. Peter Hintze, who was considered a completely subservient assistant because of his honor-student-like appearance, was already working on the screenplay for the election campaign of 1994, but it did not have a protagonist. The general secretary figured that teamwork was important; the chairperson, as some would have it, only his chancellor's bonus. It was the old story: thrown off course by bad press

The CDU chairman with his general secretary Peter Hintze, January 1993.

With Interior Minister Wolfgang Schäuble in a plenary session of the Bundestag, *October 1991.*

reports, the public relations group under Pastor Hintze in the Konrad-Adenauer-Haus lost faith in their boss's image. Hintze's mostly younger colleagues were not experienced enough in dealing with the "cumbersome commodity of Kohl" (*Süddeutsche Zeitung*). The CDU plummeted to twenty-eight percent in German Television Channel Two's political barometer a year before the big election, a terrible result considering the obvious achievements of the chancellor's party in rebuilding the East. The CDU presidium, populated almost exclusively by self-proclaimed opponents of Kohl, asked itself, "Has the Kohl era really deserved this?"[132] Speculations about an early replacement for the chancellor, or one which would occur right after a slim *Bundestag* victory, were rife. Schäuble; his CSU colleague Horst Seehofer, who had quickly made a name for himself as health minister; and FDP parliamentary party manager Hermann Otto Solms, inconspicuous almost to the point of being insignificant—but effective—were spotted as being possible heirs of the "Kohl system."

The new interior minister too, Manfred Kanther, the "black sheriff," was discussed as one of the many possible chancellor successors but was quickly dismissed. The "black sheriff," by the way, declined to "shoot from the hip." It was exactly what had been expected from him and was why all the speculations came to naught. The only thing which could not be denied was that Kohl's image had reached a new low. In the early years of his popularity, chief organizer Karl Schumacher liked to play the hit, "A friend, a good friend," over all the loudspeakers at the start of all major appearances by the party chairperson. All that was now past. The burdens of the later years were reaching out for the man from the Palatinate, and he undertook more foreign trips. His international stature was to give him a boost at home, where his few remaining friends wanted him to resign prematurely: "Where does the man get the nerve to stay away for so long when at home the mice are dancing on the table?"[133]

Almost without exception they found fault with the chancellor with a discernible loss of his grip on reality. General Secretary Heiner Geissler, who had been expelled years ago, was occasionally the ringleader, seconded cautiously by Erwin Teufel in Stuttgart. Saxony's minister-president, Kurt Hans Biedenkopf, had his *Land* interior minister, CDU deputy Heinz Eggert, say something which would have been an open declaration of war from him: "Standing next to the federal chancellor there must be people who could always be entrusted with taking over the office." In journalist circles, of which there were now so many in Bonn and Berlin that it was no longer possible to determine who they were and what their political leanings were, Biedenkopf kept talking about "political leadership." The media reports which the chancellor critics were after were equally diverse.

In these months Kohl complained repeatedly that he "had to do everything alone." He could count on no one. Or perhaps this was not the case. Government spokesperson Dieter Vogel, well versed in his job and of liberal-conservative convictions, performed his duties objectively and effectively. But the man close to Lambsdorff did not belong to the inner circle. Kohl was more certain about the loyal support of his state minister, Anton ("Toni") Pfeiffer, as well as that of head of the chancellor's office, Friedrich Bohl, who, unlike Pfeiffer could afford to crack a small joke about his top boss. Kohl was especially unhappy at that point about the lack of "staunch" figures who were self-confident enough to contradict him with good reasons when he was wrong. Pfeiffer, from a good Catholic background like Kohl himself, was a broadly educated lawyer from Baden-Württemberg who was on the board of the Konrad Adenauer Foundation and who had known the CDU leader for a long time. He rarely said "no" when the chancellor had already said "yes." Norbert Blüm was one of the few cabinet members who Kohl invited to the "holy of holies" (his office), in order to get his advice and support on a late evening. But he did not even ask Blüm when he decided on the justice minister of Dresden, Steffen Heitmann, as a candidate for the office of federal president on the recommendation of the CDU in Saxony. It is also characteristic of Kohl that he talked for quite a while about the nomination of the almost unknown CDU politician as one of his original creations (later a lot of people spoke pejoratively about a "creature"), although others had been involved in selecting the candidate. The man from the Palatinate likes to create surprises and he is quite good at it.

Kohl stated to the board in no uncertain terms that, in his opinion, Richard von Weizsäcker's successor should be an East German, since the "new" *Länder* had been only poorly represented to that point. Therefore

At the Berlin party conference in September 1993, the chancellor presents his choice for the office of federal president, Saxon justice minister Steffen Heitmann.

most of the top CDU committee voted without any reservations in October 1993 for the forty-nine-year-old Steffen Heitmann, who had a degree in theology and training in church law. By the end of the month top leaders of the CDU and CSU were discussing the candidate, who had become a "case" in the meantime, at Kohl's bungalow. Heitmann had gotten himself mixed up in an unpleasant controversy with statements on the role of women in society which he should have best kept to himself. The shy, reserved man with views suitable to the Union in the 1950s soon proved to be a bad choice. The lateral thinker of the parliamentary party, Friedbert Pflüger, former press adviser to Richard von Weizsäcker, dismissed the candidate curtly in *Die Zeit* as being "the wrong man, the wrong signal."

Already on November 10, 1993, Heitmann gave the impression through contradictory interviews that he himself had lost interest in the candidacy. At this point at the latest, Kohl dropped his "creature," of whom he had once been so proud, without sympathy, as he is wont to do. Two days before Heitmann gave up his candidacy at Kohl's request on November 25 ("my own decision") some of the papers were already speculating about Kohl's new favorite, Roman Herzog. The president of the Federal Constitutional Court was almost the opposite of Heitmann, the only thing in common being jurisprudence and their Protestant faith. If something could be said in defense of the expelled candidate Heitmann, it is that he offered insightful recommendations on how to handle the injustice of the SED. Kohl did not say much, which was probably the best thing in this unfortunate situation.

Come to the Point, Chancellor!

Helmut Kohl profited from privately funded television in the election year 1994 in several ways. In the first place, these channels' information programs had become comparable to those of the public broadcasting corporations. Secondly—and probably decisive in winning—the man from the Palatinate selected the journalists interviewing him, for example on television channel SAT 1. Andreas Fritzenkötter, the chancellor's adviser, had a good relationship with the private broadcasting networks. Formerly the Bonn correspondent for the *Rheinischer Post*, Fritzenkötter was brought to the CDU central office in 1989 by General Secretary Volker Rühe and when the latter was appointed defense minister, Fritzenkötter moved over into the central government office, initially as an assistant to Eduard Ackermann, who was due to retire shortly. The boss soon started to like the two-meter-tall man with his calm demeanor. Kohl has difficulty getting along with shorter people anyway, and logically enough, Kurt Biedenkopf was known as the "little professor" in his time. Fritzenkötter is the only person in the chancellor's office who is actually taller than Kohl. At party conferences the media adviser can occasionally be seen taking Kohl gently but firmly by the shoulders and guiding him purposefully out of a crowd that the chancellor has incautiously gotten himself into. "Fritzi," wrote Kohl in a note on the cover of a memorandum for the youngest of his media advisers; the ex-journalist had soon gained stature and respect "at court," having worked closely with the chancellor only since 1992. Kohl discovered late, and some say too late, the young people for his close staff.

"After ten years in government," Michael Backhaus wrote in *Stern*, "Kohl's relationship to *Journaille* has taken on Wilhelmenian proportions." The expression "*Journaille*" is apt: according to *Duden's*, it means "insidious, common press without scruples, and its journalists." Should the Hamburg illustrated magazine have meant this, Kohl would be well advised to give them a wide berth. But if the remark about the press refers to it in general, then "Wilhelmenian" is a complete exaggeration. The man from the Palatinate has had experience of newspapers and also with the electronic media. Could the man be criticized because he would rather talk to Heinz-Klaus Mertes (SAT 1) than to Wolfgang Herles of German Television Channel Two? During his time Kohl's predecessor Helmut Schmidt dismissed journalists wholesale as "highwaymen." Strangely enough, no one took offence at that, or at least nothing is known about it. Kohl uses his elephantine memory to good advantage with the media. He seldom participates in any media parties, anniversaries, or receptions of press or radio. When the *Mitteldeutscher Rundfunk* (MDR), which was very much inclined toward the chancellor, presented itself formally in Bonn at a party at the *Land* representation, Kohl appeared, smiling, and even gave a small speech. Naturally he was vociferous when members of the government press conference asked him indirect questions because they did not want to say to his face how little they thought of him. Kohl could be quick to retort in such circumstances and return the question with a proverbial slap in the face. One of that group earned it when he preceded a question with the arrogant phrase, "Perhaps I don't understand you correctly." Kohl answered, "You don't."

But in general the chancellor, after twelve years in office during which sixteen elections took place, was more irritable than ever. Normally he was either suspicious of or rejected anything having to do with the press or radio. He granted only a few newspaper interviews, and the journalists allowed to enter his office were carefully selected. But media policy as an instrument of influence on public opinion was perhaps his hobby. When the minister-presidents of Saxony and Bavaria, Kurt Biedenkopf and

Edmund Stoiber, went after the ADR in the spring of 1995, Kohl joined in with glee.

Even the slim victory in the *Bundestag* elections did nothing to allay his suspicions about real or suspected opponents in the media, wherever they are. While Kohl normally looked at the screen and the powers behind it, he suddenly began to pay attention to the Springer flagship, *Die Welt*, which was to get a new editor in chief, the archliberal Thomas Löffelholz, previously with the *Stuttgarter Zeitung*. The executive manager of the Springer concern, Jürgen Richter, had spotted the new man, who Kohl did not need to turn to immediately. The chancellor wrote a stinging letter of protest to the chairman of the board of Springer AG and executor of Axel Springer, Professor Bernhard Servatius, about the planned appointment of Löffelholz to the prominent position at *Die Welt*. The national paper had always served the CDU/CSU well, but in Kohl's opinion this favorable treatment could not be counted on in future. An insulted Servatius answered the chancellor, also in a letter, saying that "an independent publishing house would not be talked into his personnel politics." Kohl followed this up with a phone conversation which also did not move Servatius, at the end of which he asked Kohl to destroy the correspondence on the matter. The Springer group would do likewise out of discretion. Thomas Löffelholz became editor in chief of *Die Welt* on May 1, 1995.

Bitter Laurel Wreath, Dangerous Victory?

There was a lot of tension in the Union camp a few weeks before the *Bundestag* elections. Helmut Kohl was only a little afraid of his challenger, Rudolf Scharping. Had the SPD been able to rally around the minister-president of Lower Saxony as a top candidate, he would have been a far more serious challenger to the incumbent chancellor and his party. The very different combination of Scharping and Kohl acted like the "nephew Bräsig to Uncle Bräsig," according to J. Gross.

One of the things which bothered Kohl most was that CDU members themselves began to doubt his determination to carry on through the entire next legislative period. According to some thinking, in the middle of his final term, Kohl would suggest a successor for election as chancellor, or designate someone for the next *Bundestag* election and leave the office to him after a successful election. Even this interpretation appeared to those in Kohl's inner circle as "impossible to implement and fraught with a thousand risks." Kohl's media adviser disseminated the idea that the position of chancellor could be offered to Theo Waigel because the mood was favor-

Unimpressed with a vehement speech from his opponent in the Bundestag, *Kohl converses with his minister of the chancery, Friedrich Bohl.*

able for that in the *Bundestag Fraktion*. Schäuble's name was mentioned less frequently, but the man from Baden-Württemberg was certainly not out of the running.

But the immediate need was for the chancellor himself to counter the impression that he was tackling the autumn 1994 election only half-heartedly. Therefore the government press office published the following vague press release.

> In regard to misleading reports about the possible duration of the length of his term of office, Federal Chancellor Dr. Helmut Kohl states:
>
>> I have repeatedly stated that I am willing to be chancellor for the duration of the entire next legislative period, i.e., 1994–98, and this is so. Aside from this, I have made it clear that I do not intend in any case to become a candidate for chancellor again beyond 1998. The issues pertaining to this will be clarified in due course by the pertinent committees of the CDU and CSU as well as by the CDU/CSU parliamentary party. Any other reports are incorrect and baseless.

In late March 1995 Kohl went on the assault in the *Bundestag* against a statement by opposition leader Scharping, who would gladly have given him his pension: "The voters will determine my retirement." In essence that meant "I'll participate in the next *Bundestag* elections in 1998." A similar interpretation could be made of statements two months later, in which Kohl referred again to the government press office statement of October 9, 1994. This too could have two different meanings: Kohl would not become a candidate for chancellor again in 1998, or, more exactly, he would not serve as chancellor beyond 1998. Because "beyond 1998" could just as well be "after" 1998, the phrase "become a candidate" would not be true to the facts which the German public were determined to unearth. Giving the facts was something that Kohl was not prepared to do despite many (ambiguous) words. Whoever would like to confirm that he was no longer available as incumbent after a certain point in time (here, 1998), would only need to say this. On the other hand, whoever said that he would not in any case become a candidate again beyond 1998 would explicitly leave the question open whether he would "hold office." In another instance Kohl himself said that "should I still be chancellor in 1999," he would decide so-and-so. That was certainly stated in the conditional, thereby leaving everything in a completely gray area. Thus Kohl had not made any definite statement, and therefore at that time he was not yet thinking about retiring.

The victory of the coalition in the *Bundestag* elections on October 16 was extremely slim. The government parties CDU/CSU and FDP achieved the smallest margin of victory, 0.3 percent, ever achieved in a *Bundestag* election compared to the results of the opposition parties. At the November party conference, chairman Kohl tried to encourage the delegates who had fallen into resignation and bitterness "not to forget that we won." He did not mention the reasons why the victory had been so marginal and what needed to be done to adopt more successful strategies for the future.

Immediately before he entered the party conference the chancellor had

A beaming Helmut Kohl talks to reporters after his reelection, November 15, 1995.

praised the election results of October 16, making reference to "our friends and partners abroad," and declared that they had "received our victory as good news for Europe." On the contrary, Karl Feldmeyer wrote about the party conference, with an eye to the domestic situation, that the Union had a few bitter facts to digest.

> It is right that (General Secretary) Hintze alluded to the "intellectual and political leadership of opinions" of all things. A CDU general secretary could talk about this much more openly if it were not for conference delegates who had thereby been reminded about a promise made by Helmut Kohl. Had Kohl not promised before his election in 1982 and 1983 that he wanted to implement an "intellectual and moral change," and had he not had the best election result in his fourteen-year-term of office as chancellor, namely 48.8 percent, and thus as high as the coalition can achieve counting the FDP? The promise was never rescinded but in the view of the general secretary it was obviously not fulfilled to the extent that there is no need to call for "a battle for the intellectual and moral leadership of opinions."

Even as early as late 1994 and early 1995 and increasingly in the following months, Kohl was besieged from all sides in the party and the *Fraktion* with the demand that he forgo thinking about giving up office in the next few years and offer himself as a candidate again for 1998. During a meeting with the parliamentary party budget committee in mid-February the quiet summons had become a plea. Kohl should be there again; any other possibilities would be fairly risky. In May Kohl said that the repeated calls for him to become chancellor again were "as pleasant as a long lukewarm bath in Nivea cream." In the interim there were spirited internal party discussions about a Black-Green coalition which were directed at the November CDU party conference. The Bavarians, especially Theo Waigel, firmly rejected such speculations as misguided and illusory.

After the North Rhine–Westphalia *Landtag* elections brought heavy losses to Johannes Rau's SPD on May 14, 1995, but some substantial gains to the Greens, and a Red-Green government coalition was formed in Düsseldorf, Michael H. Spreng predicted in an editorial of the "BamS" (*Bild am Sonntag*) that "Kohl or another republic—so simple but so strong will be the message of the CDU for the next few years. Germany will be faced with controversy which will be like that of the elections of 1976 (Freedom instead of/or socialism). The bottom line is that the leaders of the Union have ascribed this to the FDP: people are nice to it, but more like they would be to a patient who is dying."

May 8: Fifty Years Later

"There can be no doubt that the liberation from the Hitler barbarianism was necessary in order to allow a free constitutional state in Germany and peace and reconciliation between the peoples in Europe." It had taken months before this unmistakable sentence could be written in the manuscript of a declaration of the federal chancellor on the fiftieth anniversary of the capitulation of the Third Reich. There had been a bitter dispute between politicians and publicists about the upcoming May 8 and its meaning for Germany: freedom or defeat, celebration or hour of mourning—it was a moving question for millions of people. For Helmut Kohl the end of the war and the National Socialist regime of terror was no longer "the long-awaited freedom." Another time Kohl spoke of "the chance of a new beginning," as a way in which to regard the day of the defeat of the Third Reich. The tactician used concepts that could be understood and were plausible, and stuck to them. Kohl had learned a lot in his thirteen years in office and now profited from his greater openness. May 8 became a quietly celebrated triumph.

Before the actual ceremonies which were to take place on this historic date in Berlin, with participation by the victors of the Second World War,

On the way to a press conference at the Wintergate Hotel in Washington, after a meeting with President Bill Clinton, February 1994.

the *Bundestag* assembled on April 28, 1995, for a special meeting with speeches by the top representatives of the constitutional organizations, Federal President Roman Herzog, Parliamentary President Rita Süssmuth, and the president of the *Bundesrat*, Johannes Rau. The guest speaker was the Polish foreign minister Wladyslaw Bartoszewski, winner of the peace prize of the German book trade association, a symbolic gesture. Bartoszewski

Official visit of an American president to Germany, July 1994. Clinton and Kohl at a demonstration in front of the Brandenburg Gate in Berlin.

The chancellor speaking to Bundestag *vice president Hans-Ulrich Klose, March 1995.*

gave a moving speech which built bridges to the future and ignored historical guilt and expiation, making his speech a "historic" one.

The writer and statesman's words of embellished frankness pleased the expellees: "We lament the individual fate of the innocent Germans who suffered the consequences of the war and who lost their homeland."

The great elder statesman of Poland who had survived the Holocaust was moved by the reception of his words, kissing the hands of Rita Süssmuth, the president of the *Bundestag*. Thanking his speaker, Kohl embraced him lightly, himself moved.

May 8 in Berlin erased the depressing memories of the events surrounding the May celebrations in Bitburg ten years earlier. There was a much better hand at work here, and the chancellor too seemed to have changed. At the Schauspielhaus at Gendarmenmarkt were all the representatives of the unified Germany and the victors of the Second World War. Speeches were made for Russia by Viktor Chernomyrdin, for Great Britain by John Major,

Helmut Kohl and François Mitterrand at a reception for the French president in Bonn, November 1994.

for the United States by Vice President Al Gore, and for France by President François Mitterrand, who left office the day after.

For Helmut Kohl, Mitterrand's speech had historic significance: the president whose name will remain synonymous with an epoch recalled his time as a soldier in Germany: "I found that the people I met were all upright people."[134]

Had Kohl foreseen the way this enormously significant day would go? He never said anything about it. In an interview with *Le Monde* two days later, Kohl said the Franco-German partnership was "incomparable." After Mitterand finished his speech at the Berlin Schauspielhaus, Kohl embraced this small man who was already touched by the hand of death. Tears were in his eyes. This scene was without parallel in the history of France and Germany, which had seen so many changes.

Appendix

Jean-Paul Picaper
Le Figaro Correspondent for Germany

Helmut Kohl has not only become the "one-man program of the CDU" and the "guarantor of the German standpoint," he has become Germany's best advertisement abroad, well ahead of Michael Schumacher, Boris Becker, Steffi Graf, Franz Beckenbauer, and Ernst Jünger, especially for us in France. Here, only Claudia Schiffer, the model, has achieved the same popularity as the federal chancellor. Both of them achieved success through their looks, embodying the new German friendliness despite their majestic appearances. Claudia and Helmut have made Europe's most beautiful story come true. The "soft giants from Germany" are respected, as one expects of Germans. What is new about them is that no one needs to be afraid of Germans anymore. They are even calming and unproblematic.

The Gentle Giant of Germany

History is naturally not determined by such superficialities as Cleopatra's nose. Nevertheless, this federal chancellor and Ms. Schiffer have something in common for public relations experts: their stature and appearance are integral parts of their images—something the brave German man and the tender German woman did not achieve during the Third Reich. It was also something that Marlene Dietrich could not achieve—she had to give up her citizenship. These two cult figures of this truly German democratic federal republic, "*die Schiffer und der Kohl*," have done it. The Germans can thank them for making Germanness in Europe an "in" thing. The "chancellor to be touched," and the "German beauty," whom many would like to touch, have collected points for their country.

For my fellow countrymen, the famous model—the Brunhilde of the catwalk—embodies German female beauty. The German chancellor embodies size and stability. Their enormous popularity probably stems from the fact that they not only correspond to the German cliché but contradict preconceived notions about Germans. In the world of fashion, the beautiful

Claudia has proved that German women can be chic and elegant. The strong chancellor is living proof that a powerful politician from Germany can also be a good democrat. Aside from that, both are good Catholics, which is never a bad thing in Latin countries in Europe.

When the socialists were ruling France, many a small businessperson or farmer sighed, "If only we had someone like Kohl! He'd bring some order into things." These reactions show that he is trusted and could be entrusted to do much more. Like the German mark, the chancellor is respected abroad. But the French people's reverence for Kohl is based on misunderstandings. Since German reunification many politicians and journalists have considered him the modern Bismarck, which he would vehemently deny. For the French Jane Doe, Helmut Kohl is the typical German chancellor: built like a Hun and stately, though good-natured and nice.

If Europe were a lot further along, Helmut Kohl could become a candidate for a top post in the French republic. Since taking office he is actually more popular in France and other countries than in Germany. His political survival and lucky star have polished his international reputation and extended it to other countries. Now that his opponent Margaret Thatcher and his friends George Bush, Mikhail Gorbachev, and François Mitterrand have exited the international political stage, he is the only surviving "*monstre sacré*." By this the French understand a "holy monster," a "*zoon politikon*." Churchill and de Gaulle, for example, were "holy monsters." In the meantime rumor had it that they existed only as fossils—until Kohl came on the scene.

The federal chancellor who is close to the people is well aware of this phenomenon. He plays at keeping a distance between himself and the normal citizen by virtue of his office. I heard him say that during a visit to François Mitterrand in the presidential palace in the rue de Faubourg Saint Honoré he had slipped off on his own to buy a present and entered a Parisian *parfumerie*. A large, statuesque woman approached him, "such a Germania," he said, and asked him in perfect German, "What are you doing here?" "The same thing as you," his answer is supposed to have been, probably meaning pursuing a career and also serving as an advertisement for Germany abroad.

After the small Mitterrand, the French have finally given themselves a president who is only one centimeter shorter than the chancellor, a considerable accomplishment in French terms. Thus Kohl has fit better into the French landscape since May 1995. We too have slowly gotten over our prejudices against oversized people, a sign of the new times. I too had been of the opinion that anyone over 1.8 meters or so did not deserve to survive.

With his Guards' height, however, Kohl has been sitting on the chancellor's throne for thirteen years. He has become more and more indispensable: there must be something to this man! Charlemagne was supposed to have been over 1.8 meters tall, and now there is a tall German chancellor who is to reinstate Carolinian Europe after one thousand years. However, he shares the prize in Charles' name with Mitterrand. The united Europe has a French and a German head as well as many limbs.

Kohl's stature is not completely un-French. My fellow countrymen and women regard him as the reincarnation of a literary figure, Gargantua, the hero of a fifteenth-century novel by François Rabelais, whose enormous appetite and fantastic thirst for knowledge are known by French people with even a halfway decent education. A friendly giant and certainly not an aesthete, the fictional character of the Renaissance who could pound mightily on the table, stuff himself, and consume whole libraries, was also the king of a prosperous realm.

The fact that "Helmut the Great" is large and powerfully built is comforting to the French. They were amazed to learn that he is a great reader, that is, also a Renaissance man. They never felt entirely comfortable with utopian Willy Brandt and activist Helmut Schmidt, not to speak of the baroque Franz Josef Strauss. They feel that someone like Helmut Kohl could do nothing untoward, that he is "someone like you and me." His cards are on the table, his aims known. And when he said in an interview (*Figaro*, June 24, 1994) that "in politics the indirect way is often the quicker way to reach the goal than the direct one," people thought, "Thank God, finally a smart neighbor."

But above all the German chancellor fills a current gap in the market: high-profile politicians have become rare in Europe. He is cut from this cloth. Was it in the stars that he should take over a leading role? Even though the chancellor emphasizes over and over that as the son of a middle-class family and a mediocre student he was not cut out to be chancellor of a unified Germany, fate seemed to have had a hand. His calling to an unusual position, however, was counterbalanced by the "human, all too human" element.

Thus the word has also gone beyond the German borders that he goes to an Austrian fountain of youth for a weight-loss program every year, returning about forty pounds lighter. The enormous weight loss and subsequent gain, this up and down in German politics, is a proof of how firmly the chancellor is rooted in the earth and in a natural rhythm such as the seasons and the flooding of the Rhine. Despite his disproportionately large physical and political dimensions he is a person who changes physically.

His structure depends on the food shoveled in, and not on a special Palatinate chromosome which makes him different from all other mortals.

Kohl's vacation spot has become part of the political scene like Adenauer's Cadenabbia and Mitterrand's Latché. When the Bonn protocol operation had to inform the newly elected Edouard Balladur in April 1993 that the chancellor could not yet receive him because he had to go to Austria for his *Kur*, this suddenly became an international issue. The Paris opposition media blew this difficulty with appointments up so that it practically looked like a declaration of war. Would the old trenches be redug? Helmut Kohl mended the fences. On January 9, 1995, he greeted Balladur at his alpine vacation spot, Chamonix, in front of journalists and cameramen with "*Bonjour mon ami, comment ça va?*" This historic hour without political consequences was also called the "harmony of Chamonix." Standing on the dizzying height of the terrace of Brévents on this auspicious day, the chancellor was surprised—or simulated astonishment with his inimitable irony—that there were so many media people at this "private" visit. I was standing near Edouard Balladur at that moment and saw him gesture—perhaps a bit enviously—toward Helmut Kohl and say that it was due to his guest that there were so many on the terrace. The following months showed that Balladur was right. He was quickly forgotten. Kohl is still standing in the limelight.

A Man with Fortune

Viewed from outside Germany, Kohl has that quality which Frederick the Great required of his officers: good fortune. Though nothing else has equaled the serendipity of German reunification which fell into his lap, other things proved fortuitous for the supposed "provincial man from the Palatinate," especially a number of factors from which he was able to profit in 1982–83 and again in 1989–90. Much speaks for Kohl's lucky star actually being his ability to deal with that which is already given, not losing sight at the same time of that which is politically feasible. He always attracts that which his opponents have prepared for him.

Three years before his election, his most serious rival, Helmut Schmidt, who despised Brandt and Kohl as well as the rest of the world equally, along with his Latin "alter ego," president Valéry Giscard d'Estaing, created the European Monetary System. This small step toward containing the intra-European currency fluctuations was the logical conclusion of the creation of a successful European internal market. It was also a step toward a European state.

Schmidt and Giscard had plowed the ground which Kohl would henceforth tread. It was Giscard who was supposed to have coined the phrase of the German-French "fateful community," even though, as in the case of many historical phrases, its parentage is uncertain. Unfortunately Giscard d'Estaing chose the unpronounceable word "*ecu*" for the future common currency, a technological concept which was a real tongue twister for Germans and others. (Gratitude is due to the European summit in Cannes of June 24–26, 1995, for having as good as done away with this horrible term, and at which it was suggested that the future European currency should be called the Euro-Mark, Euro-Franc, Euro-Pound, etc.) But the common European currency was more a precipice and a technical means to facilitate accounting in exchange and trade offices and is still a long way off from being a future common European currency.

Thus at that time people were driving in the direction of Europe in the well-worn Wankel engine of Giscard and Schmidt. Adenauer and de Gaulle had provided and stored the fuel for the journey. This machine allowed Kohl and Mitterrand to push through the Single European Act, to cement the bases of European defense and the economic and currency union, and in consideration of the British, the Maastricht Treaty of the twelve, and then fifteen, partners. But without their own contribution breakdowns would have stopped the forward motion.

Even before Kohl took office as chancellor in Bonn the French socialist government had submitted a memorandum for the revitalization of Europe to the European Community partners on October 7, 1982. These suggestions for a comprehensive economic, social, and industrial-political initiative of the European Community found little support in Germany at that time—in these times the economic recession has meant that such initiatives are no longer dismissed as directed ideology.

The chancellor maintained in several interviews that in the first few years of his term of office people were talking about "Eurosclerosis." Ten years later, after the Maastricht Treaty was signed, it was "(N)Eurose." Kohl's politics consisted of two acts of strength with long pauses for breath in between to heal the European Community and European Union of these illnesses.

The years 1981 and 1982, with the two changes of power at the top in France and Germany, naturally slowed things down. After that there were differences because of the dissimilar economic policies of the socialists in France and the Union-Liberals in Germany. These differences were smoothed over by Mitterrand's internal change of course in March 1983, though the attempted revitalization of the European Community in

Stuttgart in June 1983 was doomed. The EC summit in Athens six months later still did not achieve consensus on the Stuttgart package. But this defeat sparked a new European Community.

In January 1984, Genscher and Stoltenberg and Cheysson, Delors, and Dumas, and a month later Mitterrand, met Kohl in Edenkoben, in the Palatinate; shortly after that Kohl went to Paris. The aim was to create new initiatives to strengthen political cooperation in the EC and thus bring it more in line with the special responsibility of the two countries. In December 1982 the French government had submitted a new memorandum for a "common ground for industry and research" in Europe. The nuggets of the EC internal market and the reform of the institutions were already contained in these initiatives, likewise the "Europe of technology," which French foreign minister Roland Dumas had recommended all partners create at the behest of Mitterrand on April 17, 1985, "allowing our continent to dominate all top technologies and therefore allowing it to become the continent of the twenty-first century."

This was a promising answer to the American Strategic Defense Initiative. SDI was Ronald Reagan's space-based defense against Russian intercontinental missiles, calling for enormous research expenditure and presenting a challenge for American industry. While the German government under Helmut Kohl supported it, Hans-Dietrich Genscher broke ranks and spoke out against it. France was probably afraid of missing out on the economic and technical progress and, as ever, the French intended that the European research initiative should make Europe and their nuclear *force de frappe* independent of American dominance and allow them to keep out of the direct confrontation of the two superpowers. The French also wanted to bind the Germans more strongly to Europe. This was the root of the European Research Coordination Agency Eureka program, which furthered cooperation between European companies and research in new fields of commercial technology.

While the economic relations, youth exchange programs, and sister-city programs thrived, only one chapter of the Elysée treaty did not keep pace: military cooperation. It was no wonder that for the Germans NATO and the American nuclear shield were of critical importance. Agreements on military cooperation at the government level in October 1982 were implemented only slowly. The strategic crisis unleashed by the Soviets also precipitated a further and more important step toward integration in the EC. This progress would have ground to a halt had Mitterrand and Kohl not prepared the way. As early as December 1982 Mitterrand had said of the new strategic situation: "Pacifism is in the West, but the intermediate-range missiles are in the East." In an interview he emphasized the unilateral French nuclear deterrent, but also supported a Western European defense.

Our Best Friends

In my view cooperation between the two technocrats Schmidt and Giscard, or "men of action," as they were called then, had been furthered by a change in climate which had been brought about by many German-French micro-meetings at the local community, family, school, and student level since the signing of the German-French treaty in 1963. Up until 1978–79, opinion polls had shown that the French generally were afraid *of* the Germans. After that they were afraid *for* the Germans. Within approximately two years French public opinion made a complete turnaround, in which the Germans went from a subordinate position to that of a reliable ally and comfortable neighbor, which it has remained.

Though the "extremist directive" in Germany forbidding employment to those suspected of subversive behavior or beliefs, played up by the communists, and the extradition of the Baader-Meinhof lawyer Klaus Croissant caused a wave of anti-German sentiment in France in the 1970s, a more realistic and balanced image of Germany began to prevail by the end of that decade. Naturally there were exceptions to this, but the Barbie case in 1986–87, for example, did not cause any anti-German feelings, being considered a part of the National Socialist regime and therefore long in the past. On the day of the trial of the former Gestapo man of Lyon, Jacques Delors gave an interview to a German newspaper in which he said that the German youth could be proud of their fatherland.

When the threat to Germany by the Soviet SS-20 intermediate-range missiles became obvious a growing number of French watched this with anxiety, completely without malicious pleasure. When the German peace movement, led by the SPD and the Greens, tried to block Western rearmament, a number of security-minded French intellectuals and politicians offered to station Pershing II and cruise missiles in eastern France to protect Germany. In light of this François Mitterrand's offer in his unforgettable speech to the *Bundestag* on January 20, 1983, does not seem so surprising in retrospect. Nevertheless, this speech was the outgrowth of political expedience: Mitterrand had recognized that European countries would fall like dominoes to the Russian hegemony if Germany could be blackmailed by Moscow.

A Slap in the Face to the Pacifists

However, this speech came like a bolt out of the blue to the German pacifists. Opinion was divided even in Mitterrand's close circle and in the French diplomatic corps, so that he himself rewrote the soft speech prepared by his advisers on the flight to Germany: "It is not the moment to speak in veiled terms." To the disappointment of his colleagues in the SPD, the socialist Mitterrand staunchly supported the stationing of the Pershing missiles on German soil and thus gave Helmut Kohl invaluable assistance. Naturally he was basing this on the French postwar strategy of regarding Germany as the eastern buffer of France which must be defended out of fundamental French interests. At the same time, he elevated Germany to an essential part of French defense. Any threat to Germany was also one to France, and on this day a sort of defense identity was established on both sides of the Rhine.

This was a new kind of thinking, which many French and Germans did not immediately perceive. It also separated Mitterrand from many of his prominent countrymen, among them his predecessor Giscard d'Estaing, who had not been elected in 1981 and who held that stationing of Soviet missiles in East Germany affected West Germany and not France. At that time, no one suspected that Mitterrand's speech founded the second pillar—common defense in addition to economics and currency—of a future Europe.

In the second part of his speech Mitterrand offered the Federal Republic of Germany a common European foreign policy. "That was beyond the doctrine of binding Germany politically and ideologically to the West. It was an offer," wrote the excellent French observer, Ernst Weisenfeld. From the very beginning it was made clear that an effective European Community foreign policy could only be possible with a strong European defense force to ensure peace, which would lend it authority.

Kohl was right in implementing the deployment of the missiles, which Schmidt had initiated, in the face of strong opposition, at the same time extending a hand to the socialist Mitterrand despite opposition in his own ranks. At that time the personal relationship between the two was not so strong; what united them was political understanding.

We're Both Sitting in the Same Boat

From that time on the main thread in Franco-German relations was the assumption that in security terms Germany and France were sitting in the same boat. Up to that point, with all the good will in the world and despite the French military presence in West Germany and Berlin, the Federal Republic of Germany was a NATO member and France—from the German viewpoint—only a rebellious NATO country which liked to play the big power with its nuclear weapons—and, at least in Alfred Dregger's opinion—threaten Germany with its Pluto and Hades short-range missiles.

The new line of solidarity which began with the Kohl era led to the founding of the Franco-German brigade and the setting up the Eurocorps, leaving behind the SPD and the Greens, who opposed any military convergence. The German nationalists were also disappointed when the French withdrew the Pluto and Hades missiles to the center of the country and finally placed them in a museum.

Kohl's instinct for the important streams of history and at the same time for gaining partners who are able to accomplish something was proved for the first time in the case of Mitterrand. Certainly a number of circumstances helped the newly elected chancellor assess the situation and his new partner. Primarily it was the dispute with Giscard d'Estaing which made him think that Mitterrand's election victory in May 1981 was a stroke of luck. May 10, 1981, had been a lucky day for Kohl, since on this day in Paris Giscard d'Estaing lost the office of president, and in Berlin Richard von Weizsäcker was elected lord mayor and was thus removed from Bonn.

Once, when I was accompanying Helmut Kohl on his election campaign in 1980, he sat in a Westphalian guest house with his colleagues and journalists. He told me that Giscard d'Estaing had greatly disappointed him. In 1977 or 1978, Kohl, at that time leader of the opposition, had told President Giscard in Paris about his political plans in confidence. Giscard could not wait to reveal Kohl's plans to his friend Helmut Schmidt. The animosity between Kohl and Giscard after this breach of confidence was never reversed.

When I asked Helmut Kohl whether I could publish this story, he said, "Yes, do that," which I immediately did in *Le Figaro*. In 1982 I had the first interview by the chancellor granted to a foreign newspaper, a gesture toward France and my paper. I remember when the chancellor called my office, probably in 1983 or 1984. He asked me to inform Jean François-Poncet, former foreign minister under Giscard d'Estaing and now lead writer for our paper, that we would not grant him an interview. "Tell this gentleman who has said that Mitterrand's and Kohl's trees will not reach the sky like those of Schmidt and Giscard, that he should stick to his Giscard."

On the other hand, François-Poncet, unlike the other advisers of Giscard, preferred the alliance with Germany to any other models, such as, for example, the Franco-Soviet pseudo-alliance, the fatal illusion which has predominated since the war in certain conservative circles which blow incense in its direction, to the great joy of the communists. But Kohl's and Mitterrand's garden bloomed without François-Poncet. After the French conservative liberal government intermezzo of 1986–88, the successful gardeners were held to be Roland Dumas and Hans Dietrich Genscher.

Referring to Kohl and Mitterrand, Rudolf Augstein once said that there can never be any long-lasting friendships in politics. In this instance the *Spiegel* publisher was quite wrong. This was a friendship of life and death. I would like to turn Augstein's statement around and say that in politics there are no lasting enmities. At the latest in September 1992, when Giscard d'Estaing, along with Mitterrand, had begun to contribute decisively toward a French majority vote in favor of the Maastricht Treaty, Helmut Kohl recognized this and received Giscard d'Estaing at the chancellor's office.

Nevertheless, Kohl's earlier assessment of Giscard d'Estaing was perspicacious, since in 1990 the former French president was among those who wanted to postpone German unification. Giscard proposed calling a conference of all former allies against Germany during the war in order to sign a peace treaty with Germany. This would have postponed German reunification until the Twelfth of Never. When François Mitterrand and former defense minister François Léotard decided to allow participation of German troops in a parade on July 14, 1994, Giscard strongly opposed this with tears in his eyes on French television. He called to mind the German occupation of France by the *Wehrmacht*. Many viewers thought that his appearance was an absolute flop.

Kohl's turning to Mitterrand cannot simply be explained by his personal injury by Giscard. Over the years genuine trust and mutual respect have developed between these two very different personalities. A high point in their meetings was the gesture of Verdun of September 22, 1984, when both held hands over the mausoleum of Douaumont containing the remains of French and German soldiers, both politicians emphasizing the "reconciliation over the graves." A final highlight in the same vein was Mitterrand's remarkable speech on May 8, 1995, in Berlin, in which the soon-to-be-retired state president expressed his admiration for the German soldiers of the Second World War.

Mitterrand was obviously intent on throwing all taboos overboard and to go as far as possible in German-French relations. Did he want to prepare a fait accompli as much as possible for his Gaullist successor, or was he afraid that a neo-Gaullist, whether Chirac or Balladur, would turn back the wheel of history? Not all representatives of the political class in France approved his initiatives. After the symbolic gesture of Verdun, an Old Gaullist who had played a leading role in my paper, now since retired, said,

"That was grotesque!" Mitterrand's speech in the Berlin Schauspielhaus about the German soldiers, which was clearly aimed against a leftist campaign against the *Wehrmacht*, was sharply dismissed and declared unsuitable by such intelligent French observers of Germany as Joseph Rovan and Alfred Grosser. But this only went to show that the French president had been successful in opposing the prevailing view to bring about a change. For some time he had known that the French people—unlike certain of the Paris elite—no longer held anything against the Germans.

A similar thing happened at the German-French summit on May 31, 1994, in Strasbourg at which it was decided to ask German Eurocorps troops to participate in the military parade the following July 14 on the Champs-Elysées. Mitterrand passed this request along to Kohl at a point when the media were scornfully reporting that Kohl had not been invited to take part in the anniversary of the landing of the Allies in Normandy on June 6, 1944. But Mitterrand and Kohl knew that German troops parading in Paris pointed to the future, while the Normandy ceremony looked to the past. Helmut Kohl was visibly moved watching the parade on July 14.

In his election campaign in the summer of 1994 Kohl frequently called to mind this event, which was certainly an important milestone in European history. Despite criticism by former soldiers, opinion polls showed that the overwhelming majority of French favored this initiative.

Almost no president other than Mitterrand could have reached this decision which made history. Once when I was speaking about political friendship to the chancellor, he said that one of General de Gaulle's characteristics was being true to his friends and that Konrad Adenauer knew that he could count on him. He added that that which tied him with François Mitterrand, "had more than personal reasons."

> Mitterrand himself had suffered in the war and under the Nazi regime. With good reason we went to Verdun in 1984 in order to meet over the graves of the soldiers who had fallen in a gesture of reconciliation. We went there because we both had similar personal connections with it: my father had been in the trenches in 1916 at Verdun. As a child my father's stories about Verdun had been the embodiment of horror. When I come to Verdun and stand in front of the endless rows of graves from two world wars I think of my father. It is because of this memory that François Mitterrand and I deliberately went there.

At a Franco-German summit—I believe it was in Hanover in 1987—Mitterrand told the chancellor what had happened when the German military police had caught him after his escape as a prisoner of war. Escorted by police, starved and thirsty, he was led through the streets looking like a prisoner. Suddenly an old woman came up to him, gave him bread and sausage and said in French, "*Monsieur*, please don't believe that all Germans are bad." That was a courageous gesture in the Third Reich. Such memories can suddenly surface from the subconscious after years and decades of hectic political activities, which is probably what happened to Mitterrand, not always a friend of Germany. In the 1970s the French president had belonged to a leftist group for "Defense of Human Rights in Germany" which had been influenced by the Baader-Meinhof lawyer Klaus Croissant and the French philosopher Jean-Paul Sartre.

It had been a long way from this political opportunism to the *Bundestag* speech of January 1983 and the ceremony at Verdun.

The personal relationship between Kohl and Mitterrand became far deeper in the latter's final years in office. These two men who wished to make an impact on history also used it as an instrument in building up a Europe under the responsibility of France and Germany. How often they have shaken hands—and not just during elections, when Mitterrand was making fun of the German Social Democrats in 1994—but also when the friend was under fire from an external or internal opponent. It is possible that Helmut Kohl will some day look upon the presence of Mitterrand on the political scene during his repeated terms in office as a smile of providence.

In the latter years they were more and more in agreement. For Helmut Kohl no one can be an atheist, and friendship is holy, like the relationship with God. Thus it was a contradiction to have an atheist, Mitterrand, as a friend. I once heard him say that he once drew Mitterrand's attention to the fact that a particular library contained many religious books, whereupon Mitterrand told him he had been to a religious school and that his mother had been a strict Catholic. Aside from these meetings on the mystical level, there was a warm relationship between the two, as far as possible with the cool Mitterrand, such as when he called the Italian hospital to which the Kohls had just traveled to see their son, who had just been involved in a very serious car accident. It was moving and tragic to see at the German-French summit of November 29–30, 1994, in Bonn how difficult it was for the Frenchman to get out of his car and, obviously seriously ill, try to stand up. Helmut Kohl gave him his arm and helped him out of the car.

Before this relationship based on trust could be built up there were many barriers to be overcome which had been erected over decades between German Christian Democrats and French Socialists. A decisive role in this was played by the diplomat Alois Mertens, a state minister in the Foreign Office and a friend of Kohl's, who died at an early age. Well versed in French politics and culture, Mertens had recognized immediately that the

French Socialists were committed to Europe and could be counted on to further politics on our continent. The liberal centrists had been ousted with the defeat of Giscard d'Estaing. In terms of Europe, the Gaullists recalled only the relationship between de Gaulle and Adenauer, while the neo-Gaullist movement, the UDR and later RPR, were at that time still deeply anti-European. Had not the SFIO, the predecessor of Mitterrand's PSF, not voted for the European Defense Community in French parliament and brought down the Gaullists and communists? This ability to act jointly in security matters was the litmus test of Franco-German relations, and Kohl had always known it.

In view of European issues it was of secondary importance in Mertes's opinion that Mitterrand had allowed communists in his government or that he showed signs of having a nationalized economy—which soon collapsed, by the way. That was only internal French politics. Mertes also thought that the French Socialists had an entirely different security policy than the SPD, naive in security matters and short-sighted. Viewed thus, Mitterrand's election was a stroke of luck for Europe and Germany, while in Britain, the fanatical opponent of Germany, Margaret Thatcher continued to agitate against full European Community integration and against the Germans.

Out of the Sanctuary

Thus Franco-German cooperation arose across the political spectrum which was to last thirteen years and longer, since Mitterrand's successor, Jacques Chirac, demonstrated in May 1995 that he wants to and must continue this. The logical result of this approach was that the German economy was now wanted to support Europe, no longer causing envy, and that the French nuclear deterrent was no longer regarded as a problem, but a guarantee, because it was supposed to defend German territory against an aggressor just as intensely as it would French territory. It was predictable that the French nuclear armament would be questioned as soon as a European defense initiative was considered. For the chancellor it was clear that Germany did not strive to possess nuclear weapons and he regularly dismissed questions about it. Thus he probably followed the French debate about the definition of these weapons all the more closely in the 1980s and 1990s. Adherents of the traditional French strategy were opposed because they drew back from *la doctrine du sanctuaire*, which stated that French territory alone was worthy of being defended with nuclear weapons.

At that time there was no clear-cut change in strategy on the horizon, which had at its basis the fact that no German government could ever want control of nuclear weapons without going against the constitution; aside from this, the nature of a nuclear deterrent is left unclear in order to leave a potential aggressor in the dark.

It had nevertheless been the case that French hydrogen bombs and nuclear submarines would also defend German territory if needed, a great accomplishment of the Kohl era. German and French politicians and intellectuals such as André Glucksmann have suggested making the French force *de frappe nucléaire* available to the Germans; some even suggested sharing costs. Even though it never came to this, deliberations about a possible nuclear defense had reached this stage.

Jacques Chicac's trip to Bonn and Berlin in 1983 gave another dimension to this debate. To everyone's surprise, the head of the neo-Gaullists and mayor of Paris called for closer participation of Germany in the United States–European nuclear deterrent. After he returned to France he was, however, attacked by his own colleagues and toned down his statements toward those who took them to mean German-French nuclear control.

Chirac had talked at length with Kohl in Bonn. He had seen the Wall in Berlin for the first time and been moved in his own way. In an interview with *Die Welt*, he attacked those who believed that France had an interest in continuing the division of Germany: "No one can deny that the two halves of Germany form one nation. It is human and naturally necessary that this nation regains its unity."

Mitterrand could thus not hang back and on October 10, 1985, he paid an official visit to Berlin. Completely unlike his predecessor Giscard d'Estaing, who had not left the French sector because of the Four-Power Status and had not made contact with German officials, Mitterrand underlined the factual ties between Berlin and the Federal Republic of Germany, taking his friend Helmut Kohl along in his aircraft.

An invitation to Jacques Chirac—at that time temporary prime minister—had preceded the official visit by Mitterrand in October 1987. In Ludwigsburg the prime minister and chancellor gave speeches in front of five thousand young people on September 9, 1987, in memory of de Gaulle's visit to the castle in 1962. Thus it can be said that despite the fact that Helmut Kohl had not interfered with French internal affairs and despite his friendship with Mitterrand, he had always had a special relationship with the future French president, Chirac.

Hence it was no surprise for close observers of Franco-German relations that the two immediately started to use familiar address when they met in Strasbourg after Chirac had been elected president in May 1995. The chancellor had hardly been able to do that with Balladur.

In the two years between his visit to Berlin in 1985 and his official visit in 1987, Mitterrand had expanded the doctrine of France's "vital interests." It was no longer a case of defending the sanctuary of the motherland with nuclear weapons, but also the vital interests of France abroad. This also included the Federal Republic of Germany. He formulated this theory during an official visit to Germany in October 1987 to the chancellor and the federal president, Richard von Weizsäcker. As early as January 1986 Mitterrand had emphasized that Germany would be consulted about the deployment of prestrategic weapons on their soil "if time permitted." In October 1987 he said that France's nuclear deterrent depended primarily on submarine-launched weapons, thus making it clear that a possible battle with the Soviets on German soil would be avoided. (This was also true for the tactical weapons, since Mitterrand had already said on his state visit in October 1987 that "our prestrategic weapons are not made for our allies, but to engage and warn our enemies.") Taking the German allies into consideration in the formulation of French strategy was indeed a new element.

It is noticeable that the defense of Europe has retained this formulation of vital interest which also, for example, includes the necessary strategic supply lines of Europe. In the autumn of 1987 there was a conference of the Western European Union foreign ministers which approved a "platform of European security interests" which guaranteed each partner assistance with all possible means. It was further confirmed that "the independent nuclear forces of France and Great Britain" contributed to the defense and security of Europe. Thus the nuclear weapons remained under national control, but they protected the entire area of the WEU members.

Thus it can be asserted that Germany contributed to the change in French military strategy. Mitterrand had sharply criticized de Gaulle's nuclear policy when he was an opposition politician in the early 1960s. It was even more surprising that he took over this same strategy as president in the 1980s. Nevertheless, he made an instrument of solidarity out of an exclusively French weapon.

Helmut Kohl had appreciated French concern in March 1987 that the French—and British—nuclear deterrent could be reduced as part of East-West disarmament—the double-zero solution. He met the president and defense minister Gird several times, and then in June 1986 he met with Jacques Chirac, who followed Mitterrand in accepting the double-zero solution "out of solidarity with our partners."

At that time there must have been an assurance at the secret diplomatic level that the French and British weapons would not be sacrificed. The fact that they were quantitatively below the arsenal of the nuclear warheads of the two superpowers also lent weight to the argument against their being scrapped, unless the concept of the peace movement of a "world without weapons" had been accepted. Thus these deterrents are still protecting European soil against potential nuclear aggressors in this multipolar world in the post–Cold War era, also against chemical or bacteriological attack, should it be possible to know from whence the threat of aggression comes.

In terms of the armed forces, it was decided to start modestly and concretely in order not to put the cart before the horse, to avoid making the same mistake as the European Defense Community of 1954. Thus it was decided that all staff officers would be trained in the neighboring country until the year 2000. The first joint armament project was the combat helicopter. The bilateral exercise "*Kecker Spatz*" took place, and after the formation of a joint defense council the Franco-German brigade was formed. With 4,500 men and their high intercultural goals of bilingualism and a common uniform, the Eurocorps that was formed at the 1992 summit of La Rochelle is to continue. This corps will become operational by the end of 1995, with an integrated international general staff and 50,000 men distributed among the national units.

Taking Gorby at His Word

But a common European foreign policy took a long time. It was difficult enough with the beginnings of the joint *Ostpolitik* which became obsolete after 1990. Mikhail Gorbachev took over government leadership in the Soviet Union in 1985. Helmut Kohl had misjudged the new Kremlin leader at the beginning, and in an interview he made the famous comparison with Goebbels, for which he later apologized.

While Germany began to become more favorably disposed to *perestroika*, France continued to reject it longer, especially in regard to disarmament. The latent fear in Paris, especially during the Brandt era, of a turning away from alliances, had abated somewhat during Kohl's time, especially since a strong relationship had developed between Kohl and Mitterrand. But Genscher's politics were viewed as duplistic, and were mistrusted. Moreover, strong internal opposition to Kohl in those years made his stay in office uncertain. It was not until 1988 and the return of Mitterrand's trusted colleague Roland Dumas to a top French diplomatic position that these fears were finally laid to rest. During the bourgeois government of 1986–88 Genscher had maintained close contact with Dumas on a personal level. But France never shared Germany's enthusiasm for rapprochement.

At that time only a very few observers suspected that German reunification was just around the corner, still less that it would happen with Western approval. Heiner Geissler and his friends had even wanted to strike reunification from the CDU's platform in 1987, which Helmut Kohl was able to prevent. German reunification stayed on the program in a quote from Adenauer, which said volumes. Had it not been Adenauer who had prevented an early reunification by rejecting a note from Stalin in 1952?

As a result of the unconventional attitude of the new communist party leader in the Soviet Union, France began to suspect that Moscow was going to offer Germany reunification in exchange for neutrality. Thus in 1986–88 the background music to loud political drumming became the reinstated "*incertitudes allemandes*." As if people in France had known in 1987–88 about the Soviet offers, there was a heated debate in Paris as to whether the Soviets would allow German reunification in order to break up the Western alliance. In 1986–87 it had become obvious that the Soviet leadership under Gorbachev had started to distance itself from the GDR Politburo, as Beria had done with Ulbricht in 1952–53; he had been ready to sacrifice the German dictatorship to ensure a more open relationship with the West. Had the top French leaders of the time not received confidential reports that the Kremlin had made the German government an offer to this effect? It was not provable at the time, but there are indications, especially in a speech by Mitterrand's close associate Pierre Bérégovoy in 1987, in which the former finance and foreign minister and future prime minister said, "Gorbachev can propose reunification to the Germans in exchange for their neutrality. It is therefore necessary to couple West Germany to Western Europe and to unify the European Community in terms of every state, currency, and defense."

The Germans misunderstood this French attitude. The French government—less so the French people—were not so much against German reunification as against the unified Germany's possible withdrawal from existing treaties. Fear of German withdrawal from the West certainly gave great impulse to Western European integration in those years. This is the explanation for the French zeal to demonstrate to Germany its solidarity and to give the European Community more life. At any rate, Chirac, like de Gaulle ever a supporter of the German nation, has clearly shown that France's political right was not necessarily against reunification in principle.

Thus he said in Berlin on July 2, 1987, "Freedom is never truly achieved; people must always be ready to defend it. France is on your side in this battle. As long as Berlin remains a divided city, things are not normal; as long as a wall divides a people and they have to pay bitter tribute with their lives if they want freedom. The feeling of being residents of one and the same city and citizens of the same nation will last longer than a wall, steel, and concrete." Such a standpoint was very different from that of many

Germans at the time; the SPD in particular believed that the East Germans had come to terms with the communist regime and no longer wanted national unity.

If it is true that Helmut Kohl directly or indirectly rejected a proposal or suggestion by Gorbachev at that time, then he had acted no differently than had Adenauer in 1952, who rejected Stalin's offer of reunification which was obviously directed at preventing Germany from joining NATO. Should this be the case, Kohl's contribution to reunification is greater than has been hitherto acknowledged, since he achieved it by retaining Western ties and in keeping with the democratic principles of the Federal Republic of Germany. Should the secret diplomacy behind the scenes really have been such, then it is easier to understand why so many Franco-German initiatives came about in the early Gorbachev years, such as the European acts and the Franco-German brigade. It certainly cannot be denied that the trust in Mitterrand was such that Kohl had not needed to tell him about the Soviets' actions, and Mitterrand would have to have informed his prime minister of such an important issue.

Mitterrand's hesitation was thus all the more surprising in November and December 1989 when the slogan "*Wir sind* das *Volk*" (We are *the* People) was changed to "*Wir sind* ein *Volk*" (We are *one* People) on the placards of demonstrators in Leipzig and Berlin. It contrasted with the opinion of the French people who were happy about the opening of the Berlin Wall and who were not against German unification. The president flew to Kiev to meet Gorbachev in order to revitalize the long-outmoded Russian-French "power-sharing plan" on Germany, which he fortunately was unable to do. He traveled to the GDR, paid homage to the tatters of its last communist regime, and had dinner with its representatives such as Modrow, Gerlach, and Krenz, applauded by the crypto-communist "GDR-French Friendship Society." The day after that he did not walk through the Brandenburg Gate with Helmut Kohl.

Since late November Kohl and Genscher had known the French condition for German reunification: that Germany would not go its own way and leave NATO, the WEU, or the European Community treaties. A corollary by Paris was recognition of the western border of Poland. When Bonn finally showed that these conditions would be met, French diplomats began supporting German reunification as much as possible. With U.S. president George Bush's approval, Kohl and Mitterrand, Genscher and Dumas acted, despite the protests of Margaret Thatcher, whose adherents have probably never forgiven the French for this "treason."

Helmut Kohl himself has indicated that the European Council of Ministers meeting of December 9, 1989, was extremely frosty because the German chancellor had presented his ten-point program of November 28, a great step forward toward German unification, without consultation with his partners. Margaret Thatcher's comments on German unification expressed what others were only thinking.

On the other hand, the ten-point program contained nothing other than that which the allies themselves had said in a number of declarations, and, as a matter of fact, this road map toward German unity was extremely modest. It was also overtaken in a month or two.

Mitterrand broke ranks and soon openly supported unification, for which the "Iron Lady" and her friends never forgave him. Ministers of this energetic lady denigrated him as a "poodle of the chancellor," attesting to the British conservatives' conviction that he had led the German chancellor by the nose and played a double game against England.

An important day in Franco-German understanding on reunification was January 4, 1990, when Kohl and Mitterrand met at the French president's country home at Latché to discuss the European confederation which Mitterrand had proposed on December 31. It was an exceptionally warm and sunny winter's day and the two statesmen went for a walk with journalists and photographers to the beach of Vieux-Boucau, with Mitterrand's dog Baltic running around them. Kohl assured Mitterrand that he had spoken to nobody about the ten-point program. "It is a German matter," he said, "but you can be certain that my intentions are in keeping with the spirit of Franco-German friendship and cooperation." Both of them emphasized that "German confederation" and "pan-European confederation" meant two different things. With these words Mitterrand left the Germans to achieve unification, and this day can thus be regarded as a turning point. Thereafter the only problem to be solved was the German-Polish border, but Hans Dietrich Genscher had been set on its recognition for a long time.

German Patriotism

The chancellor also had characteristics which he shared with other Europeans even before the discussion arose in Germany. One of these is his patriotism, which makes contact with the French, British, Dutch, Spanish, and others much easier. The Christian Democratic chancellor preached a type of republican patriotism which is well understood in France. At the same time he turned against national socialism and national egotism. When he was elected chancellor, the German and French leftist media and political scientists spread the rumor that Germany would descend into evil national socialism—as if these "observers" had not realized that election of this chancellor had meant a step toward normality!

As one of Kohl's closest colleagues, Michael Mertes, admitted, "patriotism" is a word heavily loaded with prejudice in "postnational" Germany, so that it was suggested in all seriousness that the Day of German Unity, October 3, should not be celebrated in exchange for its happening, an idea which would seem ridiculous to the French and Americans if someone had tried to do away with the *Quatorze Juillet* or Thanksgiving Day or Independence Day.

It took many years for intellectuals, whose profession it is to think, to realize what Kohl's patriotism actually meant. Even today not everyone has understood this. It was necessary for unification to be achieved before minds were opened—a spontaneous movement, but one in which Kohl masterfully steered the German ship. French and Germans had become closer in 1989, not just because of the congruence with 1789, the year of the French Revolution, but because the East Germans accomplished the first successful revolution in the history of Germany. For seventeen million people this meant recapturing the basic rights from the declaration of 1789, which our democrats still adhere to.

German unification did not happen as the German left—the SPD and the Greens—had imagined it. They had believed the only thing possible was a compromise between communism and socialism in a sort of "*democratur*" and tolerance of some sort of division. The GDR revolutionaries achieved unity in freedom without spilling blood, from which the CDU/CSU and FDP never distanced themselves. Kohl, whose love of his homeland and fatherland has always ruled out radicalism, was immediately understood in France, especially by circles around François Mitterrand and naturally also by other liberals and conservative parties.

Superpower in Europe

American and other foreign journalists sometimes complain that since German reunification they are not being treated as sensitively and gently by Germany government authorities as they were earlier. As the victims of a less easy access, they are perhaps noticing a change in behavior which does not correspond to reality, but to their own fears. A typical example of such superficial and global judgment is *After the Wall: Germany, the Germans and the Burden of History*, published in 1995 by Marc Fisher, a correspondent for the *International Herald Tribune*, which naturally enough was strongly praised by *Der Spiegel*. The American has picked out a number of real weaknesses in the German mentality but ones which are more likely to make the reader smile. However, he has lumped them with past and present political problems which he is completely unable to discuss in terms of weight and priority.

To be sure, despite all the official relations, the Americans are no longer at the center for the Germans as they had been at the height of the Cold War. NATO has lost significance since 1990—to this was also added the sad death of the German general secretary, Manfred Wörner, a personal friend of the chancellor. European integration has now become the center. The American backdrop for interviews and background information has shrunk somewhat, while it has been expanded in Europe from the initial twelve to fifteen countries.

The prevailing historical situation has certainly decisively influenced the actions of the politicians, even if they wish it were otherwise. It is inevitable that foreign relations will take a less central position than in the time of the limited sovereignty of the Federal Republic of Germany. Germany is a complex society with an extremely complicated history, which correspondents based there for only a short time—many of whom have blinkers—cannot comprehend. There is also the frustration of the old correspondents who are suffering because life in the highly taxed, more crime-ridden, and poorer postreunification Germany is not as pleasant as it had been. But a wave of national socialism has not happened. There are more books and articles than before on the chronic problem of the German intellectuals and the search for the German identity. Why should German academics not be allowed this favorite game? On the other hand, Helmut Kohl and his ministers as well as federal president Roman Herzog have done everything to contain this unavoidable surge of German excess.

As a counterweight on a European scale Germany is trying to achieve restraint and there is much evidence of this. In this regard, Germany's absence from the Normandy ceremonies on June 6, 1994, was good. It served as a basis for the chancellor's doctrine, according to which Germany would not participate in any victory celebrations, but should mourn in the cause of peace and reconciliation. Kohl also acted in this way when he and François Mitterrand did not review the military parade on May 9, 1995, in Moscow, attending only the official reception and the wreath-laying at the German and Soviet memorials.

No politician—whether American, Russian, or whoever—can disregard Kohl. His blessing was sought by Bill Clinton after his election, and Jacques Chirac made his first foreign trip a meeting with Helmut Kohl at Strasbourg Kohl lays great store in these personal contacts, which lend a "human" touch to the otherwise cold relations between states. The visits to the sauna with Boris Yeltsin, the meal with Bill Clinton at the "Philomena" in

Washington and at "Yvonne" with Jacques Chirac in Paris will go down in the annals of history. Such approaches by foreign politicians to Germany's senior leader make liars of the right-wing radicals who have been spreading the myth of German degradation "on the nose ring." Putting the minds of neighbors to rest, especially the smaller neighbors, that Germany does not intend to go a separate way, is currently the foremost aim of German foreign policy.

Unreformable Britain?

There are Britons who can never forget the past conflicts in the old Europe. Their thinking is stuck in a groove, like that of the Allies who did not offer any assistance during the Second World War to the democratic opposition to Hitler: "*alles Deutsche*" . . . "all of those Huns" . . . "*tous des Boches*." Aside from the communist KPF, only a very small majority in France, on the other hand, always supported the Ulbricht and Honecker regimes at the cost of German unity and the democratic Federal Republic of Germany. These people, primarily concentrated in the GDR-French Friendship Society and their publication, *Allemagnes d'aujourd'hui*, founded by Georges Castellan and Jérôme Vaillant, had had a certain amount of media influence through various channels. This remained small, however, because the *ressentiments* against Germany in France did not last as long as they had in Britain or other smaller countries such as The Netherlands or Denmark, which feared a supposed German dominance. Thus it was somewhat surprising that John Major was more friendly than ever at the British-German consultations in May 1995—though this visit took place after the embrace by Chirac and Kohl in Strasbourg. In an interview with the *Bild-Zeitung* the British prime minister offered "to change the quiet German-British alliance into a partnership which everyone would talk about." He mentioned the "love story" between Britain and the German football star Jürgen Klinsmann and added that "both countries had the same way of pursuing politics and economics." After Jacques Chirac, who speaks Russian, Arabic, and good English, but no German, had suggested several times that Britain should be brought more strongly into the European fold, it appears that a sort of competition has arisen between London and Paris in front of the chancellor's throne. In the autumn of 1994, however, former foreign minister and now prime minister Alain Juppé made assurances on television that "the French and British entente is not directed against Germany and that Europe can make progress only when Germany and France are in accord." What do France and Britain have in common? The same defense doctrine?

They were together in the Gulf War and have closed ranks in Bosnia—but the *Bundeswehr* has also been there since June 1995.

France, like Germany, wants a strong Europe, but, like Britain, with weak institutions. France wants Europe to become a "superpower," but Britain wants it to become a "world power," as John Major has said. The Germans steer clear of using the word "power" at all. This European concept as a whole is in contrast to the politics of the two nations, "to develop its own emanation and be able to make specific contributions to international politics," a "dilemma on which the Maastricht Treaty is silent," as Norbert Prill, a colleague of the chancellor, ascertained in April 1995.

The Gaullist Jacques Chirac had a head start in confidence over Major. Even when he took office the French and German concepts in matters such as currency and economic union and Europol were similar, which was not the case with Britain.

The oath of confidence is given at the moment at which the decision is made about the acceptance of majority vote and dispensing with the national veto in the EU Council of Ministers. Can Chirac come to terms with the idea of expanding majority decisions so valued by Kohl and Kinkel? Despite everything, those in the know think that Chirac and not Balladur is the better European. The chancellor would have had more difficulty with Balladur, who is hard to assess, than with the "bulldozer" Chirac, who shares many of Kohl's characteristics: closeness to the people, roots in the provinces, belief in principles and ideals, ability to tackle things, and belief in his own fortune.

The so-called Lamers or Schäuble paper led to controversy in the summer of 1994. It presented the German concept of a federal Europe, centered on Germany, France, the Benelux countries, and perhaps Austria, thus excluding Italy, Greece, Denmark, and Spain. The British, the French Gaullists, and the Bavarians in Germany were unhappy about this concept of a European federal state and the others felt themselves to have been relegated to the role of satellites or extras. Only France had read this text more with approval in the beginning, though its enthusiasm waned when the chancellor himself began to distance himself from it due to negative reactions.

The latest version of June 1995 takes these reservations into consideration. It also put to rest the minds of the many pro-Europeans in France that the 1995 version of the paper on Europe which Kohl approved was no longer as "supranational" and "center European" oriented as the Schäuble-Lamers paper of the previous year, but which nevertheless led more certainly to a united Europe: the chancellor had obviously recognized that it was better to take a few steps backward to get a running start.

Europe's shortcomings are often discussed and the EU thoughtlessly criticized for having been a failure in the Bosnia conflict like the United Nations and NATO. Thus it is necessary to point out the great success of the Kohl Mitterrand team: the Serbs and other states of the former Yugoslavia were not able to split France and Germany. Bosnia was the first example of unanimous EU foreign policy.

At the beginning France and Britain had had a certain amount of sympathy for the Serbs for historical reasons which François Mitterrand, well versed in history, brought up in the first phase of the conflict. This was why Paris regretted Bonn's early recognition of Slovenia and Croatia. Aside from the fact that France and Britain did not want to support any Serbian guerrillas who fired on children in Sarajevo like rabbits and set up concentration camps, people in Western Europe had learned a great deal. The decisive factor is that on our continent conflicts of interest are no longer allowed to be solved with weapons. War in Europe is no longer the extension of politics by other means. The Serbs who are fighting in this war do not appear to have understood this. Fortunately they were unsuccessful in driving a wedge between Germany and Austria on the one hand and Britain and France on the other. This diabolical plan, which smacks of 1914, was stopped at the very latest by Mitterrand on September 18, 1991. On a visit to Bonn the president made it clear that France held the same views on the former Yugoslavia that the Federal Republic of Germany did.

Thus Paris approved Germany's decision of June 25, 1995, to finally send German troops, medical personnel, and above all, *Luftwaffe* aircraft to Bosnia. The fear often expressed by Defense Minister Volker Rühe and Foreign Minister Klaus Kinkel that the presence of German uniforms in the Balkans could recall the terrible time before 1945 proved to be groundless. Aside from Serbian propaganda, no one in Europe identifies the *Bundeswehr* with the *Wehrmacht* any more.

Even in 1987, when five European minehunters were sent to the Gulf during the Iran-Iraq war, the lack of German naval units was sharply criticized in France. The German contribution to the Gulf War beginning in 1990 was the checkbook. The chancellor was aware that this must have left a dubious impression in many people's minds, but a decision was needed first by the German Federal Constitutional Court on July 12, 1994, in order to be allowed to send German troops in support of the United Nations. This also gave the green light for a European defense which would be possible outside the NATO region.

After July 14, 1994, when German, French, Belgian, and Spanish troops paraded in Paris, the taboo of "the German uniform" was finally laid to rest. In the years after German reunification there have been fundamental changes in thinking which allow the Germans and all other Europeans, especially the French, to again play their part in world history. Why should the two most intelligent nations of the world, Germany and France, not combine forces and win other partners in order to survive? Firming up this pact and building a dynamic Europe are the final tasks for Helmut Kohl, which he had started to do with François Mitterrand and will now complete with Jacques Chirac.

This is the background against which the German and French governments should look to achieve consensus in the important question of the nuclear defense of Europe. This chapter presupposes that the Europeans, especially the Germans and the French, want to achieve a common European reconnaissance satellite which would protect us against surprise attack. There is also the question of conventional armaments—especially construction of a future large transport aircraft by Dasa and Aerospatiale—for peacekeeping outside Europe, which also impinges on our security.

Nevertheless, Bonn must steer a decisive course against the widely indoctrinated ecological-peace movement. In June 1995 Jacques Chirac's announcement of eight nuclear tests in the Pacific was received with mixed feelings in Germany. With the exception of the FDP there were no German government protests, which leads to the suspicion that the mere existence of the French nuclear arsenal is not entirely unwelcome at a time in which radical military forces and politicians in Russia threaten to use nuclear force and there is talk about the threat of nuclear armed terrorist states.

But the chancellor distanced himself from these nuclear tests and said only that he respected Chirac's sovereign decision (I am writing this in August 1995). Perhaps more agreement could be expected as a "return" for Mitterrand's *Bundestag* speech of January 1983. To be sure, however, the initial French position was difficult to defend. Only when it became clear that these nuclear tests had become a welcome pretext on the part of the peace movement and the Green and SPD leftists to drive a wedge between France and Germany and to lead a massive anti-French campaign, making the establishment of an integrated European defense impossible, did it become possible and necessary to hinder with every means and argumentation possible the destruction of a Franco-German friendship that had been built up slowly over three and a half decades.

The direction changed too on the French side. After his relatively bombastic and premature announcement of his intentions at a press conference on June 13, 1995, Chirac later made it clear that the French nuclear force was a European one. This was also emphasized by the French foreign minister, Herve de Charette. Then the formerly anti-European Philippe Seguin clearly defended in *Le Figaro* the "Europeanization" of the French—and later the British—nuclear forces. This was not a turning point because the expansion of the nuclear shield to Germany had already happened in 1987, as we have seen. But the fact that the Gaullists were supporting this doctrine was an important new development. Equally sensational was the fact that Chirac indicated his support for a common European currency and politics of stability right after taking over office.

It is naturally very necessary that German politicians—and not the blind proponents of the peace movement who do not wish to see the danger in the southern and southeastern Mediterranean, but those who are realists and wish to survive—react to these offers. In the summer of 1995, *Bundestag* member of parliament Friedberg Pflüger, defense spokesperson for the CDU/CSU parliamentary party, said: "By doing this, Seguin has given the French nuclear force, previously reserved for national defense, a clearly European function. In an uncertain world, the express and full protection of the French nuclear deterrent—as well as the American one—is an important offer. We must discuss this objectively with the French. There are still many questions to be clarified. This clarification is the need of the moment, not the excited public protest against the last eight underground tests—after practically no one protested against the eighty-six tests carried out on Muroroa under Mitterrand.

But only Helmut Kohl can take this great step with Jacques Chirac in the direction of a unified Europe. Only his word would be trusted by the French, since he has consistently pursued a policy friendly toward France. Countries outside Germany especially hope that he will run again in 1998. This time too the French, Poles, Czechs, Russians, and Americans have appreciated what they have in Helmut Kohl, ahead of the Germans.

The Only Prominent Frenchman in Germany

The head of an institute for German-French consulting, Jochen Peter Breuer, who has been trying to instill the practicalities of working together in French and German managers in a suburb of Paris—which is certainly not easy with such complex people as the French and Germans—once gave me a plausible explanation for Kohl's popularity with my people: "Kohl," this German management consultant said, "is the only prominent Frenchman in Germany. He has French characteristics which are lacking in the Germans today. He goes against the currently prevailing opinion, he even has his own opinion, which is very rare in my country. As a political statesman he is bold and courageous. He is a leader, but has remained a democrat. He does not allow himself to be influenced by his critics."

Breuer's judgment of Kohl is politically neutral. In his opinion he can be compared only to another prominent German who was active in a different area and also a member of the SPD: the former chairman of the board of Daimler-Benz, Edzard Reuter. Reuter had been as popular with his fellow board members of large companies as Kohl is with other politicians, because he is different. "There is a distinct lack in Germany of personalities who buck the prevailing trend." After Reuter left his position as head of the company in May 1995, he too was vilified and criticized. Will Kohl suffer the same fate?

> Aside from this," the consultant said, "Kohl acts naturally, which is rare in this country. In our training seminars we often have a test. We show the participants a video with an interview with Kohl on the French television program "The Hour of Truth." We turn the sound off, show the picture only, and ask them, "What is the chancellor talking about now?" The Germans answer that he was talking about his last vacation or that he was telling a joke. Actually, though, he was speaking about German reunification.

Breuer continued:

> Kohl lets himself get carried away by his own gestures and spontaneity. But naturalness is not popular in Germany: it supposedly makes things less believable. On the other hand, when the French see and hear him, they find him likable, lively, and clever. Mitterrand was, to be sure, not an extrovert. This damaged his image with his fellow countrymen for a long time and they called him "the sphinx." But compare if you will the New Year's speeches of Mitterrand and Kohl! In Mitterrand's final years of office he practically fell out of the television into the arms of his audience, because he had been told to loosen up. On the other hand, Kohl is motionless and fixed in front of the camera, because his advisers have probably told him that a serious face is needed in Germany.

In general, Breuer said, Kohl does not usually stick to this demeanor and the German commentators harshly criticize this breach of the codex of their country. In this regard his situation is like that of Franz Josef Strauss, whose habits were also the target of withering criticism, especially from North Germany, and this observer regrets that Kohl is not able to be himself in front of his fellow countrymen. The Germans button up and say that a person is no longer in control of him or herself. Helmut Kohl obviously feels much more comfortable talking to French people because he can be more natural with them, whereas in Germany he has to always watch his expressions and gestures and control his temperament, the behavioral psychologist believes.

It may be due to this that in June 1994 the chancellor gave my editor in chief and me an interview the like of which would never appear in the German press. This long interview has become legendary in recent press history as the "refrigerator interview," since the chancellor answered our question of what he was thinking when he got up in the middle of the night in regard to the "mantle of history." "That is a question I don't ask myself. When I get up at night, I'm not thinking about history, but plundering the refrigerator. When I go to the refrigerator, history is not at all important to me," he said, and laughed heartily.

Despite his close connections with religious and political ideals, Helmut Kohl is a pragmatist. He stands with both feet on the ground and therefore is a member of an endangered species whose characteristics were once toughness, good common sense, and a feeling for reality. "He does not often parade his firm beliefs, such as in the dream of a united Europe, since the Germans measure every political belief with the yardstick of totalitarian music," said my discussion partner. I do not agree with this judgment of the Germans. Roman Herzog once criticized the Germans for not being pragmatists. Ideologies and messianic ideas have indeed not disappeared completely in this country, as proven by successful campaigns by the peace movement and the German Greenpeace activists. Kohl's democratic pragmatism is clearly an anathema to these politico-mystics. On the other hand, political enthusiasm in Germany had been forced on the people by the government for too long for the people to now approve of the emotional side of politics.

On the contrary, the main characteristic of a politician in France is that he is able to win many adherents for an idea or a challenge, and thus create change, by virtue of his emotions.

The Germans, who had at first tipped Jacques Delors and then Edouard Balladur in the French presidential elections of April–May 1995, misjudged the power that Jacques Chirac had of addressing the emotions and frustrations of his fellow countrymen, particularly the younger ones. Thus Federal President Richard von Weizsäcker was more popular than Helmut Kohl, because he was the typical, cool "anti-Kohl" or, more correctly, "unKohl." Von Weizsäcker acted like the Germans imagined themselves to be. At first they turned away from Kohl because he is like them. Perhaps the Germans do not like themselves. They do not want to be like themselves. Thus they like the theatrical and affected Weizsäcker, but do not approve of the natural and spontaneous Kohl. This attitude is prevalent among intellectuals and Protestants. German intellectualism is a constant battle against reality.

In the meantime they have gotten used to Kohl. They have had enough time for that. When the German citizen casts his vote, he can acknowledge his identity and dare to follow his interests in the anonymity of the voting booth. Thus it is that Kohl loses the opinion polls and wins the elections. The voter thinks, “This man will represent our interests with no ifs, ands, or buts,” because the German people as a whole have a strong sense of the concrete and of reality. Moreover, Kohl, who opponents have often accused of “sitting out” decisions, is a “reactive” man who is able to quickly adapt himself to new situations without losing sight of the fixed points of his vision. It is for this reason that J.P. Breuer said that Kohl is a “German Frenchman,” who combines German staunchness and exactness with French flexibility and strength of vision.

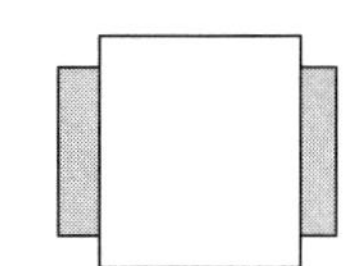

NOTES

1. Rudolf Pörtner, ed., *Mein Elternhaus* (Düsseldorf and Vienna, 1985).
2. Ibid.
3. Ibid.
4. Werner Filmer and Heribert Schwan, *Helmut Kohl. Eine Biographie* (Düsseldorf, 1987).
5. Willy Zirngibl, *Gefragt: Helmut Kohl* (Bonn, 1972).
6. Pörtner, *Mein Elternhaus*.
7. Personal communication, 1984.
8. Werner Masur, *Helmut Kohl - der deutsche Kanzler* (Frankfurt am Main, 1990).
9. Klaus Hoffmann, *Helmut Kohl - Kanzler des Vertrauens* (Stuttgart, 1984).
10. Masur, *Helmut Kohl*.
11. Zirngibl, *Gefragt*.
12. Hoffmann, *Helmut Kohl*.
13. Filmer and Schwan, *Helmut Kohl*.
14. Ibid.
15. *Focus* 16, 1994.
16. Berhard Vogel, ed., *Das Phänomen. Helmut Kohl im Urteil der Presse* (Bonn, 1990).
17. Reinhard Appel, ed., *Kohl im Spiegel seiner Macht* (Bonn, 1990).
18. Supplement to volume 13 (1965) of the *Frankfurter Allgemeine Zeitung*.
19. Zirngibl, *Gefragt*.
20. Vogel, *Das Phänomen*.
21. Hoffmann, *Helmut Kohl*.
22. Interview with Peter Hopen.
23. *Süddeutsche Zeitung*, February 25, 1970.
24. Ibid.
25. This interview occurred on December 18, 1970.

26. *Hannoversche Allgemeine Zeitung*, January 1, 1971.
27. *Süddeutsche Zeitung*, January 7, 1971.
28. Protocol of the CDU party conference, Düsseldorf, 1971.
29. *Stern*, February 7, 1971.
30. Protocol of the CDU party conference, Düsseldorf, 1971.
31. *Westdeutsche Allgemeine Zeitung*, September 25, 1971.
32. Brügge's text quoted from the reprint in: Vogel, *Das Phänomen*.
33. Ibid.
34. Ibid.
35. Ibid.
36. Zirngibl, *Gefragt*.
37. *Frankfurter Allgemeine Zeitung*, November 13, 1972.
38. Ibid.
39. *Süddeutsche Zeitung*, July 7, 1972.
40. Ibid.
41. *Die Zeit*, May 4, 1973.
42. Unpublished statement by Professor Biedenkopf.
43. J.W. Goethe, *Faust I, Vorspiel auf dem Theater*.
44. The speech was first published in its entirety in the CDU's newsletter, *Union in Deutschland*, June 13, 1973.
45. Interview of the Week, *Deutschlandfunk*, June 17, 1973.
46. The complete text can be found in issue 8 (1976) of *Die politische Meinung*.
47. *Tageszeitung*, Munich, February 23, 1974.
48. Ibid.
49. *Westfälische Rundschau*, May 20, 1975.
50. Ibid.
51. *Frankfurter Rundschau*, October 30, 1974.
52. Ibid.
53. *Frankfurter Rundschau*, March 11, 1975.
54. *Der Spiegel*, March 17, 1975.
55. *Frankfurter Rundschau*, April 4, 1975.
56. Protocol of the CDU party conference, September 1976.
57. *Der Spiegel*, June 21, 1976.
58. *Die Weltwoche*, Zurich, October 31, 1976.
59. *Die Welt*, May 21, 1970.
60. *Die Welt*, May 31, 1979.
61. *Der Spiegel*, February 16, 1981.
62. *Frankfurter Allgemeine Zeitung*, January 23, 1981.
63. *ARD Tagesschau*, June 18, 1982.
64. *Die Zeit*, July 2, 1982.

65. *Frankfurter Neue Presse*, October 5, 1982.
66. Karl Carstens, *Erinnerungen und Erfahrungen* (Boppard, 1993).
67. Quoted from the *Bundestag* protocol.
68. Paul Pucher, *Der letzte Preusse* (Berlin, 1995).
69. *Die Welt*, August 26, 1983.
70. The quotes stem from an unpublished text which was produced in the chancellor's office for documentary purposes.
71. *Die Zeit*, March 2, 1984.
72. Wolfram Bickerich, *Der Enkel. Eine Analyse der Ära Kohl* (Düsseldorf, 1995).
73. *Die Welt*, May 11, 1984.
74. *Der Spiegel*, March 4, 1985.
75. *Union in Deutschland*, April 25, 1985.
76. Ronald Reagan, *An American Life: The Autobiography*. New York: Simon and Schuster, 1990, p. 377.
77. Ibid., p. 377.
78. Ibid., p. 378.
79. Ibid., p. 378.
80. Ibid., p. 379.
81. Ibid., p. 382.
82. Ibid., p. 382.
83. Ibid., p. 383.
84. *Der Spiegel*, May 6, 1985.
85. *Stuttgarter Zeitung*, May 30, 1985.
86. Filmer and Schwan, *Helmut Kohl*.
87. From the personal documents of Heinz Schwarz.
88. All quotes in the previous paragraphs come from *Der Spiegel*.
89. Ibid.
90. *Die Welt*, March 29, 1986.
91. Christiane Schatzmann, personal communication.
92. Eduard Shevardnadze, *Die Zukunf gehört der Freiheit* (Hamburg, 1991).
93. Documentation from the *Bundeskriminalamt* (BKA)1995.
94. Wolfgang Schäuble in a press interview, 1990.
95. Mikail Gorbachev, *Erinnerungen* (Berlin, 1995).
96. Ibid.
97. Ibid.
98. *Deister- und Weserzeitung*, March 16, 1989.
99. *Bremer Nachrichten*, March 29, 1989.
100. *Der Spiegel*; confirmed by Jürgen Merschmeier.
101. *Nürnberger Zeitung*, August 30, 1989.
102. Told to Gerhard Löwenthal, German Television Channel Two.

103. *Die Koalition der Vernunft. Deutschlandpolitik in den 80er Jahren* (Bonn, 1995).
104. Helmut Herles and Ewald Rose, eds., *Parlamentsszenen einer deutschen Revolution* (Bonn, 1990).
105. Documentation from the BKA, 1995.
106. Horst Teltschik, *329 Tage. Innenansichten der Einigung* (Berlin, 1991).
107. Documentation from the BKA, 1995.
108. Ibid.
109. *Süddeutsche Zeitung*, November 3, 1989.
110. *Weltbild*, November 17, 1989.
111. Gorbachev, *Erinnerungen*.
112. *Die Welt*, December 5, 1989.
113. *Frankfurter Rundschau*, December 13, 1989.
114. According to H. Klein.
115. Documentation from the BKA, 1995.
116. Ibid.
117. *Weltwoche*, Zurich, February 2, 1990.
118. Friedrich Schorlemmer, *Meine Jahre mit Helmut Kohl* (Mannheim, 1994).
119. Lothar de Maizière, personal communication.
120. *Der Spiegel*, June 25, 1990.
121. *Erinnerungen*.
122. Teltschik, *329 Tage*.
123. Documentation from the BKA, 1995.
124. Hans Klein, *Es begann im Kaukasus* (Berlin, 1990).
125. *Die Woche*, February 18, 1993.
126. Ibid.
127. Ibid.
128. *Frankfurter Allgemeine Zeitung*, October 15, 1990.
129. dpa (*Deutsche Presseagentur*) story, May 13, 1991.
130. *Bundestag* protocol, session of June 20, 1991.
131. *Süddeutsche Zeitung Magazin*, December 2, 1994.
132. *Die Zeit*, March 5, 1993.
133. Ibid.
134. All quotes in the preceding paragraphs from documentation of the Press and Information Office of the federal government, Bonn, May 8, 1995.

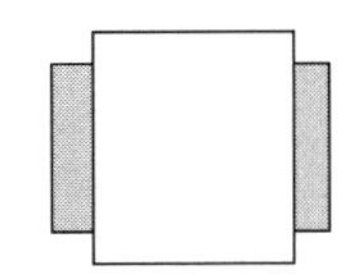

Chronology

1930	Born in Ludwigshafen on April 3.
1936–1940	Attends primary school in Ludwigshafen-Friesenheim.
1940–1944	Attends secondary school in Ludwigshafen.
1944	*December:* Evacuated to Erbach, in the Odenwald, until May 1945.
1945	*August to December:* farmer's apprentice in Düllstadt. The fifteen-year-old Helmut considers becoming a farmer. *December:* returns to the secondary school in Ludwigshafen.
1946	Joins the Christian Democratic Union as member no. 00246.
1947	Co-founder of the *Junge Union* in Rhineland-Palatinate. Deputy chairperson of an Initiative for Europe, which was quickly forbidden by the French occupation forces.
1948	*Autumn:* Kohl organizes a tea dance at the Weinberg guest house in Friesenheim and meets Hannelore Renner, aged fifteen, who later becomes his wife.
1950	*June 8: Abitur* (secondary-school diploma) in Ludwigshafen. *Autumn:* Beginning of studies at the Johann-Wolfgang-Goethe University of Frankfurt, majoring in law.
1951	Continuation of studies at the University of Heidelberg, majoring in history and minoring in public law, government law, and political science.
1953	Member of the management board of the CDU of the Rhineland-Palatinate.
1954–1961	Deputy chairperson of the *Junge Union* of the Rhineland-Palatinate.

1955–1966 Member of the board of the *Land* CDU of the Rhineland-Palatinate.

1956–1958 Assistant at the Alfred Weber Institut of the University of Heidelberg.

1958 Awarded Doctor of Philosophy degree by the University of Heidelberg. Dissertation topic: "Political Development in Rhineland-Palatinate and the Resurgence of Political Parties after 1945."

1958–1959 Assistant to the management at the Willi Mock iron foundry in Ludwigshafen.

1959 Chairperson of the CDU county organization of Ludwigshafen.

1959–1969 Adviser to the Organization of the Chemical Industry, based in Ludwigshafen. Learned about environmental protection.

1960 *June 27:* Marries Hannelore Renner thirteen years after having met her. They had two sons, Walter (born in 1963) and Peter (born in 1965).

1960–1969 Chairperson of the CDU city council parliamentary party in Ludwigshafen, with a view toward becoming mayor of the city.

1961 *October 25:* Elected by a slim majority as deputy chairperson of the CDU *Landtags* parliamentary party.

1963 *May 9:* Elected CDU parliamentary party chairperson with thirty-eight of forty-one votes of the CDU *Landtag* members of parliament.

1964 *October 13:* Elected chairperson of the CDU district organization in the Rhineland-Palatinate with 236 out of 250 votes at a special party conference.

1965 *November 7:* Elected again as chairperson of the region with 263 out of 274 valid votes.

1966 *March 6:* Elected chairperson of the *Land* CDU of Rhineland-Palatinate at the thirtheenth party conference with 415 out of 477 valid votes. Kohl finally becomes the designated successor of minister-president Peter Altmeier.
March 21–23: Kohl makes an unsuccessful bid for a seat in the CDU federal-level presidium at a party conference in Bonn, but by virtue of his position as chairperson of the *Land* CDU he becomes a member of the board of the party at the federal level.

1967 *April 23:* The CDU again wins the *Landtag* election of Rhineland-Palatinate with 46.7 percent of the vote.
May 23: Kohl elected to the board of the party at the federal level with 398 out of 566 votes at the fifteenth CDU national party conference at Braunschweig.

1968 *April 27:* Again elected chairperson of the *Land* CDU of the Rhineland-Palatinate with 347 out of 428 votes cast.

1969 *May 19:* Elected minister-president of Rhineland-Palatinate with fifty-six out of ninety-seven votes cast, thus ending Peter Altmeier's era in Mainz.
June 1: Kohl ends work for the Organization of the Chemical Industry.
November 17: Elected deputy chairperson of the CDU with 392 out of 476 votes cast at the party conference of the federal-level party in Mainz.

1970 *May 25:* Confirmation as chairperson of the *Land* CDU of Rhineland-Palatinate.
May 29: Helmut Kohl declares that he intends to become a candidate for chairperson of the CDU at the federal level.

1971 *January 25–27:* Kohl fails in his presentation at the CDU party conference in Düsseldorf with his model for co-determination favoring the employee, against the conservative model of Alfred Dregger and others.
March 21: In the *Landtag* elections the CDU wins an absolute majority with fifty percent of the votes.
October 4: At the party conference in Saarbrücken, Kohl loses the election as chairperson of the party at the federal level to Rainer Barzel. Out of 520 valid votes, 344 were for Barzel and 177 were for Kohl.

1973 *January 21:* Kohl again says he intends to run for chairperson of the CDU at the federal level.
June 12: Barzel resigns as chairperson of the CDU at the federal level and leader of the CDU/CSU *Bundestag* parliamentary party. Kohl is elected chairperson of the CDU at the federal level with 520 of 600 valid votes. Kurt Biedenkopf becomes his general secretary.

1975 *March:* The CDU of Rhineland-Palatinate has the best election result ever in the *Landtag* election under Kohl with 53.9 percent of the votes.
May 20: Confirmation of Kohl as minister-president with 55 out of 105 votes cast.

June 19: After a dispute the presidia of the CDU and CSU confirm Helmut Kohl at a joint meeting in Bonn as candidate of the Union parties for the next *Bundestag* elections.
June 23–25: The CDU issues a declaration on "The New Social Question" at the Mannheim party conference. The party conference confirms Kohl as chairperson of the party at the federal level with an overwhelming majority of 696 out of 707 valid votes.

1976 *October 3:* With 48.6 percent of the vote the CDU/CSU just misses an absolute majority in the *Bundestag* elections, the second best result ever for the Union in *Bundestag* elections.
November 19: At a closed meeting in Kreuth the CSU serves notice that it intends to terminate the joint parliamentary party in the *Bundestag* in the so-called "Kreuth resolution."
November 24: "Wienerwald" speech presented by Franz Josef Strauss to the *Junge Union* of Bavaria, with a strong defamation of Helmut Kohl.
December 1: 184 out of 189 CDU *Bundestag* members of parliament vote for Kohl as successor to Karl Carstens as chairperson of the parliamentary party.
December 2: Kohl resigns as minister-president of Rhineland-Palatinate.
December 12: CDU and CSU agree to again become a joint parliamentary party.
December 15: The CDU/CSU *Bundestag* parliamentary party elects Kohl as chairperson by 230 out of 241 valid votes.

1977 *February:* Due to a crisis in confidence general secretary Kurt Biedenkopf announces he is resigning. Kohl wants to propose the social minister of Rhineland-Palatinate, Heinrich (Heiner) Geissler.
March 7: The CDU party conference again confirms Kohl as party chairperson. Geissler becomes the new CDU general secretary.

1978 *January:* A group of CDU/CSU *Bundestag* members of parliament, among them Helmut Kohl, are not allowed to enter East Berlin.
October 23–25: The CDU agrees on its first basic program at the party conference at Ludwigshafen.

1979 *March 5:* Kohl again confirmed as party chairperson at the party conference at Kiel with 617 out of 740 votes.
May 28: After strong internal party debate the federal-level CDU board nominates Ernst Albrecht as candidate for chancellor.

July 2: The CDU/CSU *Bundestag* parliamentary party nominates Franz Josef Strauss, making him the joint candidate.

1980 *October 5:* The CDU/CSU loses over 4 percent of the votes in the *Bundestag* elections, achieving 44.5 percent of the votes. The SPD/FDP coalition are thus able to continue in government.

1981 *March 9:* Kohl confirmed for the fourth time as chairperson of the CDU at the federal level at the Mannheim party conference with an impressive 689 out of 715 votes.

1982 *September 20:* CDU/CSU and FDP begin negotiations on forming a new coalition under Kohl's leadership.
October 1: Constructive vote of no-confidence in the *Bundestag*. Helmut Kohl is elected chancellor of the Federal Republic of Germany.
December 17: As agreed, the chancellor poses the question of confidence in the *Bundestag* to have early elections on March 6, 1983, allowed.

1983 *January 7:* Federal president Karl Carstens dissolves the *Bundestag*.
March 6: In the *Bundestag* elections the Union achieves a triumphant victory just short of an absolute majority: CDU/CSU, 48.8 percent; SPD, 38.2 percent; FDP, 7.0 percent; and (for the first time) the Greens, 5.6 percent.
March 29: Parliament confirms Kohl as chancellor.
May 25: The CDU party conference in Cologne confirms Kohl as chairperson of the party at the federal level.
June 29: The federal government grants a one-billion-mark credit to the GDR via Strauss and Bavarian banks; East Berlin pledges transfer costs from the federal budget.
July 4–7: Chancellor Kohl and Foreign Minister Genscher make their first joint official visit to Moscow.

1984 *February 13:* First meeting of Kohl and Honecker at the funeral of the Soviet general secretary, Andropov, in Moscow.
September 22: François Mitterrand and Helmut Kohl shake hands at Verdun as a symbol of the reconciliation of their peoples.

1985 *March 12:* Second meeting of Kohl and Honecker in Moscow at the funeral of General Secretary Chernenko. Kohl meets his designated successor, Mikhail Gorbachev, for the first time.
March 22: Again confirmed as chairperson of the party at the federal level at the party conference in Essen.

May 1–5: U.S. president Ronald Reagan visits the Federal Republic of Germany at Kohl's invitation. Both visit the concentration camp at Bergen-Belsen and the military cemetary in Bitburg (the "Bitburg drama").

1986 *February:* Horst Sindermann, the president of the GDR *Volkskammer*, meets with Helmut Kohl for two hours on a visit to Bonn.
June 3: Kohl appoints his party friend Walter Wallmann to be the first environment minister on his cabinet.

1987 *January 27:* The CDU/CSU loses votes in the *Bundestag* elections and achieves 44.3 percent. Continuation of the coalition with the FDP.
September 7–11: Helmut Kohl receives the SED general secretary Erich Honecker for a "working visit" in Bonn.
September 12: Der Spiegel publishes serious accusations against the CDU minister-president Uwe Barschel, which rocks Helmut Kohl's party as a whole.

1988 *October 3:* Kohl offers condolences to the CSU leadership on the death of Franz Josef Strauss.
October 24–27: Official visit by the chancellor to Moscow. Kohl and Gorbachev have cordial discussions.

1989 *April 13:* Kohl reshuffes his cabinet: Waigel becomes finance minister, Stoltenberg takes over as defense minister from Rupert Scholz, and Wolfgang Schäuble takes over the interior ministry from Friedrich Zimmermann, who takes over transport.
August 22: Kohl announces that he will dismiss Geissler as general secretary at the next party conference and wants to appoint in his stead Volker Rühe, previously deputy chairperson of the *Bundestag* parliamentary party.
September 11: The new general secretary is confirmed by the party conference in Bremen; his opponents Lothar Späth and Ulf Fink lose their seats in the party presidium.
September 30: At the height of the twelve-month drama of the GDR refugees, the chancellor and Foreign Minister Genscher arrange the emigration of about ten thousand East Germans from the embassies of the Federal Republic of Germany in Prague and Budapest.
October 26: After the fall of Honecker on the eighteenth Kohl speaks on the phone with his successor, Egon Krenz, who resigns (on December 12) shortly after the fall of the Berlin Wall on November 9.

November 28: Kohl presents his ten-point plan on German unification to the *Bundestag*, which foresees a "federal organization" for both German states.
December 19: Kohl meets the GDR prime minister, Hans Modrow, in Dresden to examine the possibility of a "community under a treaty." In the evening the chancellor gives an internationally noted speech in front of the ruin of the Church of Our Lady. The Germans are on the road to a "single Fatherland."
December 22: Kohl and Modrow open the Brandenburg Gate in Berlin; Kohl speaks of "one of the happiest hours of my life."

1990 *February 10:* Kohl and Foreign Minister Genscher travel to Moscow. Gorbachev indicates that the Germans themselves are to determine unification.
February to March: Helmut Kohl campaigns in eastern Germany for the "Alliance for Germany," a joint party of the CDU/East and the *Demokratischer Aufbruch* (DA).
March 14: Kohl and Lothar de Maizière speak to a crowd of three hundred thousand on the Opernplatz at Leipzig.
June 5: Kohl visits U.S. president George Bush in Washington: the unified Germany is to remain a member of NATO.
July 15: Gorbachev and Kohl agree in Moscow on the modalities for German unification; the negotiating delegations subsequently travel to the Caucasus.
October 1–2: At the unification party conference in Hamburg Helmut Kohl joins the CDU West with the CDU East in a ceremony.
October 3: Kohl celebrates Unification Day with his family and closest associates in Berlin.
October 4: Statement on the government by Kohl at the first session of the *Bundestag* in a reunified Germany.
October 14: The CDU wins in the *Landtag* elections in four of the six new *Länder*.
December 2: The Union wins the first all-German election with 43.8 percent of the vote; the coalition with the FDP can continue.
December 17: Lothar de Maizière resigns as minister (without portfolio) due to accusations of Stasi affiliation.

1991 *January 17:* Kohl elected the first chancellor of a united Germany.
May 12: Kohl attacked by leftist radicals in Halle; he defends himself personally. Press photos of the incident circulated internationally.

June 20: The *Bundestag* decides with a slim majority (the balance being tipped by the FDP and PDS) on Berlin as a capital. On a vote by name Kohl votes for Berlin.
November 26: Kohl reshuffles his cabinet: Seiters becomes interior minister, and Friedrich Bohl succeeds him at the chancellor's office. Schäuble becomes chairperson of the CDU/CSU parliamentary party.
December 9-11: At the European Community summit in Maastricht Kohl finally takes a key role in the process of European unification.

1992 *February 7:* Kohl signs for Germany the treaty on the foundation of the European Union (EU).
March 31: Kohl appoints Volker Rühe to replace Gerhard Stoltenberg at the Ministry of Defense; Rühe's successor as CDU general secretary is Peter Hintze.
April 27: Foreign Minister Hans Dietrich Genscher states that he will retire on May 17; his successor is Klaus Kinkel.
October 1: The CDU celebrates ten years after the "change" or "turning point" of 1982 at a large party at the Maritim in Bonn with about three thousand guests; Helmut Kohl has been chancellor for ten years.
December 14: Minister for Post Schwarz-Schilling resigns in protest of the German policy on the former Yugoslavia.

1993 *May 5:* Kohl appoints Matthias Wissmann as transport minister after Günther Krause resigns.
July 4: Cabinet again reshuffled after the resignation of Seiters as interior minister due to mishandled GSG-9 action in Bad Kleinen; Kohl appoints Manfred Kanther his successor.
October 3: At Kohl's suggestion the CDU board appoints the justice minister of Saxony, Steffen Heitmann, as candidate for the office of federal president. After an internal campaign against him Heitmann gives up his candidacy on November 25.

1994 *May 23:* The former president of the Federal Constitutional Court, Roman Herzog, is elected the first federal president of a unified Germany in Berlin by the Federal Convention.
October 16: The coalition under Kohl achieves a slim majority in the *Bundestag* elections; the Union receives 41.5 percent and the FDP 6.9 percent of the vote.
November 15: Helmut Kohl is confirmed as chancellor with 338 votes for and 333 votes against.

November 17: Kohl presents his new cabinet; surprise appointments are Jürgen Rüttgers as "future" minister and Claudia Nolte as minister for women.
November 28: Kohl is again confirmed as chairperson at the CDU party conference with 94.4 percent of the vote.

1995 *April 3:* Helmut Kohl celebrates his sixty-fifth birthday; it becomes clear that he intends to become a chancellor candidate again in 1998.
May 8–9: In Berlin Kohl celebrates a "Rendezvous with History" on the fiftieth anniversary of the end of the Second World War. Speeches are made by François Mitterrand, U.S. vice president Al Gore, as well as the prime ministers of Russia and Great Britain, Viktor Chernomyrdin and John Major; on May 9 Kohl takes part in a ceremony with President Yeltsin in Moscow.

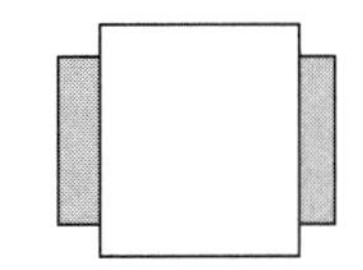

Index

C

H

L

M

N

O

P

Q

R

S

T